GENIUS
IN DISGUISE

To Werd Payton
from
Martha & Bob

Xmas 1997

THOMAS KUNKEL

GENIUS IN DISGUISE

HAROLD ROSS OF
THE NEW YORKER

CARROLL & GRAF PUBLISHERS, INC.

NEW YORK

Originally published in hardcover by Random House, Inc.

First Carroll & Graf trade paperback edition 1996.

Carroll & Graf Publishers, Inc.
260 Fifth Avenue
New York, NY 10001

Grateful acknowledgment is made to the following for permission to reprint both published and unpublished materials: The Estate of E. B. White: Excerpt from articles by E. B. White from May 28, 1927, September 9, 1939, February 17, 1945, and December 15, 1951, issues of *The New Yorker*. Reprinted by permission of the Estate of E. B. White. Jacqueline James Goodwin: Excerpt from "Dayton, Tennessee" by Marquis James from the July 11, 1925, issue of *The New Yorker*. Reprinted by permission. *The New Yorker:* Drawing of Eustace Tilley courtesy of *The New Yorker* magazine. All rights reserved. Memo (February 9, 1944). Copyright © 1944 by *The New Yorker* magazine. Excerpt from book review of *Ross and The New Yorker*. Copyright © 1951 by *The New Yorker* magazine. Excerpt from letter from Harold Ross to E. B. White (April 1943), excerpt from letter from Harold Ross to Charles Morton (April 3, 1950), memo (June 25, 1951), excerpt from letter from Harold Ross to H. L. Mencken, memo from James Kevin McGuinness to Harold Ross (undated), memo from Fillmore Hyde to Ralph Ingersoll (1926), memo to Ralph Ingersoll (1926), memos from Harold Ross (May 1931), memo from Harold Ross to Eugene Spaulding (March 12, 1930), excerpt from letter from Harold Ross to Lloyd Paul Stryker (July 25, 1944), excerpt from letter from Harold Ross to Arthur Kober (December 9, 1946), excerpt from letter from Harold Ross to Joseph Mitchell (February 13, 1945), excerpt from letter from Harold Ross to Marjorie Kinnan Rawlings (November 30, 1945), excerpt from letter from Harold Ross to Emily Hahn, excerpt from letter from Harold Ross to Rebecca West (January 7, 1948), excerpt from letter from Harold Ross to Samuel H. Adams (February 4, 1943), memo (September 6, 1940), excerpt from letter from Harold Ross to Henry Luce (November 23, 1936), excerpt from letter from Harold Ross to Katharine White (1939), excerpt from letter from Harold Ross to Frank Sullivan, excerpts from letters from Harold Ross to Gluyas Williams (August 7, 1934), excerpt from letter from Harold Ross to James Thurber (December 13, 1944), excerpt from letter from Harold Ross to E. B. White (June 24, 1941), excerpt from letter from Harold Ross to Alexander Woollcott (May 19, 1942), cable from William Shawn to John Hersey (March 22, 1946), excerpt from letter from Harold Ross to E. B. White (1946), excerpt from letters from Harold Ross to Lloyd Paul Stryker (July 4, 1945, and October 29, 1945), excerpt from letter from Harold Ross to Julius Baer (November 12, 1945), excerpt from letter from Harold Ross to Rebecca West (October 4, 1949), excerpt from letter from Harold Ross to Elmer Davis (September 13, 1949), excerpt from letter from Harold Ross to W. Averell Harriman (November 15, 1949), excerpt from letter from Harold Ross to Howard Brubaker (January 22, 1951), excerpt from letter from Harold Ross to E. B. White (October 1943), letter from Harold Ross to Rebecca West (June 20, 1951), excerpt from letter from Harold Ross to E. B. White (September 1951); Harold Ross's query sheets. Copyright © 1955 by *The New Yorker* magazine. All rights reserved. Reprinted courtesy of *The New Yorker* magazine.

ISBN 0-7867-0323-7

Library of Congress Cataloging-in-Publication Data is available.

Manufactured in the United States of America.

For Deb—
and her little women

I was going to wire you, but I couldn't think of anything to say that would sound tactful; I'm hypersensitive because I hear *Harper's* said I wasn't tactful, which is the grossest misstatement ever made about me. I am the God damnedest mass of tact known to the human race. That's about all I am. *Fortune* said I never read a book and *Harper's* says I'm tactless. American reporting is at a low ebb.

—*H. W. Ross to E. B. White*

CONTENTS

III / SEASON IN THE SUN: 1939–1951

GENIUS
IN DISGUISE

A HELL OF
AN HOUR

IN EARLY 1950, PRECISELY AT THE MIDPOINT OF THE AMERICAN
Century, New Yorkers were of a mind to build. They got that way
from time to time, and after slogging through two world wars and a
global depression, with vacant apartments nonexistent and business
desperate for more space, they could be forgiven for being more concerned with their future than with their past. Still, even hardened
New Yorkers were unsettled by the announcement, in January, that
the landmark Ritz-Carlton Hotel would soon be pulled down to
make way for another nondescript steel-and-glass box. The hotel, on
Madison between Forty-sixth and Forty-seventh streets, was only
forty years old, and while it was nothing special architecturally, in
that short time it had attained a kind of venerability. Many considered the Ritz, with its storied debutante balls, lavish parties, and state
receptions, the most glamorous venue in the city. "In no other country of the world, and indeed in few cities of this country, would it be
conceivable that a block-long, eighteen-story building in excellent

condition and housing a world-famous hotel would be torn down after a life of only forty years," commented *The New York Times,* managing to sound a little proud and ashamed all at once.

More openly sad about the whole business was *The New Yorker.* Ahead of the wrecker's ball, staff writer Geoffrey Hellman produced not one but two "Talk of the Town" lamentations on the Ritz. Beyond their obvious bond of a shared clientele, the magazine and the hotel had more or less grown up together, custodians of a distinctive urban gentility now in eclipse, and here one of them was about to be knocked down. It was fitting, then, that the last major fete in the hotel's grand ballroom, on March 18, 1950, was *The New Yorker*'s twenty-fifth anniversary gala.

This being *The New Yorker,* the invitation said in nonchalant fashion, "Dress or not, as you like." Given the poignance of the occasion, few took this seriously, and it was very much a night for black ties and beautiful gowns. Seven hundred people crowded into the ballroom, and by almost every account, whether contemporaneous or recollected four decades later, it was that rare magical evening, the kind of party where everyone drank but not too much, the music played without end, and the toast beneath the lobster Newburg was crisp even at two in the morning. With the apparent exception of the Pecksniffian Edmund Wilson ("Prominent persons whom I will not name were guilty of wholesale malignant rudeness"), a splendid time was had by all. Every staff writer, every artist, every contributor, every editor who had had anything to do with the magazine through the years, was invited. Conspicuous by her absence was *The New Yorker*'s first lady, Katharine White, who bought a new gown for the party, only to come down with flu at the last moment. But her husband, E. B. White, was there. So were most of the other old hands, reaching all the way back to the magazine's colicky infancy in 1925, and a few, it seems, from even before: John Cheever reported hearing Wolcott Gibbs say, "I danced with Harriet Beecher Stowe twice."

Harold W. Ross had spent the better part of his life avoiding such high-profile affairs as this. The editor of *The New Yorker* liked parties well enough, but he was so self-conscious about the spotlight that he categorically declined speaking engagements and once fled the funeral of his dear friend Heywood Broun for fear that he might be asked to say a few words. This night, though, he was unavoidably, and for the most part happily, the center of attention. Still wan from his own case of flu earlier in the week, Ross was tugged at, toasted, and passed around the room. He made a great fuss over his special guest and crony, Mayor William O'Dwyer, who was just months away from resigning, under gathering clouds of scandal, to become Truman's ambassador to Mexico. Ross formed up along the grand staircase a rather tipsy greeting party of writers Joseph Mitchell, Philip Hamburger, and John McNulty, then popped in and out with frequent updates on O'Dwyer's motorcade, as if it were ferrying not the mayor but the pope.

Spirits ran so high that Ross was even persuaded, for the first time in years, to have a drink, which provoked his ulcer, but he didn't mind. He was among friends, in a warmly familiar place. From time to time through the years the Ritz had been his home. He'd been here often for other functions, or just to have drinks in the bar. Then

A rare snapshot of Ross in black tie.

there was the memorable day in 1936 when he sat down to lunch in the basement grill with H. L. Mencken. Though it was their first meeting, the two men fell into such easy conversation that before long they were comparing their respective kinds of boobery. "I'm the boob who asks the waiter what is especially good on the menu," said Mencken. Countered Ross, "I'm the boob who says 'Fine' when the barber holds the mirror so I can look at the back of my neck."

The night passed in surreal fashion, Ross wrote two days later to his friend Rebecca West, "like a movie film running at five times its normal speed." The party was different from its predecessors, and not just in its scale or ostentation. For instance, *The New Yorker*'s tenth anniversary, in 1935, was basically a group of still-young people celebrating survival—the magazine's survival, survival of the Depression, even personal survival. But the twenty-fifth was about accomplishment, about creating something of enduring importance. Those who had been present at the Creation were no longer young, and they were beginning to realize that their lives had been circumscribed by, and would be remembered in terms of, *The New Yorker.*

Standing behind them—or more typically just off to the side, casting anxious glances from time to time—was Harold Wallace Ross, the unlettered immigrant's son from Colorado who blew out of the West to create what was then, and many still consider to be, the most influential magazine in American history. Though in time *The New Yorker* came to fulfill all the rash promises Ross had advanced in the magazine's famous 1924 prospectus, he could never have imagined what his little fifteen-cent "comic paper" would come to do, or how robust its legacy would be. Ross's *New Yorker* changed the face of contemporary fiction, perfected a new form of literary journalism, established new standards for humor and comic art, swayed the cultural and social agendas, and became synonymous with sophistication. It replaced convention with innovation. And while Ross was never as interested in great names as in great writing, what indelible names paraded through his *New Yorker.* There were the storytellers: E. B. White, James Thurber, Dorothy Parker, Alexander Woollcott, John O'Hara, Ring Lardner, Clarence Day, Emily Hahn, Sally

Benson, Arthur Kober, Leo Rosten, Kay Boyle, John Cheever, Irwin Shaw, J. D. Salinger, H. L. Mencken, S. N. Behrman, Frank Sullivan, S. J. Perelman, Ogden Nash, Shirley Jackson, Shirley Hazzard, Vladimir Nabokov, William Maxwell, Eudora Welty, Frank O'Connor, Jerome Weidman, Mary McCarthy, Jean Stafford, Niccolò Tucci. The reporters: Janet Flanner, John Hersey, A. J. Liebling, Joseph Mitchell, Rebecca West, St. Clair McKelway, Meyer Berger, Mollie Panter-Downes, Philip Hamburger, E. J. Kahn, Jr., Brendan Gill, Lillian Ross, Andy Logan, John Lardner, Berton Roueché, John Bainbridge, Richard Rovere. The critics: Robert Benchley, Wolcott Gibbs, Clifton Fadiman, Lewis Mumford, Edmund Wilson, Louise Bogan. The artists: Peter Arno, Helen Hokinson, William Steig, Saul Steinberg, John Held, Jr., Gluyas Williams, Gardner Rea, Otto Soglow, Miguel Covarrubias, Mary Petty, Charles Addams. The editors: Katharine S. White, Ralph Ingersoll, James M. Cain, Gustave S. Lobrano, Rea Irvin, James Geraghty, Rogers E. M. Whitaker, William Shawn.

A more unlikely literary avatar than Harold Ross is hard to imagine, for he was a man of spectacular contradictions and wondrous complexities. *The New Yorker* aside, Ross's personal reading ran to dictionaries (Fowler's *Modern English Usage,* particularly) and true-detective magazines. He was a prototypical westerner whose magazine embodied eastern urbanity. He was a coarse, profane man with a near-perfect ear for language. He was equally capable of the rude or the gracious gesture, a charming weekend host who nonetheless could not—would not—abide fools ("We don't run our magazine for dumbbells," he was known to bark more than once). In the throes of concentration, Ross would absentmindedly cluck his tongue in the great yawning gap between his two front teeth. Looking upon these anomalies, some found it hard to believe that this peculiar man could be responsible for *The New Yorker.* But this was Ross at the margins. Anyone bothering to see beyond, to the core, found a keen native intellect, a searching curiosity, and a droll humor—qualities Ross imprinted onto his magazine. He conducted himself like what he was, a man with a very personal, even mystical, mission, that being

The New Yorker. From Ross emanated a strength that creative people found reassuring and an artistic freedom they found intoxicating. In return, they advanced the mission with work of surpassing quality and taste. Richard Rovere, who began *The New Yorker*'s "Letter from Washington" in 1948 (in the beginning neither he nor Ross thought it an especially good idea), later would say that beyond his obvious contributions to journalism and letters, Ross was, at a more fundamental level, fighting to save the dignity of the printed word. Andy White, as was his wont, said it differently, and perfectly: "In retrospect I am beginning to think of him as an Atlas who lacked muscle tone but who God damn well decided he was going to hold up the world anyway."

Such was the wide affection and esteem for Ross that more than a few people at the Ritz gala actually had been fired by the editor in his early and most manic incarnation, in the years when it was a week-to-week proposition whether there would even be a *New Yorker* and Ross was grinding up editorial talent like so much pork butt. One of these was Charles Morton, who by 1950 was a respected editor at *The Atlantic Monthly* but who as a budding reporter in the early days of the Depression made an unsuccessful attempt to join the staff of *The New Yorker*. After the party Morton sent Ross a note of thanks. "The main satisfaction of it for me was the chance to see you at the end of a twenty-five-year hitch firmly possessed of every one of the objectives you set out to reach, still breaking new ground, never lowering the standard. . . . Your anniversary guests were a talented lot, no doubt, but every one of them is probably further in your debt than you could ever bring yourself to believe." He added that Ross needn't reply, but not replying went against Ross's compulsive nature, and so shortly thereafter Morton got a letter i i which, in a rare instance, Ross commented on the job he had do ie at *The New Yorker*.

"I guess we've made most of our objectives; I hould say two-thirds of them, which is probably pretty good, and n some instances we've exceeded them, as I appraise things now," Koss said. "I hadn't thought of it that way before, being, of course, g iellingly unsatisfied most of the time, which must be the case with anyone getting out a magazine and shooting high. Getting out this magazine has been a tour de force, of course, and a tour de force of twenty-five years is wearing."

Anyone who knew Ross was accustomed to his organic complaining—all his life this Atlas had, in fact, walked in the stooped fashion of a man carrying too much weight—but in this instance the weariness he professed was real. It was true that to all outward appearances, Ross, at fifty-seven, was at a pinnacle. Aside from his professional accomplishments, he had a beautiful wife and an adoring teenage daughter. If he was not as wealthy a man as many assumed, his holdings were substantial enough, including a sumptuous Park Avenue apartment and a country estate of more than one hundred acres in north Stamford, Connecticut. As editor of *The New Yorker* he made fifty thousand dollars a year, plus twenty-five thousand dollars for expenses. His collection of friends reached from the White House to Hollywood, from industrialists to retired railroad men in Nevada, the "one-armed poker companions" he loved so well. And of course he was on a last-name basis (Ross's address of choice) with many of the best writers in the world.

Yet within a year his life would be slipping away. In the spring of 1951, Ross, a heavy smoker for more than forty years, would be told he had cancer. He kept his condition from family and friends, but his absences from the office grew so frequent and long that colleagues knew something was amiss. (Thurber guessed the worst about Ross when his old friend confided that sardines were the only thing he could still taste.) Not long after, Ross left his third wife, Ariane. She would eventually sue him for divorce on grounds of abandonment, and press on him a series of lawsuits alleging that he had cheated her out of tens of thousands of dollars. He would wind up back in a suite, alone, at the Algonquin Hotel, where he read manuscripts, took infrequent meals, and saw a few intimate friends. By Christmas, he would be dead.

Yet even in death there was indignity. In reminiscences, various colleagues caricatured Ross—some affectionately, some not, but all along the same general lines. This cartoon Ross was said to be aggressively ignorant, unfailingly rude, sexually naïve, and generally intolerant. His comic tendencies were exaggerated, his editing acumen trivialized, and his achievements laid to dumb luck and the skill of his bemused, solicitous associates. As with all caricatures, there were nuggets of truth underlying each of these assertions, but on the whole they were rubbish. Even so, this deleterious view of Ross took such firm hold that today, if he is remembered at all, it is as Ross the Wonder Editor, the literary equivalent of the precocious pony at the sideshow who taps out sums with his hoof.

So perhaps it was a touch of foreboding, or maybe sheer wistfulness, that Rovere detected in Ross as the glittering twenty-fifth anniversary gala moved into the small hours. He would write, twenty years later, "All that remains with me is a picture of Ross looking balefully over the ballroom, consulting his watch, and saying that it was one hell of an hour for his young daughter to be at the Ritz Hotel."

PART I

CHILD
OF THE WEST:
1892–1924

CHAPTER 1

THE PETTED

DARLING

ON THE CORNER OF FIFTH AND BLEEKER STREETS IN ASPEN, Colorado, is a small frame house, utterly nondescript save for its pleasant color of pale rose. Its drab style is only underscored by the fanciful Victorians and neo-Victorians surrounding it in the West's trendy capital of conspicuous consumption. Though the house has been added on to repeatedly through the years, in today's real estate parlance it is a "tear-down," the true value of the property being not in the structure but in the dirt beneath it. In 1991, Pitkin County's appraisers reckoned the house was worth thirty-five thousand dollars—and the small lot $675,000.

A century before, caught up in Aspen's first real estate boom, a Scotch-Irish immigrant from Ulster named George Ross paid a tidy one thousand dollars for the squat little cottage at 601 West Bleeker, and was doubtless glad to have it. Like the homes around it, it was thrown up in a hurry in the late 1880s, made from rough-sawn Colorado spruce harvested from the lush mountains girdling the mining boomtown. The house was situated facing north, but it was scarcely equipped to take the bitter winter winds; the plank walls were insulated with oilcloth, wadded newspapers, and pages ripped from old mining magazines. The current owners, who have renovated the house extensively, have even come across the occasional playing card nailed up over a hole, a pitiful pasteboard barrier against the unremitting draft. It's not hard to imagine George Ross awakening in the middle of the night and, seeing his breath, rising to rekindle the stoves that heated the few small rooms. On November 6, 1892, a boy was born in this house. His mother, Ida, christened him Harold, a name meaning "leader of men."

In temperament, Harold was very much his father's son; in his upbringing, he was very much his mother's.

Like most of the nine thousand or so Aspen residents in 1892, George Ross was there in search of fortune, a very long way from home. He was born in 1851 in County Monaghan, on a farm that had been in the family for five generations. Eldest of three boys and seven girls, George as a young man was swept up in the great Irish emigration to America (in time a half dozen of his siblings, one by one, would follow him). George came by way of Canada. At various times in his life he was a carpenter, grocer, contractor, scrap dealer, and, it was said, supervisor of a mental hospital in Toronto. But according to his son, George Ross was always, at heart, a miner, and he drifted from boomtown to boomtown across the West. Judging from his résumé, the elder Ross was a handy and resourceful man, if not especially lucky where prospecting was concerned. Voluble and gregarious, with a sharp tongue and a gift for sarcasm, he liked a good joke almost as much as a good argument. But he was said to be so genial that even his forensic adversaries admired him.

Sometime around 1885, George Ross's wandering brought him to Aspen, where he worked the mines and eventually staked some claims. A few years later—no one is sure of the circumstances, whether he was traveling or she was—he encountered a schoolteacher from Kansas named Ida Martin. As Ida would recount to her daughter-in-law, Jane Grant, the courtship that ensued was an unorthodox one, even by the standards of nineteenth-century

Colorado. Their brief meeting evidently left a much stronger impression on George than on Ida: a few weeks later he sent her a postcard pressing his suit and even proposing marriage, but her recollection of him was so dim that she had trouble making out the signature. Ida responded by offering to provide George some writing paper so that he might conduct a proper correspondence. He, in turn, mustered a charming apology. The epistolary courtship advanced through the school year and culminated with their marriage in June 1889 in Salina, Kansas, where Ida was then teaching. The groom was thirty-eight, his bride thirty-four. The formal announcement of their wedding concluded, "At Home, After June 25th, Aspen, Colorado."

Ida Martin Ross came from old New England stock. She was born in Amesbury, Massachusetts, north of Boston, in 1855, but her father moved the family to Kansas and she was raised in McPherson, not far from Salina. She was the embodiment of the prairie schoolmarm: prim, thin, plain, a little austere, recipient of a normal-school educa-

George Ross and son Harold, around age nine.
(Courtesy of Patricia Ross Honcoop)

tion. She was also outspoken and clearly unintimidated by adventure. Before working in Salina, it was said, she taught for several years in the Oklahoma Indian territory. Writer friends of Harold Ross who met Ida in her old age in New York often described her as naïve, as she no doubt was in the ways of speakeasies and cocktail-party protocol. But the woman who emerges in a handful of her surviving letters, written to Jane Grant when Jane's marriage to Ross was foundering, is anything but naïve. This is a concerned mother and compassionate mother-in-law, a sensible woman plainly familiar with marital tribulation and other hard ways of the world. Besides, if there ever was a naïve side to Ida Ross, frontier Aspen would have ground it away.

Aspen, situated on the Roaring Fork River and circumscribed by mountains, is a place of surpassing beauty. Yet for all its natural appeal, it owes its existence to brute commerce, the mining of silver.

Ida Ross was the product of New England ancestry and prairie upbringing. *(Courtesy of Patricia Ross Honcoop)*

Aspen sprang up in 1879, when its potential attracted a dozen silver prospectors who had been crowded out of Leadville, the boomtown just across the Continental Divide. By the time newlyweds George and Ida Ross arrived, in the summer of 1889, Aspen not only was bustling but was beginning to make the transition from mining camp to civilized town, with some gaslights, the occasional stone building, even social clubs. But no amount of makeup could disguise the truth of it: with its smokestacks, dirty air, rutted avenues, and noisy, ore-laden trains, Aspen was all about silver. Those establishments not in mining directly were in its service, from the new Hotel Jerome to the East End brothels.

In the cumbersome grantee books in the Pitkin County Courthouse in Aspen, one still finds George Ross's claims on silver lodes with such romantic names as the Little Anney, the Sarah Jane, the Bartelett, the Bob Tail, and the Bonteet. There was nothing remotely romantic about the work, however, which was backbreaking and dangerous. Main shafts were dug hundreds of feet into the mountainsides, with short tunnels spurring off every so often, like the stubby teeth of a comb. Miners chiseled holes into the rock to set the charges, which generated tons of rubble that had to be cleared. Miners were completely at the mercy of mine owners, grantees, and supervisors for their hours, working conditions, and pay. Leases were arranged in various ways. For instance, George Ross's 1891 leases on the Sarah Jane and Bartelett cost him twenty percent of the value of all ore he extracted. (He also agreed to work at least four miners per shift, to conduct eighty shifts a month, and to keep the three-and-a-half-feet-wide shafts clear of debris.) In 1892, leasing the Little Anney, he paid a flat five hundred dollars for rights, with no royalties.

George Ross never found his fortune in the mines, though he did make enough to hold a small interest in some camp boardinghouses, as well as to buy the modest house on Bleeker. The couple took possession in August 1892, when Ida was six months pregnant. After all the hard work, after three years of living in rental property, and with their first child on the way, the Rosses might have been completely

content had it not been for the pernicious rumor racing around
Aspen about this time that the government was about to demoneta-
rize silver. And in fact, with the economic panic of 1893, Aspenites'
worst fears were realized. Congress repealed the Sherman Silver Act,
which for years had required the federal government to buy much
more of the metal than it really needed. Aspen's sole commodity
plunged in value, and the town began a long, slow decline.
Thousands were driven from the mines, including George Ross.
Rather than leave town, as many did, the Rosses responded, in 1893,
by opening a meat market and grocery. Still, a service establishment
in a dying community is a dubious proposition in its own right, and
there was no more income to be had from the boardinghouses.
Within a few years, as Harold Ross himself would say later, "everybody in town was broke, including my father."

―――

HAROLD WALLACE ROSS WOULD ALWAYS RELISH PLAYING THE ROLE OF
the country boy abroad in the big city. But it was just that—an act—

The Rosses outside their home in Aspen, Colorado.
(Courtesy of Patricia Ross Honcoop)

and Ross got a little testy whenever someone bought it too well, as if the turnip truck had made no stops on the trip from Bleeker Street to Park Avenue. "I may well have been the boy from Aspen, all right," he told his friend the writer Margaret Case Harriman, "but I point out that I left at the age of six and thereafter lived in cities—Salt Lake City, Denver, San Francisco, Panama, New Orleans, New York, and Paris, more or less in the order named. I was really just the petted darling of world capitals." It is inarguably true that by the time he came to start his own magazine, the well-traveled Ross had attained a kind of careworn worldliness that most New Yorkers, as parochial then as now, could only imagine. But it is just as true that Ross was, and would always be, a child of the frontier.

His first years were full of privations, though of course young Harold didn't realize they were hardships at the time because everyone he knew lived the same way he did. There was no indoor plumbing, and water had to be drawn and hauled daily. The house was cold and drafty. When Ross was three his mother gave birth to a second son, Robert, but the child died on his first birthday. (Ross later said one of his earliest memories was of his brother's tiny white coffin in the parlor.) There was little money and provisions were thin. Ross would remember his mother as an unaccomplished cook but add that she "didn't have much of a chance, because of the limited provender of the mountains." Ida Ross, like all frontier wives, developed of necessity a steely frugality that, in later life, even prosperity couldn't dent. In the Thirties, when she visited her son in New York and he put her up in the better hotels, Ida refused to pay the shocking prices they charged for meals. Instead, she would sneak a hotplate into her room to cook her own. She was always found out and a few times even asked to leave, to the mortification of the editor of *The New Yorker.*

The young Harold (he was almost always Harold; never Harry, and seldom Hal) adored Aspen. He enjoyed fishing the creeks and mountain lakes with his father and exploring the endless hillsides. If his mother was overly protective—she wouldn't let him run barefoot, even in summer, and refused to let him swim lest he drown—

out of her sight he indulged his more mischievous impulses. Harold and his best friend and cousin, Wesley Gilson, who was two years older, liked to go into the countryside and pepper the sides of barns with their shotguns (at other times they fired small snakes stuffed down the barrel). Once, while visiting his favorite uncle, John Ross, who lived near Denver, Harold captured an eagle, but Uncle John made him set it free.

In school Harold did well, scoring high grades in every subject except, notably, deportment. But his education scarcely stopped at the classroom door. As soon as he was old enough to be of help, he ran errands for his father's grocery. So at ages six and eight, he and Wesley found themselves hauling buckets of beer to the town's saloons, careful not to spill any lest they get their ears cuffed by thirsty patrons. Harold also toted groceries to the brothels in Aspen's red-light district. He liked the prostitutes right off because they invited him in to warm up on cold days, gave him candy, and invariably tipped better than the churchgoers across town. This exposure marked the beginning of Ross's lifelong fraternal fascination with prostitutes and their lot. Years later he would tell the story of how, as a boy, he once overheard his mother and her friends buzzing over the scandalous news that a prominent politician was about to wed a local madam. How were they expected to respond, the ladies asked themselves, when they encountered the newlyweds on the street? As he told it, the young Ross found their perplexity amusing but their hypocrisy troubling.

Even so, Ida Ross, a proper woman with proper friends, was merely being true to her values, which were firm and strongly held. She doted on her only child and worked hard transferring her views to him. If not everything took hold, much did. For instance, she imprinted on Ross a puritanical strain that was remarked on as a quaint, albeit sometimes annoying, trait all his adult life. Just as passionately the former schoolteacher drilled into her son a love of reading and language. He was taught to read at a young age, and Ida regularly exposed him to books that would have been well over the heads of his classmates. She took pains that Harold respect not just the ideas therein but the words themselves. In grammar as in life, she believed, there were firm rules to be followed. She augmented Harold's schoolwork with grammar lessons at home, making him parse sentences until their fundamental structure became second nature. This builder's approach to language appealed to Harold's logical mind and would become a signature of his professional editing style.

Curiously, one book Ross was *not* exposed to, at least in any depth, was the Bible. Though George and Ida Ross both came from Presbyterian backgrounds, it seems the family practiced no formal religion, and for his entire life Ross, despite his strong moral ethic, never belonged to any denomination. George, who enjoyed referring to himself as a "blackmouth Presbyterian," was familiar enough with the Bible to argue with his Catholic friends about their dogma and, after the family had moved to Salt Lake City, with Mormon friends about theirs. Harold delighted in listening to his father in these contentious sessions—George Ross was a "violent anti-Mormon," his son said—and grew up with the idea that a person's convictions were more important than his affiliations, be they religious, political, social, or otherwise. Remembering Ross years after his death, Rebecca West, who never knew Ross's parents but who from time to time heard him hold forth on matters spiritual and even theological, said, "At some time an impressive nineteenth-century rationalist, of the sort not rare in the West, must have had the shaping of him, for he knew nothing about the Bible and an emotional block prevented him from repairing this lack in his later life. He could not pronounce phrases such as 'the cherubim and seraphim' without stammering, and he never recognized the most familiar texts."

His father was not the only contrarian influence on the young Ross. Religious skepticism, not to say mischief, ran in the family. This is clear from an amusing and telling encounter that *New Yorker* writer Joseph Mitchell had in 1940 with Bishop Alma White, founder of the Pillar of Fire sect. At the time, the Pillar of Fire had forty-three temples in the United States, Canada, and England, broadcasting and publishing holdings, and two colleges. The movement had originated in Colorado but was then based in New Jersey, and Mitchell decided to write a Profile of Bishop Alma. When, after some negotiation, Mitchell was introduced to the cleric, he found a woman in her late seventies and rather infirm, "a buxom old Roman emperor . . . lying in bed, propped up on pillows." Bishop Alma invited Mitchell to sit down, then asked him directly, "Did Harold W. Ross send you out here?"

Mitchell was taken back. "Not exactly," he said, endeavoring to explain how someone at *The New Yorker* must have approved his Profile idea, but that person was not necessarily Ross.

"That's a sorry paper," Bishop Alma continued. "Somebody from Colorado told me that Harold W. Ross was associated with it, and I bought a copy, and I was certainly disappointed. There's nothing about the Lord in *that* paper. The reading matter is on a very low level, and the ads are worse than the reading matter. Every page you turn there's a big bottle of whiskey staring you in the face. Harold W. Ross came from one of the finest families in Colorado, a good old Scotch-Irish family, but looking at *The New Yorker* you'd never know it."

Mitchell asked the bishop if she knew Ross.

"I do not, but I knew an uncle of his, Mr. John Ross, out in Morrison, Colorado, and I owe a great debt of gratitude to him. If it wasn't for him and his help, I might not be here today and the Pillar of Fire might not be in existence." John Ross was the second-born of his family, one year younger than George. He had come to Denver as a miner and had prospered. He moved to Mount Morrison, west of Denver, where he developed an extensive logging operation, accumulated vast landholdings—he sold the city of Denver the acreage for what became the Park of the Red Rocks—and became one of the community's leading merchants. Bishop Alma went on to explain to Mitchell that before the advent of the Pillar of Fire movement, she and her husband, a Methodist minister, were sent to a church in Morrison for her health. Once there, a bitter fight arose within the congregation over a proposed church festival, replete with dancing and gaming, that was intended to raise money for the pastor's salary. The Whites so vigorously protested this sinful enterprise that the majority of the congregation not only turned against them but threatened to cut off the pastor's support altogether. Salvation, she said, arrived in the person of John Ross. "I don't think he had ever made any profession of Christianity whatsoever," said Bishop Alma, "but he called my husband into his store and put a twenty-dollar gold piece in his hand, and encouraged him, and said that as long as he had a store we shouldn't want for anything. He continued to give liberally to our support, and we weathered the winter, and I went on from there to found the Pillar of Fire." The bishop then handed Mitchell a copy of her autobiography, *Looking Back from Beulah,* in which she recounts the benefaction of John Ross. "I want you to take it to Harold W. Ross. Take it to him, and tell him it's from me. Tell him to read it, and study it, and think on it. And tell him I'll pray for him."

Mitchell told Ross the story and gave him the book. The editor was amazed, then began to laugh.

"My Uncle John was a sly old man," said Ross, "and he liked to stir up trouble. He always kept out of trouble himself, but he would look pious and stay on the sidelines and egg others on. He didn't belong to a church, and he had a low opinion of preachers in general, but he took a lot of interest in religious affairs. There was nothing he enjoyed so much as a religious controversy—a fight in a congregation, or something like that. He'd watch the fight, and keep it going, and if it died down he'd find some way of starting it up again. Well, he's the first person in my family who ever amounted to anything. From now on, when I hear people bragging about their ancestors, I'm going to claim that an uncle of mine was partly responsible for the Pillar of Fire movement. That's something they can't take away from me."

Ross took home *Looking Back from Beulah* and reported to Mitchell that he enjoyed it as much as any book he'd ever read. "She doesn't write quite as well as Cardinal Newman," Ross said, "but she'll do."

———

GEORGE ROSS, LIKE MANY ASPENITES, HELD ON TO THE SLENDER HOPE that one day the price of silver would rebound, and Aspen with it. The recovery never happened. By 1901, the Rosses, broke and without prospects, had had enough. That spring, after Harold finished out the third grade (despite what he told Margaret Harriman, he was eight, not six, at this time), the Rosses sold their house at a big loss and left town. After residing briefly in tiny Redcliff, and then Silverton in southwest Colorado, the family finally settled on Salt Lake City as its permanent destination. Why they chose Salt Lake is not really clear. It appears that another of George's siblings may have owned a store there at the time, and so perhaps had bragged about the town's prosperity. Certainly what would have appealed to George, after eight marginal years as a grocer, was the fact that the copper mining in Salt Lake was going strong, and there were plenty of opportunities for enterprising men in related trades. Though founded by Mormons, Salt Lake at the turn of the century contained many non-Mormons and was, in fact, one of the West's more wide-open cities.

Whatever his reasons, George Ross went ahead alone to Utah to get established, then sent for his wife and son. The move was traumatic for Harold, beyond the normal trauma any child experiences at leaving behind friends, pets (in Harold's case a shepherd dog named Sam), and the only world he has known. As the Rosses' stage-coach was navigating a mountain pass, a sudden storm blew up; the coach slid off the road and crashed. A fellow passenger was killed, and Harold was badly roughed up, sustaining many cuts and bruises. Years later, when he was sporting a distinctive three-inch pompadour, Ross liked to say it was the stagecoach accident that caused his hair to start growing straight up.

George Ross at first worked in and around Salt Lake's mining trade, turning up in the annual city directories variously as "carpenter," "miner," "molder." Within a few years he moved into general contracting, and as a sideline he began doing demolition work. Then in 1911 he formally established the business that would occupy him the rest of his life. The Ross Wrecking Company was a house-demolition and scrap enterprise, although it's clear George Ross was willing to do almost anything to bring in a few dollars, including stabling horses and selling kindling. But the company specialized in used building materials: "We Buy and Sell Everything," it advertised. House wrecking made the Rosses no wealthier than did silver mining or selling meat, but evidently it did afford a good living. They were able to buy a home, at 622 Elizabeth Street, on a high hill overlooking the city; George became a Mason and a respected businessman; and the family was even able to take a trip back to New York. It's not known what the purpose of this trip was—perhaps to pick up or drop off another of George's migrating siblings—but merely having the wherewithal to travel so far as a family is some indication of their relative prosperity.

It took Harold some time to adjust to Salt Lake. The stagecoach accident had complicated matters, of course, but so did Harold's emerging shyness. The young Ross was gangly and awkward, self-conscious, and constantly fidgeting. He was also terribly bright and rather inventive; for instance, it was said he outfitted his bedroom with contraptions to open the windows automatically. But Harold was, above all, headstrong. Increasingly he argued with his father—Ross always said they were too much alike—and he got into the habit of running away from home.

The boy was a voracious reader, feeding his emerging sense of wonder with biographies and tales of adventure and romance. He carefully followed the Russo-Japanese War of 1904–1905 in the newspapers and magazines, being intrigued especially with the accounts of correspondent Frederick Palmer of *Collier's*. But his interest waned in what he considered mundane school subjects, like mathematics or science, and he often played hooky. One day when Ida Ross was informed of her son's truancy, she set out after him, only to be relieved when she found him in the public library, absorbed in *The Luck of Roaring Camp*, by one of his favorite writers, Bret Harte—who, Harold pointed out ominously, had quit school at thirteen. It's difficult to say just how wide a rift developed between the rebellious teen and his father, but Salt Lake's directory for 1907 indicates that at fourteen Harold was residing away from the family in a boardinghouse. The following year, however, he was back home.

It was during this difficult adolescence that several events pushed

Ross toward his eventual life's work. In the fall of 1904, when Harold was just shy of twelve years old, he entered Salt Lake's old West High School. (Ross was always big for his age, and in the family's moves Ida had managed to advance him one grade.) As a freshman he joined the staff of the school newspaper, *The Red and Black*. Also on the paper, three grades ahead of Harold, was John Held, Jr., the artist who in the Twenties created the ubiquitous symbol of the Jazz Age, the flapper, and whose comic woodcuts were among the most distinctive features of the infant *New Yorker*. Ross and Held became friends and, beyond their work for the school paper, participated in an innovative apprentice journalism program at the *Salt Lake Tribune*. For a dollar or two a week, dozens of high-school-age reporters fanned out across the city to gather news items, which were collected and published the following Sunday. It was Ross's first exposure to newspapering, and he was smitten. He began to hang around the paper so much that the older men more or less adopted him. As they slipped off after midnight to play cards and drink, they let their enthusiastic young charge "cover" the police beat for them, and he thrilled to ride along on their emergency calls. If the sports editor had need of a local fighter, he had Harold make the rounds of the saloons—once he ran into his own father—until the pug was found. Then there was the time, Held recalled, when the young Ross was sent into the Stockade, Salt Lake's red-light district, to interview one of its more flamboyant madams, Helen Blazes. Ross was familiar with the district from his days as a delivery boy for a local drugstore, but now he was there as a working journalist. Not wishing to give offense, he was on his best behavior, still wearing his uniform pants from school and carefully couching his questions in the most delicate euphemisms. At last Ross's politesse got on Miss Blazes's nerves. "Jesus Christ, kid, cut out the honey. If I had a railroad tie for every trick I've turned, I could build a railroad from here to San Francisco."

Ross's attention to schoolwork, always tenuous, began to erode in direct proportion to his newspaper activity. As he said, "I had accumulated so many miles of walking the path for punishment that it was hopeless to remain in school." A love of pranks, which he indulged all his life, proved a turning point. Toward the end of his sophomore year, he set off a stink bomb ("a vile smelling chemical," he said) in the manual-training room and was invited to leave school. "But the real trouble," he would explain later, "was that I was bitten by the newspaper bee, and I spent more time hanging around the police station than I did attending classes."

At this point, Ross either ran away to his uncle Jim in Denver or was sent there by his angry parents. (In recounting his childhood, which Ross enjoyed doing, he typically offered slightly different variations on a theme.) Through his uncle's connections, he worked briefly as an errand boy at the *Denver Post*. He returned home determined to quit school and be a real newspaperman, and eventually he wore his parents down. He would always remember the day they consented as one of the happiest of his life.

So rather than return for his junior year, Ross became an apprentice reporter for the *Salt Lake Telegram,* then owned by the *Tribune.* His precocity notwithstanding, he learned the trade from the ground up. His first job was as a legman, a reporter who gathered the facts of a story but turned them over to a more experienced colleague to write up. He wrote obituaries, still the dispiriting proving ground for aspiring journalists. In time he was trusted to do his own feature stories. More significant, he was coming under the charismatic spell of a colorful, and now long-extinct, fraternity, that of the tramp newspaperman. A tramp was a freelance reporter who, in the early years of the century, more or less rode an erratic circuit, not unlike an itinerant preacher. He worked at one paper for a few weeks or months, until he was no longer needed or himself felt the urge to move on. Tramp newspapermen were common in the West, and their number swelled predictably every year as they migrated toward California ahead of the winter. Ross was transfixed by their fabulous, often fabulist, tales and by the glamorous prospects of life on the road.

After several years of this, Ross decided it was time to see what he'd been missing. In 1908 he and an older boy set off for California. After stopping in Morrison to visit Ross's uncle John, the pair moved south to Albuquerque, New Mexico. There Ross's companion absconded with their money, leaving Ross to hobo his way alone to California. Hopping the infrequent freight train but mostly walking, Ross got as far as Needles, in the broiling Mojave Desert. There he found work as a timekeeper—the person on a construction site who keeps track of everyone's hours, a task he had done for his father. When he had enough money to buy a new suit of clothes, he returned (by first-class train this time) to Salt Lake.

He would not stay long. As it had his father so many years before, wanderlust had taken hold of Harold Ross. Sometime in the latter half of 1910 he bounded aboard a train, knowing only that it was headed west.

CHAPTER 2

TRAMP

ON A CLEAR SUNDAY MORNING IN MARCH 1911, SOME THREE DOZEN anxious people crowded onto a smallish gasoline-powered freighter, the *Sioux,* which was docked on the Feather River in tiny Nicolaus, California, just north of Sacramento. The short trip they were about to make, upriver to Marysville, would take only a few hours, but there was a great deal more at stake than a diverting excursion. The passengers were rivermen, engineers, business leaders, the merely curious, and a handful of newspaper reporters. Representing the *Marysville Appeal* was H. W. Ross, as his byline had it, a gangly, gawky man-child of eighteen.

Marysville had a problem: it was a river town whose river had silted up, useless, from years of unrestrained hydraulic mining. This had the effect of marooning Marysville from Sacramento (and therefore San Francisco), and put its future directly into the unwelcome hands of the railroads. With the mining finally shut down, there was new cause to think the Feather might again accommodate big steamers, but it all depended on whether the *Sioux*—which, though small, had a deep draft—could make it all the way upriver without getting stuck. As Ross summed it up in the *Appeal* two days later, "The re-navigating of the Feather is one of the most important moves in the history of Marysville—probably the most important. . . . When boats are again running shippers will not be at the mercy of the railroads." And beyond the obvious business ramifications, Ross reminded his readers, there were "unbounded" social possibilities: "The excursion of the future will not be made in a small launch with a dozen or so passengers, nor in a fifty- or sixty-foot pleasure craft—but it will be possible for excursion boats carrying hundreds of passengers to ply between this city and Sacramento—yes, even to [San Francisco] bay."

The news that day, as duly reported by H. W. Ross, was good: the *Sioux* had been unimpeded. The *Appeal* signaled the importance of the story not only with big headlines and top-of-the-page treatment, but by attaching Ross's byline to it. At this time in American journalism, a byline—the writer's name at the beginning of a story—was rare, for the most part reserved for articles of real significance or distinction. This is just one of the reasons it is difficult to follow the zigzag, vaporous trajectory of Ross's newspaper career; he left behind little telltale evidence, even at those papers where he is known to have worked. Between the time he left Salt Lake and the spring of 1917, when he enlisted in the army, Ross the tramp reporter worked at so many newspapers—about two dozen—and usually for such short durations that before long he himself couldn't reconstruct the bewildering itinerary precisely. Not entirely in jest he would say later, "If I stayed anywhere more than two weeks, I thought I was in a rut." Documented stopovers included San Francisco, Sacramento, Santa Rosa (at the *Republican,* whose politics, Ross was amused to discover, were Democratic, while its rival, the *Santa Rosa Press-Democrat,* leaned Republican), Pasadena, Panama, New Orleans, Atlanta, Brooklyn, and Hoboken, New Jersey. It appears he also worked in Arizona and New Mexico, and at one or both of the major wire services of the day, the Associated Press and the United Press.

As it happened, one of Ross's most significant assignments turned out to be one of his first, at the *Marysville Appeal.* Small as it was (population 6,000), Marysville at this time supported two daily newspapers. The editor of the *Appeal* was John H. Miller, a likable, sympathetic man and a widely respected journalist whose career had rubbed up against that of another California newspaperman, Mark Twain. Ross would have been aware of Miller's reputation, and not long after he left Salt Lake he bounded into Marysville and persuaded the editor to take him on as the *Appeal*'s lone full-time reporter.

There was genuine affection between Miller, who was sixty-two, and his teenaged protégé. In a short time Miller taught the eager young man a great deal about the down-and-dirty newspaper arts, and Ross, for his part, was a quick study. He had to be, merely to survive the grueling regimen. The *Appeal* published six days a week, eight pages a day. Since it specialized in local news (said one headline: BEGGARS HAVE COME TO TOWN) and competed with the evening paper for readers, exhausting hours were required to report and write enough material to fill that maw.

Ross's account of the *Sioux* expedition is less interesting for what it is—a straightforward, inelegant, and predictably boosterish piece of work—than for what it reveals about the apprentice himself. First, one is struck by an uncommon seriousness of purpose in one so young. Beyond that, Ross's story is fully reported, providing perspective and demonstrating an impressive grasp of the shipping trade. Of most interest, however, is early evidence of what Rebecca West would describe as Ross's "clear, hard, classical American style" of writing: a formal syntax, a rigid (rather than conversational) tone, and the directness and clarity he would later demand as an editor. Read this, the opening phrase from his first sentence—"The fact that the Feather is navigable, and henceforth will be open to steamboat communication the year round, was undisputably proven Sunday"— and it is clear that John Miller had no more use for ambiguity than did Ida Ross.

Five weeks after Ross wrote that story, Miller took ill. He was hospitalized in Sacramento but died on May 31. Out of respect (if not out of printer's inertia), Miller's name remained on the newspaper's masthead until June 3. Then, on June 6, it is replaced with this: "H. W. Ross, Editor." Still learning the finer points of eluding railroad Pinkertons and scarcely old enough to shave, Ross suddenly found himself in charge of a daily newspaper. Almost certainly he gave himself the battlefield promotion, but he had little choice: when Miller died, the *Appeal*'s owner, Colonel E. A. Forbes, adjutant general of the state of California, was traveling on military business. At the time it all must have been a little terrifying, but two decades later Ross recalled the episode with the newspaperman's sangfroid: "Someone had to edit the paper. The only part I couldn't do was write the editorials—we got a man for that and I did the rest."

However he managed, Ross didn't do badly. Under its new editor the *Appeal* was just as newsy as before, and perhaps a little edgier as the chamber-of-commerce tincture faded. Certainly he did a workmanlike job under difficult circumstances. Even so, after two months Ross's name disappeared from the mast without explanation. Whether the colonel was dissatisfied with Ross or, quite reasonably, wanted an editor of slightly more experience isn't known.

It's also just possible that Ross decided two months was enough management to last him for a while. From Marysville it is thought he made the short trip west to take in a few haunts of his current idol, Jack London: Santa Rosa, in the idyllic Sonoma Valley, and San Francisco. From there it was back to the Central Valley and the *Sacramento Union*, where his city editor was Kenneth Adams, who became Ross's friend and later worked with him on *The Stars and Stripes*. Adams shared Ross's fondness for pranks and one day caught him in a beauty. For a feature story, he assigned Ross to stow away aboard a Southern Pacific freight train crossing the Sierra Nevada. Ross accepted with alacrity, unaware that Adams in the meantime had tipped off a friendly sheriff to the stunt. Shortly after midnight outside Auburn, California, deputies intercepted the train and hauled Ross, hands skyward, out of his cozy boxcar. Tossed into jail, he proclaimed his innocence to no avail. When he finally persuaded his jailers to telephone the *Union*, Adams denied knowing him, at which point Ross realized he'd been had. Rather than sulk, he decided to play the role for all it was worth. The next morning when Adams's sheriff friend asked the jailer how Ross was getting along with his cellmates, all petty offenders, the jailer replied, "He's got them convinced that he's wanted in Salt Lake City for three murders." Back in Sacramento, he signed an account of the adventure "Hobo Ross," a sobriquet that, to his regret, stuck for years.

One day Ross failed to show for work. Thinking his friend might be on a bender, Adams wasn't especially concerned. But Ross wasn't drunk; he was gone. Adams eventually got a postcard from Pasadena, then another from Needles. Ross seems to have worked his way across the desert through early 1912, in Arizona and New Mexico, before turning up in, of all places, Panama. A few years earlier Adams himself had traveled through Central America, and he had mesmerized Ross with his recollections; Ross wrote his friend that he simply had to see if the stories were true. In Panama he worked at the English-language *Star and Herald* until anti-American rioting forced the *yanquis* on the staff to leave. He trooped up to Paraíso, where he got a job on the canal, which was still under construction. Years later Ross often bragged about how he had bossed a work crew of natives there, but this struck many listeners as a Rossian tall tale. Whatever he was doing, there is no question he was in the Canal Zone long enough to learn his way around. In a 1951 query sheet on a story dealing with the canal, Ross corrected some mistakes of geography, noting, "It so happens that I am quite familiar with the region the author is writing about in this piece. I worked on the Pedro Miguel locks and lived in Paraíso. . . . The way the author has it, he ignores the Pedro Miguel locks, which are between the Miraflores locks and the beginning of the Gaillard Cut. I regard this as a personal slight."

After he was felled by a serious fever, Ross began to have second thoughts about the tropics. He decided to return to the States and see something of the South, a part of the country he knew only second-hand. He arrived by steamer in New Orleans on Thanksgiving Day, 1912, and went to work covering the police and the courts for the *Item* "at the lowest pay I ever got on a newspaper anywhere, before or since." In New Orleans he demonstrated the agile reporter's trick for manufacturing news where none exists. He noticed that the doorway of a popular saloon displayed carvings of fetching nudes. If the saloon's clientele had ever noticed the carvings before, they certainly didn't mind them. But when Ross brought them to the attention of the city's leading society matrons, a minor scandal—which is to say, a story—ensued.

That spring Ross was among several newsmen enticed to Atlanta to work for William Randolph Hearst's splashy new paper, the *Georgian*. On arriving, however, he found that the man who had recruited him had been recalled to New York, and the promise of a job had gone with him. Ross got a reprieve from a competing Atlanta paper, the *Journal*. It hired him as its new police reporter— just in time, as it happened, for the most notorious crime in the city's history.

———

IN THE SPRING OF 1913, HAROLD ROSS WAS TWENTY YEARS OLD AND had been on the road without stop for nearly three years. He had grown to his full height, just under six feet, and full weight, a lean 160 pounds, which is more or less what he remained the rest of his life. He was already walking with a trademark slouch. His arms and legs were so long that when he sat in a deep chair he resembled a tent folding in on itself. His unruly jet hair and high cheekbones gave his face an Indian cast. He was a little self-conscious about his smile because it revealed a pronounced gap between his two front teeth, easily wide enough to pull ten-penny nails. His best feature was his eyes, alternately penetrating and dancing.

Transient and habitually broke, Ross owned a skimpy wardrobe. What clothes he had were loud and reflected dandyish tastes, a country boy's idea of how a city boy should dress. He was especially remembered for a favorite pair of yellow high-button shoes. He was still young by the standards of the tramp brethren, but in their company he worked hard—a little too hard—to mask his innate shyness and be one of the boys: he was loud, boisterous and profane; he smoked heavily; he drank regularly, if not regularly to excess; and he could scarcely be dragged away from a poker table or dice game. He could be explosively funny and was regarded as excellent company, at least among other men. (There is no particular record of his amorous activities around this time, but given his choice of associations and off-duty milieus, he almost certainly wasn't monastic.) He was considered a competent if not spectacular reporter, though he had a growing reputation as a capable "picture swiper," a handy skill in those rough-and-tumble newspaper days.

At about six o'clock on Sunday morning, April 27, Ross was rousted from bed by the telephone. It was his editor, instructing him to hustle down to Bloomfield's Funeral Home. In its very late editions that morning, the rival *Constitution* had managed to print a short front-page story about a brutal murder that had occurred the day before. A thirteen-year-old girl, Mary Phagan, had been found dead in the grimy pencil factory where she worked, and the *Journal* was playing catch-up.

At the ramshackle mortuary Ross saw Mary Phagan's lifeless and mutilated body lying atop a circular "cooling slab." He was present as authorities led in the superintendent of the pencil factory, a reserved, soft-spoken man named Leo M. Frank, who within a week would become a prime suspect. As Frank gazed upon the dead girl, Ross made a point of studying him.

The murder of Mary Phagan and the subsequent arrest and trial of Leo Frank made for one of the most sensational crime stories of the early twentieth century. Unfolding against a charged Georgia backdrop of racial prejudice, political intrigue, and sexual anxiety, the Frank case quickly built to such a lurid, hysterical pitch that it became a national fixation. As one of the *Journal*'s lead reporters on the story, Ross understood its complexities better than most. While not exactly a naïve man, he was shocked and deeply affected by much of what he saw transpire. This shock was still evident two years later when he wrote an analytical recapitulation of the case for the *San Francisco Call and Post*.

Ross wrote that immediately after the murder, "the police did what they always do in Georgia—arrested a Negro." This first suspect was Newt Lee, the factory night watchman who found the girl's body and reported the murder. In quick succession several more black men were held on suspicion. Rather than reassure the community, however, the arrests seemed to fuel its outrage. Said Ross, "The police realized the truth which determined their whole future course of action: The murder of Mary Phagan must be paid for with blood. And a Negro's blood would not suffice."

The investigation came to focus on Frank, the plant superintendent. He had admitted giving the girl her week's pay in the near-deserted factory the morning of the murder, and he was the last person to see her alive. Frank was also a Northerner, a Jew, and, to many angry Georgians, a nearly ideal villain. On May 24, he was indicted for the murder.

According to Ross, the decision to prosecute Frank was not made lightly, for even though the evidence against him was far from conclusive, authorities knew there could be no turning back once he was

Ross, back row center, poses with other reporters covering the Leo Frank trial in Atlanta in 1913. *(Atlanta Constitution)*

accused. That Sunday morning at Bloomfield's, Ross had talked to Frank. He had doubts about the man's guilt, doubts that the *Journal* returned to during and after the trial, despite the prevailing anti-Semitism and the overwhelming public sentiment that Frank was guilty.

One reason for Ross's apprehension was that Frank's indictment was based in large part on the testimony of a black suspect, Jim Conley. Conley, who swept floors at the factory, changed his story about Frank repeatedly, and to Ross it seemed that each change "eventually dovetailed into the theory of the prosecution." Also about this time, rumors began to circulate that Frank was a philanderer and, worse, a sexual deviate. When Conley was transferred to the county jail, police briefly made him available to reporters, and Ross got right to the point:

> I was, I think, the first newspaper man to talk to him after his series of confessions.
>
> "Is Frank a pervert?" I asked flatly.
>
> "No," was the reply. Moreover the Negro exhibited surprise at the question. Obviously he had never even thought of such a thing before.

Like its competitors, the *Journal* covered the case in staggering, at times even stenographic, detail. Ross himself contributed hundreds of inches' worth of feature stories, background, and examinations of legal strategy. Throughout, the *Journal* took a less frenzied, more evenhanded approach than its competitors did. For instance, after interviewing Conley, Ross and a *Journal* colleague, Harlee Branch, wrote long, side-by-side analyses on the hypothetical impact of Conley's ever-evolving statements to police. One argued the position that the evidence tended to exculpate Frank, the other that it tended to convict him. At any rate, before long Conley altered his story again, now contending that Frank *was* a pervert. (He later testified to this effect in court.)

The trial took place in a jammed courtroom through most of a sweltering August. Newspaper coverage was in the sensational, over-wrought style of the day. Exacerbating the emotional situation was the fact that the two established Atlanta newspapers were tied to different factions within Georgia's Democratic Party, so the trial coverage also was slanted for maximum political gain. The rhetoric proved nearly as hot as the weather.

On August 25, Frank was convicted of murder and sentenced to hang. But it had been obvious to many, including Ross and editorial writers at the *Journal*, that the trial had been a farce. Nearly two years of appeals ensued, during which public sentiment remained incendiary. When Frank's last court appeal failed, he turned to Governor John M. Slaton, who was under enormous pressure to let Frank hang. However, on June 21, 1915, Slaton commuted his sentence to life imprisonment. On this news, Ross's reminiscence appeared two days later in the *Call and Post*, which billed it as "the whole famous and dramatic chain of incidents as seen by a man trained in gathering correct impressions and deducing correct conclusions from tangled evidence." Ross's account is a fascinating if lumbering document. Typically, his main points are contained in the first three paragraphs:

One who saw Leo M. Frank as he looked upon the mutilated and abused body of Mary Phagan in the morgue at Atlanta three hours after her remains had been found, who talked to him afterward, who observed his conduct in detention and under arrest, who listened to his remarkable statement at his trial and heard his intensely dramatic appeal when the death sentence was passed upon him for the first time, can not today believe him guilty.

Without making the assertion that Frank is innocent, it may be said that his conduct from the outset was that of an innocent man, that he did not have a fair trial, that the evidence against him was not conclusive and that it did not prove him guilty beyond that "reasonable doubt" required by law.

He begins his life sentence in prison after two years of suspense, a possible—perhaps a probable—victim of circumstances, and, incidentally, the living proof of the assertion that if juries convict men upon evidence such as was adduced against him, and judges uphold them, no man is absolutely safe from paying the penalty for a crime he did not commit. Because the evidence against Frank might, conceivably, grow up about any man.

Ross went on to say that "Frank, of course, could not be hanged" under such circumstances, and he applauded Governor Slaton's commutation, concluding, "His act will receive the endorsement of the American people, with a notable exception perhaps in his own state."

On August 16, a mob stormed the Georgia state prison at Milledgeville, retrieved Leo Frank, took him back to Mary Phagan's childhood home of Cobb County, just outside Atlanta, and hanged him.

The Frank case was so controversial that in some corners of Georgia it can still provoke an argument. His guilt was neither proved nor disproved, and the fact is that eighty years after the crime no one is really sure who killed Mary Phagan. Ross's involvement in, and thoughts about, the case are significant on several counts. Most obvious, again, is the maturity evident in a reporter who, it must be remembered, was only twenty years old when entrusted with this incendiary story. Ross not only had to master the intricacies of the case but, as an outsider, had to sort through the shadowy forces behind it. Second, he demonstrated genuine courage in forming, and then maintaining, the belief that Frank just might be innocent, a decidedly unpopular view. Third, the *Call* piece is compelling for what it says about Ross's fundamental democratic values, especially in light of the fact that twenty-five years later he himself would be accused of anti-Semitic and racist views. Like many men of his time and background, Ross held some prejudices, and they surfaced to sting him a few times when he was the editor of *The New Yorker*. But as the Leo Frank piece (not to mention countless friendships and professional associations) demonstrates, Ross was in no way anti-Semitic, and if he sometimes made thoughtless personal utterances about blacks—which he did—this shortcoming was more than offset by his unstinting insistence that *New Yorker* writers, virtually all more liberal than he, say what they liked in the pages of his magazine.

There is one last noteworthy aspect of Ross's stay in Atlanta: he produced some obvious forerunners to *The New Yorker*'s Talk of the Town stories. For the Sunday feature section of the *Journal,* he wrote a handful of offbeat pieces that employed the editorial "we" and a tone of detachment. One, written shortly before the Frank trial began, was a visit to Atlanta's notorious police court, Judge Nash Broyles presiding, where the city's detritus washed up for penance. The newspapers ran daily vignettes from the court, and Steve Oney, a writer who has studied them, says, "Usually these pieces were full of Uncle Remus dialect and illustrated by Little Black Sambo–like line drawings. Thus, in context, Ross's piece strikes a more sophisticated—or scared—tone." An excerpt:

> Being of that vast class of society which calls itself respectable, we have never been in police court before and are, therefore, shocked by what confronts us. Negroes—scores of them—banked up on tiers of benches on one side of a railing which divides the room in half, a dozen policemen lolling in chairs, and the judge's rostrum on the other side—all this is disconcerting. It is not even a pleasing sight. But we are out to see the police court! So we will subdue for the nonce the just and decidedly respectable inclination to leave, and take seats among the policemen.
>
> Court has begun. The clerk from beside the judge's chair calls a name without looking up from his docket. An attaché automatically opens a door on one side of the room and repeats the name raucously. His tone grates on our nerves. And then we have the opportunity of seeing one of those notorious people, a police court character.
>
> He comes out through the door—out of the cage—blinks, glances furtively around and then, probably having been there before and knowing the way, walks straight up to the judge's stand. He looks human, that is about all we can say for him. . . .

Full of himself after covering the first truly important story of his career, Ross decided to make his stab at the big time, New York City.

He didn't think he'd much like New York; he had a westerner's prejudice against the city and the dudes, as he called them, who populated it. On the other hand, to work in New York was to establish one's bona fides, and if he could show the city slickers a thing or two in the process, so much the better. He repeatedly tried to crack Manhattan from temporary assignments at the short-lived *Hudson Observer,* based in Hoboken, New Jersey, and the *Brooklyn Eagle.* He applied at the *Times,* and most likely to many of the dozen or so other dailies then publishing in New York. But the New York newspapers never had much need or use for transient help, and he was sent away discouraged.

About the same time, Ross got a rather insistent plea from home: his father, now in his sixties, wanted him to come back to Salt Lake and join him in the family business. Unsurprisingly, Ross was dubious. He had been home a few times between jobs in the West; George and Ida were always glad to see him, and he was thankful for a few weeks of hot meals and clean sheets, but everyone understood the visits were temporary. What his father proposed now was different, permanent—working in a business he had never cared for, side by side with a man just as stubborn and cantankerous as he was. Still, down on his luck and tired of the road, Ross was inclined to be the good son this once. Setting aside his reservations, he returned to 622 Elizabeth Street, a footsore and worldly man of twenty-one back under his parents' roof. He spent the better part of 1914, it appears, trying to make the arrangement work, but he couldn't. He simply found the business of knocking down houses and peddling scrap too dull. Making matters worse was the buildup and outbreak of war in Europe, which he followed carefully in the papers and dreamed of covering. He knew too well that he lacked the necessary credentials to be a foreign correspondent, but the reveries nonetheless reinforced just how much he missed journalism. Informing his disappointed parents of his decision, he set off again for the most romantic destination within reach, San Francisco.

———

COVERING THE WATERFRONT WAS AN IMPORTANT BEAT FOR THE SAN Francisco papers, and good duty for any reporter, and this was the assignment Ross wangled from the *Call and Post*. If the city's notorious Barbary Coast was in its death convulsions, its waterfront was busier than ever. Everywhere one looked were sailors and sea captains, visiting dignitaries, good restaurants, and accommodating saloons. The glittering Panama-Pacific Exposition of 1915 was reacquainting the world with San Francisco, which less than a decade before had been buried by earthquake and fire. Add to this the general to-and-fro of a busy harbor and it was a lot for a waterfront reporter to stay on top of. Ross thrived on it. Though one San Francisco colleague remembered him as "a picture-chaser and a rather grubby and not too efficient reporter," others said that after his brush with the prosaic world of house demolition Ross brought a reinvigorated interest to his reporting. Certainly the *Call* of this period is full of (unbylined) news from the waterfront: sailors demanding better wages from shipowners; personnel changes at the shipping lines; the arrival of new steamers and exotic visitors. Ross made friends easily and was a good talker, qualities he used to get information from people. He cultivated contacts all along the waterfront. Long after he was gone, young reporters would hear about the man from the *Call* who prowled the piers and warehouses in a trenchcoat, battered hat pulled down mysteriously over his eyes.

Of course, the Ross legends had as much to do with his talent for horseplay as anything else. Even by San Francisco's estimable standards, he was considered a character. He navigated the city in a temperamental Stutz roadster, and if he wasn't playing cribbage at the tony Bohemian Club he might be sitting in on a poker game in a pineapple warehouse. His antics are suggested by some of the nicknames he acquired at this time: "Punk" Ross, "Roughhouse" Ross, "Hangover" Ross. When the local press club needed new furniture, it was Ross who led a midnight raid on the Danish exhibit of the (by then closed) Panama-Pacific Exposition, relieving it of its wicker furnishings. On another occasion, he stumbled onto a bewildered Polynesian chieftain who had been diverted, somewhat against his will, to San Francisco. For several days he assumed personal custody of the chief, who spoke no English. Ross took pains to introduce him to department stores, cable cars, and, most satisfyingly, bock beer.

Almost without his realizing it, a year went by, then two, and Ross was still in San Francisco. For the first time in his career, he was not impelled to try the next town over the hill. He was thoroughly captivated by the city's climate and civility, its cosmopolitan charm, its expansive cultural menu. He began to get a reputation as a ladies' man after he was caught sending flowers to the receptionist at his dingy residential hotel. San Francisco was taking off some of the frontiersman's rough edges and imposing a little discernment on his palate (an education that would resume soon in Paris, then in postwar New York). Beyond this, he continued to read hungrily—so much that his blowsier friends began to wonder if he might not be a closet intellectual. He read Conrad, Kipling, O. Henry. He rejoiced, predictably, in Twain's surgical examination of James Fenimore Cooper's "literary offenses." But what he read most avidly was the work of Herbert Spencer, the English positivist who is credited with the concept of social Darwinism. Spencer's philosophy became the single biggest shaper of Ross's own worldview. He had been reading Spencer since his teens, perhaps steered by the testimonials of such devotees as Clarence Darrow and Jack London. On the other hand, at that time in America Spencer's influence could be found everywhere. This was especially so in the West, where his ideas about the survival of the fittest married very nicely with the code of rugged individualism. "The generation that acclaimed Grant as its hero took Spencer as its thinker," explained the social historian Richard Hofstadter. Spencer offered a comprehensive explanation of the world, but he wasn't technical or overly intellectual. This accessibility attracted Ross and countless others of limited formal education. Spencer's profound influence is apparent not merely in Ross's political outlook, which was classically laissez-faire on everything from war to income tax, but in the fact that all his life he would drop Spencerian aphorisms into conversations or correspondence where he felt they were appropriate.

In the early months of 1917 it became obvious that America would join the World War. Ross had ample time to consider what he would do upon the formal declaration of war, which came on April 6. A few days later he passed by an army recruiting station for a railway regiment, the Eighteenth Engineers. He was drawn to the placard's boast: "First to France; First to Fight." Persuading half a dozen friends to join him, he enlisted.

A railway unit appealed to Ross. After six years of following train tracks, he had become something of an expert on the subject. Years later, as a passenger in the private car of W. Averell Harriman, whose father had built the Union Pacific, he regaled his host with reminiscences of his tramp days. Harriman was so taken that he gave Ross the car's brass nameplate as a souvenir.

So it was that Ross left San Francisco, bound not for another newspaper this time, but for boot camp.

CHAPTER 3

THE STARS
AND STRIPES

ABOUT THAT SLOGAN: IT WAS THE "FIRST TO FRANCE" PART, NEEDLESS to say, that spoke more seductively to Ross's soul than the "First to Fight" part. This is not to suggest he was a coward, because he wasn't, or that he didn't sincerely believe it was America's duty to bring the Boche to heel, because, by God, he did. But for Ross, as for countless thousands of other American provincials, motivation to march off to war had less to do with getting shot at or gassed than with the opportunity to see something of the world. The enterprise had a romance attached to it that no amount of carnage would wring out.

The Engineers were true to their word: Ross was, in fact, one of the first twenty-five thousand Americans in France. In getting there, however, he outsmarted himself twice over. He was induced by a common sucker's promise—a quick corporalcy—which didn't materialize, and he somehow got the impression that a railway regiment meant relatively cozy duty. "He and a pal had put one over the Army by enlisting in *the Engineers*, and he told it as a good joke," said the artist and writer Cyrus LeRoy Baldridge, who roomed with Ross in France and whose wife had worked with him in San Francisco. "Little did he know the Army! The Engineers being one of the hardest worked units. I guess he thought it would be some kind of paper work." Soon enough he would learn otherwise.

After boot camp at Fort Lewis, Washington, the regiment spent what seemed like an eternity traveling in the dead of summer—a week on a train to New York; another train to Canada, where they boarded a transport ship for surreptitious passage to Britain; then finally to France. The transatlantic crossing, in August, was especially unpleasant. "There were 2,600 troops aboard—my own regiment and another—quartered between decks in what originally provided space for one thousand steerage passengers," Ross wrote to friends back in San Francisco. "The first morning all my stuff, carefully stowed under the bunk, was under two feet of water and some of it floated off." The Engineers came to be stationed in Bordeaux, where, by late summer, Ross's supposedly cushy unit was building port installations and spending much of its time literally digging ditches. If he was humbled by this ignominious turn of events, he was at least thankful for being beyond harm's reach. He closed an early letter to his parents by saying, "By way of comfort—mutually—may [I] remark that I have it on rather good authority that this railroad regiment never will get in the danger zone. Good night."

The Eighteenth Engineers comprised ragtag, undisciplined westerners, men whose personal wear and tear matched or exceeded Ross's own. Many were surly and/or alcoholic; ditch-digging did nothing to improve their outlook. The argumentative, unsoldierly Ross fit in well enough, though he did distinguish himself with a measure of natural leadership. For instance, he helped start up a respectable regimental publication, *The Spiker*, and was its second editor. This initiative perhaps explains why he was nominated for officer's training school—though it was also suggested, not altogether facetiously, that the commanding officer hit on the idea to get Ross out of his hair. Either way, Ross was delighted; aside from escaping manual labor, he would be in for a second lieutenant's commission if things worked out. But that was before he got to the officer's training camp itself in Langres, high in the foothills of the Vosges range in northeastern France. Arriving with the onset of winter, he soon realized he had been consigned to hell without the heat. Langres was wet, cold, muddy—in a word, miserable. Ross proceeded to flunk the officer's examination—"I was too flip with my answers to the goddamn silly questions"—but stayed on as a company clerk. Paperwork better suited the cerebral private than spadework, but there was nothing to be done about the dank chill. Even Christmas at Langres was depressing. After sitting down to a holiday meal of beans, Ross and a friend decided they might at least wash down this indignity with champagne. They scrounged a bottle, but the military police warned them not to drink it on the premises. "For two hours we hunted for a place to down it comfortably, eventually consuming it standing in the snow behind the Army Staff College, drinking out of one mess cup by turns. After eating *deux oeufs*—omelette—*et pommes frites*—*oui, oui*—*oui, oui*—I went back to the barracks. The stove was as cold and the room as dismal as the rest of the day had been. The whole room—twenty men—went to bed at eight o'clock to keep warm."

As yet Ross was unaware of an idea that was hatching, at this same time, at the American Expeditionary Forces headquarters of General John J. Pershing in Chaumont. An official A.E.F. newspaper was under consideration. The notion had been kicked around before, but now an ambitious second lieutenant in the army censor's office, Guy T. Viskniskki, was pressing for it. The idea appealed on many counts. News from the States was hard to come by in Europe, and outdated in any case. American troops already were complaining about being out of touch with home. Beyond that, Viskniskki argued, the paper would be an effective tool for purposes of morale and propaganda, not to mention an efficient vehicle for disseminating army directives. Pershing was persuaded. Shortly after Christmas of 1917, he approved a weekly publication; it would be called *The Stars and Stripes,* and Viskniskki was ordered to get it up and running as soon as possible.

The Stars and Stripes would have appropriate military supervision, of course, and censorship would be applied as necessary. To Pershing's great credit, he saw to it that even though the newspaper was formed under the auspices of the A.E.F. general staff, his officers for the most part resisted the military impulse to meddle. Pershing also knew that if *The Stars and Stripes* was to have credibility with the soldiers it was intended for, the reporters and editors needed to be chosen, by and large, from the enlisted men themselves. Even with the commander in chief's blessing, however, staffing proved difficult. Viskniskki culled the ranks for experienced journalists, but even when they could be found, their commanding officers often were reluctant to lend them out.

Back in Langres, this was not exactly the problem for Private Ross. As company clerk, he had seen some of the earliest communiqués about *The Stars and Stripes* and recognized it as his ticket back to civilization. He immediately put in for a transfer and formally applied to the paper, characterizing his newspaper career in as flattering terms as he could muster. But going by the book got him nowhere; all his requests were ignored. His frustration mounted until direct action was required, and one night he simply walked away from Langres. "Without saying goodbye, go to hell, or anything else to the commandant, he caught a truck for Paris," a colleague marveled. Actually, Ross tended to avoid trucks, trains, and other official conveyances because he was, after all, A.W.O.L., so he mostly stuck to the back roads, on foot, for the one hundred fifty miles to Paris. After a few days, on or about February 15, 1918, he turned up at the newspaper's makeshift offices at the Hôtel Ste.-Anne, not far from the Louvre and the Palais Royale, a portable Corona in hand. The second issue of *The Stars and Stripes* had just gone to press, produced by an exhausted start-up staff so small that it could be numbered on one hand. They were so glad to see Ross—they would have been glad to see anyone, much less a man with a typewriter—that Viskniskki promptly squared away Ross's transfer papers ex post facto.

As the officer in charge of *The Stars and Stripes,* Viskniskki— invariably just "Visk" except to his face—was responsible for its staffing, production, distribution, and, at least nominally, its content.

He was an efficient bureaucrat. He was also bullying, humorless, officious, and, alas, regular army (a veteran of the Spanish-American War). In civilian life he had worked for a newspaper syndicate, but to the newspaper's staff, most of whom were masquerading as soldiers anyway, the gaunt Visk was a "military son of a bitch" to whom they took an instant dislike. They especially resented, and endlessly thwarted, his attempts to run the paper on something like a military basis. (Visk once placed Ross under house arrest because the Paris edition of the *New York Herald* beat him on a story. After a few hours of watching Visk scurry back and forth, Ross stopped him to ask, "May the private have the lieutenant's permission to go to the can?")

Another private, Hudson Hawley, an ersatz machine gunner from the Twenty-sixth Division, was one of the earliest recruits and wrote most of the first two issues. Arriving with Ross was Private John T. Winterich, 496th Aero Squadron, a versatile writer and editor. Two weeks later there appeared a short, corpulent sergeant, most recently an orderly with a field hospital and, before that, theater critic of *The New York Times*. Alexander Woollcott had a moon face, and with round wire-rim eyeglasses sitting atop his hook nose, he looked to Ross like nothing so much as "a human owl in sergeant's stripes." Woollcott had taken the once-lowly theater job at the *Times* and, by

Private H. W. Ross
of *The Stars and Stripes*–
and his calling card.
(Brown Brothers)

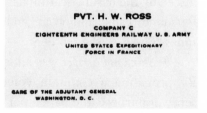

dint of his hyperbolic prose and personal audacity, made something of a reputation on Broadway. Rejected for combat duty because of poor eyesight, he had signed up with a medical unit, performing admirably enough to be promoted to sergeant. *The Stars and Stripes* had gotten wind of Woollcott's transfer, and Ross especially, still smarting from his New York rejection, was none too pleased. He strode up, towering over the new arrival. "Where'd you work?" Ross demanded. "*The New York Times*—dramatic critic," replied Woollcott evenly. With this Ross threw back his head and broke into exaggerated laughter—until Woollcott cut him dead. "You know," he said, "you remind me a great deal of my grandfather's coachman." In this way Ross and Woollcott began what would become a long, mystifying, and, it must be said, ultimately perverse friendship.

With the addition of two exceptional artists—Albian A. Wallgren, whose forte was comic drawing, and Baldridge, whose illustrations were more serious and inspirational—Ross, Hawley, Winterich and Woollcott formed the editorial core of *The Stars and Stripes*. There would be other notable staffers. Captain Franklin P. Adams, whose bags Private Ross lugged from the train station, was in civilian life the popular *New York Tribune* columnist F.P.A. And Lieutenant Grantland Rice arrived just after the paper decided to suspend its sports page (a symbol of frivolity) until hostilities ended, so he contributed some fine combat reportage instead. Yet even as the overall employment of *The Stars and Stripes* swelled into the hundreds, Ross, Winterich, Woollcott, Hawley, Baldridge and Wallgren remained an ad hoc editorial council that essentially decided the content and set the tone of the paper. They were much more dedicated to the men than to the military. Rank meant little to them, to the utter consternation of some of their superiors. Their rogue behavior was reinforced by the harum-scarum nature of the *Stars and Stripes* operation. Personnel came and went, and the office itself was moved three times. The first, the Hôtel Ste.-Anne, also housed German prisoners.

The Stars and Stripes was a happy marriage of form and function. By providing a common voice and articulating an unwavering sense of purpose, the paper, perhaps more than anything other than combat itself, coalesced the disparate, cobbled-together American units into an army. As predicted, it became instantly popular, and for one overriding reason: it was relentlessly, unapologetically in the service of the enlisted man. It was a good newspaper, equal parts news service, bulletin board, department store, advice column, and inspiration sheet. It ran to eight pages and appeared every Friday. It cost a dime—a great deal considering that English-language Paris papers could be had for a few pennies—but the soldiers paid gladly. As promised, there was much news from the States; *The Stars and Stripes* even maintained a "correspondent" in New York who regularly cabled long features and shorter news items of interest from the home front. Dispatches from the war itself were most prominent, of course, with related editorials and the inevitably bracing tales of courage. The paper was informative, brash, and sometimes blunt. It tweaked the brass when necessary. Unfailingly, the tone was soldier-to-soldier.

Arguably the most important features of the paper were those that allowed enlisted men to speak for themselves. Their letters to the editor, jokes, stories, and poetry offered trench-level perspectives on the war, and they accounted for much of the paper's appeal. Predictably, there were many gripes: about the food, mess sergeants, "cooties" (lice), the cumbersome headgear, and the hated spiral puttees—leggings which inexplicably were adapted from the uniform of British troops in India who had worn them as a precaution against snakebite. But it was the "doughboy doggerel" more than anything else that revealed the heart and soul of the A.E.F. Soldier-poets were so numerous that the newspaper got more than five hundred submissions a week. Two samples from the issue of September 6, 1918, typify the general tone:

> Goodbye, pal; I don't know where you're camping now,
> Whether you've pitched your tent 'neath azure skies,
> Or whether o'er your head bleak storm winds blow.
> I only know
> That when they sounded final taps for you
> Something within my heart died, too.
>
> —*From "Requiem," Fra Guido*

Fighting Germans is what I crave,
But fighting cuckoos makes me rave.
I'll save them till I find a Boche,
And plant them in his shirt, by gosh!
—*From "The Cuckoos," John J. Curtin*

Still, it was only when the Americans began fighting in earnest that *The Stars and Stripes* came into its own. This was during the last great German offensive, in the spring of 1918, and the Allied counteroffensive of that summer. These were long, horrific, storied battles: Château-Thierry, Belleau Wood, the Argonne Forest, St.-Mihiel. Reporting on them, *The Stars and Stripes* moved well beyond a mere service publication to a unique chronicler of history. Reporters rode to the battlefields in cars and, when they couldn't find haystacks, slept in the backseats. Dozens of staffers contributed to the war coverage, but it was the ubiquitous Woollcott, the paper's chief correspondent, who became the pudgy symbol of *The Stars and Stripes* for enlisted men (in part thanks to Wallgren, who routinely caricatured Aleck in his cartoon strips). Woollcott truly was fearless, to the point at times of foolhardiness. Ross traveled with him often and carried away the image of Woollcott "trundling along in some exposed spot amidst calls of warning and shouts of 'Get the hell out of there!' "

But for all his enthusiasm, even valor, it took Woollcott a while to get the hang of combat. Winterich accompanied him on his first battlefield trip, to Château-Thierry. "Far off to the left, toward dawn, three guns, friendly or hostile (or one gun firing three times), went pop . . . pop . . . pop, with intervals of perhaps five seconds between the pops. A hand nudged me in the darkness and a courteous voice inquired, 'Is that a barrage?' "

Woollcott showered his readers in glory—and in prose that was treacly even by the estimable standards of the day. But he was only giving the men what they wanted, and the proof was in the numbers. In a year the circulation of the paper, which started at thirty thousand, soared past five hundred thousand. Given this kind of growth and an army on the move, delivery of the paper was often a nightmare. Resourceful field agents did what they had to—including once, in the Argonne, enlisting Captain Eddie Rickenbacker to air-drop two thousand copies.

Later in his life Ross was often credited with "editing" *The Stars and Stripes,* and eventually he did become its top editor. For the most part, however, his leadership was manifested more by example than by title. Like everyone else in the place, he reported and wrote stories, made assignments, edited copy, and wrote headlines, but his greatest value was in generating ideas. More than anyone else on staff, Ross had an uncanny sense of what enlisted men would and wouldn't read. It was the commoner's touch, which sprang from his own background as well as his multifarious professional experience. He himself recognized this singular capability and asserted it from the beginning.

Just one month after he arrived, Ross conceived a campaign that turned out to be one of the boldest public-relations strokes of the war, not to mention one of its most poignant legacies. He proposed that A.E.F. troops donate money to "adopt" French war orphans. (More accurately, the Red Cross–administered fund cared for children who had had one or both parents killed or disabled in the war.) Ross hoped the modest campaign, announced in the paper on March 29, 1918, would spur friendly competition among the doughboys—the original goal was one thousand adoptions—as well as raise their consciousness of the French plight. He could not have imagined, even as he prodded readers with a weekly ration of heartrending stories, how enthusiastically the campaign would be embraced, not just in the ranks but even stateside. (Pershing himself adopted two orphans but ordered Ross not to make a fuss over it, so his contribution was simply recorded like every other on the list, between "Y.M.C.A. Secretaries, Base Camp No. 1" and "Aero Const. Squadron.") By December, more than two million francs had been raised on behalf of nearly 3,500 French children. The French themselves were flabbergasted and genuinely touched. Ross's commanding officer later would say that Ross had contributed "more than almost any individual in the A.E.F. to the cordial relations between the U.S. and the French republic."

Gratifying as this was, Ross derived as much or more pleasure

Ross tours a World War I battlefield in France. *(Courtesy of Patricia Ross Honcoop)*

from his opportunity, at last, to be a war correspondent. He turned up at most of the hotspots, usually to help report and contribute secondary stories. In September, for instance, he recounted the success of an American cavalry regiment at St.-Mihiel, and in October, at the Argonne, he helped produce the paper's expansive account of the fabled "Lost Battalion." About this same time he got a call from the provost marshal's office. They had an American soldier who had just escaped, via Switzerland, from a German prison camp; was *The Stars and Stripes* interested? Ross and Winterich rushed down immediately to take custody of one Private Frank Savicki. They debriefed him, then kept him under wraps for several days to thwart the civilian competition. Savicki's escape was indeed dramatic, and Ross told the story in brisk, occasionally breathless detail. Clearly his narrative sense had come a long way since that boat ride on the Feather River. This passage picks up Savicki as he encounters his last, most treacherous obstacle:

In the cover of the bushes he remained all day. Across the valley he could see the peasants tilling the soil. They, he knew, were in Switzerland. Before him, in the foreground, too, he could see the river and the difficulties before him in crossing it. Paralleling the river was a railroad, the string of sentry boxes and a wide belt of barbed wire, obviously put there to prevent the escape of such as he. At noon he saw the sentries changed, and again in the evening.

The sentries, he discovered, did not walk post, merely maintaining a watch from their boxes. The wire, he decided, he could get through. The river, he calculated, was too broad to jump—but it could be vaulted. He stirred during the afternoon just enough to get a sturdy stick and trim it for a vaulting pole.

After dark he started. He crawled. So slowly and cautiously did he go that the trip to the edge of the barbed wire took five or six hours. There he rose and threaded his way through the strands, pausing after each step to unfasten the barbs which clung to his clothing.

He came to the railroad track and crawled over that. He could dimly discern the sentry boxes. He heard a guard cough in one of them. He crawled on, laying a course midway between two of them.

He gained the edge of the river. He stood on the bank. The other bank, ten feet away, was Switzerland and safety. He poised his vaulting pole and sprang for the further side. The pole sank four feet into the mud of the river bottom. Private Frank Savicki landed, belly deep, in the water with something of a splash.

There was a tense minute. Clinging to a clump of grass on the Swiss bank, Savicki waited for the bullets he was certain were coming. But none came. Evidently the Boche had not heard him. Finally, he pulled himself on to the land. He was a prisoner no more.

War might be hell, as Private Savicki could testify, but Private Ross was having the time of his life. He adored Paris (and became a lifelong Francophile), he was a war correspondent, and he was a key player in an enterprise that he believed in completely. In retrospect some have called *The Stars and Stripes* insufficiently critical and overly gung-ho, and certainly to anyone from the Vietnam generation the innocence one finds in the newspaper is as suspicious as it is beguiling. But it accurately reflected the emotion and sentiment not just of its staff but of the A.E.F. generally. Ross's own letters home were full of passages that Hollywood might have been tempted to crib. In July 1918, smack in the middle of the Allied counteroffensive near Soissons, he wrote his parents: "The Americans were in it strong, of course, and fought wonderfully—so well that I don't believe anybody will be able to fully describe it. I saw some of the soldiers as they came out of the line. They were jubilant, enthusiastic and confident. When the American army gets going full blast, it won't take long to defeat the kaiser." The flip side of his ardor was that Ross scarcely could look on such a scene without feeling guilty. At Belleau Wood, Woollcott found him sitting by the side of a dusty road, tired and disconsolate as he watched the American wounded being carried away. When Woollcott asked what was wrong, Ross fired a string of profanities at him, then said, "At home I was always a nonproducer and here, on a battlefield, I'm a noncombatant."

———

THE ONLY TIME THE GERMAN ARMY CAME CLOSE TO KILLING PRIVATE H. W. Ross was one pleasant Saturday morning in the middle of Paris. In March 1918, not long after he had arrived from Langres, the Germans began shelling the capital with the fearsome long-distance gun that the French nicknamed Big Bertha. This particular Saturday was her debut, and so Ross and all of Paris were caught unawares. He was sleeping late on his day off when he was awakened by an air-raid siren. He ran into the street and looked up for airplanes, but there were none. He continued to scan the skies. "I was standing with my mouth open, as I say, when *whango!* one of the shells dropped right behind me, so close I was spun around with the concussion." He staggered to a subway station for shelter. Emerging two hours later, still shaken, he went off and, as he said, "consumed a whole bottle of 'morale.' " (Ross's friend Marc Connelly, the playwright, used to tell another Big Bertha story so exquisitely surreal that it more than likely comes from the thick Ross Apocrypha. In this version, Ross decided one afternoon that he would see Paris from the city's Ferris wheel, made famous in the exposition of 1900. Once he reaches the top, the wheel stops and, of course, Big Bertha roars into action. He was said to be stuck there for an hour, feeling like the fattest duck in the shooting gallery.)

The longer Ross was in Paris, the more he grew in savvy and repute, but to all outward appearances he remained the Colorado Kid. The artist Charles Baskerville, who would be one of Ross's important early contributors at *The New Yorker* and who was a decorated soldier in World War I, remembers running into Ross in Paris at the time. Ross was sociable enough, he said, but "a rough guy, uncouth. He was a very ordinary farmboy-type [who] just happened to turn up in this extraordinary situation." Ross's French, what he tried of it, was terrible. In Rossian dialect, a favorite bar, Monsieur Jacques, became simply "Monjacks." His hair was an unruly thatch, and his ill-fitting uniform was known to prompt gasps: blouse usually unbuttoned, shoes unshined, leggings droopily telescoped around his ankles.

In time the *Stars and Stripes* regulars (and some irregulars, such as civilian correspondents Heywood Broun and Ring Lardner) fell into the pleasant habit of spending Saturday evenings at a Montmartre bistro, known as Nini's after its accommodating owner. The soldiers provided Nini with extra ration tickets for sugar and bread, and she in turn provided them with sumptuous (for wartime) meals, good wine, and an intimate place to play cards and dice. Dinner and gaming typically stretched well into Sunday morning.

One night in November, just after the armistice was declared, Woollcott turned up at Nini's with a young woman on his arm. She was Jane Grant, an old friend from New York. Attractive and outgoing, she soon had all the poker players vying for her attention in their best schoolboy fashion. Ross especially made an impression on her. "As I peered at him from across the table, slumping over his poker hand like a misshapen question mark, I decided he was really the homeliest man I'd ever met," she later wrote. Nonetheless, before long Ross had finagled the seat next to her, and as he talked she found herself rather charmed. At dawn, he escorted her (with Winterich in tow) back down the hill to her hotel.

Jeanette Cole Grant had come to France two months earlier as a clerk with the Y.M.C.A.'s Motion Picture Bureau; with Woollcott's help she was now transferring to the Y's entertainment division. Born in Joplin, Missouri, and raised in Girard, Kansas, she was a gifted singer, and after high school her family had sent her to New York to study voice. She did some professional singing, but to make ends meet she took a job writing short notices for the society pages of *The New York Times*. Intelligent and independent, Jane eventually earned

Jane Grant, here in her Y.M.C.A. service uniform, considered Ross "the homeliest man I'd ever met." (*Jane Grant Collection, University of Oregon*)

a general assignment job, in so doing becoming the first full-time female reporter in the *Times* city room. (She later teased Ross that she probably saw him the day he applied unsuccessfully for a job at the *Times.*) At the paper she became fast friends with Aleck and joined his widening coterie. She was thrilled with the transfer to the entertainment division because it meant she could perform for the troops and see Paris to boot. Woollcott was her only friend there, and she looked him up the moment she arrived. Early in their relationship, Aleck persuaded himself that his interest in Jane was more than platonic; he even spoke of marriage. Naturally enough, Jane was either confused or amused by this pose—Woollcott was a sexual neuter who tended to derive emotional gratification by arranging couplings and uncouplings among his friends—and shrugged it off. Though he remained close to her, Aleck never quite forgave her that. For now, however, he was satisfied to play matchmaker between two of his best friends.

The courtship advanced in fits and starts. Jane was coy, and Ross, never articulate anyway, could be positively opaque when it came to matters of the heart. Neither quite knew where they stood with the other. Even as he felt himself tumbling into his first serious relationship, Ross was suspicious about it all. In February, when Jane was on the road performing, he wrote to her, "I haven't laughed much since you left town. Funny coincidence, isn't it?" Yet in the same letter, in the fourth of seven giddy postscripts, he says, "I can't make up my mind about you." He *had* made up his mind, of course, and presently he was doing everything he could think of to ensure that the feeling was mutual. Jane had become close to all the *Stars and Stripes* staffers, and she never lacked for beaus. This, as well as Ross's expanding role at the paper, complicated his efforts to see her, but he was nothing if not persistent. He commandeered a Cadillac to give her a personal tour of the battlefields at Belleau Wood and Château-Thierry. Fortunately, the armistice was making it possible to enjoy France in a more conventionally romantic fashion, so in time they were sailing along the Seine, visiting Versailles, and dining in the Bois de Boulogne. To impress Jane, Ross even pretended to enjoy things he actually despised, like the opera. (As many an officer had discovered, he could be charmingly disingenuous when it suited him.) From this proximity Jane began to appreciate what an extraordinary paradox Ross was—as she said, "brave and fearful, kind and brusque, attentive and indifferent. He was as profane as a man can be—but he was never smutty. In the presence of women he was especially puritanical and I always found him excessively modest." (Years later she told James Thurber that Ross had never tried to sleep with her until after they were married.) She knew things were getting serious when she found herself chipping away at Ross's prejudices against New York, where she intended to resume her reporting career after the war. When he discussed his postwar plans in any detail at all, they usually involved a quixotic, Jack Londonesque South Seas sabbatical. Gradually his resistance to New York softened, however, and he began to talk to Jane in vague terms about things "they" might do once back home. Indeed, Jane probably didn't even realize it at first, but Ross and Woollcott, in their café reveries, already had kicked around an idea for a magazine devoted to New York. They hadn't taken the concept far, but they knew it would involve some new wrinkles, like criticism of the New York press. And it must have humor, they agreed, lots of humor.

———

WITH THE ARMISTICE, PARIS EXPLODED IN CELEBRATION. "IN A restaurant today an old Frenchman got up and shook hands with me and (I think) would have kissed me if we hadn't had the table between us," Ross told his parents. "I'm onto the kissing dodge, however, and am always elusive." He was glad for an end to the fighting, he added, not so much for himself as for "the fellows who have been up on the front for months under fire and in the mud and cold which induces as high a degree of physical misery as can be imagined."

At *The Stars and Stripes,* meanwhile, the cease-fire was kindling the spirit of insubordination. If they didn't have to shoot Germans anymore, the staff figured, they could finally concentrate on their real enemy, Visk. Nine months of working with Captain (for he had been promoted) Viskniskki had only intensified their disdain. They called him rude and arrogant, a schemer and a meddler. Looking back on the insurrection, Woollcott would finger Ross as the protagonist, and Ross Woollcott. It's impossible to know who was right, though the episode certainly anticipates some of Ross's deep-cover sorties against Raoul Fleischmann at *The New Yorker*. In any event, both men heartily endorsed a bill of particulars that the editorial council drew up against Visk and sent to the army command. Ordinarily such insolence might invite some time in the stockade, but the general staff knew full well that it was Ross and company, not Visk, who were more critical to the production of *The Stars and Stripes*. Visk was promoted up and out.

This left the small problem of who was to run the paper. Ross, Woollcott, Winterich, Hawley, Baldridge and Wallgren met to decide. Ross, who was said to resemble a Bolshevik anyway, suggested a soviet-style solution: create a managing directorate, he said, from which one member would serve as managing editor, but only for as long as he pleased the group. The idea was accepted. Ross nominated Winterich for the top job, for he was generally regarded as the steadiest and most technically capable editor, but the shy Winterich demurred. Instead, Ross was chosen by acclamation, and his leadership was never again put to a vote.

At thirty-eight dollars a month, Private Ross was suddenly the lowest-paid managing editor of a major American newspaper. (He stubbornly resisted efforts to promote him to a more respectable rank, though he did have his own business card.) There was something exhilarating about a private—"the lowest form of human life in the A.E.F.," Woollcott said—consigning a captain's lovingly wrought poetry to the circular file. Still, Ross's friends had done him no favor. With the war on, the paper's direction had been obvious, but with peace breaking out, what was the staff supposed to write about? The only thing the two million Americans in Europe wanted to know was when they were going home. Ross saw that the paper's focus must change, and it did. *The Stars and Stripes* covered the peace talks— Ross and crew carried off pieces of the German flag of truce as souvenirs—drummed up interesting feature stories from the field, and resumed the sports pages. It examined, and tried to combat, growing anti-French sentiment in the American ranks, especially among those units posted in or near Germany. The paper also published as much information as it could to smooth the enlisted man's reentry to civilian life.

All this amounted to an incredible education for Ross. He became intimately familiar with the production, personnel, and advertising demands of a big publication. Naturally hardheaded and sometimes abrasive, he learned something about the requisite diplomacy of command, especially since he had to manage both up (with army censors and the general staff) and down (with his own staff and readers) at the same time. He began to indulge his finickiness about grammar and punctuation; that Christmas as a present he gave Winterich a page of commas. Most significant, he began to see the possibilities of some unfamiliar journalistic forms. Because *The Stars and Stripes* was a weekly, it had to find ways to distinguish itself from its hard-news-oriented daily competitors. One way was to exploit their inherent superficiality, so features, personality pieces and substantial behind-the-scenes stories all became part of the paper's menu, with a high premium placed on storytelling. In other words, for the first time Ross was encountering story forms that in a few years he would resurrect and polish at *The New Yorker*.

About this time Ross learned one other useful thing about himself: inside the editor lurked a bit of the entrepreneur. Many of the American units in France produced their own publications, as Ross had *The Spiker*. They all published jokes, and they all piled up in *The Stars and Stripes* offices. Why not cull the best of them, he wondered, put them into an anthology, and sell it to the troops for a franc? (Twenty-five years later, interestingly, he would excoriate DeWitt Wallace for doing basically the same thing with the *Reader's Digest*.) Ross put the idea to Winterich, who said it was crazy and also found the notion of selling soldiers their own jokes vaguely repugnant, so Ross set to cutting and pasting on his own. In the space of a few nights he had produced the pamphlet, which he called *Yank Talk*. There remained some hurdles. For one thing, since the pamphlet was to be typeset in a French printshop, he had to borrow English quote marks from the newspaper that printed *The Stars and Stripes,* then safely return them each night. For another, he had to set up a dummy French firm, the Lafayette Publishing Company, to skirt army regulations against engaging in trade. And beyond that, would anyone buy it? To his astonishment, and that of just about everyone familiar with the scheme, the Red Cross was so taken with *Yank Talk* that it ordered fifty thousand copies. Ross's windfall, after paying off expenses and investors, was twenty thousand francs.

A few weeks later, Ross was chatting with *New York Times* correspondent Walter Duranty, who casually suggested that the franc was on the verge of "going to hell." Since he still had some seventeen thousand francs on deposit, an alarmed Ross pressed Duranty for particulars. The next day he withdrew the francs and hurried to the army post office, where he asked that they be converted to dollars— they amounted to nearly $3,100—and sent home in a money order.

"Oh, I can't do that," said the clerk. "The maximum permitted is one hundred dollars."

Though Ross was accused of selling doughboys their own jokes, his *Yank Talk* was a huge success.

YANK TALK

A REVIEW OF A.E.F. HUMOR — TRENCH AND BILLET

PRICE, ONE FRANC

So Ross patiently spent the next few hours filling out thirty-one money orders. A few days later the franc started going to hell.

The men of *The Stars and Stripes* were as anxious to get home as everyone else, and they were irked at the army's insistence that the paper continue publishing. But at last their discharge papers came through, effective April 30, and for the next two weeks they saw France in style. Ross bought himself a snappy gray suit, and wrote home that "although my stock of shirts, ties, etc. isn't very large yet I'm able to put up a pretty good appearance on the boulevard. Have bought myself a cane and am cutting a wide swath." The boys lazed in the cafés, took in the racetrack, and saw something of the south of France. This last was as they made their way to Marseilles, where they would embark for home. Through a friend in the shipping business back in San Francisco, Ross had arranged passage for himself, Woollcott, Winterich, and Baldridge on a freighter bound for New York by way of North Africa, Gibraltar, Portugal, and the Azores.

This would have to do in lieu of Ross's South Seas odyssey, because he had made a career decision: he would be returning to New York after all. Not long before, the Butterick Publishing Company, which produced the popular *Delineator* magazine, had approached him about the idea of publishing a postwar version of *The Stars and Stripes,* a magazine aimed at returning veterans. He agreed to edit the publication (annual salary ten thousand dollars), and in turn signed up Winterich as managing editor and the other cohorts as contributors. Originally, Butterick apparently intended to appropriate the unprotected *Stars and Stripes* name, but the staff objected strongly to anyone in the private sector doing this. Ross in particular feared that hucksters would exploit the *Stars and Stripes* name, and he argued that the army should reserve it in case the paper ever had to be resurrected. Through military channels he even appealed to Congress, which, while sympathetic, took no action. Even so, Butterick changed its mind and decided to call its new magazine *The Home Sector.*

Seventy-one issues of *The Stars and Stripes* were published in all, and at a profit, it turned out, of $700,000. The staff was adamant that the money go to the orphan fund, but the Judge Advocate General's office determined instead that by law the money must be returned to the U.S. Treasury. Ross and company appealed to Congress on this question too, but again to no avail.

This disappointment notwithstanding, it had been a heady two years for Private H. W. Ross. His work had been praised by President Wilson and General Pershing. He could truthfully be called "the most widely known private in the American Expeditionary Forces." Promotions and commendations had been proffered, and resolutely ducked. Yet even Ross must have been stirred when his commanding officer, Major Mark Watson, recommended him for the prestigious Distinguished Service Medal. Ross didn't get it—the DSM seldom was conferred to men below the rank of colonel—but Watson contended that his work "stood out so conspicuously as to entitle [him] to special mention above even the admirable work performed by [his] associates."

On May 15 Ross and entourage sailed from Marseilles. Jane Grant, still entertaining the occupation troops, would follow two months later. The freighter put in at the Algerian port of Oran to take on coal, but a longshoremen's strike kept it there five days. At a bazaar the group bought some inexpensive bathing suits, broadly striped in pink and baby blue. "Clad in these," Woollcott wrote later, "both Ross and I aroused unfavorable comment as we sported in the waves of the gulf of Mers el Kebir."

CHAPTER 4

NEW YORKER

THE GRANDEST NON SEQUITUR OF NEW YORK'S YOUNG 1923 SEASON
played out on a cool Sunday evening late in September. A crowd that
looked to be dressed for a Broadway opening was instead piling into
a party in the middle of Hell's Kitchen. Musicians, actresses, newspaper columnists—people who otherwise wouldn't be caught dead
here, lest they be caught dead—turned up by the score at the double
brownstone on West Forty-seventh Street, just beyond Ninth
Avenue. In truth, the area's most violent days were behind it, but the
notoriety remained; more trepidatious guests had the option of being
led into the rough neighborhood by guides from Times Square. In
front of the building, a carousel provided by Harpo Marx and
Dorothy Parker occupied the local urchins who otherwise might pelt
the glitterati with insults or worse. Down the street, the ever-helpful
Charlie MacArthur passed out invitations to strangers. Inside, the
revelers were gambling and gamboling, fueled by good bootleg
liquor. And for their further amusement there were theatrical traves-

ties. Woollcott, after threatening to boycott his own party in a fit of pique over the guest list, was the hit of the evening as he played Nurse to Peggy Wood's Juliet. After a full year of demolition, construction, and exasperation, the communal house owned by Ross, Jane Grant, Woollcott, and their friend Hawley Truax was at last being warmed in style.

Of necessity, Ross and Jane had become urban pioneers long before the concept was fashionable. In the summer of 1922, fed up with temporary living arrangements, they wanted their own home. Like everyone else who has ever lived in Manhattan, all they wanted was a place with lots of space, close to work, and cheap. Given the postwar housing crunch, that pretty well narrowed their options. Truax, an old friend and Hamilton College classmate of Woollcott's, was a lawyer who had gone into the real estate business. He had been scouting around in Ross and Jane's behalf and eventually found the side-by-side tenement buildings in Hell's Kitchen, at 412 and 414 West Forty-seventh. Ross and Jane paid $17,000 for the filthy, rickety properties, with a metamorphosis in mind: to fuse them magically into a single stylish cooperative. In turn the couple sold one-fourth interests to Woollcott and Truax, who would also live there. Two other small apartments would be let to friends.

In the intervening year the transformation at 412, the address of record, was as stunning as it had been endless. The cooperative was capacious yet warm, formal yet inviting, a splash of elegance in the middle of a slum. The buildings were renovated with entertaining as much in mind as everyday living, so the common, or shared, spaces—living room, dining room, kitchen—were spacious and comfortably appointed. The big dining room doubled as an after-hours gaming parlor. The living room, twenty-five feet square with fireplaces at either end, was dominated by a secondhand concert grand on which Irving Berlin sometimes entertained and George Gershwin previewed *Rhapsody in Blue* for a handful of friends. French doors opened onto a small Spanish-style courtyard, with fountain and loggia. Each of the residents had an individual apartment as private quarters. For a while Ross kept a stray cat he called Missus

(Frank Adams's Persian was Mister), but she turned out to be a promiscuous he and broke Ross's heart.

Ross called 412 essentially Woollcott's idea, "an early manifestation of his innkeeping instinct." Woollcott was born and raised in the Phalanx, an experimental Fourier commune in New Jersey, and indeed all his life arranged to be surrounded by guests, friends, or, in a pinch, mere acolytes. Originally Ross, Jane and Truax had contemplated a simpler arrangement—that is, one without the demanding, temperamental Woollcott. But when Aleck found them out, which they all knew was inevitable, he invited himself into the ménage and took charge of the plans. Thus 412 grew more communal, and decidedly more grandiose.

Jane agreed to run the household's domestic affairs, and Truax the finances. The collective arrangement permitted them certain amenities beyond their individual means, like a few servants. They ran through a series of Chinese houseboys—a concession to Ross's fascination with all things Oriental, a taste he had cultivated in San Francisco—before finding a black couple, Arthur and Marie Treadwell, who would become their permanent butler and cook, respectively. Later their son, Junior, became Woollcott's valet.

The denizens of 412 might be living in a slum, but they were doing it in style, which was the important thing. As for the cold, damp discomfort of wartime France—well, that already seemed a lifetime ago.

The moment Ross had stepped off that freighter from Marseilles, in early June of 1919, he threw himself into *The Home Sector*. Launching a magazine is round-the-clock, migraine-inducing work, never more so than when, as in this case, there is virtually no lead time. Ross knew that if the returning veteran was *The Home Sector*'s target, it was best to catch him before the war became just a particularly vivid memory. So with Winterich, his managing editor, Ross took a small apartment on West Eleventh Street in Greenwich Village and set to work.

Butterick may have forgone the *Stars and Stripes* name, but in every other way it intended to trade on the paper's reputation and

formula. The cover of the first issue, dated September 20, 1919, announced that the magazine was "Conducted by the Former Editorial Council of [in conspicuous large type] *The Stars and Stripes.*" Lest anyone miss the point, the headline on its mission statement declared, "By the Same Bunch, for the Same Bunch, in the Same Spirit." And in that spirit, Ross and Winterich succeeded remarkably in replicating the look and feel of their old paper—succeeded too well, actually. With Baldridge's trademark illustrations, Woollcott's recycled battlefield yarns, Wallgren's cartoons, the comic stories and poetry, there was a musty whiff about *The Home Sector* from its opening number. For the first and perhaps only time in his life, Ross's instinct was trailing his audience, not leading it. The five million American veterans had undeniably warm feelings for *The Stars and Stripes,* but it belonged to a part of their lives that was now thankfully behind them.

Which is not to say there wasn't much commendable about *The Home Sector*; there was. Its forty to forty-eight pages (with a conspicuous dearth of advertising) were well written, thoughtful, and fun.

When feeling particularly frisky, it delighted in skewering "Scare-devil" Jack Dempsey, the heavyweight boxing champion, who Ross—a sometime acquaintance of Dempsey's from their days in Salt Lake—and other veterans believed had ducked the wartime draft. (The merciless ragging convinced Ross's staff that one day Dempsey would simply turn up and exact his revenge. Capitalizing on the anxiety, Woollcott had a business card printed up with Dempsey's name, secretly persuaded a secretary to slip it to Ross, and then watched gleefully as all the blood drained from the editor's face.) In time, perhaps to counterbalance the overly reminiscent quality of the early issues, *The Home Sector* became a vigorous pulpit for veterans' issues, something Ross cared about passionately.

In retrospect, *The Home Sector* is most interesting from a genealogical standpoint, as it contained many *New Yorker* precursors. First there is the format itself: a weekly magazine blending the serious and the comic, reportage and reminiscence, book reviews and opinion, with cartoons throughout. Its "editorial" pages suggest the later "Notes and Comment" of E. B. White, in that they offer opinions on eight or ten miscellaneous subjects in a light though hardly trivial vein. In the third issue Ross introduced a department called "Casuals," his term for those distinctive short-storylets or life sketches (three hundred to five hundred words, thereabouts) that would become so familiar in the *The New Yorker*. The magazine's covers, too, in time got away from strictly military themes to broader subjects and began featuring artwork that was more stylized, impressionistic, and whimsical. Several of the covers—a man and a woman in enigmatic embrace; a sidewalk-level view of a craps game; a John Held, Jr., view of the galaxy—might easily have made early *New Yorker* covers. If *The New Yorker* was still five years into the future, *The Home Sector* offered ample evidence that Ross was already giving it, or at least its formula, a great deal of thought.

What little spare time Ross had he devoted to rekindling his relationship with Jane. The two had corresponded in those few months when Jane stayed behind in France, but her letters were curiously noncommittal. She had never intended to become so serious about

Ross, and she decided to use the physical separation to add some emotional distance as well. Impishly, she even slipped back into New York without telling Ross she was coming. When he found out from a mutual friend, he was in a dark humor for weeks.

Jane returned to the *Times,* which assigned her to cover hotel news, and resumed a busy social life. Once Ross got over his pique, he doggedly tried to resume the courtship, only to find that Jane always seemed to be otherwise engaged any night he asked her out. After one such rebuff he blurted, "Goddammit, it's a pretty howdy-do when I have to date you three weeks in advance!" After another, he simply asked, "Don't you ever buy your own dinner?"

As in Paris, however, Ross rose to the competition. He blandished Jane with flowers, candy, and childlike notes of love. He tried to persuade her of their innate compatibility, and when he was in persuasion mode, a friend said, "his words hit the listener like hail in a high wind." He became, in short, as irresistible as a homely, gap-toothed man can be—though it must be said that his rubbery face was always redeemed by those mischievous hazel-brown eyes. Soon the two were seeing each other steadily again. They went to the theater, which they both enjoyed, and even the Philharmonic, where Jane would listen intently to the music while a bored Ross surveyed the house and estimated the theater's take. Sometimes she cooked meals for him and Winterich. On weekends the two might visit Coney Island or take long walks through Chinatown and the Lower East Side, or along the waterfront. Slowly, deliberately, Jane began to unlock New York for the insatiably curious Ross. His infatuation with the woman and the city advanced in lockstep.

In his delightful 1949 monograph *Here Is New York,* E. B. White contends there are three New Yorks: that of the native, who takes the city for granted; of the commuter, who sees only narrow, unchanging pieces of it; and of the settler, who comes to New York on a kind of quest. This last New York is the greatest of the three, he says, because it is the settlers who give the city its passion and lend it achievement. "Each embraces New York with the intense excitement of first love, each absorbs New York with the fresh eyes of an adventurer, each generates heat and light to dwarf the Consolidated Edison Company." White may have had any number of *New Yorker* colleagues in mind when he wrote these words, but they were true of Ross most of all. For the rest of his life the man from Aspen was an outsider set loose in New York, exhilarated, intimidated, and appalled by turns at what he saw, but never, ever bored. It would prove to be a felicitous match: a city constantly revealing itself, and a man who couldn't stop watching.

Of course Ross's timing was impeccable, what with Edith Wharton's New York giving way to Scott Fitzgerald's. In the Twenties, the postwar, Prohibition generation was ready to raise some hell, and New York was obliging. Speculators on Wall Street, Jimmy Walker at Tammany. Dempsey-Tunney (twice). Ruth, Gehrig, Meusel, and Lazzeri on Murderer's Row. American literature and painting were newly ascendant, nightclubs were stomping, jazz was raging, and Broadway was king. Skyscrapers rose up like steel sequoias; at their feet, speakeasies sprouted like so many mushrooms—thousands in midtown alone, clustered mostly between Fifth and Sixth avenues. "It was an intimate world of young people," suggested Charles Baskerville, "trying to create, and have, a happy life."

In this fizzy climate, Ross and Jane decided to elope. Their relationship had advanced to the point where, by March of 1920, they were discussing marriage. In such matters Ross was the soul of convention, and he proposed an engagement, with the usual ring and six-month incubation. But Jane despised convention and offered a counterproposal: why don't we get married this Saturday? The idea rattled Ross, not only for its rashness but because just then the future of *The Home Sector* had become quite precarious; he literally didn't know how much longer he would have a job. But Jane had an answer for that, too: they could keep the marriage secret until Ross's future cleared up. He would continue to room with Winterich, Jane would keep her own small place, and they would steal away on weekends. The elopement was on.

Needing help with arrangements on such short notice, they

brought Woollcott, a conspirator of the first rank, into their confidence. He enthusiastically helped Jane select a wedding ring, found a minister, and arranged for a discreet little ceremony at the Church of the Transfiguration (better known as the Little Church Around the Corner) in Murray Hill. So it was that on Saturday afternoon, March 27, 1920, Jane and Ross were married—and immediately afterward returned to their respective jobs pretending nothing had happened. That evening Woollcott dined with the newlyweds at the Waldorf-Astoria before putting them on a train to Philadelphia, where they had a one-day honeymoon at the Bellevue-Stratford. That Monday, Woollcott presented them with an itemized, $218.85 bill for services rendered—including $18.75 for dinner at the Waldorf and $100.00 for "personal wear and tear." The bill was tossed onto a tall pile of gambling IOUs between Woollcott and Ross and reconciled later with the rest of the debts.

As a wedding present, Ross surprised Jane with his new contract, signed that very morning, as editor of the *American Legion Weekly.* The *Weekly,* the official organ of the fast-growing new veterans organization, had preceded *The Home Sector* by several months and now wanted to expand its reach. Ross's magazine had gone gamely along for twenty-three issues, but it simply never caught on. Beyond the question of editorial focus, *The Home Sector* sustained an early devastating blow; after just four issues, a New York printers' strike forced it to suspend publication for two months. By March 1920, Butterick was looking for an exit, and when the *Weekly* offered to absorb *The Home Sector,* it jumped. Ross was offered the editorship of the combined publication, at the same salary as before.

It was a melancholy decision. As much as Ross supported the American Legion and believed in the cause of veterans, he didn't really want to edit a house organ. His own magazine interests were broadening, and this was the narrowest kind of endeavor. But with marriage pending and no other immediate employment prospects, and with much still to learn about publishing, he bowed to expedience. He packed up his *Home Sector* staff and editorial backlog and, without missing a beat, settled into his prosaic new job. His office was

Ross and Jane Grant's elopement didn't surprise their friends, but her decision to retain her maiden name did. *(Jane Grant Collection, University of Oregon)*

in a dingy building on West Forty-third Street almost at the Hudson River. There was a constant clatter from the freight trains just outside, as well as the vivid aroma of a neighboring slaughterhouse.

It took only two uncomfortable weeks of sneaking around for Jane and Ross to decide to divulge their secret. Besides, his immediate future, unappetizing as it might be, had firmed up faster than either of them had imagined. Their friends were hardly surprised at the marriage but were taken aback by Jane's news that she would be retaining her maiden name. It turned out the bride had been jarred when, after the ceremony, she was congratulated as "Mrs. Ross." (The phrase rattled the groom, too, for that matter.) Jane was proud of her independence, and one of her guiding principles was that a woman's worth had nothing to do with whom she happened to marry. It was Jane Grant who had abandoned Kansas for the big city, fought her way up through the oppressively chauvinist *Times,* and taken care of herself in the middle of a war, and Jane Grant she would remain. As for Ross, in this instance his appreciation for non-conformity outweighed his traditional bias; he was both amused by and proud of his wife's brave decision and seems to have been generally supportive—despite the confusion it invariably caused when they registered in hotels and the steady ribbing Ross took from friends. For instance, in 1926, when the *New Yorker* staff marked Ross's birthday with a lampoon edition, a Talk of the Town item referred to the editor as Harold Grant, but quoted him saying, "I'm calling myself Ross now, you know."

Jane had a kindred spirit in friend Ruth Hale, a theatrical press agent who was married to *New York Tribune* (later *World*) columnist Heywood Broun. Her brand of feminism was so ardent that she even insisted her husband see other women, though the reluctant libertine often just looked up a poker buddy instead. In mid-1920, when Ross and Jane's hunt for a suitable apartment was stymied by the housing shortage, it was Broun and Hale who came to their rescue by letting them stay awhile in a spare bedroom. Between Ruth and Jane the man-bashing got intense at times. After one particularly ferocious discussion, Ross said, "Aw, why don't you two hire a hall?"

The following year they did. The two women founded the Lucy Stone League, an advocacy organization named for the New England feminist who a century before had fought for women's rights, including that of keeping her maiden name after marriage. Ruth Hale was president, Jane Grant, secretary.

———

IN THE SUMMER OF 1919, JUST AS ROSS, WOOLLCOTT AND COMPANY were getting reacquainted with civilian life, a Broadway press agent named John Peter Toohey was contemplating a problem. He was trying to drum up publicity about a precocious new playwright, Eugene O'Neill, whose dark work had yet to attract any Broadway producers. By this time Woollcott was back at the *Times,* and Toohey wanted to plant an item about O'Neill in Aleck's Sunday column, "Second Thoughts on First Nights." Since Toohey didn't know

Woollcott, he called Murdock Pemberton, who handled public relations for the Hippodrome and had known Aleck since childhood.
Pemberton set up lunch for the three at the Algonquin, a small but
stylish hotel on West Forty-fourth Street, across from the Hippodrome and also convenient to the *Times*.

Woollcott wasn't overly interested in what Toohey had to say
about O'Neill; instead he turned the conversation, as was his wont,
into a monologue about his own wartime exploits. Afterward Pemberton and Toohey conspired to good-naturedly prick Aleck's self-
absorption. They drew up a gag press release for a luncheon the
following week that would feature a dozen different reminiscences of
the war. All twelve speakers were Alexander Woollcott, his name
mangled twelve imaginative ways. Invitations to the lunch were sent
to theater journalists and friends. Algonquin owner Frank Case gave
over the Pergola Room (later renamed the Oak Room) to the affair,
and the Hippodrome's prop department festooned it in military
bunting. A huge, gold-embossed banner read "AWOL—COTT."
Three dozen people attended and Woollcott, far from being offended,
was delighted. The gathering was so much fun that Toohey, it is said,
suggested they meet again soon. And they would—over and over
and over again.

So much has been written and recounted about the Algonquin
Round Table—true, false, and somewhere in between—that it is
easy to forget that, for all the eventual fame and forced drollery, in
the beginning it was simply a high-spirited gathering of friends at a
convenient, affordable restaurant. Of course it didn't take these
savvy, ambitious people (least of all the opportunistic Case) long to
realize the self-promotional value of their association. But the Round
Table didn't start out to be a salon, or a cascade of wit. Ross once
described it this way to Mencken: "I was there a lot and I never heard
any literary discussion or any discussion of any other art—just the
usual personalities of some people getting together, and a lot of wisecracks and quoting of further wisecracks. It was always about the
same as a dinner with you, Nathan, and a couple more—Grant Rice
and Paul Patterson, say—at '21.' No cosmic problems settled; merely
laughs."

It is easy to forget, too, that in that summer of 1919 the principals were mostly young—late twenties and early thirties—not terribly accomplished, and little known beyond their circle. Of the core group, the venerable F.P.A. (a graybeard at thirty-seven) was the only genuine celebrity and serious wage-earner, and thus the informal dean. Woollcott, who tended to preside like an impertinent ringmaster, was just thirty-two and years away from his "Town Crier" fame. Ross, twenty-six, and Jane, just turned twenty-seven, toiled in good, albeit nondescript, jobs. Heywood Broun, thirty-one, had yet to reach his peak popularity as a columnist and champion of labor. George S. Kaufman, twenty-nine, was a second-string drama critic for the *Times* who on the side had written several undistinguished shows. His soon-to-be collaborator, Marc Connelly, twenty-eight, also had a few flops to his credit. Harpo Marx, thirty, and his funny brothers were still waiting for a breakthrough show. Robert Benchley, twenty-nine, and his attractive, brooding sidekick, Dorothy Parker, twenty-five, were working for proletarian wages at the aristocratic *Vanity Fair*.

Others in the circle included the Pemberton brothers—Murdock, who would become *The New Yorker*'s first art critic, and Brock, soon to bolt the *Times* to become a producer; the dapper editor of *Vanity Fair*, Frank Crowninshield; music critic and composer Deems Taylor; *Harper's Bazaar* editor Arthur Samuels; Robert Sherwood, later editor of the original *Life* and a Pulitzer-winning dramatist; writers Edna Ferber, Alice Duer Miller, Donald Ogden Stewart, and Herman Mankiewicz; playwright-to-be Charles MacArthur; and the beautiful artist Neysa McMein, already a successful illustrator for such magazines as *Woman's Home Companion* and *The Saturday Evening Post*. Eventually Ring Lardner joined in, and there was a corps of Round Table irregulars, many of them performers. These included the Lunts; Helen Hayes (later Mrs. MacArthur); Paul Robeson, whose singing career Woollcott championed; and Noel Coward, who became especially friendly with Ross.

Two other irregulars were Raoul Fleischmann and his wife, Ruth. Through Adams, Fleischmann had joined via the Table's ancillary poker game. He managed his family's large East Side bakery, but his extended family had famously made its fortune in yeast. Raoul Fleischmann was Harold Ross's obverse: as polished as Ross was rough, as polite as Ross was profane. But they had one thing in common: both loved to gamble.

On any given day the number at lunch was usually ten or twelve; admission was more or less by invitation and subject to the whim of the court. One must be amusing, preferably witty, and somewhat masochistic, for no foible or accident of birth was beyond the Round Tablers' needle. They made sport of Parker's pitiful suicide attempts ("Dorothy, if you don't stop this sort of thing you'll ruin your health"); Kaufman's Jewishness; Broun's dubious hygiene; Woollcott's dubious sexuality ("Louisa May Woollcott"). They jabbed at one another's neuroses, clothes, even bridge skills (when his partner asked if he might be excused to go to the bathroom, Kaufman snapped, "Fine, this is the first time this afternoon I'll know what you have in your hand"). Those among them who had spent the war toting a pen instead of a rifle—an enduringly sensitive issue—were targets too. At a poker game Woollcott was riding publicist David Wallace mercilessly about his infantry career. At last the normally mild-tempered Wallace could hold his tongue no longer. "At least I'm not a *writing* soldier," he blurted. There was a long and awkward silence, until Ring Lardner finally said, "You sure swept the table that time, Dave."

To enhance the luncheon's visibility, Case moved the group from a long table in the Pergola Room to a round table in the back center of the Rose Room. There they dubbed themselves the Vicious Circle.

Though a founder, the unlikeliest member of the circle was Ross. To this day when the Round Table is recalled he is generally relegated to something like junior-partner (or, less charitably, mascot) status. Even Case, who was close enough to Ross to know better, described him as "a sort of adopted child, taken in on approval before the final papers were signed."

The slight is unfortunate but understandable. By this time, Ross had taken to wearing his hair in a tall, stiff pompadour, a shock-coif that seemed as implacable as a privet hedge. The extra three inches conveyed the impression, no doubt intended, that Ross was even taller than he was. (It was this remarkable thatch that the actress Ina Claire had in mind one spring day when she declared to Case, "Frank, I feel so wonderful I'd like to take off my shoes and stockings and wade in Ross's hair!") The quality of his clothes was improving with his station, but his slouch and his ill-proportioned, Lincolnesque body—overly long arms, thin legs, big hands and feet—always made tailoring a challenge. His fashion sense remained so retro that he still wore high-top, lace-up shoes.

Kibitzers marveled at Ross's gat-tooth countenance and curious behavior—long periods of quiet punctuated by "teamsterlike snorts" or explosive, left-field interjections. He did not seem as intellectually agile as his friends. Rebecca Bernstien, who lunched at the Round Table occasionally in the company of her newspaper colleague Broun, said of conversations with Ross, "He looked at you as if he were listening hard, not quite getting whatever you said." He laughed often, but sometimes too heartily, betraying a trace of insecurity. Ross's intellect was as keen as any at the table, but he wasn't suited to verbal swordplay. His humor tended to be offbeat, understated, evident in his "daring felicity of phrase and freshness of thought" (Edna Ferber's assessment) and, unique for this group, in his self-deprecation. For instance, Ross once received a manuscript from a writer who had included some of his credits in the letterhead. Immediately thereafter, when friends got letters from Ross, these testimonials appeared beneath his name: " 'A splendid fellow.' —*Alexander Woollcott*" and " 'Among those present was H. Ross.' —*F.P.A. in the New York World.*"

As Margaret Case Harriman, Frank's daughter and chronicler of the Round Table, would later point out, it was easy to underestimate Ross, but anyone who did so simply wasn't looking hard enough. His friends prized him, and not just because he was a good audience. They appreciated the qualities that escaped others: his droll sense of humor, intense powers of observation, and a wide playful streak.

It didn't take long for the luncheon rondelet to become celebrated in New York for its wit, both mirthful and lacerating. For this celebrity the Round Tablers had largely themselves to thank. With a handful of influential newspapers and magazines represented in the circle—the *Times,* the *Tribune, Vanity Fair, Harper's Bazaar, Life*—the wits cross-pollinated feverishly. Shrugging off charges of logrolling, they quoted one another in their columns, reviewed one another's shows, publicized one another's books. To be fair, many of the glowing notices were deserved—and in any case not all the notices were glowing. Depending on who was feuding with whom, reviews could be as catty and personal as their uglier lunchtime digs. On the whole, however, the arrangement suited everyone nicely.

By far the most powerful transmitter of Round Table wit was Adams, whose column in the *Tribune* (and later the *World*), "The Conning Tower," was scoured by tens of thousands of New Yorkers for its dollops of quippery and clever verse. Young writers conspired to break into the column, and the appearance of even a four-line snippet was regarded as a triumph. Writers as diverse as E. B. White and John O'Hara always remembered F.P.A. fondly for cracking open the door to them when they were struggling. The formation of the Round Table supplied F.P.A. with a freshet of material, and he wasn't bashful about using it. A particularly good line from Parker or Kaufman or Benchley might turn up in "The Conning Tower" within hours of its utterance. Similarly, F.P.A.'s "Diary of Our Own Samuel Pepys," which appeared on Saturdays and recounted his comings and goings in the archaic fashion of the seventeenth-century diarist, was a virtual calendar of the circle's social whirl. Readers came to follow the Round Tablers as if they were the crazy kids down the hall. Here is an entry from Sunday, March 7, 1920:

> To J. Toohey's, for a short and silly game of cards, which I ought not waste my time at, and nobody gaining aught but H. Ross, by stupid good luck, too, albeit he prates ever of his skill and acumen.

And another, from Saturday, February 9, 1924, when the group had taken the train to Atlantic City:

> So to our inn, and I for six miles of walking with Jane Grant, and pleasant enough when we drew away from the vast crowds of the

dullest-looking people ever I saw in one place, and so with H. Ross and H. Broun and George Kaufman to dinner, and we went to a strange and costly inn, and had a fine dinner and cast dice for the reckoning, and some luckless wight paid.

As is clear, the Vicious Circle worked hard at play; a moment of solitude was a moment wasted. Lunch at the Algonquin, cocktails at Neysa's studio, après-théâtre at 412. They were crazy for games—cards, charades, cribbage, backgammon, or croquet (at which Ross was routinely accused of advancing the ball with his foot). This was matched only by their passion for pranks, to which Woollcott and Ross were especially addicted. Countless examples, from the sophomoric to the inspired, are recorded, but this is fairly typical: when Woollcott let it be known how thoughtful it would be if his friends banded together to give him the multivolume *Oxford English Dictionary* for Christmas, they presented him with ten copies of the first volume.

Perhaps the ultimate expression of the Algonquin set's exuberance—critics were already calling it obnoxiousness—was a comic revue they wrote and staged, for one night only, in April 1922, before a handpicked house at the Forty-ninth Street Theatre. Their show, called *No Sirree!*, sent up a Russian revue then popular, *Chauve Souris*. Described in the program as "An Anonymous Entertainment by the Vicious Circle of the Hotel Algonquin," *No Sirree!* was a pastiche of sketches, blackouts, monologues, and musical numbers. Ross was virtually the only Round Tabler who didn't have a featured spot. His acting was considered so hapless that he was relegated to the role of Lemuel Pip ("an old taxi-driver"), who is referred to repeatedly but never appears on stage. Amusing as it all was, the only truly noteworthy act was provided by Benchley. He had promised to write a skit but, as was his custom, blew his deadline so badly that he wasn't even listed on the program. Nonetheless, he debuted his celebrated comic monologue "The Treasurer's Report," which scored such a success that Irving Berlin immediately signed him to perform it for five hundred dollars a week in his *Music Box Revue*—and in so doing launched Benchley's bittersweet career as a performer.

Theater and journalism were two Round Table pillars. The third was gambling. In their Village apartment, Ross and Winterich revived the old Nini's Saturday-night poker game. Frank Adams, borrowing from *Main Street*, christened the gathering the Thanatopsis (meaning "contemplation of death") Pleasure and Inside Straight Club. Other permutations included the Thanatopsis Literary and Inside Straight Club and the Thanatopsis Chowder and Marching Society, but to the players, sensibly enough, it was always just Thanatopsis. As the popularity of the game grew, it began to float from place to place. In fact, the first time Kaufman laid eyes on Ross he was shooting craps on the floor of Kaufman's own apartment, having pulled the spread from the host's bed to use as a playing surface. Harpo Marx also first encountered Ross at Thanatopsis, remembering that he looked for all the world like "a cowhand who'd lost his horse."

In the beginning it was typical for big winners or losers to be up or down several hundred dollars at the end of an evening. But the stakes skyrocketed when some wealthier players, like Fleischmann, composer Jerome Kern, and *World* executive editor Herbert Bayard Swope, joined the game. Thousands of dollars began changing hands. Some, like Ross and Woollcott, unable or unwilling to play at this level, eventually left the Thanatopsis game for others. The mere mortals who stayed on played at their peril. Ross later recalled how Broun lost thirty thousand dollars one evening and had to sell his apartment.

The Round Table lasted twelve years, but Ross began pulling away from the group shortly after launching *The New Yorker* in 1925. He remained friends with the individuals, though, and a handful— but only a handful—were important to his magazine's success. In general, however, their support for him was halfhearted at best, and he had his eyes opened. Beyond this, Ross came to abhor the logrolling and to see the Round Table's dissolute lifestyle for what it was—an insidious cannibalizer of energy and talent. Perhaps this is one reason why the unlikely Ross, of all those in the circle, would leave the most profound and lasting cultural legacy.

FOR GOOD AND BAD, LIFE AT 412 WEST FORTY-SEVENTH INEVITABLY began as an extension of the Round Table. Shortly after they married, Ross was abashed when Jane, who loved dancing, would step out for the evening just as he was getting ready for bed. But often she needed to go only as far as her living room. People showed up at 412 at all hours because they knew they could. There they found ready companionship and liquor, as at a favorite bar that never closed. Between the formal entertaining and the walk-in traffic, the array of guests was a New York Who's Who. On any given night you were as apt to find Father Duffy, the storied World War I chaplain, as you were heavyweight champion Gene Tunney or nightclub owner Texas Guinan.

Jane enjoyed the folderol as much as anyone, but as the person responsible for keeping the household stocked in food and drink she

Jane and Ross at home at 412 West Forty-seventh Street.
(Jane Grant Collection, University of Oregon)

found the revolving door a constant challenge. She once came home to twenty-eight unanticipated dinner guests. Another time she was cited for buying bootleg liquor (the charge was dropped after her boss at the *Times* intervened). Ross, who seldom drank to the point of stupefaction, was put off by those who did. He even suggested to Jane that they stop serving liquor. They didn't, but the rowdier drunks were not invited back.

Under the circumstances, no one at 412 stood on formality. Visitors got accustomed to being greeted by Woollcott in open robe and pajama bottoms. And Ross, as always, could be counted on to be himself. "I remember having dinner there a couple of times in the communal dining room," said Russel Crouse. "On each occasion when we got back to the living room Ross stretched out on the floor and went to sleep, ignoring the conversation even though the conversation didn't ignore him."

The entertaining grew more lavish. One reason is that shortly after they moved in, Woollcott jumped from the *Times* to the *New York Herald,* one of the underachieving newspapers owned by the oleaginous press lord and ex-greengrocer Frank Munsey, for a staggering increase in pay—from one hundred to five hundred dollars a week. The calculating Munsey wanted Woollcott for his insightful and popular theater column, but Ross later told Aleck's friend and biographer, Samuel Hopkins Adams, that Munsey also had an ulterior motive, one not untypical in that very cozy period. "It was Anna Case, the opera singer, who nominated Woollcott for the Munsey job," Ross wrote Adams. "Mr. M. was courting her at the time in a mammoth way. I think Anna did more than nominate; I think she insisted. Aleck is one of the few dramatic critics who ever got a job so his employer could get a piece of nookie."

Beyond the revolving door, inevitable personality conflicts kept 412 in an uproar. Even something as simple as the dinner menu became a source of irritation. Both Ross and Truax already had developed bad stomachs, and they required bland diets. For the gluttonous Woollcott, however, no food was too rich, and the mere presentation of broth at the table would send him storming out. But when he came back, he often was of a mind to play, no matter what the hour. If he saw Ross and Jane's lights burning—the bedroom of their apartment faced the street—he'd barge in and drag Ross away for cribbage.

The ménage staggered along this way for four years, but nerves were fraying, sleep becoming scarce, and space cramped. "We adored Aleck, you know," Jane told Margaret Case Harriman. "He was perfectly fine in almost every way. He didn't drink, to speak of, and he was meticulous about money matters, and God knows he was entertaining. I don't know *why* there always came a time with Aleck when you couldn't *stand* it anymore." For Jane, Ross and Truax, that time arrived in the summer of 1926, when Ross had given over body and soul to keep his new magazine alive. Ross, who didn't mind a philosophical fight but was constitutionally incapable of confronting intimates, asked Jane to ask Aleck to leave.

Woollcott took it well enough at first, but when the question of settling up finances and household furnishings arose, compounded by a bollixed dinner between Ross and Woollcott, he turned characteristically splenetic. He fired off a letter to Ross that began, "I agree

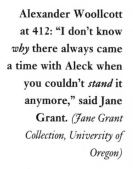

Alexander Woollcott at 412: "I don't know *why* there always came a time with Aleck when you couldn't *stand* it anymore," said Jane Grant. *(Jane Grant Collection, University of Oregon)*

with you that the fewer dealings one has with you and the fewer debts one permits you to incur, the less chance there is to be subjected to your discourtesy. I have enjoyed your company so much that I have been one of the last to make this simple discovery." Then he slapped Ross for his behavior after the bobbled dinner. "And your subsequent paroxysms of mirth made me a little sick. Any tyro in psychology recognizes that urchin defense mechanism, but the person who jeers at me when there is a good audience and waits for privacy to apologize is manifesting a kind of poltroonery I find hard to deal with." He closed, "I think your slogan 'Liberty or Death' is splendid and whichever one you finally decide upon will be all right with me."

Such a bilious epistle would have been the last word in most relationships, but it was just another blip between the two men. Within a few years, Woollcott would be writing "Shouts and Murmurs," one of the most popular features in Ross's *New Yorker*.

———

WHEN THEY WED, ROSS AND JANE AGREED TO LIVE ON HER SALARY and salt away his against that dream publication, whatever it turned out to be. Overwhelmed by the expenses of 412 but determined to hold up her end of the bargain, Jane sought out other moneymaking opportunities. In addition to her *Times* job, she began to write syndicated features, then magazine pieces, in time becoming a contributor to the high-paying *Saturday Evening Post*. All the while she encouraged Ross in his entrepreneurial aspirations, even as he slogged away at the *Weekly*.

That Ross cared deeply about the veterans of World War I there is no doubt. He spoke out at Legion meetings and wrote impassioned letters to New York newspapers in their behalf. The *Weekly* thumped for the highly controversial veterans' bonus and published two flinty series, written by Marquis James (who would twice win the Pulitzer Prize for biography), about American war profiteers. But Ross was becoming increasingly disillusioned with the Legion itself, which was turning more political, and editing its magazine had become a thoroughly unsatisfying grind.

Unlike *The Home Sector,* which reflected an independent editorial judgment and creativity, the *Weekly* was clearly an institutional mouthpiece. Its single greatest concern, judging from the insistent cover reminders, was that Legion members pay their dues. Here and there were nice flourishes, like contributions from Ross's old friend John Held, Jr., but on the whole the magazine was uninspired. The doughboy humor, collected in "Bursts and Duds," was mostly the latter, and the topical material was often a reach ("Didn't Uncle Sam Hand Out Some Promises Four Years Ago About Farms for Soldiers?"). Vain Legion executives began to send Ross speeches to print, many of which he found so dull or wrongheaded that he read them aloud sarcastically to friends. He wearied of finding new ways to say the same things. His desperation was evident when, nearly five years after the armistice, the *Weekly* was soliciting readers for "your most thrilling experience" from the war.

Increasingly Ross pondered his options. Besides the New York weekly idea, he had considered publishing a shipping-news journal, an ad-free newspaper (that would carry an advertising insert), or inexpensive paperback books. He even toyed with the idea of a syndicated comic strip. That he considered so many ideas bespeaks his uncertainty of mind. He pleaded with Jane to help him decide—or really, she felt, to tell him what to do.

She thought Ross's most promising concept by far was the metropolitan weekly, and in his heart so did he. Though the broad outline of the idea reached back to wartime Paris, Ross's experience in New York only reinforced its soundness. No single magazine spoke directly to him or his generation. The more he looked about him, the more he was persuaded that a magazine managing to tap into this new energy, and reflect it back, couldn't help but find a receptive audience.

Ross also was well aware that fortunes were being made in the magazine industry. For one hundred and fifty years, American magazines had been limited by cost and other obstacles to small curiosities. But by the early Twenties, favorable postal rates and a wave of technological innovation, including fast rotary printing presses, conveyor systems, and multicolor picture reproduction, had paved the way for the great national magazines such as the *Post, Collier's, Liberty,* and *McCall's.* By 1926, there were twenty-five domestic magazines with circulations exceeding one million. With commercial radio in its infancy and television a futuristic fantasy, magazines represented the lone true national medium, the only efficient way for major advertisers to reach audiences from coast to coast. For magazine publishers, this combination caused an explosion of prosperity. But to Ross, it presented an obvious opportunity. Why would an upscale New York department store or other retailer want to reach readers in Duluth and Denver? he asked. This was what happened when they advertised in national magazines. Even if they advertised in the New York newspapers, they still bought primarily "waste" circulation, because most newspaper readers couldn't afford their goods. The magazine he had in mind—glossy, intelligent, and cheeky—could deliver quality New York merchandise to a quality New York audience.

Ross was just as dissatisfied with most magazine content, which he found overly sentimental and often subliterate. He considered the two big surviving humor magazines, *Life* and *Judge,* tubercular. H. L. Mencken and George Jean Nathan's *Smart Set* and its successor, the *American Mercury,* certainly were sassy and provocative, and Crowninshield's *Vanity Fair* glittered, of course, but these again were national magazines.

Jane ran Ross's idea by the brilliant managing editor of the *Times,* Carr Van Anda. He saw a certain shrewdness in the plan but pronounced it prohibitively expensive; it would take five million dollars, he estimated, just to break into the black. Since Ross and Jane were hoping to start with one one-hundredth that amount, this news was discouraging.

But apparently not so discouraging as working at the *Weekly,* for by the summer of 1923 Ross clearly was more focused on his magazine dream than on his magazine reality. That July, Alice Duer Miller steered her cousin Edward Weeks—then fresh out of Cambridge, in later life editor of *The Atlantic Monthly*—to Ross to discuss job prospects. Ross was cordial and told Weeks that he would be starting his own magazine in the near future, but he added that he was only just beginning to put together a dummy of it. In the meantime, he was working up a business plan and refining his concept. Copies of *Life, Judge, American Mercury,* and *Smart Set,* as well as *Punch* (a major influence) and other foreign humor magazines, were strewn about his apartment at 412. He and Jane were reading everything they could find on the subject of magazine publishing. They forged ahead, agreeing that fifty thousand dollars, while probably inadequate, would have to do.

Once Ross produced the mock edition, he peddled it among his circle but found no enthusiasm remotely approaching his own. Few were willing even to concede Ross's market assumptions, much less invest their own money in his enterprise. "He carried a dummy of the magazine for two years, everywhere, and I'm afraid he was rather a bore with it," Kaufman wrote later. Even Woollcott, who was so close to the concept and who could be counted on to vouch for Ross's editorial acumen even if the two men didn't happen to be speaking, was skeptical. He refused to introduce Ross to the influential publisher Condé Nast.

No one questioned Ross's inherent editorial abilities. He was known to be good with a pencil, efficient, hardworking, and a fair judge of talent. If you needed someone with a grasp of military issues or shipping news, there was none better. No, his skill wasn't the question. This was: "How the hell could a man who looked like a resident of the Ozarks and talked like a saloon brawler set himself up as pilot of a sophisticated, elegant periodical?" This was how playwright Ben Hecht put it, adding, "It was bounderism of the worst sort." Hecht and sidekick Charlie MacArthur (they would later write *The Front Page*) felt so strongly about the matter that they spent a boozy, three A.M. session on a Broadway curb in front of an all-night drugstore trying to dissuade the delusional Ross.

The skepticism was everywhere. Though outwardly Ross parried it, inwardly it fed his own mounting insecurity. After all, he, otherwise so sure of his editorial capabilities, was smart enough to know that a high-school dropout from Colorado who still referred to romance as "spooning" had a lot to learn about urbanity. How could he presume to tell New York about sophistication?

Just then an opportunity arose which looked to obviate the need for Ross to start his own magazine. The same company that printed the *Weekly* took a financial interest in the lately shaky *Judge* and asked Ross to be coeditor. (There are some indications that he considered buying the magazine himself, with investors, but this is unclear.) He was well known to the people at *Judge* because its offices and the *Weekly*'s were in the same building. He had good reason to be wary: *Judge* embodied everything he found wanting in American humor. It was wheezy and out of step, with its Krazy Kracks and cartoons that were mere appendages to stale "he-she" gags. It spoke to Middle America, not Manhattan. Yet it was a venerable, respected title, and Ross thought some of his fresh ideas might help resuscitate it. Beyond that, he was so desperate to make a change that he couldn't resist. In March 1924, the faithful Winterich took over the *Weekly*, and Ross moved down the hall to *Judge*.

Almost immediately he realized it was a terrible mistake. He fought constantly with coeditor Norman Anthony, as well as with the new owner, both of whom had little use for his newfangled ideas about humor. Ross, that rare editor who was always solicitous of his contributors, was appalled to find that at *Judge* they had to camp out in the lobby to get paid. He complained that originality was treated like a disease.

He made a valiant try, but the pre-Ross/post-Ross schizophrenia in *Judge* is plain. After his arrival, the humor tries to move from the turn-of-the-century to the more topical. He leans heavily on some of the contributors who would help define the early *New Yorker*, such as humorists Corey Ford and Howard Dietz and artists Held, Ralph Barton, Perry Barlow, and Gardner Rea. (At Woollcott's urging, he also tried to persuade an up-and-coming vaudeville cowboy, Will Rogers, to write for him, but the droll young man went to *Life* instead.) There are elements that Ross would appropriate for, or refine in, *The New Yorker*: casuals, "Newsbreaks" (those column-ending tweaks of newspaper mistakes), movie reviews, celebrity news.

On the other hand, the magazine retained plenty of the dreadful standbys, like "Funnybones," which were jokes literally printed inside a drawing of a bone ("A red nose indicates a horn of plenty these days!").

One of Ross's boldest strokes at *Judge* was an issue given over to satirizing the Ku Klux Klan; it appeared one week after he left but undoubtedly was produced on his watch. The racist organization is lampooned on the cover and in cartoons, jokes, and stories. From the content, and in view of Ross's background, one senses that the spoof derived less from any personal outrage over Klan persecution of blacks, Jews and Catholics than from the inherent silliness and comic possibilities of a hate group in bed linen. Nonetheless, it was a powerful statement in 1924 and tends to mitigate, again, later suggestions that Ross himself was racially intolerant.

Even so, Ross was desperately unhappy at *Judge.* He was frustrated by the low common denominator required of its humor, and the steady erosion of ads merely validated his views about national versus local advertising. When Ford walked in one day with a smart article on New York's problem with snow removal, Ross had to say no because the subject was too parochial. Then he exploded at Ford as if it were his fault. "That's the trouble with this goddamn magazine! If it went after a local audience, it would get local advertising."

Ross walked away from *Judge* in August, after just five months. Right away he had attractive offers from Hearst's *Cosmopolitan* and other publications, but by now he was determined to go out on his own. It was time to test his theories in the marketplace. Besides, he had decided that the only way to have a completely independent magazine was to start your own. He had seen how business-side pressures and advertiser complaints had led to Parker and Benchley's departure from *Vanity Fair,* and of course he had had a full quota of interference himself at both the *Weekly* and *Judge.* At his own magazine, he vowed, there would be a wall between editorial and business as if between church and state.

Ross now set about finding an angel. He met with several New York "risk" capitalists but got no bites. Then one evening he and Jane attended a party given by Raoul and Ruth Fleischmann. During a lull in a bridge game Jane casually began chatting with Fleischmann about Ross's idea for a New York magazine. For some reason—perhaps because he was so far removed from the publishing world—Ross and Jane had never considered Fleischmann a potential backer. But Raoul (pronounced like "growl") hated the baking business, and Jane could see he was intrigued by the idea. He urged her to have her husband come by.

Ross went over the next day, but in what amounted to a last-minute failure of nerve, instead of pitching the New York weekly, he tried to sell Fleischmann on the shipping newspaper. Fleischmann, who knew and cared nothing about that subject, was baffled, and Jane was flabbergasted. For a week she badgered Ross to go back, and finally, sheepishly, he did.

Fleischmann listened, then asked how large a stake Ross required. Twenty-five thousand dollars should do it, Ross said, and he and Jane would put up a like amount. To Fleischmann, who then had a net worth of nearly a million dollars, this seemed reasonable enough. They shook hands.

Fleischmann could not have imagined how many hundreds of thousands of dollars were to follow before he ever got a cent back. As someone who knew virtually nothing about publishing, he had walked into the deal blithely. He regarded it as a lark, not unlike a wager—albeit a very heavy one—on one of his beloved Thoroughbreds at Saratoga. But as soon as word of his participation began circulating, Fleischmann was teased enough, and was asked enough questions he didn't have answers for, to start worrying.

To placate his skittish new partner, Ross lined up an "advisory board" of ten celebrated friends, who presumably would lend the sophistication to this self-styled "magazine of sophistication." The ten were Woollcott, Broun, Parker, Connelly, Kaufman, Ferber, Alice Miller, dramatist Laurence Stallings, and artists Ralph Barton and Rea Irvin. Ross badly needed their credibility, but he knew the board was at best a fanciful ruse, and at worst plain dishonest. "Some of them didn't really work on the magazine, and others I had no expectation of getting actual help from," Ross said years later. "It was one of the shoddiest things I have ever done. I have been ashamed of it ever since."

In the late summer of 1924, Ross took a small office in a building owned by the Fleischmann family at 25 West Forty-fifth Street. By now he had everything he needed for his new magazine but a name. The Round Tablers proffered many suggestions, among them *Manhattan, New York Life,* and *Our Town.* But it was Toohey, the man who five years earlier had inadvertently begun the Round Table, who asked the obvious: Why not call it *The New Yorker?* With nothing of real value left to him, Ross compensated Toohey with a few shares of stock in the new magazine, a gesture the Vicious Circle found as hilarious as it was most assuredly empty. (None of them realized it then, but this was not the first time the name had been used. Horace Greeley published *The New-Yorker,* "a weekly journal of literature, politics and general intelligence," from 1834 to 1841. Proof again, if any were needed, that there are no truly new ideas in publishing.)

Presently all that remained was for Ross to write a prospectus, a mission statement cum sales pitch for the embryonic publication. What he produced, in fits and starts, would become the most famous magazine prospectus in history. (See Appendix I, page 439.) It represented the first and only time Ross articulated his goals for *The New Yorker* in detail. When the prospectus is referred to these days, the passage usually singled out—invariably out of context—is the one dealing with that famous reader Ross was *not* interested in, "the old lady in Dubuque." (He went on to explain, "This is not meant in disrespect, but *The New Yorker* is a magazine avowedly published for a metropolitan audience and thereby will escape an influence which hampers most national publications.") Much more pertinent was his lead: "*The New Yorker* will be a reflection in word and picture of metropolitan life. It will be human. Its general tenor will be one of gaiety, wit and satire, but it will be more than a jester. It will not be what is commonly called radical or highbrow. It will be what is commonly called sophisticated, in that it will assume a reasonable degree of enlightenment on the part of its readers. It will hate bunk." *The New Yorker,* Ross went on to brashly pledge, would be "so entertaining and informative as to be a necessity for the person who knows his way about or wants to."

At the bottom of the prospectus were listed the ten advisors, most of whom were well known to the public, and "H. W. Ross, Editor," who wasn't.

Fleischmann had been considerably bucked up by the advisory board. Like casual readers of the prospectus, no doubt he believed they would have a lot to do with fulfilling the document's bright promise. Nonetheless, he continued to hear from assorted second-guessers and tongue-cluckers. One friend who knew something about publishing gave Fleischmann this piece of advice: Get a satchel, fill it with your twenty-five thousand dollars, board a ferry, and throw the bag over the side. This will be quicker, he said, and ultimately much less painful.

PART II

A MAGAZINE OF SOPHISTICATION: 1925–1938

CHAPTER 5

LABOR PAINS

Pop: A man who thinks he can make it in par.
Johnny: What is an optimist, pop?

THE JOKE WAS LAME EVEN BEFORE IT WAS UPENDED, WHICH WAS THE point, really, and so it appeared, in just this way, on page twenty of the first issue of *The New Yorker*. The transposition was not a mistake, as some have suggested, but was Ross's way of tweaking what was still passing for humor in *Life* and *Judge*, implicitly proclaiming that in his *New Yorker* readers could expect such a stale convention to be stood on its head. The idea was amusing, even passing clever, done once. But Ross thought it so precious that he repeated the upside-down joke in twenty-six straight issues, until someone—possibly an appalled Katharine S. Angell, who, though just arrived, knew a sub-collegiate gesture when she saw it—persuaded him to stop.

On one level the case of the optimist joke is little more than a tri-fling footnote, but on another it represents something significant about the excruciating birth of *The New Yorker*—a year of good intentions gone wildly, very nearly fatally, amok. In 1925, even when Ross hit on a good idea, he didn't always know what to do with it.

The pallid, labored first issues of *The New Yorker* failed the magazine's prospectus in every conceivable way. However, the most misleading aspect of that document wasn't any individual promise but its underlying tone of confidence—because now it is clear that while H. W. Ross, Editor, may have had a grand cosmic vision, what he didn't have was a game plan. He was of necessity making up *The New Yorker* as he went along, week by week, story by story, sentence by sentence.

The first issue hit the newsstands on Tuesday, February 17, 1925, dated the following Saturday. Traffic did not stop, crowds did not gather, attention generally was not paid. What immediate reaction there was from passersby was surely puzzlement. Though Ross and Jane had hurriedly gotten out some promotional placards, and though a few advance notices had appeared in the newspapers, now *The New Yorker* was on the streets—and really, what *was* it?

Beyond the name of the magazine itself, the only element on the glossy cover was a curious illustration of a Regency fop examining a butterfly through his monocle. No headlines or promotional blurbs hinted at what lay inside. Ross had toyed with various concepts for this crucial first cover, and he asked several artists to work up sketches on what amounted to a dreadful visual cliché, a curtain going up on Manhattan. What he got back was predictably static and maddeningly literal. At the very last moment Ross prevailed on his art editor, Rea Irvin, to come up with something—anything—that might suggest sophistication and gaiety. Irvin responded with the high-collared character who a few months later would be christened Eustace Tilley, the elegant model of insouciance who thereafter appeared on *The New Yorker*'s anniversary numbers. (Irvin studied pictures of historical dandies for inspiration, and Tilley bears a remarkably strong resemblance to an 1834 caricature of the French Comte d'Orsay. Irvin added the monocle and butterfly.)

The optimist joke notwithstanding, that first *New Yorker* was distressingly derivative of *Judge* and *Life*. It led off with "Of All Things," a weak potpourri of anecdote and josh signed by "The New Yorker," followed by "The Talk of the Town," an even longer potpourri of

UNCLE: *Poor girls, so few get their wages!*
FLAPPER: *So few get their sin, darn it!*

This "he-she" cartoon from *The New Yorker*'s first issue would have been right at home in *Judge* or *Life*.
(By Ethel Plummer, ©1925,1953 The New Yorker Magazine, Inc.)

anecdote and josh signed by "Van Bibber III," a character appropriated from Richard Harding Davis. "The Story of Manhattankind" was a satiric thrust that missed. The first "Profile," of Metropolitan Opera impresario Giulio Gatti-Casazza, was trailed by "The Hour Glass," which offered thumbnail sketches of the likes of runner Paavo Nurmi and mayor-to-be Jimmy Walker. There were peeks at the latest theater, books, and "moving pictures," as well as light verse, scattered anecdotes, and Round Table travel notes under the heading "In Our Midst." A few sharp illustrations were offset by some dumb jokes of the "he-she" and tipsy-Irishman variety. What signed contributions there were were signed at the end of a piece, usually with pseudonyms. Ross employed the pseudonyms for several reasons: because they focused attention on the work rather than the writers; because he thought them sophisticated; and because some of the contributors didn't want to be, or couldn't be, named. Likewise, there was no staff box or other identification of the perpetrators. This, Ross explained, was because "there were no proven editors" and because "I wanted to avoid a great mass of mail coming in here personally addressed to me."

The New Yorker contained some interesting bits, but on the whole it was a confused and confusing jumble. There was no meat to it—or, for that matter, raison d'être. It was an ominous sign that Ross felt compelled to apologize, in "Of All Things," for what he knew was a marginal beginning: "*The New Yorker* asks consideration for its first number. It recognizes certain shortcomings and realizes that it is impossible for a magazine fully to establish its character in one number."

All of which was true but surely didn't mollify anyone who had shelled out fifteen cents, particularly those who had expected better. George Horace Lorimer, editor of *The Saturday Evening Post,* bluntly told his contributor Jane Grant, "I threw it across the room in disgust." *Vanity Fair*'s Crowninshield paged through the issue with one of his writers, Margaret Case Harriman, and declared, "Well, Margaret, I think we have nothing to fear." Even F.P.A., who could usually be counted on to find an encouraging word where his friends were concerned, dismissed *The New Yorker* as "too frothy for my liking," and his true disdain may be inferred from the fact that for the next year or more the magazine never resurfaces in his diary.

The sharpest rebuke to *The New Yorker*'s first number arose from within the very same building. Ross's office was one floor above that of two other magazine dreamers, Briton Hadden and Henry Luce, who were nursing along the two-year-old *Time.* The precocious Yalies were considerably further along than Ross, and Hadden especially had taken exception to the snobbish tone of Ross's prospectus. He handed the first issue to one of *Time*'s best writers, his cousin

Niven Busch, instructing him to work it over. Consider what the old lady in Dubuque would think of it, Hadden goaded.

Busch's vivisection was as artful as it was thorough. Summing up, he purported to speak for dowager Iowans everywhere: "I, and my associates here, have never subscribed to the view that bad taste is any the less offensive because it is metropolitan taste. To me, urbanity is the ability to offend without being offensive, to startle composure and to deride without ribaldry. The editors of [*The New Yorker*] are, I understand, members of a literary clique. They should learn that there is no provincialism so blatant as that of the metropolitan who lacks urbanity."

Ross appreciated the writer's way with the lash, even if he was the one being flayed; before long he would be hiring away Busch to work for *The New Yorker*. But the criticism hurt, all the more for being so true.

Then there was perhaps the most telling reaction, that of Ross's already nervous partner. Fleischmann didn't merely hate the first issue; he was terrified by it. What he had undertaken as a lark was looking more and more like a very expensive fool's errand. He was in a gray frame of mind anyway because, just as *The New Yorker* was preparing to launch, his cousin and close friend, Julius Fleischmann, fell from his polo pony, dead, in Miami Beach. The colorful Julius, former president of Fleischmann's Yeast Company and twice mayor of Cincinnati, was fifteen years older than Raoul but had been something of a mentor and big brother to him all his life. Raoul was shaken badly by Julius's death, and his personal despair made his mounting disillusionment with *The New Yorker* that much harder to take.

By now most of Fleischmann's initial stake was gone; worse, he knew that if the magazine was to stand any chance at all, he would have to pump in a good deal more. It was also clear that Ross, as technically capable and occasionally charming as he might be, either had been dreaming about how much capital would be required, or had flat-out misled him. And now that the first issue was out, Fleischmann knew one other thing: if *The New Yorker* didn't get any better than this, it wouldn't survive.

With these sobering thoughts in mind, Fleischmann immediately rang up a man named John Hanrahan, who had been referred to him as a "publisher's counsel" but who really was one of the first magazine doctors. In exchange for a ten percent stake in *The New Yorker*, Hanrahan, a wiry business-side veteran of various newspapers and magazines, agreed to help dig the F-R Publishing Corporation out of this hole. The R, Ross, was president, and he was none too pleased at what he regarded as a rash and unilateral move by F, the vice president and publisher. But being in no real position to squawk, he responded the only way he knew how: by taking an instant dislike to Hanrahan.

Immediately Hanrahan found a handful of capable managers to shore up the magazine's advertising and circulation departments (till then Fleischmann had been concentrating on negotiating the important printing contract, as well as soliciting ads). Hanrahan even had the temerity to offer editorial advice, which only made Ross angrier. In time his antipathy for Hanrahan would develop into full-blown hatred, but for now he stayed out of the savvy Irishman's way.

Hanrahan's other major contribution to *The New Yorker* was a promotional campaign that, nakedly and unapologetically, welded the magazine to a discerning, monied readership. The expensive campaign, launched that fall, succeeded in persuading the city's high-end advertisers that *The New Yorker* was uniquely positioned to help them. If Hanrahan's copy was less subtle than the editor might have liked, his message was precisely what Ross himself had been preaching for years. In spite of this, Ross would later declare, "My personal opinion of our promotion is that it was terrible and probably gave unobservant people the notion that we were frivolous." Whether he hated the promotion or just the promoter, the overriding point is that before *The New Yorker* was one week old, the first crack had appeared in the relationship between Ross and Fleischmann.

———

THE SHAKY LAUNCH OF *THE NEW YORKER* SURPRISED NO ONE WHO HAD been watching the countdown, which was erratic enough to discourage Horatio Alger himself. Certainly it had unsettled Fleischmann. "I am free to admit I didn't think for a moment we'd make a go of it," he wrote in a private memoir near the end of his life. "I wasn't at all impressed with Ross's knowledge of publishing. I had no reason to doubt his skill as an editor, nor any reason to believe in it. I had merely got into something I couldn't get out of gracefully, and Ross was so hell-bent on going ahead—and we were very friendly—that I was in, and that's all there was to it."

Ross and Fleischmann each had taken ten percent of the company's stock, leaving the remaining eighty percent to distribute later as necessary. But as 1924 had drawn to a close, Ross and Jane had been able to scrape together only twenty thousand of the twenty-five thousand dollars they had pledged, so Ross agreed to draw just one-third of his three-hundred-dollar-a-week salary and put the rest into the magazine. There wasn't really adequate time for the February launch, but there also wasn't enough money to push it back. Ross was broadcasting all over town for help, but with little money to spend and mostly part-time positions to offer, he was able to gather about him only a motley and overmatched staff. One young man, Philip Wylie, later a popular novelist but at the time a down-on-his-luck publicist (he had been unjustly tarred in a paternity scandal), even offered to work free on a trial basis for three weeks. The sympathetic Ross took him on and was immediately impressed when Wylie arranged for the first copy of *The New Yorker* to be delivered to Governor Al Smith. "This feat slightly stunned Ross," Wylie said later, "though any press agent . . . could have pulled it off, as I did, with a phone call." Within days, Ross put him on the modest payroll, and before long Wylie was responsible for coordinating the magazine's illustrations and running the weekly art meeting.

Ross's first coup was to persuade the gifted Irvin, formerly of *Life*, to be his art editor. Irvin was not so much an employee as a permanent consultant: for seventy-five dollars a week and stock, he came in every Tuesday to adjudicate the week's art submissions and generally lend his expertise where it was needed. Other charter members of the editorial staff included Tyler (Tip) Bliss, a gag writer and utility man who had worked with Ross at *The Stars and Stripes* and *The Home Sector*; Helen Mears, Ross's first secretary and later a contributor to the magazine; and Gladys Unger, a receptionist/switchboard operator—surely unnecessary in so small an office but for Ross's compulsive rearranging of the magazine's few phone lines, an early manifestation of his obsession with "systems" of every kind. In time Ross would hire *The New Yorker's* first de facto managing editor, Joseph Moncure March, a poet and unaccomplished artist whose only experience was editing a house publication for the New York Telephone Company. But he was the son of General Pershing's chief of staff, which was good enough for Ross. His first Talk of the Town writer and editor was James Kevin McGuinness, a temperamental young sportswriter and humorist who, Ross presently discovered, intensely disliked Joseph Moncure March. And though she was still at the *Times,* Jane Grant spent every spare moment at the magazine, lending Ross a hand with copy and trying to put a circulation department on its feet.

Just as Ross had badly underestimated *The New Yorker's* financial requirements, so too was he naïve about the editorial demands—though it may have been less naïveté than the brand of wishful thinking that an empty pocketbook can induce. For instance, he had hoped an inexpensive source of material would be back-of-the-notebook items from the city's army of newspaper reporters, and he posted solicitations in newsrooms all over town. But this reaped little of use. He was also still counting on his Algonquin friends to lend a hand; if they wouldn't invest in the magazine, they might at least write for it. There were problems here, too, however. Besides their continuing skepticism over the project, by 1925 the Round Tablers were genuinely preoccupied with their own busy careers, and some, like Broun, were contractually precluded from associating with what amounted to a competitor. By the magazine's launch the ten advisory editors had dwindled to seven; gone were Broun, Ferber and Stallings.

Some have maintained that the Round Table completely abandoned Ross in his hour of greatest need, but this is not quite fair. True, he certainly was made to understand that he couldn't build the magazine on his famous friends—which in the long run was a blessing since it forced *The New Yorker* to find fresh voices of its own. On the other hand, the Round Tablers did pitch in here and there, turning up just often enough in the nascent magazine for it to maintain a shred of credibility with the reading public. Dorothy Parker supplied about the only readable material there was in the first two issues: droll theater reviews under the pseudonym Last Night ("It is the sort of well-mannered piece that ought to have Bruce McRae in it, and, oddly enough, always does have him"), a poem ("Cassandra Drops into Verse"), and a satiric thrust at the superficial life of a club-woman. Woollcott anonymously (a wise move, given its obsequiousness) profiled his old boss Carr Van Anda in issue three, and a few months later sketched penny-books tycoon Emanuel Haldeman-Julius. Humorist and lifelong Ross friend Frank Sullivan sparked the sixth number with a whimsical look at convoluted cab fares. Ben Hecht got over his abashment to contribute a casual in issue nine. Murdock Pemberton was there almost from the start, recruited by Jane as the first art critic. Ferber profiled editor William Allen White in issue fifteen, and Benchley's first humorous essay, "Sex Is Out," appeared in the last number of 1925. Herman Mankiewicz was also present at the creation, cranking out everything from funny promotional ads to theater criticism, as was Marc Connelly. He was an especially diligent handmaiden to Ross, writing anonymous pieces, editing, even mediating. One day as he was taking a pencil to a piece Ross had written, Jane walked up and asked if he intended to trim it back. Connelly said yes. "I told Ross to cut it," she replied, "but that man is wife-deaf."

Ross spoke constantly, almost mantra-like, of hitting on the right "formula"—that magical mix of words, pictures, and attitude that gives a magazine its identity. It is an alchemy difficult for any magazine to achieve, much less a new one with groundbreaking aspirations. Even so, one cannot help but be struck by how many of the now-familiar elements were in place from the start. Rough as it was, that first number is immediately recognizable as *The New Yorker*. Beyond the distinct "look" of Irvin's typography and text-driven design, one finds Talk of the Town; cartoons and comic illustration;

cultural reviews and notes; the "Goings On" calendar of events; light verse; very brief (albeit thoroughly aimless) casuals; and Profiles, which in the beginning truly were what that name implies—subjects sketched quickly, in outline. (It is said that McGuinness first suggested the name "Profiles" to Ross, who rather reluctantly concurred. Later he became so proprietary about the name that *The New Yorker* copyrighted it and fought its appropriation by other publications— though in time, of course, "profile" as a literary form simply passed into the lexicon.)

Ross nonetheless juggled the magazine's disparate parts like so many china plates, and more than a few crashed to the floor. Many early departments that had seemed indistinguishable either were sharpened (Talk of the Town, Of All Things), or pitched out ("Behind the News," "And They Do Say," "New York, Etc."). Columns were named and renamed; page headings constantly metamorphosed. For nearly a year Ross lumped together the cultural reviews under a single rubric, "Critique," before separating them again. The Story of Manhattankind and In Our Midst mercifully died quick deaths. With each departure came an addition, and usually it was an improvement in the formula. In July the first letter from overseas, "From Paris," arrived (though not from Janet Flanner), and in mid-August "Notes and Comment" showed up for the first time, forever after to lead Talk of the Town. A general sports column debuted early, as did "The Sky-Line," an innovative commentary on building design and its impact on the cityscape.

One crucial and telltale entry appeared in the eighth number. "When Nights Are Bold" was a witty and genuinely informative assessment of the nightclub and speakeasy scene, and *The New Yorker*'s first real lurch toward its true, nouveau-society audience. Signed by "Top Hat," the column was conducted by the debonair Charles Baskerville, who also provided the accompanying sleek drawings under his real name.

Baskerville, Ross and Jane Grant had come to know one another socially in New York after the war. Ross was not a dancer or a habitué of the better clubs (he *was* known in some of the rougher speakeasies), but he was aware that Baskerville was a genuine man-about-town and asked the young artist if he would cover the clubs for his new magazine. The decision marked Ross's first real effort to link *The New Yorker* to the Jazz Age milieu, and he clearly hoped some of its excitement and illicit glamour would rub off on the magazine.

Ross paid Baskerville little and gave him the most cursory instructions. "He never told me anything except just to go out and 'report what you think would be amusing,' " the artist recalled. He happily complied, dropping off his copy at the magazine each week and seeing it come out more or less the way he had written it. Later that year Baskerville headed back to Europe, and the column was taken over by a recruit from *Vanity Fair*, the glamorous Lois Long, who wrote under the pseudonym Lipstick. Soon after the column was renamed "Tables for Two."

So Ross's problem was not so much *The New Yorker*'s format, which was slowly gelling, but its execution, which wasn't. It wasn't that he didn't know what he wanted. He dreamed of toppling conventions. He envisioned news and comment and a dash of gossip, delivered with cheek. He wanted *The New Yorker* to be informed but offhand ("We were on our way to the Winter Garden when we overheard . . ."), and humorous throughout. And he wanted it all bent to his own peculiar notion of a sophisticate's world. "Ross had a map in his mind of the things *The New Yorker* should be covering," explained the writer William Maxwell, a longtime fiction editor for the magazine. "Florida, the West Indies, California and Europe were on it, but Illinois and Canada were not."

All this would have been a very tall order in the best of circumstances, but for a handful of undercapitalized, underexperienced newcomers, conjuring the *New Yorker* of Ross's glib prospectus would require something closer to prestidigitation. But magic, alas, was in short supply.

For one thing, Ross was unsure of his audience—was he supposed to be courting established society or mocking it?—and therefore uncertain what he wanted to say, or even how to say it. The tone of the early issues was less informed and offhand than smug or shrill. The magazine trafficked endlessly in Round Table notes and journalistic inside baseball, and wasted entirely too much buckshot on obvious or dull targets like Mayor John F. Hylan. Profiles, while a good idea, were uneven, fawning (except for yet another trashing of Jack Dempsey in issue four), and predictable (Alice Roosevelt Longworth, Giants manager John McGraw, Charlie Chaplin). The magazine also exhibited virtually no modulation in tone. Pieces meant to be subtle were so understated as to be baffling. Yet when Ross wanted to draw blood, subtlety went out the window. Thus William Jennings Bryan, creationist symbol of the Scopes trial then unfolding in Tennessee, wasn't nicked in a single cartoon but harpooned in four in the same issue. Ross, a man who spent a career counseling writers to "use the rapier rather than the bludgeon," had yet to grasp this lesson himself.

The only major piece of the formula that worked almost from the start was "art"—then and now *The New Yorker*'s term for cartoons, covers, and illustrations. Likewise, these important contributors were never the "cartoonists" or the "illustrators," but the "artists." This respect, then rare in the magazine world, owes much to Ross, but it is also one of the many important legacies of Rea Irvin.

Irvin was a large but soft-spoken man, with a twinkling sense of humor. A onetime actor, he had a theatrical presence that he enhanced with a flamboyant wardrobe. He was eleven years older than the editor and came from San Francisco, so Ross listened to him where often he wouldn't to others. Like some other important early contributors who stayed too long at the magazine, Irvin in time came to an unhappy parting with it. Doubtless this is one reason he has never been given his full due in various accounts of its history.

Rea Irvin contributed four crucial things to Ross, without any one of which *The New Yorker* would have been diminished. First, of course, was that inaugural cover. Tilley not only effortlessly conveyed everything Ross wanted his magazine to be—smart, enigmatic, relaxed, observant, amusing, yet somehow detached—but in time literally came to embody *The New Yorker,* a familiar icon to this day.

Second, Irvin designed the unique, casually elegant headline type (still known as "Irvin" type), and created the magazine's clean design, down to its squiggly column rules, against which the cartoons and high-priced advertising could pop out in crisp relief. Third, he spent much of his time in the early years teaching Ross about art. Philip Wylie, who sat in on the first one hundred or so of those weekly art meetings, attests that Irvin "rubbed most of the uncouthness and corn-love out of Ross's mind in the all-afternoon Tuesday conferences." Ross was a very quick student, and his own taste in comic art would become superior, but the fact remains he had a patient, expert teacher.

Irvin's fourth contribution, of course, was the art itself. From the beginning, the art in *The New Yorker* was much closer to Ross's elusive aims than the prose. "Irvin always knew what he wanted Ross to

Rea Irvin. *(Keystone)*

want," Ralph Ingersoll observed, "which was why *The New Yorker*'s art took off first." The primordial *New Yorker* is full of the best comic artists of the day—among them Ralph Barton, Al Freuh, Miguel Covarrubias, and John Held, Jr. By the summer of 1925 they were joined by the likes of Gardner Rea, Garrett Price, and Johann Bull, as well as such promising newcomers as Peter Arno, Helen Hokinson, Carl Rose, and Alice Harvey. It's a good thing for Ross they *were* there, for the delightful covers and witty cartoons made the magazine worth perusing even in those instances when there was little in it to read.

Though many of these artists had worked with Ross prior to *The New Yorker*, it was Irvin who had the credibility to pull them into this experimental, low-paying magazine, and who, just as important, pointed them in the right direction. Almost immediately the artists demonstrated a willingness to depart from orthodoxy that their writing counterparts couldn't muster. For instance, when Held drew for the magazine, Ross and Irvin eschewed his overexposed flappers, instead publishing his contemporary twists on the Gay Nineties woodcuts Ross had loved as a boy. Under the guidance of Ross and Irvin, *New Yorker* cartoonists would abandon the standard two-line joke in favor of the single-line caption; suddenly the drawing was intrinsic to the gag, not just an illustration of it. Also in that first year, the artists reflected the permissive times by celebrating the female form in surprisingly risqué illustrations—surprising given the reputation for prudery, both in word and picture, that Ross earned in later years. All the while, Irvin was practicing what he preached. He produced some of the best *New Yorker* cartoons of 1925, such as his delightful "Social Errors" series that featured the classic "The Young Man Who Asked for a Pack of Camels in Dunhill's."

There was good reason why, in those early days, Ross was often heard to mutter, "We need to get the words like the art!"

———

THE ART NOTWITHSTANDING, BY THE SPRING OF 1925, NEW YORKERS were not reading *The New Yorker* in droves.

In retrospect, an early slide in circulation might have been predicted. Even had the magazine offered sturdier fare from the very beginning, it clearly meant to be something new, and therefore an acquired taste.

True to form, Ross and Fleischmann hadn't permitted themselves to consider the worst, but after ten or so issues they were staring at it. The press run, which had started out at fifteen thousand, was down to eight thousand and falling. Unpurchased copies piled up. Advertisements grew scarce and were not always collectible in any case. The book shrank to an anemic twenty-four pages. The magazine's initial capital was long gone, and Ross was presenting Fleischmann with bills of five thousand dollars a week and more.

Late one evening Marquis James was having a drink with Ross. As they parted well after midnight Ross casually said, "Have to dig up a thousand dollars before breakfast."

The next morning James found Ross back at his desk. "I got it," he said. He had sold a complete bound set of *The Stars and Stripes*—which the artist LeRoy Baldridge suggested that Ross had pilfered from him after the war—to his old friend Theodore Roosevelt, Jr., founder of the American Legion.

Still, the pressure to find new money built in inverse proportion to readership. Finally Ross's desperation led him to a disastrous evening of cards at the home of Herbert Bayard Swope. It was Swope's custom to entertain lavishly on weekends, and on this Sunday evening Ross and Jane were among a number of couples there, including the Fleischmanns. As usual, a high-stakes poker game began. By now, Ross generally had given up the richer games, but this night, with *The New Yorker* hanging in the balance, he believed he was gambling on the side of the angels.

And in fact, Ross *was* ahead when Jane indicated she was ready to leave. He rose to go, but after the other players challenged his manhood, not to mention his poker etiquette, he sat back down and Jane left alone. The game wore on through the night, past dawn, and into Monday morning. Ross finally stumbled home, drunk, at noon. As he slept it off, a horrified Jane fished IOUs out of his coat and pants pockets that totaled nearly thirty thousand dollars.

"This added debt gave me a feeling of utter despair," she wrote.

"We were disgraced. I could think of nothing left for us to do but commit suicide." When her husband awoke they contemplated the grisly solution, but fortunately as he sobered up their conversation turned instead to how they might reconcile the debt.

Having watched it all, Fleischmann was angry—not so much at Ross but at those players he believed had callously taken advantage of his partner's financial plight and drunken state. He managed to get some of Ross's debts absolved, repaid others himself, and then arranged with Ross to square the remainder between themselves. Ross was relieved, obviously, but also ashamed and embarrassed. More ominously, it began to dawn on him that suddenly, after a lifetime of independence, he owed his entire existence to this man Fleischmann. The perverse resentment of his partner deepened.

For his part, the Swope debacle may well have been the last straw for Fleischmann. On Friday, May 8, he called together Ross, Hanrahan and Truax, one of the magazine's directors, for a meeting at the Princeton Club. (Ironically, this occurred just as the magazine was publishing the first major contribution by a promising young humorist, E. B. White, called "Defense of the Bronx River.") The four men chewed over their limited options, including suspending publication through the dog days of summer, but nothing seemed plausible. With great reluctance, they agreed to kill *The New Yorker*.

On their desultory walk back to the office, Fleischmann overheard Hanrahan say to either Ross or Truax, "I can't blame Raoul for a moment for refusing to go on, but it's like killing something that's alive." The remark sent a shudder through him, but he walked on in silence.

As it happened, the following day Frank Adams was getting married in Connecticut, and Ross and Fleischmann both were there. In this convivial atmosphere and plied with champagne, the two began to revisit their decision. If there was some way to get the magazine into the lucrative fall season, they believed, it might survive. They left the reception having agreed to talk further on Monday, and two days later they devised a plan to give the magazine one last try.

Years later, in a private history of the Fleischmann family, Raoul conceded that had his cousin Julius not died that February, he might not have permitted himself second thoughts about *The New Yorker*. "It is a pretty good chance that had he lived I would have spoken to him about the rough days we were going through by June of that year," he wrote. "And if he had made any suggestion that I drop it and come into the Fleischmann Yeast Company, the chances are mighty good that I would have done so."

But Julius wasn't there, and Raoul's only real alternative to publishing *The New Yorker*—a return to the bakery—was intolerable, so for very different reasons he was as motivated as Ross to find a way to keep the magazine going. Their plan was to limp along as best they could through the summer, operating as inexpensively as possible while husbanding their best material and cash for a big push in September. The press run would be kept low—with circulation eventually slipping below three thousand copies, this was not a big problem—and Ross would continue to hone the format. They also agreed to set aside sixty thousand dollars for Hanrahan's promotional campaign.

Of course, still to be solved was the little problem of money. Fleischmann had continued to pour in more of his own, in exchange for a growing mound of the dubious F-R stock, but there was a limit to his personal largess. He couldn't really turn to his family because they thought he had taken leave of his senses. However, his wife, Ruth, had wealth independent of Raoul's, and now for the first time she put money into *The New Yorker*. Truax and his brother-in-law, the respected Wall Street attorney Lloyd Paul Stryker, came in with about fifteen thousand dollars between them. Meanwhile, the intrepid Jane had managed to secure promises of capital from a Texas oilman, and there was talk that financier Bernard Baruch, a friend of the Round Table, was prepared to throw a lifeline, too. By then, however, the reinvigorated Fleischmann had pulled together enough money to keep the magazine closely held.

Thus did *The New Yorker* teeter on the abyss, never again to be so near death.

Which is not to say the problems were over. It was, in fact, a hellish summer, and not only because New York was sweltering through one of its periodic heat waves. On a personal level, Ross was anxious for his father back in Salt Lake. George Ross had been gravely ill for months with cancer of the stomach, and in early June Ida telephoned to say that his death was near. Telling his staff, "Keep it going if you can," Ross boarded a train for Utah and arrived on June 19, just hours after his father expired. George Ross, at seventy-four a relatively prosperous businessman and a respected member of the community, was laid to rest by his fellow Masons. Personal grief aside, the timing could hardly have been worse for Ross, with his magazine foundering two thousand miles away, but he stayed on for two weeks to comfort his mother and help settle the family's affairs.

On his return, Ross found the coffers so low that the July 11, 1925, cover of the magazine, a satire on the Scopes trial, actually ran in black and white. Advertising had atrophied to practically nothing. Things reached such an embarrassing pass that many weeks the magazine couldn't even sell its premium advertising positions, the back page and front and back inside covers. In a reverse of the customary procedure, it was often frantically calling agencies at the last minute, offering to run ads free of charge just to maintain appearances.

To help camouflage the dearth of advertising, Ross asked Corey Ford to come up with some promotional, or "house," ads. Ford's response was the "The Making of a Magazine" series, which not only represented some of the cleverest writing in the 1925 *New Yorker* but went a long way toward establishing the magazine's droll, self-deprecating tone. The series, which began August 8 and ran in twenty issues, took readers on a tongue-in-cheek tour of "the vast organization of *The New Yorker*," from the squid-tickling factory, where ink is collected, to the Emphasis Department, where italics are forged, to the punctuation farm, where commas, quotation marks, and semicolons are scrupulously cultivated under the watchful eye of "our Mr. Eustace Tilley, General Superintendent." Each article was accompanied by a Johann Bull illustration featuring the ubiquitous Tilley, who was based on the Rea Irvin dandy. Ford had simply made up the moniker (" 'Tilley' was the name of a maiden aunt," he explained, "and I chose 'Eustace' because it sounded euphonious"), and soon it came to be identified with Irvin's monocled figure. Tilley began turning up by name in Talk items, and Ross listed him in the telephone directory.

Another piece of luck that hard summer was the sensational Scopes trial. If Ross still wasn't sure exactly where the magazine stood in relation to New York society, lampooning the yokels down in Tennessee was a no-brainer. As with the cartoon digs at Bryan, most of the early efforts were clumsy and heavy-handed. Then, in that July 11 issue with the black-and-white cover, there was a breakthrough. Ross dispatched Marquis James to Tennessee to have a look at the Scopes hoopla for himself. The piece he produced was, in essence, *The New Yorker*'s first real "Letter" or "Reporter at Large," though Ross had yet to invent those labels.

James's account, titled simply "Dayton, Tennessee," vividly described the carnival-like atmosphere surrounding the trial, and how the good citizens of Dayton had pressed a case against the unassuming biology teacher John T. Scopes—"twenty-four and young for his years"—more on a whim than out of any moral indignation. The story is noteworthy for many reasons, but primarily as a forerunner of the classic *New Yorker* fact tradition: it was well-written, detailed, understated, amusing, and serious without being sober. James achieved that *New Yorker* vantage point, a certain comfortable detachment, from which to make his observations. One can easily imagine this description of Dayton being written fifteen years later by A. J. Liebling or Joseph Mitchell:

> This town differs from other east Tennessee towns because it is newer and more progressive. It was founded in the eighties when the railroad came through from Cincinnati. It belongs to the twentieth century. It ought to have a Rotary Club and Mr. Robinson, the hustling druggist, ought to be the president. Dayton took the county seat away from Washington, which is more than one hundred years old, but has no railroad, no hustling druggist and will never catch the eye of Rotary International. It is a restful Southern

hamlet of character. You couldn't get up an evolution test case there on a bet.

Gradually, pieces like this helped *The New Yorker* find its voice. Just as important, Ross was beginning to assert what was perhaps his greatest editorial gift—the instinctive ability to find talent, sometimes in the oddest places, and to cultivate it.

There is no greater example of Ross's spotting raw potential than his hiring, that August, of a remarkable young woman, ostensibly to be a part-time reader of manuscripts. Katharine Sergeant Angell was a refined and darkly beautiful woman, born to a prominent Brookline, Massachusetts, family and educated at Bryn Mawr. In the summer of 1925 she was brought to Ross's attention by Fillmore Hyde, who was the capable first writer of Notes and Comment and a summer neighbor of the Angells. The mother of two young children, Katharine Angell felt trapped in a deteriorating marriage, and she yearned to be back in the workplace. Her eclectic résumé included a job surveying all the disabled residents of Cleveland, Ohio, but her only real publishing experience was several articles and reviews for *The New Republic, The Atlantic Monthly,* and *The Saturday Review of Literature.* She was everything Ross was not: cultured, classically educated, stylish, well-spoken, but with a New England reserve that was often mistaken for aloofness. She might have been expected to be put off by Ross's gruff, antic manner; instead, she was attracted by his energy, humor, and sense of mission. She also shared his conviction that a literate journal of humor was not only doable but important. Against the advice of *Saturday Review* editor Henry Seidel Canby (his judgment was that *The New Yorker* was "nothing"), she jumped when Ross offered her the part-time job at twenty-five dollars a week. Almost immediately Ross made her full-time, doubled her salary, and broadened her role. She found herself "doing everything—as we all did at the start." In her case, this included editing stories, working with artists, even contributing some of her own modest verse and casuals.

When Katharine Angell arrived, Talk of the Town was being conducted by another fortuitous recruit, a young Yale graduate, Ralph

McAllister Ingersoll, whom Ross had hired only two months earlier. Though a plodding writer, Ingersoll was intelligent, ambitious, and, perhaps most of all, confident beyond his years. Trained as a mining engineer, he also had limited publishing experience—a smattering of reporting and a light-selling novel. But his lineage was impeccable: the McAllisters were among the New York Four Hundred. Ross thought that perhaps Ingersoll, who moved so easily in New York society, might lend a knowing and sophisticated air still badly missing in *The New Yorker*. Then, too, Ross had spilled ink all over Ingersoll's newly purchased pale-gray suit during his first job interview, and this sealed it. As Ingersoll walked out of the editor's office, he heard Ross growl, "Jesus Christ, I hire anybody!"

RALPH INGERSOLL FIRST ENCOUNTERED HAROLD ROSS THROUGH mutual friends just before *The New Yorker*'s launch. He was unimpressed with the new magazine and gave it little more thought—until that June, when he was still unimpressed but more desperate to secure work. He went to see Ross, but during their conversation Ingersoll was preoccupied—he was in the clutch of some romantic entanglements—and Ross, misreading Ingersoll's distraction for lack of interest, observed, "You look a little vague about it." The editor's candor impressed Ingersoll enough that he made a note of it in his diary.

In their various discussions Ross focused on the weak Talk section, and Ingersoll agreed to do some sample pieces for it. Soon after, he was hired—at twenty-five dollars a week, half what he had asked for—with the specific aim of resuscitating this department.

Ingersoll arrived in the middle of Ross's personal calvary. It was in *The New Yorker*'s first year that Ross's now mythic reputation as a wild, erratic manager took root—and not without some reason. In previous jobs he had always demanded as much from his staff as he did of himself, but even allowing for his eccentricities, he was considered a fair and reasonable boss. Now, however, with his own money and reputation at stake, he was more driven and single-

Ralph Ingersoll
just prior to joining
The New Yorker.
*(Ralph Ingersoll Collection,
Boston University)*

minded than ever. Like most entrepreneurs, he believed the product was everything, and he cared not a whit about what people thought of him or his methods. Natural tics—flailing his arms, running a hand throughout his unkempt hair, jingling the coins in his pants pocket—became more pronounced. Friends who casually asked how he was doing got back a litany of despair. His patience, never a long suit anyway, evaporated, and as his exasperation mounted he gave full rein to his anger. His criticisms tended to be intemperate and laced with sarcasm, and he sometimes kept mistakes tacked up over his desk to remind himself to chew out the miscreants. This Ross represented the unflattering marriage of perfectionism and panic.

There were other factors, too. A man trying to invent a new magazine form, Ross wasn't sure how to achieve it, much less articulate it to others. Even if he had known exactly what he wanted, in those early days and months he certainly didn't have the staff talent to pull it off. For reasons of sentiment and economy, he at first turned to many old newspaper friends and castoffs, then let them go as they proved too alcoholic or prosaic to advance his cause. He also dug up some genuine eccentrics, which was to become as much a *New Yorker* tradition as Eustace Tilley. One writer was said to have the shakes so bad that an office boy had to roll the paper into his typewriter. Old-timers especially liked to recall the otherwise normal young woman, never identified, who at the same time each day removed her jewelry and wristwatch, walked to another office, telephoned her husband, and gave him a brutal tongue-lashing. She then calmly put her jewelry back on and returned to work. "The cast of characters in those early days," E. B. White would write, "was as shifty as the characters in a floating poker game."

Then there was the problem of copy. There was never enough of it, it was never good enough, and yet there was never enough time to fix it. A pernicious cycle developed: the shortage of ads left too much editorial space to fill, which meant too many weak stories were published, which further alienated readers, which caused more advertisers to drop out, which created more space. . . . Ross found himself in the uncomfortable position of running almost every borderline piece he received. One reason why he (and more notoriously, his successor, William Shawn) came to develop such a huge backlog of material—more than the magazine could ever use—is that in those desperate days, the editor, like a profane Scarlett O'Hara, vowed he would never go hungry again.

It was unsurprising, then, that Ross constantly badgered the few capable contributors he did have. After her initial flurry of pieces, Dorothy Parker, despite her assurances to Ross, fell out of the magazine for months. In an exchange that passed instantly into *New Yorker* lore, when Ross ran into her one day and inquired why she hadn't been by the office, Parker replied, "Someone was using the pencil." The remark was hardly the exaggeration most people assume. In the first *New Yorker* office, space and supplies were nearly as scarce as cash. There were only a handful of typewriters, and one was kept in reserve for those contributors who *did* stumble in and felt disposed to bat something out. One day, after he'd become managing editor, Ingersoll arrived to find this still-smoking note, in Ross's distinctive scrawl, on his desk: "Ingersoll, the typewriter and stand are gone again from the end room, God damn it!!!"

Such was the office environment—desperation with an overlay of loopiness—that Ingersoll encountered that hot, unpromising summer. Notes he recorded in his sporadic diary of 1925 provide a glimpse of the pressures and anxiety.

Ross still hoped to make Talk of the Town the signature of *The New Yorker;* indeed, throughout his entire career he would devote more personal attention to it than to any other portion of the magazine. He was distressed that under McGuinness Talk had gotten off to such a choppy start, and for days he, Ingersoll and March discussed what might be done about it. Ingersoll was anxious. He wasn't exactly certain what Ross wanted; besides, how was he supposed to

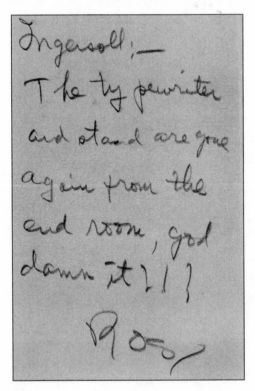

Micromanagement: a Ross memo to Ingersoll, probably from 1926.
(Ralph Ingersoll Collection, Boston University)

insinuate himself into Talk without alienating McGuinness? More broadly, the whole magazine had so far to go. In talking over *The New Yorker* with his family just after he'd started there, Ingersoll had to concur with their assessment that the magazine not only wasn't smart but betrayed the staff's "too-recent escape from Middle Westernness."

Because it was supposed to be the "newsiest" and most topical department, Talk was always one of the last pieces of the magazine to close, at week's end, before it went to the printers. After a few weeks Ingersoll was contributing Talk items along with McGuinness; Mankiewicz did some rewriting, and Ross edited it all himself. On July 3, a Friday morning, just as everyone was looking forward to a sorely needed holiday, Ross "read Talk, went in the air and ordered the whole thing done over again." This was bad enough, Ingersoll continued, "but then he took McGuinness and March and me 'in conference' and for six hours talked—not on this week's issue but on policy—vague and anecdotally-flavored until my head went round—and still no this week's Talk."

That Sunday Ross and March were back in the office, "at it hammer and tongs." Then on Monday Ingersoll noted: "This last week marked the definite failure of my attempt to swing Talk. The last of [this week's department] went in with McGuinness, Mankiewicz and Ross all in a frenzy of contribution, driven by the last. At that it was about half my stuff—but Lord what a mess. When it was over I went out to lunch alone, immensely relieved and dizzy. Why the hell they don't fire me, I don't know."

Despite those occasional bouts of self-doubt, Ingersoll persisted, generating his own Talk items and working over McGuinness's. The latter's irritation with the situation is evident in this complaint to Ross over a clumsy change that Ingersoll had made:

Memorandum from McGuinness.
    To all concerned, from the Hon. Ross down.
    In re: editing.
    1. In this week's Talk of the Town, under heading Rabelaisian,

in paragraph containing comment by Mr. David H. Wallace, I wrote "will be valuable as source material only," etc.

2. I note this has been changed to read "as *a* source *of* material only, etc."

3. I meant "will be valuable as source material," etc.

4. "Source material" means, in the jargon of the literary profession, if such, original sources to which writers repair for material. In other words, the origins consulted (old documents, histories, etc.) are "source material."

5. The change makes the phrase high schoolish instead of informed.

6. For the love of Mike.

McGuinness stewed over this unhappy state of affairs for weeks until one day he exploded. "Goddammit, every bit of my copy for a month has been rewritten," he snapped. "I don't consider Ingersoll competent to rewrite my stuff." Rising to Ingersoll's defense, March looked as if he might hit "his old enemy" McGuinness. The confrontation dissolved into a spate of grumbling, and that night Ross tried to patch things up by taking both Ingersoll and McGuinness to his house for drinks. After McGuinness left, however, Ross expressed his support for Ingersoll—who was to note later, "The more I see of Ross the more I like him and want to work for him." Not long after, McGuinness absconded for the saner and more financially rewarding life of a Hollywood writer.

With deadlines looming daily—magazines are produced and printed in sections that close throughout the week, rather than all at once—the work regimen amounted to a veritable treadmill. It seemed to Ingersoll that he was constantly meeting with Ross—during, after, and even before work; the editor was known to conduct meetings at 412 while still shaving. On a Saturday afternoon in August, Ingersoll found Ross and March in the office, "wan-faced with exhaustion, counseling each other not to work tomorrow." As Ross's top lieutenant, the sensitive March was the magazine's first so-called Jesus, and therefore drum major in that ignominious procession that came to be known as the Jesus Parade. In the *New Yorker* lexicon, "Jesus" was a corruption of "genius," but the term was less sacrilegious than apt because it characterized Ross's constant search for that editorial messiah who was as good with a production schedule as he was with a blue pencil. But divinity being a rare commodity in publishing, he was forever let down, and he systematically ground the spirit out of one Jesus after another. March was only the first to buckle under the pressure, and one afternoon, according to Ingersoll, he "was actually removed from the office by little men in white coats."

As Talk grew more confident, so did Ingersoll, and in October a staff reorganization gave him more responsibility; his ascendance had become apparent. It had been Ingersoll's intent to make Talk a "magazine within the magazine," and he was the principal architect of the format that became such a success: a menu of alternating short essays and anecdotes, "visit" pieces, mini-profiles, and background news pieces. He extended Talk's reach from Broadway to Wall Street to Park Avenue. "Done right," Ingersoll said, "the whole would give the reader—unobtrusively—the feeling that he had been everywhere, knew everyone, was up on everything. And each week a different locale and subject pattern—so that over, say, a month or six weeks with Talk, a reader really did get around."

To secure this range of items, Ingersoll recruited a number of strategically placed people around town into a kind of information exchange. Ironically, one of his first and best sources was a young Walter Winchell, who in a few years would become New York's biggest and most feared gossip columnist and a passionate enemy of Harold Ross.

Ingersoll's mind was at once logical, analytical, and obsessive (when in later years he covered college football games for *The New Yorker,* he scrupulously diagrammed each individual play in his notebook). His peccadilloes matched or exceeded Ross's own and were guaranteed to set the editor's teeth on edge. In meetings he would nervously chew on paper clips until Ross yelled at him to stop. Then he would start chewing on paper, neatly lining up the little wadded balls before him on the table.

But Ingersoll was organized and, above all, got results. In November Ross made him his second Jesus, appointing him managing editor. In five months he had gone from new hire to senior staff member—though in fact the government's postal regulations forced the question of his title because they required that the name of the managing editor appear in the magazine's statement of ownership. Ross took great pleasure in reminding Ingersoll not to read too much into the gesture; next time, he said, he was thinking of naming his butler the managing editor.

———

AS *THE NEW YORKER* POISED FOR ITS FATEFUL AUTUMN PUSH, ROSS could truthfully say he had upheld his end of the bargain. The magazine's tone had become more natural and self-assured. The basic format was in place, and so were many of the key people who could at last help Ross put it across.

On the art front, the first of Helen Hokinson's popular dowagers and clubwomen had begun to appear, as had the promising offerings of a former jazz-band piano player, Curtis Arnoux Peters, who called himself Peter Arno. (Inevitably, the dashing and roguish Arno soon took up with beautiful Lois Long, one of the first of many dreaded office liaisons to plague Ross. "There'll be no sex, by God, in the office!" he was to insist in vain.)

A defection, and one with violent consequences, was that of the resourceful Mankiewicz. It was Mankiewicz who had consoled Ross when his Round Table friends let him down ("The half-time help of wits is no better than the full-time help of half-wits," he remarked), but despite his commodious talent he had proved an intimidating, unsettling presence in the tiny office. Even Ross was unnerved at times by his patronizing tone. That fall, needing money, Mankiewicz was also seduced by Hollywood. He fully expected it to be a temporary diversion, however, and was stunned when Ross sent him a telegram firing him. That February, when he returned to New York, Mankiewicz regaled his Algonquin friends with how he planned to take his revenge by caning Ross. Legend has it that when he came

Helen Hokinson. *(AP/Wide World)*   **Peter Arno.** *(AP/Wide World)*

An early Hokinson cartoon shows that she was already in firm control of her unique and gentle humor.

(By Helen Hokinson, ©1928, 1956 The New Yorker Magazine, Inc.)

"They serve this so nice at
Battle Creek, in just a little butter sauce."

around looking for the editor, Ross hid in his closet, leaving Mankiewicz no option but to rap his cane on the editor's desk and depart. Indisputable, however, is the fact that Mankiewicz eventually caught Ross in the office, and the two squared off in a vitriolic argument that Ingersoll and a few others overheard in shock and wonder. Mankiewicz left in a rage, still fired, but Ross was exhausted and bruised; Ingersoll said that the ugly confrontation was one reason Ross began to have underlings deliver his unpleasant tidings for him. Mankiewicz was replaced as theater critic by the novelist Charles Brackett.

Meanwhile, Jane Grant had written to a friend living in Paris, Janet Flanner, practically pleading with her to begin contributing a regular "letter" to the magazine. Ross was looking for someone there who could pull together smart items about the arts, fashion, and other subjects of interest to worldly New Yorkers, but he had been disappointed by the superficiality of some early freelance submissions. Jane pitched hard. "Certainly you know your Paris, better than anyone I can think of," she wrote, "and while I know it is difficult to make long distance arrangements, I feel sure you can get the idea if anybody can."

The Indiana-born Flanner had fled to New York after the war; there she became friends with Jane and Neysa McMein, joined the Lucy Stone League, and moved on the periphery of the Round Table. When she fell in love with another writer, Solita Solano, they moved to Paris in 1922 in order to live more openly. Flanner was a vigorous personal correspondent, and Jane felt that any of her newsy, idiosyncratic letters "would be just the thing" for *The New Yorker.*

Flanner always said that Ross's only directive to her was "I don't want to know what *you* think about what goes on in Paris. I want to know what the French think." She retained this as her charge for the next fifty years. In exchange, Ross was prepared to offer her forty dollars per submission, every other week (it was later cut to thirty-five). Flanner agreed to try. Ross cobbled together her first two efforts into a single column, which appeared on October 10, 1925. By now Ross was, logically enough, calling the department Paris Letter, and it was signed Genet (sans circumflex; this oversight would not be corrected for two more years). Ross never explained to Flanner what Genêt was supposed to connote, but she assumed, almost certainly correctly, that "to his eyes and ears [it] seemed like a Frenchification of Janet."

While Jane wooed Flanner, Ross worked diligently on another important recruit. As he combed the newspapers for talent, he had taken note of a young reporter and rewrite man at *The New York World,* Morris Markey, who possessed a writing style more graceful, even literary, than that of the usual inky wretch. Markey had other job opportunities and was perfectly aware of *The New Yorker's* wobbly gait. But Ross was at his persuasive best, and he uttered the words that every journalist longs to hear but seldom does: "Write exactly what you see, exactly the way you feel." The young man was hooked.

Markey was a rock for Ross in 1925, week after week pounding out sassy commentaries and reliable news features about New York—on the Chinatown tongs, on Tammany, on the futility of Prohibition enforcement—and gave the otherwise feather-light magazine some badly needed gravitas. In the longer run, he helped Ross establish the standards and expectations of *New Yorker* fact pieces and was the first in its long and distinguished line of resident journalists. In hiring Markey, Ross had urged him to disinter some of the fascinating stories that the dailies had buried, and to tell them fully and in detail—even to employ the fiction techniques of narrative and mood. Markey's initial pieces that summer were news features, under the heading "In the News," which more or less alternated with criticism of New York's newspapers, in a department called "The Current Press," the forerunner of Benchley's (and later Liebling's) "The Wayward Press." Then that December Markey officially became *The New Yorker's* first "Reporter at Large."

Ross made good his promise of editorial freedom, and Markey thrived on it. But the editor, still somewhat unsure of himself when staring at a piece of fiction or satire, was wholly comfortable with news reporting, and Markey therefore was one of the first *New Yorker* writers to get the full brunt of Ross's confrontational challenges.

When Ross edited a Markey story, he would grasp the manuscript firmly and cite its alleged shortcomings line by line. Both men would dig in their heels, and the haggling might go on for days. (In the parody issue the staff prepared for Ross's birthday in 1926, Markey's contribution was entitled "A Reporter in Chains.") Like so many of Ross's reporters, however, Markey was ultimately philosophical about, even grateful for, Ross's sometimes maddening ministrations. "The only thing I had a talent for was looking at a thing and trying to tell people exactly what I saw," Markey would say. "Ross knew that, and I suppose he was trying to sharpen it."

The fall push began with the September 12 issue, and its ad-filled forty pages are eloquent testimony to the effectiveness of Hanrahan's promotional campaign. At the same time, *The New Yorker* stepped up an existing program of celebrity endorsers, which presently included Jimmy Walker, Irving Berlin, and George Gershwin. If business still wasn't thriving, it was definitely improving, and for the first time in a year Ross, if he squinted, could detect light at the end of the tunnel.

Then in November, the hard-luck *New Yorker* finally got a genuine break. Ellin Mackay, daughter of wealthy New York socialite Clarence Mackay and one of the city's most celebrated debutantes, sent Ross a handwritten, leather-bound manuscript. What she had produced was a shrill attack on the hypocrisy and torpor of society's private parties and balls, and a defense of the democratic nightclubs she and her friends frequented instead. Even as the author slapped her elders, her bred-in-the-bone elitism shone through: "We do not particularly like dancing shoulder to shoulder with gaudy and fat drummers. We do not like unattractive people," she wrote. But wasn't the cabaret hoi polloi infinitely preferable to the dreary stag lines at the white-tie functions, she asked, where "a young man who is well-read in the Social Register . . . prays that you won't suspect that he lives far up on the West Side."

Ross disliked the writing but was otherwise mystified what to make of the manuscript. He sought Ingersoll's opinion, deleting the author's name so as not to bias his judgment. But even without knowing the writer, the socially savvy Ingersoll recognized the material's explosive value. "It's a *must!*" he told Ross.

Ross had the piece rewritten, but when Ellin Mackay objected, he published it as submitted, under the title "Why We Go to Cabarets: A Post-Debutante Explains." From the vantage point of seventy years later, "Cabarets" seems little more than a quaint, even puzzling, museum piece. But in its time it had roughly the same scandalous effect as would be produced today if, say, John Kennedy, Jr., wrote an op-ed piece in *The New York Times* trashing Cape Cod aristocracy, or a Hollywood starlet explained "Why We Smoke Crack."

Indeed, the Mackay article, published on November 28, at the height of the debutante season, provoked a sensation. This was largely because, through Jane's public-relations cunning, the *Times, World,* and *Tribune* on the same day ran front-page advance stories on it. Editorials and rebuttals followed. For once, a copy of *The New Yorker* was hard to find on a newsstand.

Two weeks later Mackay followed in the same vein with "The Declining Function: A Post-Debutante Rejoices." But it would seem this time that her intended audience was her famous father. To his horror, Ellin had been seen around town with Irving Berlin, who to most was the millionaire toast of Broadway but to Clarence Mackay would always be Izzy Baline of the Lower East Side. Wrote the rebellious daughter, "Modern girls . . . marry whom they choose, satisfied to satisfy themselves." Months later when she eloped with Berlin, the newspapers erupted again. Ross and Jane helped the newlyweds slip out of town until the tabloids could find something else to write about.

Ingersoll and others later suggested that the Mackay stories were critical to *The New Yorker*'s success. This is crediting them too much, for it is clear the magazine was well on its way to stability by the time they appeared. Still, there is no question that the publicity was invaluable and helped fix the upstart magazine in the public's consciousness.

Another Ross masterstroke that fall was more calculated. In addition to Tables for Two, Lois Long kicked off a second popular service column, this one devoted to the subject of discerning shopping. Eventually known as "On and Off the Avenue," the column was of particular value because it was honest. At the start, Long had asked Ross what she should say if certain merchandise was terrible. "Say it's terrible," he replied.

This was at a time when it was commonplace for major retailers to expect, as a quid pro quo, favorable mentions in the magazines in which they advertised (cynics would say times haven't changed much). Likewise, it was not unheard of for magazines to threaten reluctant advertisers with less than flattering publicity. Ross, whose own view of advertising was that it was at best a lamentable, unavoidable necessity, loathed this kind of blackmail. He was so concerned for *The New Yorker*'s integrity that on the first page of the first issue he took the remarkable step of putting his own advertising staff on notice. Addressing New York's business community, he wrote: "If … someone should ask you to advertise in *The New Yorker,* and throw out the hint that your refusal might lead to some unwelcome public-

Lois Long. *(©Harold Stein)*

ity, you wouldn't shock us much if you poured him into the nearest drain."

Long, while mostly upbeat, was always honest ("Peck & Peck has broken a series of rather mediocre window displays with an exhibit of women's sports things done in blacks, white, and greys—most effective"). Most of all, she was enthusiastic about the sport of shopping, treating it as intelligently as *The New Yorker* did the latest bestseller or the U.S. Open finals. In a short time the column became a popular fixture.

By the end of the year, *The New Yorker* was over the hump and took more space in the same building in order to expand. Big advertisers like Saks and B. Altman's were signing fifty-two-week contracts for 1926. The Christmas number was a fat, fifty-six-page issue chockablock with ads for French perfumes and luxury automobiles. The same issue featured a Ralph Barton Christmas card to *New*

"The old lady in Dubuque," as seen by Ralph Barton for *The New Yorker*'s 1925 Christmas issue. *(By Ralph Barton, ©1925, 1953 The New Yorker Magazine, Inc.)*

Yorker readers from "the old lady in Dubuque"—a busty, cigarette-smoking dame who in her tipsy excitement has just dropped a cocktail shaker.

Country boy Harold Ross was finally growing into *The New Yorker*. For forty-six weeks the names of the advisory editors had appeared on the opening editorial page in the magazine. With the issue of January 9, 1926, their names were gone.

CHAPTER 6

CAVALRY

H. L. MENCKEN ONCE FELT COMPELLED TO OFFER A FRIENDLY PIECE OF advice to William Saroyan. "I note what you say about your aspiration to edit a magazine," said the man only a few years removed from guiding the groundbreaking *American Mercury.* "I am sending you by this mail a six-chambered revolver. Load it and fire every one into your head. You will thank me after you get to Hell and learn from other editors how dreadful their job was on earth."

Given the chance, Ross would have concurred with his friend Mencken. His perspective is plain in one of *The New Yorker's* few funny Newsbreaks of 1925. Said the news item, "A magazine written and edited by lunatics has been started in England." *The New Yorker's* heading: "A Big Step Forward."

Ross had come through the trauma of near-demise. Now he was confronting something altogether scarier: survival. Failure at least would have afforded him the respite of the dead; no more work, no more worry, no more pain, no more eight A.M. strategy sessions with

Ingersoll over the washbasin. The specter of success, on the other hand, promised no such relief and gave rise to all sorts of pesky questions—like, What now?

Through stubbornness and sheer force of will, Ross and Fleischmann had gotten *The New Yorker* up onto its thin, unsteady legs. The magazine at last had the public's attention, and Ross had constructed a formula with earmarks of durability. *The New Yorker*'s first-anniversary number strung together advertisements from Bonwit-Teller, Pierce-Arrow, Helena Rubinstein, and other purveyors of premium goods like so many pearls. Advertisers were buying not only *The New Yorker* but also its presumed cachet, or that quality Ross simply called "snob appeal." Thus an ad for one of the day's ubiquitous self-improvement courses could proclaim with a straight face, "You are judged by the French you speak." (It's a mark of Ross's sense of mischief and editorial temerity that only a year later he had

For a burlesque edition of the magazine to mark Ross's birthday in 1926, Rea Irvin rendered the editor as Eustace Tilley. The insect under inspection is Alexander Woollcott.

E. B. White parodying this very type of ad.) Circulation bounded higher by the week, to fifty thousand by the end of 1926. Business, in fact, was *too* good, since *The New Yorker*'s paltry charter ad rates—$150 a page—were guaranteed through the second year. No matter: by that spring the magazine was widely regarded as a rousing commercial success.

Yet if Ross had learned anything in 1925, it was that nothing is more fickle than a magazine's momentum. He was proud of his accomplishment, certainly, but far from satisfied with it. For all the talent he had brought together, *The New Yorker* still didn't crackle. There were weak departments, the humor was uneven, and most important, the distinctive stylistic identity he sought for the magazine continued to elude him. *The New Yorker* might skate along as the charming parvenu for an indeterminate while, but he knew that long-term success depended on carrying the magazine to the next plateau, to the status of "must" reading in New York.

All of which meant that prosperity, rather than calming Ross, only made him more manic. For one thing, *The New Yorker* was quickly becoming the biggest editorial organization Ross had ever been responsible for, and he was having an immensely difficult time making the adjustment. He constantly wrestled with questions of how best to structure the staff and use his own time. What should he tend to himself, and what should he leave to others? He had yet to learn the manager's essential trick of staying involved in the magazine's routine without undermining his lieutenants or usurping their authority. The supervisor in him tried again and again to delegate and to establish personal priorities because he knew he must, but the entrepreneur in him was almost incapable of letting go. He found himself spending as much time reconciling a secretary's vacation time as he did editing a Profile.

This situation, exacerbated by Ross's perfectionist streak and the ever-evolving cast of characters, kept the editorial offices in a constant stir. The editor lurched backward and forward on assignments, stories, covers, cartoons—everything he touched. Robert M. Coates, whose dark fiction would become a *New Yorker* staple but who first came to the magazine in the late Twenties as a part-time Talk writer, likened the frenetic decision-making of Ross's early years to "the chargings-about of a man in a canebrake, trying blindly to get through to the clearer ground he is certain must lie beyond."

To the staff, Ross's manic performance was exasperating—and worrying. Fillmore Hyde, the first writer of Notes and Comment (always referred to internally simply as Comment), was an old friend and colleague of Ross's from San Francisco and Panama. About this time, the two had a falling-out over Hyde's pay and his suspicions that Ross was souring on Comment; in fact, the editor was seriously thinking of discontinuing the department. When Hyde tried repeatedly to confront him about their differences, he was always steered to Ingersoll instead. Eventually Hyde spilled out his frustrations to Ingersoll, as well as his candid concerns about Ross. "I think the organization, instead of being gradually got in hand by Ross, is constantly confusing him more and more. It appears too big for him; he is on the verge of a nervous and abnormal condition," said Hyde. "I have a great deal of sympathy for Ross, whom I regard as facing difficulties too great for him just at present. But he won't let anybody help him. It's his magazine."

However erratic Ross's demeanor behind the scenes, it must be said that in the magazine his touch only grew more sure. Perhaps the greatest dividend of *The New Yorker*'s improving fortunes was that now he could afford to be a good bit choosier about what he published and whom he hired. It was also becoming clearer to him what *The New Yorker* should, and shouldn't, be. He was more than happy to arch some eyebrows, for instance, with a refreshingly saucy Profile of First Lady Grace Coolidge. Among other things, the piece politely chastised Mrs. Coolidge for her bland couture and asserted that "her own mother [had] objected to her marrying Calvin Coolidge. Mrs. Goodhue has been quoted as having said that she 'never liked that man from the day Grace married him, and the fact he's become President of the U.S. makes no difference.' "

The New Yorker's artwork, meanwhile, was continuing to elevate the magazine above its competitors, as fresh artists seemed to turn up every few issues. In 1926 these included a prolific pair, Otto Soglow and Alan Dunn, and the following year, Dunn's future wife, the brilliant Mary Petty. At the same time two naughty Peter Arno biddies, the Whoops Sisters, were creating a mild (if now somewhat inexplicable) sensation. More significant were Arno's witty and graphically bold cover illustrations, which Ross particularly fancied. (One autumn cover featured a gardener, rake in hand, patiently waiting for the final leaf of the season to drop; the following April the same fellow was back on the cover, this time holding a watering can as he hovered over the first spring bud on the same tree.)

A Dorothy Parker casual, "Dialogue at Three in the Morning," was a dark little piece and a faint precursor of the phenomenon that came to be labeled the "*New Yorker* short story." The "dialogue" is really a drunken, self-pitying monologue by a woman in a speakeasy, whose companion ("the man with the ice-blue hair") cannot get a word in edgewise. Parker was no stranger to late-night conversations in speakeasies, and it was said her protagonist's boozy soliloquy was more recollection than invention. As for Parker's Algonquin pals, Ross finally imposed a moratorium on all the Round Table fluffery, and likewise began to replace the newspaper gossip with stepped-up criticism of the New York press. Not only was he trying to raise the overall tone of the magazine, but he was consciously setting out to demarcate *The New Yorker*'s brand of journalism from the prosaic norm in the dailies. Manuscripts that struck him as too superficial or mundane he began to tag as "newspaper-conscious," and before long the phrase became a virtual *New Yorker* epithet.

And Ross was continuing to make some astute hires: George F. T. Ryall, who began "The Race Track" column, which he would produce for fifty-two years under the pseudonym Audax Minor (an homage to British turf writer Arthur Fitzhardinge Berkeley Portman, whose pen name was Audax); John Mosher, a versatile writer and critic, but perhaps most influential as the longtime first reader of unsolicited manuscripts ("I must get back to the office and reject," he liked to say after a leisurely lunch); and most significant, the redoubtable Rogers E. M. Whitaker, who would enhance *The New*

Yorker in so many guises—as the first head of the magazine's vaunted fact-checking department, as a brilliant and acerbic editor, as a football writer ("J.W.L."), jazz and nightclub writer ("Popsie"), train buff nonpareil ("E. M. Frimbo"), and Talk's "Old Curmudgeon."

In his quest to find new talent, Ross had the good sense to look under his nose. In those days he had a firm rule: if *The New Yorker* purchased three pieces from any contributor, he invited the writer down for a get-acquainted session. Emily Hahn, a young geology teacher at Hunter College, sold the magazine three short casuals in its early years and was excited by the prospect of meeting the editor. Whatever she expected Ross to be, it wasn't what she found. "He was very earthy, like an old shoe," she recalled. "I was sitting on the edge of my chair. He said, 'Young woman, you have a great talent. You can be cattier than anybody I've ever read, with the possible exception of Rebecca West. Well, keep it up.' Then he turned down my next three pieces."

Emily Hahn.
(UPI/Bettmann)

Ross's hands-on style, laudable in so many ways, invariably proved a sore point for his current Jesus—in this case Ingersoll. Ross said he wanted a man to whom he could, in confidence, turn over the entire magazine, because down deep that's what he wanted to do: he always told himself, and Fleischmann, that he wanted to run *The New Yorker* until it was stable, then retire gracefully into the role of a consulting editor while he pursued new projects. To everyone else, however, it was plain that as long as he was on the premises, no one but Ross would ever really be in charge, and this reality made being his executive officer an ordeal. Over the first ten or so years of *The New Yorker*'s existence, Ross exhibited an almost pathological pattern: he built up impossibly high expectations in a Jesus, only to hasten along the poor bastard's downfall when he saw, inevitably, that he was going to be disappointed. Failure became a self-fulfilling prophecy; Jesus tenures were brief and generally unhappy. One subsequent Jesus, a dour man named Bill Levick, perhaps summed it up best. Whenever James Thurber passed him in the hall and asked how things were going, Levick would invariably reply, "One day nearer the grave, Thurber."

In 1926, it was Ingersoll who was making this mortal trudge. By that spring, the major editorial duties of *The New Yorker* were roughly divided between Ingersoll and the estimable Mrs. Angell, who before long was given the title of co–managing editor to reflect her status. For the most part she handled what was considered the more "literary" material—casuals, longer Profiles, and verse—and dealt directly with many of the artists. As the Jesus, Ingersoll was responsible for the reporting and other nonfiction, such as Talk of the Town and cultural criticism, as well as for the physical production of the magazine.

A passionate man in all things, Ingersoll devoted himself to Ross and *The New Yorker*. He was constantly at the editor's side—even at meals, when, if the two weren't talking about *The New Yorker*, they kicked around ideas for future publishing ventures. For Ingersoll, Ross became almost a surrogate father. Yet for his part, Ross always regarded Ingersoll with a nagging ambivalence. He respected the younger man and relied on him completely, but he never developed for him the genuine affection he later had for other important associates, such as Andy White or Wolcott Gibbs. Part of it was that Ingersoll, in one lanky frame, embodied two New York types that Ross always purported to suspect and disdain—fancy college men and society "sophisticates." But part of it appears to have been nothing more than incompatible personal chemistry: Ingersoll simply drove him crazy. Whatever the reasons, he just couldn't keep himself from deriding Ingersoll. He teased the sensitive young man about everything from his hypochondria to his thinning hairline. Once at the weekly Talk meeting, where the editors critiqued past departments and discussed upcoming ones, Ingersoll told Ross he had the information that the editor had wanted about Harry K. Thaw, the famous killer of architect Stanford White. Alas for Ingersoll, who had a slight lisp and the New Englander's penchant for sounding *R*s where *W*s should go, "Thaw" always came out "Thor." Hearing it again, Ross said, "I'll have no mythological characters in this magazine." And in a truly stunning double standard, Ross—the original "systems guy," the man who hired a switchboard operator in a five-person office—professed disdain over Ingersoll's parallel impulse. In the early Forties, when Gibbs profiled Ingersoll (by then the crusading founder of the newspaper *PM* and a globe-trotting war correspondent), Ross volunteered this recollection: "Ingersoll was a great man for system. If I gave him a thousand dollars a week just to sit in an empty room, before you know it he'd have six people helping him."

However much they annoyed each other, Ross and Ingersoll more or less had a rapprochement until that June, when Ingersoll had the temerity to become engaged. Ross, who preferred his fealty complete, was apoplectic, though his ire is partly explained by the fact that he first learned the news from the papers. Nonetheless, Ross's response, conscious or unconscious, was to tighten the screws on his callow managing editor: the teasing turned more cutting, the hard workload more burdensome yet. Ingersoll considered Ross's response irrational, and his actions those of "a tyrant and sadist." In Ross's view, Ingersoll would later write, he had committed an act of treachery. "I had no right to take such a step without consulting him . . . I was crazy . . . I was going to ruin a life he thought might have promise. It was even worse than that. It was—goddammit, there wasn't any other way of putting it—just plain *disloyal!*"

That July, in the midst of this intensifying war of nerves, Ross developed an impacted wisdom tooth—bad teeth, a legacy of his frontier upbringing, were a lifelong curse—that quickly degenerated into a serious infection. He wound up in the hospital for surgery and, with his recovery, was away from work for nearly a month. As it happened, Katharine Angell was then out of the country on vacation, so it fell to Ingersoll to pull three times his weight. To do so, he worked seven days a week, sixteen hours a day, and in the process exhausted himself.

Upon his return, Ross hastily pecked out a note commending Ingersoll for his yeoman work. He also apologized—sort of—for his boorish behavior. "If I have been cranky I am sorry and I haven't intended to be. Please don't think I am because I am not although I may indicate impatience, even exasperation at times and on the whole this is good for the business if nobody minds it because we are not making Ford automobiles. I admit that frequently I make unwarranted criticisms, etc. but it is the way I am and please don't mind."

The peace offering, such as it was, came too late. Ingersoll proceeded to have "a nervous breakdown the likes of which I never want to come near again," he wrote. "Its first—and gentlest—symptom was a conviction that I had no legs below the knees, even though I could see and pinch them." He hied himself to his father's farm, where he chopped wood and entertained malicious thoughts about Harold Ross for a month. He seriously considered not coming back. In the end he did, but inevitably his role changed and he became something of a senior editor, handling special tasks and doing some writing. Years later Ross quietly helped Ingersoll get *PM* off the ground, and the latter's respect for his old mentor was such that he dedicated his 1961 autobiography to him. But the two men would never again have the joined-at-the-hip relationship that built so much of *The New Yorker*. Ross had broken his second Jesus.

That November, Ingersoll went through with his marriage. The wedding was an elaborately formal affair, as was the reception at the

Plaza Hotel. In the reception line, when a butler announced Ross to the bride and groom, he found the whole picture so funny that he began laughing uncontrollably—to the point where Ingersoll, his bride, and the entire wedding party were soon laughing with him.

———

AS 1926 DREW TO A CLOSE, *THE NEW YORKER* WAS REGULARLY PUSHING one hundred pages a week. The next year Ross's little magazine actually would rival the vaunted *Saturday Evening Post* for total ad linage (though not, obviously, for revenues), and for the first time it broke into the black. But if 1927 was arguably the most important year in the long history of *The New Yorker,* the reason had to do less with the balance sheet than with a remarkable and serendipitous burst of recruiting. Within a matter of months, Ross managed to assemble a quartet of unlikely people who at last would be able to translate *The New Yorker* of his imagination to the printed page.

The first of these, Katharine Angell, was already on the premises. For all of Ross's innate qualities—passion, audacity, humor, and a breathtaking capacity for hard work—he still lacked confidence in what constituted "sophisticated" work. In Mrs. Angell he found a helpmate who more than compensated for this shortcoming. As William Shawn would observe, "When he was unsure of himself, he was sure of her."

As Ross went about the shaping of his magazine, Katharine Angell was his one truly indispensable editor. She had a hand in everything—because she wanted to be involved, and because Ross, having made her his de facto arbiter of taste and style, wanted her involved. Her discernment was so respected that even Fleischmann came to rely on her to adjudicate the acceptability of borderline advertisements. Katharine used to say that when Ross howled that he was "surrounded by women and children," as he often did in those days, she looked around and was fairly certain she was the "women" he was inveighing against. But Ross knew he was lucky to have her.

Though her sensibilities were far different from Ross's, Katharine prized humor as much as he did, and she was the single biggest reason *The New Yorker* moved so quickly beyond the *Judge-Life* school to something altogether different and refreshing. Her prodding took various forms, direct (such as editing and recruiting humor writers) and indirect (for instance, quietly prevailing on Ross to phase out baser stereotypical humor in the cartoons). She also encouraged new artistic talent, such as George Price. In 1931, after he had been contributing "spot" illustrations to the magazine for a few years, Mrs. Angell challenged him to try his hand at cartoons. His first one appeared in 1932, and he stayed at it for six decades.

Whether he realized it or not, Ross—an only child who even as a man was never quite comfortable without his mother's approbation—almost certainly was reassured by the many similarities between Mrs. Angell and Mrs. Ross. Born within forty miles of each other, both women were intelligent, no-nonsense, opinionated. Both could come across as imposing, even austere. And both possessed a strong sense of right and wrong where the written word was concerned—just the type of certitude to ease Ross's perpetually uneasy mind. In the end, they would be the two most influential women in his life.

The relationship between Ross and Katharine was unique and complex, often remarked on by fellow staff members but never really understood. (Even Shawn, who knew them both so long and well, described their bond as "ambiguous.") In a way, Ross and Katharine had a much more successful "marriage" than Ross ever did in the conventional sense. As with a venerable couple, their relationship transcended respect and affection; it was the kind of commitment that, over twenty-six years, endured every conceivable crisis—their respective physical and emotional traumas, relocations, even hair-pulling editorial disagreements. Later, after his own critical judgment had matured, Ross could be irritated with Katharine's editorial limitations (as she could be with his, such as his perpetual suspicion of serious poetry). At times he even found her manner intimidating, as did some other *New Yorker* writers and editors. But Ross never stopped relying on her as a trusty compass. Such was his regard that while other editors typically came down to his office for discussions, Ross unfailingly went to Katharine's.

Rumormongers at the infant magazine wondered if the attraction

Katharine Angell and Ross, circa 1927. His inscription reads: "To Katharine Angell, God bless her, who brought this on herself."
(E. B. White Collection, Cornell University)

wasn't more than a professional one. While there is absolutely no evidence that this was so, there does seem to have been some kind of subterranean charge between Ross and the pre–E. B. White Katharine. This would hardly have been surprising. When they first met, they were young (both were thirty-three) and full of zeal. She found him delightful, if not especially handsome, and he of course recognized her for the beautiful, intelligent woman she was. When Katharine and Ernest Angell were about to travel to Paris, Ross gave her a letter of introduction to Ralph Barton, who was living there. It began, "This is to introduce Mrs. Angell, who is not unattractive," an uncharacteristically forthright declaration from Ross. Katharine would prize the letter, calling it "the highest personal comment I ever got from him."

Less enamored of Katharine was Jane Grant. She was somewhat jealous, as Ross himself conceded, although it's not clear whether this was jealousy over a perceived rival or only the understandable resentment of a wife who saw as much of Ross's editors as she did of

Ross himself. (Jane never really liked Ingersoll, either.) By now, their marriage was fraying at the edges.

In any event, things were about to change all around, for in 1926 Mrs. Angell did a most propitious thing, both for *The New Yorker* and for herself. She urged that Ross hire a young writer named Elwyn Brooks White.

In the last issue of 1925, *The New Yorker* had published a casual called "Child's Play," signed by "E.B.W." This was White's amusing, self-deprecating account of a real-life mishap, when a waitress spilled buttermilk down his blue serge suit. The story's protagonist, with cool head and great savoir faire, comforts the distraught waitress, refuses to be fussed over, and in general manages to turn the embarrassing situation into a "personal triumph." White had been reading *The New Yorker* from its inception, and Ross had already published some of his light verse. But "Child's Play" was a breakthrough for White, and in it Ross and Mrs. Angell recognized a fresh voice and clarity of style that approached their ideal. The following spring, after the magazine accepted two more White casuals, Mrs. Angell suggested to Ross that perhaps they should hire the mysterious contributor, whom neither had met as yet.

E. B. White was born in 1899 to a well-to-do family in Mount Vernon, New York, in suburban Westchester County. By nature a nervous and diffident young man, he was so painfully shy that at times, when unfamiliar visitors called on him at *The New Yorker*, he would outwait them on the fire escape. He was only truly at ease when he was with family or close friends, or when he was in the country, pursuing farm chores or sailing his boat. His iron resolve, his inner confidence, seemed to surface only when he was expressing himself on a piece of yellow copy paper.

At Cornell, White edited the campus newspaper and picked up his nickname (students named White tended to be dubbed Andy, after the university's first president, Andrew D. White). Upon graduation, he worked at a series of tedious jobs—including, briefly, the American Legion News Service, housed in the same shabby building where Harold Ross was publishing the *American Legion Weekly*. But for

White, who aspired to write, public relations was the dullest kind of work, and in the spring of 1922 he quit in order that he and a friend might embark on a grand adventure—crossing the country in White's Model T Ford roadster, "Hotspur," living by their wits and on pawned personal goods. Landing in Seattle, he worked for a while at a local newspaper, with indifferent results, before booking passage on a steamer to Alaska. But by the fall of 1923, broke and really no closer to his writerly goals, he returned to Mount Vernon to move back in with his parents.

White took a nonwriting job at a New York City advertising agency but on the side continued to turn out light verse and gentle humor. These he regularly sent off to his heroes, the great newspaper humorists of the day—F.P.A., Christopher Morley, Don Marquis— and their occasional publication, more than anything else, sustained his ambition.

When Ross invited White to come down to *The New Yorker* to talk about a job, he was looking for someone to handle a number of chores, among them Newsbreaks—those unfortunate newspaper gaffes—and various kinds of rewrite. However, as much as White admired *The New Yorker*, he proved a difficult sell. By now he had moved to a different ad agency, J. H. Newmark, where for thirty dollars a week he was writing automotive copy, and his organic insecurity was not easily overcome. There were many lunches with both Ross and Katharine, and much arm-twisting, before White, in late 1926, agreed to a compromise: he would come to work part-time at the magazine, but he would retain his Newmark job until it was clear to one and all that things would work out.

White immediately justified Ross's patience and in early 1927 came on full-time. He wrote like an angel, and there was little he couldn't do. Soon the magic White touch was all over the magazine, from sharper Talk stories to his doctored cartoon captions to the instantly crisper Newsbreaks. An early example:

Station WJAX will use 10,000 watts on a Sioux City woman charged with 1:45 Central Standard Time.—*Sioux City (Iowa) Tribune*
That's hard on any woman, no matter what she's charged with.

White would handle Newsbreaks for more than fifty years; it is estimated that he wrote more than thirty thousand of them. In good times and bad they remained for him a kind of creative umbilical cord to the magazine.

So confident was Ross of his prodigy that he quickly turned over to him the magazine's most prominent department, Comment. In White, he miraculously had found that thing he wasn't sure existed, a seemingly effortless producer of crystalline prose that was at once unforced, bemused, ironic. White, in Marc Connelly's words, "brought the steel and music to the magazine."

In Comment, employing the editorial "we," White ostensibly spoke on behalf of the magazine, but the views therein were always his own, not Ross's or anyone else's. He might solicit the editor's "guidance," but he wrote what he pleased. As the title "Notes and Comment" suggests, his paragraphs were less conventional editorials than quirky, elegant observations on the passing parade. It was not White's style—or Ross's—to crusade in Comment, and if they did, it was in some suitably amateur pursuit (a big early success was their campaign to get the information kiosk at the old Pennsylvania Station moved to the center of the terminal). Neither innocent nor naïve, White nonetheless brandished a charming, otherworldly idealism that once led Ross to observe that he was "as impractical as Jesus Christ." Still, it was an attractive quality, and one that helped explain White's delightfully unorthodox worldview. As his biographer, Scott Elledge, points out, this was already apparent in one of his earliest Comment paragraphs. When in the wake of Lindbergh's transatlantic flight in May 1927 the newspapers were filled with soaring prose about the self-effacing aviator, Ross doubtless fretted over what was possibly left to be said. White knew:

We noted that the *Spirit of St. Louis* had not left the ground ten minutes before it was joined by the Spirit of Me Too. A certain oil was lubricating the engine, a certain brand of tires was the cause of the safe take-off. When the flyer landed in Paris every newspaper was "first to have a correspondent at the plane." This was a heartening

manifestation of that kinship that is among man's greatest exalta-
tions. It was beautifully and tenderly expressed in the cable
Ambassador Herrick sent the boy's patient mother: "Your incom-
parable son has done me the honor to be my guest." We liked that;
and for twenty-four hours the world seemed pretty human. At the
end of that time we were made uneasy by the volume of vaudeville
contracts, testimonial writing and other offers, made by the
alchemists who transmute glory into gold. We settled down to the
hope that the youthful hero will capitalize himself for only as much
money as he reasonably needs.

The preceding February, White had attended a friend's party in
Greenwich Village, where he was introduced to another aspiring
humorist, James Thurber. Though meeting only now, the two knew
a great deal about each other; in 1925, White's newly married sister,
a woman with "the lilting name of Lillian Illian," had become
friendly with Thurber and his wife on a cruise to Europe (Thurber
was to spend the next year in France trying to become a "real"
writer). After the party, White encouraged Thurber, who had
already sold Ross one or two slight pieces, to come down to the magazine. Meanwhile Ross had somehow got it into his head that
Thurber and White had been bosom pals for years, and this was
enough for him to hire Thurber on the spot.

Two years younger than Ross and five years older than White,
Thurber was from a Columbus, Ohio, family whose sundry eccentricities fueled four decades of Thurberiana. He was inventive, wildly
funny, and extremely sensitive. The last quality derived partly from
a dreadful childhood accident; when he was six, a brother shot him in
the left eye with a blunt homemade arrow. The injury blinded that
eye, and years later rendered him completely sightless.

After attending Ohio State, Thurber, like White, worked as a
newspaper reporter, though with considerably more success (despite
the fact that the *Christian Science Monitor,* for whom he was a stringer,
consistently credited his stories to "Miss Jane Thurber"). Also like
White, he wanted to write humor; he too had had submissions

accepted by "The Conning Tower" and had watched the growth of the young *New Yorker* with more than idle interest.

Unfortunately, Ross hired Thurber not as a writer—such creatures were "a dime a dozen," Ross would famously, if not entirely seriously, maintain—but as an editor. The imaginative Thurber, forever prone to exaggeration even where his own life was concerned, made a great point (in *The Years with Ross* and elsewhere) that Ross had hired him as a Jesus. It is true that by this time the bruised Ingersoll had relinquished the role, meaning Ross may well have been on the lookout for another victim. But the position Thurber actually filled was Sunday editor, the person whose job it was to process late reviews and tend to the many last-minute details as the magazine was rushing to close. And if Thurber had any spare time, Ross had added unhopefully, he could write. In a short time, however, it became apparent to everyone that Thurber was no editor. He may have been a man of action—he was known to deal with reader complaints by burning them—but the administrative discipline and adherence to rules (in Gibbs's memorable phrase, "insect routine") required of *New Yorker* editors was antithetical to Thurber's restless nature. He was miserable, able to do little original writing and working so many hours that he piled his soiled shirts in the corner of his cubicle rather than haul them to the laundry. Finally Ross relented; poking his head into the doorway of Thurber's office one afternoon, he barked, "All right then, if you're a writer, write! Maybe you've got something to say."

In emancipating Thurber, Ross did him a second great favor: he gave him Andy White as a roommate. The gifted Thurber scarcely needed anyone to teach him to write, but proximity to White naturally had a tonic effect on his own style, which he was always quick to acknowledge. "The precision and clarity of White's writing helped me a lot," Thurber explained to a friend, "slowed me down from the dogtrot of newspaper tempo and made me realize a writer turns on his mind, not a faucet." Free to write, he unleashed a torrent of casuals and original Talk stories, in addition to his Talk rewrites.

E. B. White,
left, and James
Thurber, shown
here in 1929.
White "made me
realize a writer
turns on his mind,
not a faucet,"
Thurber would
say years later.
*(Courtesy of Mrs.
Milton Greenstein)*

Already friends, Thurber and White now became soulmates. By
the end of 1927 they were collectively responsible for most of the
front of the book—Comment and Talk—and it was starting to
sparkle. If White provided the steel and music, Thurber contributed
the right amount of phosphate and mischief. They spurred each
other on, wrote to please each other, and soon came to form a kind of
double helix at the core of *The New Yorker.* As Brendan Gill said, at
some point Ross realized that "though the magazine was his, the persona of the magazine must be White-Thurber."

The salutary impact of these two men transcended the pages of
the magazine to the office itself. In an environment that was beginning to look like any other thriving commercial enterprise—dozens
of somber people scurrying about, constant discombobulations from

expansions and renovations—White and Thurber helped ensure that none of it was taken too seriously. White presented Ross with the decapitated head of a department-store mannequin (named Sterling Finny) that the writer had used to illustrate his parodies of the self-improvement ads; Finny remained on permanent display in the editor's office, wearing a filthy wig, there to mystify many a guest. Thurber was a more devious cutup, as is evident from a prank he played on Rogers Whitaker. Whitaker edited copy forcefully and, with red pen, flamboyantly. One day Thurber burst into his office, leveled a (toy) pistol at Whitaker, and shouted, "Are you the son of a bitch that keeps putting notes in red ink on the proofs of my Talk stories?" Whitaker fainted.

The fourth member of the Ross Quartet, arriving close on Thurber's heels, was Wolcott Gibbs. Actually, his full name was Oliver Wolcott Gibbs, after the signer of the Declaration of Independence, but he hated the first name so much that he always went by the second. This he pronounced the same way Alexander Woollcott pronounced his surname—*Wool*-cut—which would lead to no end of confusion in the minds of readers, especially after Gibbs moved into Aleck's old domain of theater criticism. Neither man was flattered by the unintended comparisons.

Like every other person in New York, it seemed, Gibbs was a relation of Alice Duer Miller, and as she had with so many others, she sent Gibbs over to see her friend Harold Ross. Even by the editor's inscrutable standards, it would seem Gibbs was spectacularly unqualified to work at *The New Yorker*. He was born in New York in 1902, but when he was a boy his family moved all around the Northeast and Midwest. Bright but a borderline ne'er-do-well, he was in and out of a succession of boarding schools, where he earned his spending money by selling Latin translations to classmates. Once out in the world, he had been, among other things, an insurance clerk, a chauffeur, an architect's apprentice, and a brakeman on the Long Island Rail Road. In Gibbs's one stint as a reporter, on a small suburban newspaper, his employer had hired him more for his tennis prowess than for his way with words.

Still, somewhere in the high-strung, witty young man Ross divined potential, for he hired Gibbs as a copy editor. After he had covered the ground rules, such as they were, he dismissed Gibbs with a little headmasterish wave of the hand that was his trademark way of ending a conference, as if to shoo one from his office. Then as Gibbs reached the door, Ross piped up, almost as an afterthought: "I don't give a damn what else you do, but for God's sake don't fuck the contributors." It was clear, Gibbs later wrote, "that he spoke with the memory of some previous and painful experience in his mind." He added that this was "the closest approach to a coherent editorial policy I ever discovered."

In many ways, Wolcott Gibbs was Ross's most versatile hire. Quickly rising to become Mrs. Angell's assistant, he proved a brilliant editor of fiction; like Ross, he had an instinctive and unerring sense for how words should go together on a page, and he was known to excise whole paragraphs from a manuscript with no one, including the author, the wiser. For several years, in White's absence, he wrote Comment. He was an accomplished short story writer, an unequaled parodist, a discerning and feared drama critic. Gibbs led something of a sad life and turned a sour eye on the world, but this darkness manifested itself in some of the most acerbic and wickedly funny writing of his generation.

These four lieutenants—Mrs. Angell, White, Thurber, and Gibbs—formed the foundation on which Ross could comfortably rest his magazine. Like their editor, each brought an outsider's perspective to New York City, helping to inform *The New Yorker* with an appealing openness and inquisitiveness. More important, they gave Ross standards as high as his own, a common appreciation of the magazine's possibilities, and phenomenal editorial range. In return, Ross gave them the extraordinary opportunity to invent themselves. Before Ross, all four had been somewhat adrift, personally and professionally, unknown and unfulfilled. After him, each had a hand in shaping contemporary American letters. For this precious gift, each repaid Ross with a lifelong devotion that bordered on hero worship.

Wolcott Gibbs: Ross would come to say of him, "He can do anything."
(Culver Pictures)

———

TWO YEARS INTO THE GREAT EXPERIMENT, THEN, THE MATTER OF *New Yorker* personnel was falling into place, but there were still bugs to be worked out. That February saw a rare star turn. Ross published an odd little parody from Ernest Hemingway that may have persuaded the celebrated young novelist to stick to his day work; it would be his lone contribution to *The New Yorker*. At about the same time, the magazine ran a Profile of Edna St. Vincent Millay so riddled with factual mistakes that the poet's mother trooped down to the office in person to protest. Ross sent out Katharine Angell to placate Mrs. Millay, and Katharine later said the embarrassing episode might have prompted Ross to start the fact-checking department.

In the main, however, the magazine was charging confidently to that next level. When examining a weekly magazine, which in the course of a year publishes thousands of stories, drawings, poems, and miscellany, one must resist the impulse to read too much into any single gesture. Every now and again, however, Ross printed something that clearly signaled a shift in attitude. The Scopes report in 1925 was one, and in April 1927 there was another, a huge Profile of the enigmatic publishing titan William Randolph Hearst. Heretofore *New Yorker* Profiles were rather superficial: glib, not particularly probing, and running at most a little more than two pages. Now, suddenly, readers were treated to a five-part extravaganza. At a total of thirteen thousand words, the Hearst portrait was many times over the most substantial piece *The New Yorker* had published to date. Aside from compelling reading, it amounted to a declaration from Ross that some people, sometimes, warranted more serious scrutiny. Hearst, who no doubt had fascinated Ross from his San Francisco days, was a perfect candidate: millions knew the legend, but almost no one really knew the man.

This Profile, written by John K. Winkler, was generally favorable but not altogether flattering, and was notable chiefly for its extraordinary detail (all it seems to have overlooked was Marion Davies) and the length it went to put the extravagant publisher into contemporary context. Here is Winkler on Hearst's role in promulgating the Spanish-American War:

> The little shindig with Spain that followed the destruction of the *Maine* would have been pure *opéra bouffe* except for its accompaniment of political and bully beef scandal. Although today he might not be so eager to claim the credit, the Spanish-American conflict *was* W. R. Hearst's war. He spent half a million dollars on cables and correspondents and spectacular stunts. He fed raw meat to his hirelings and roused even the dignified, deliberate Richard Harding Davis to extraordinary efforts.

These were heady days around *The New Yorker*. Most of the magazine's staffers were young, single, inexperienced, woefully underpaid—and thrilled to be in the service of a publication that Ross once said was not a magazine but a movement. Marcia Davenport, who would go on to win acclaim as Mozart's biographer and chronicler of the Communist overthrow of Czechoslovakia, was typical; her first professional job, in 1927, was as a Talk reporter. She prowled the city at all hours to dig up the information that Thurber and White turned into Talk stories. In her memoirs, Davenport recalled becoming swept up in the excitement and commotion. "We thought nothing of working from early morning until nine or ten at night, with a sandwich for lunch at our desks. Then after a dinner break the proofs would start coming in. They had to be corrected and rewritten in whole or in part after Ross got his hooks into them, so it was the rule rather than the exception to work from eleven or twelve at night until dawn. Three or four hours' sleep and we were at it again."

Of course, when they did get a little spare time, these red-blooded youngsters tended to drift into the city's speakeasies and other dark nooks and crannies. Keeping track of his feckless children brought out the worrier in Ross. Certainly on principle he didn't mind their carousing; he had simply learned that too much of it often kept them away from their typewriters, and this was not good for the magazine. S. N. Behrman recalled an evening at "21" with Ross and a party-prone *New Yorker* writer who had managed to stay on the wagon for more than a week. Another friend came up to their table and persistently pressed them all to join him in a glass. The abstinent writer begged off repeatedly, but it was clear that his resolve was flagging. Exasperated, Ross finally growled, "When one of my writers, no matter how insincerely, refuses a drink, don't you go urging it on him!"

It was at about this time that Ross's Mother Hen tendencies reached a ridiculous extreme. He decided that the most efficient way to monitor his staff's off-hours activity was for *The New Yorker* to establish its own speakeasy. He appropriated the basement of another Fleischmann building just down the street, furnished it with a bartender-bootlegger and battered secondhand tables and chairs, and then advertised it to his writers and editors as a counterpart to

Punch's famed literary salon. The noble experiment ended abruptly the morning Ingersoll, the nominal proprietor, came in and found two contributors passed out behind a sofa in clothesless embrace.

If Ross wasn't busy parenting, he was prodding. This was especially true in the case of two Round Tablers who were just joining the staff to produce some of *The New Yorker*'s most popular early departments. In 1927 Robert Benchley, a voracious reader of newspapers, began his irreverent Wayward Press column, under the pseudonym Guy Fawkes, and then two years later took over the magazine's theater criticism from Charles Brackett. Also in 1927, Dorothy Parker began regular book reviews for Ross under the name Constant Reader. She tended to overlook the serious literature of the day, preferring to squelch more popular titles. Her tart opinions were meant more as entertainment than as criticism, however, and her column, like Benchley's, was immensely well-received at a time when *The New Yorker* was still searching for an audience. In fact, a decade later, Ross went so far as to say that Parker's "Constant Reader, in the early days, did more than anything to put the magazine on its feet, or its ear, or wherever it is today."

This was quite a concession, considering the lengths Parker went to goad Ross—she called him Junior, for instance—and how difficult her chronic procrastination made his life. He emerged from his office one day with a big grin, reporting that he had just telephoned Parker to inquire about the whereabouts of her overdue column. "Aw, Harold," she replied, "I've been too fucking busy. Or vice versa, if you prefer." But then, she had learned at the feet of the master deadline-pusher himself, Benchley, who once reported to his editor that his theater column would be late because he was in Philadelphia and there didn't seem to be any typewriters there. Like all ex-reporters, Ross had a grudging respect for creative foot-dragging, and he happily tolerated such shenanigans from his stars.

On a deeper level, however, the overall grind was beginning to wear on Ross. It had been three years (if one includes the start-up) of relentless pressure, and increasingly he wondered if all the aggravation was worth it. His marriage was strained, his stomach was worsening, he was tired all the time, and he could see himself becoming a nervous wreck. Besides, he had always maintained that he never intended to make *The New Yorker* a permanent career. Indeed, he continued to nurse along the idea of starting up his own true-crime magazine; it would be a stylish, well-written variation on the familiar pulp model, and he was thinking of calling it *Guilty*.

Ross wasn't dwelling on his problems simply out of morose habit. An unforeseen development had suddenly forced the issue: a syndicate had approached Fleischmann in the latter part of 1927 with an offer to buy *The New Yorker* for three million dollars. Still nagged by the guilt of dragging Fleischmann so deeply into the hole, Ross assured his partner he would not stand in the way of a sale, and even urged him to accept the offer. If Fleischmann sold out for a nice profit, he figured, his own obligation would be erased once and for all. Conversely, if Fleischmann passed up the money, any future indebtedness would belong to his own conscience, not Ross's.

As it turned out, Ross's departure was the last thing Fleischmann wanted. Now that *The New Yorker* was finally profitable, he preferred to hang on to it, but only if Ross committed to stay. No fool, Fleischmann understood that for all its success the two-year-old magazine likely couldn't survive the loss of its eccentric creator. As Jane Grant explained in a letter to Ross's mother, "Fleischmann frankly said that he would not for a moment entertain a thought of selling if Ross would only agree to stay with it. And that he has refused to do." Ross's waffling, whether out of coyness or genuine indecision (or most likely both), maddened Fleischmann. He "begged" Jane to try to persuade Ross to sign a new contract—with disastrous consequences for her. Ross already felt under attack, and now it appeared that the gang included his own wife. "That was one of the factors that made Ross think we were all trying to double-cross him and say that he wanted nothing to do with any of us," Jane wrote. "He really fancies that he is being tricked."

Fleischmann was panicked by the prospect that Ross would walk away, and this may well have been the first time—there would be others—that he approached Katharine Angell about assuming the editorship should it be necessary. It wasn't. In the end, as he always would when forced to choose between staying or leaving, Ross stayed and Fleischmann turned down the offer to sell *The New Yorker*, but the tense interlude was not without its ramifications, both professional and personal.

————

THE FAILURE OF A MARRIAGE IS NEARLY ALWAYS SAD, AND THAT OF Ross and Jane seems especially so because there was no single promulgating trauma, no "other woman," no real end to their affections. The dissolution played out like a slow-motion wreck that no one— neither Jane, nor Ross, nor their despairing friends—seemed able to stop. If there was a true third party in the breakup, it was *The New Yorker*, which was consuming Ross. "I'm married to this magazine," he told Thurber once in a melancholy moment. "It's all I think about."

By 1926, when Jane asked Woollcott to leave 412, a visible crack had developed in her marriage—she and Ross used the vacated space to establish separate bedrooms—and the vindictive Aleck proceeded to drive wedges into it. According to Jane, Woollcott went out of his way to invite Ross along to dinners, parties, and first nights, while pointedly leaving her out. Meanwhile, Ross was tiring of Jane's increasingly shrill feminist cant, not to mention the incessant teasing from his friends. And the noisy household was making it impossible for him to work at home. He was known to lug his typewriter from room to room in search of a little peace.

Jane concurred that the success of the magazine was paramount, but she resented that her husband was obsessed with it to the exclusion of all else. Who but Ross, for instance, would call a staff meeting at his house on Thanksgiving morning? Her resentment extended to the editors. As Ross told Marc Connelly, "Jane just doesn't understand how I can dislike some of the people she likes, and I suppose I get on her nerves—no, goddammit, I *know* I do—with some of the people I want to bring home. She hates Mrs. Angell and Rea Irvin. Well, goddammit, I've got to be nice to them—they help me all the

time in my work, and I ought to be able to bring them to dinner anytime, goddammit."

Desperate for some quiet space, Ross eventually took a hotel room
near the magazine. This had been intended as nothing more than an
adjunct office; increasingly, though, he was calling Jane to say he
wouldn't be home that night.

Matters worsened dramatically over Christmas of 1927. After the
412 ménage threw its traditional holiday party, Ross essentially
walked out on his wife. He and Charlie MacArthur spent several
days in Atlantic City; when Ross returned he suggested to Jane a
temporary separation. He urged that she take off three months to
travel and rest up from a mysterous ailment that had nagged her,
time he would use for some badly needed solitude at 412. Jane realized better than anyone how much stress Ross was under, and she
had become accustomed to his stubbornness, grumbling, and alternating moods, one minute lashing out at her and the next apologiz-
ing, holding out the promise of better days just ahead. But his new
proposal genuinely took her aback. She asked Connelly, their mutual
friend, if he might ascertain what was really going on inside Ross's
head.

In an angst-ridden three-hour conversation, Ross complained to
Connelly about the usual things: the Lucy Stone business, his and
Jane's growing incompatibility, the pressure to make a commitment
to Fleischmann. In reading between the lines, though, Connelly
probably came closer to the true cause when, reporting back to Jane,
he said:

> Of course, I don't know how close these observations are to his
> main trouble. I am beginning to believe he is unconsciously passing
> off on you (because of convenience and tangibility) the strain he
> feels around the magazine. Ross really has no business trying to
> mold himself into a sedentary business man, which his job essen-
> tially demands he be. I think he's just tired, but that he doesn't dare
> admit it to himself because of the material responsibilities he faces
> here every day. Of course that doesn't help your problem.

Under the circumstances, Jane reluctantly acceded to Ross's wish for a trial separation. She arranged for sick leave from the *Times,* and while she headed for Palm Beach, Ross moved back into 412. In late March, having been away less than a month, Jane quietly returned. Ross had not expected her back so soon. In a brief note, she informed him that she had taken a room of her own at the Barclay Hotel; he still would have his full three months to sort things through, she assured him.

Caught off guard, Ross responded with a hastily written and heart-breaking letter—a primal, careening document that was part indictment, part recrimination, part apology. It was the anguished cry of a man who thought he wanted to leave his wife but was still trying to convince himself:

> We have different tastes, different interests, different instincts, different ideas. We are distinctly two entities, two personalities. We differ in almost everything. We are both terribly sot. Living with you on the basis that I have in the past is, I have concluded, impossible. You are a disturbing and upsetting person. From your standpoint I undoubtedly have most objectionable characteristics. I truly realize that I must be almost impossible. In the past I have yielded much to you, much, much more than I now am willing to yield. My brief period of freedom from you, while it has frequently left me at a loss, has convinced me that I am quite capable of arranging my own life on a much more satisfactory basis than it has been on in the past seven years.

Ross went on to propose that they continue living apart indefinitely, but asked that he retain 412 in order to have a place to work and carry out "certain social obligations" that a magazine editor must undertake. He closed:

> The fact is that I feel hopeless about the whole thing. . . . My opinion is that [a definite separation] would be best. We are so far apart in most respects that compatibility is probably impossible. As for myself, I am a monstrous person incapable of intimate association.

In a postscript Ross urged Jane to reply by note rather than in person because this would "bring in the emotional element, which is the last thing that ought to be brought in." Clearly he was not so confident in his decision that he believed he could withstand seeing her. Jane sensed his wavering, of course, but she also knew that soon sheer stubborn pride would be governing his actions, and that reason was useless. In desperation, she appealed to Ross's mother, something she had promised Ross she wouldn't do. (He had assured Jane he would tell Ida of their problems, but he hadn't.)

The news from Jane upset Ida Ross but didn't terribly surprise her; she had detected something wrong, even at her long remove. In a tender reply to "my dear little girl," Ida said she knew her son was under great strain. "I have worried ever since he has been on that mag. that there was a danger of a nervous breakdown, as I know how he works his brain on things he undertakes." Then she promised to intervene and help in any way she might.

Jane was greatly relieved by Ida's offer, not to mention by her sympathy. "I did not know how you would feel toward me in this matter," Jane confessed. "Mothers are so apt to think their sons are faultless." She went on:

I am sure now that if he did not write to you it was because he dreaded telling you. He does not feel right about the whole affair, but in his behalf I want to say that he can't seem to help what he is doing. At the moment he is so nervous that half the time he does not know what he is doing. I cannot tell you the agony I have suffered. . . .

The whole thing is that he has done a superb job on something that is foreign to his nature and is at the moment unable to rise above it. He is a simple and direct person and a sophisticated and biting mag., such as *The New Yorker* is, is unnatural for him and the undertaking has almost got the better of him. . . .

Together, I am sure we can accomplish something. I do not want to hang onto Rossie. If he is happier without me I can regulate my life, of course, but so far I have not been able to convince myself that we have come to the parting of the ways. Of course, this will leave such a hurt that I fear it will never be healed, but then time does wonderful things.

One can see that as much as Jane was wishing for the best, she had begun bracing for the worst. And when Ida at last did talk to her son, she, like Connelly, came away with no cause for hope. "My heart ached for Harold," she wrote. "He seemed so nervous, and his doctor told me that he was dreadfully overworked, and I think that *New Yorker* was too much strain on him and on you both."

So it was to be divorce. It was not generally Ross's style to discuss his private affairs, but years later he did touch on this subject in a letter to Woollcott's biographer, Samuel Hopkins Adams. He was remarking on the disparate 412 personalities, specifically on Aleck's talent for rationalization, which he said was matched or exceeded by Jane's. Then he engaged in a little rationalizing himself. "The reason I left Jane Grant, or whatever it was, was that I never had one damned meal at home at which the discussion wasn't of women's rights and the ruthlessness of men in trampling women. You go through several years of that and you can't take it anymore."

The particulars notwithstanding, once the matter had been decided it was all rather amicable (with the exception of some of the financial loose ends, which dogged Ross for years). "Never for a moment did Ross lack consideration," Jane would say. This was fortunate, for in New York State at the time, obtaining a divorce was no simple matter. Serious grounds had to be alleged—in this case adultery—and ostensibly proved; in friendly partings this generally required some artful choreography all around. There is no indication that Ross was in truth unfaithful to Jane, though it would not have been surprising if he had been, especially toward the end. For instance, in the spring of 1928, when Hecht and MacArthur's *The Front Page* was trying out in Atlantic City, Ross was among a number of their buddies who came down to frolic, according to Ben Hecht, while "a small harem . . . was kept out of sight."

The divorce decree was final in the summer of 1929. Ironically, Jane was in the hospital at the time; her illness had finally been diagnosed as operable cancer. When Ross found out, he reverted to gallant form: he called in several specialists to corroborate the diagnosis, sent for Jane's sister from Joplin, lavished flowers and presents on the patient, and helped arrange her lengthy recuperation.

Jane Grant would remarry happily, and as a special consultant to Fleischmann she proved instrumental in *The New Yorker*'s explosive growth after World War II. For all their problems, Ross never forgot that, in his own words, "there would be no *New Yorker* today if it were not for her."

———

CONSIDERED IN A MORE MERCENARY LIGHT, THE DISINTEGRATION OF Ross's marriage in the late Twenties was just another facet of his brutal on-the-job training. In managing creative people, who can be overly sensitive, given to self-doubt, and capable of leading messy personal lives, hand-holding is as critical an editorial skill as blue-pencil editing. If Ross's grasp of interpersonal relations was still infirm, soon enough he became something of an expert. He had to; about this time his office was turning into a precursor of Peyton Place.

Not that it showed in the magazine, which in 1928 and 1929 cruised blithely on. Mrs. Angell embraced the work of a prolific and desperately ambitious newcomer named John O'Hara, whose naturalistic stories would pave the way for so many *New Yorker* writers to follow. In Paris, Janet Flanner was gradually moving beyond fashion and the arts to a meatier correspondence. Morris Markey's Reporter at Large subjects too were steadily more wide-ranging ("Markey's gotten to the point where he thinks everything that happens to him is interesting," Ross grumbled). The magazine was printing the initial pieces of a dazzling new breed of reporter, Alva Johnston—at the *Times* he had garnered one of that paper's first Pulitzer Prizes—whose Profiles would set the *New Yorker* standard. And Thurber and White were rapidly becoming reader favorites.

Also in 1929, Ross overcame his own editorial ambivalence toward his friend Woollcott—according to Samuel Hopkins Adams, Ross once said that no other living writer had so successfully mined so thin a vein of ore as Aleck—and gave him a regular column, "Shouts and Murmurs." The column was unalloyed Woollcott; in it he used some pretext to recycle old stories or wax extravagant about the latest great thing to confront "these old eyes." Nonetheless, it was a savvy play on Ross's part, coming just as Woollcott's personal popularity was about to explode on the radio. Shouts and Murmurs had the distinction of being the only *New Yorker* feature ever written to a preset length—one page. The job of enforcing this, as well as excising the blue stories Woollcott tried to slip in, fell to Mrs. Angell. Ross was willing to run Shouts only on the condition that she take complete responsibility for it. This Mrs. Angell didn't mind because she got on well enough with Woollcott, despite his best attempts to rattle her—such as the time she came by his apartment to go over a column and he answered the door naked. Unfazed, she said, "Go back and put your clothes on, Mr. Woollcott."

By now Ross's formula was beginning to look like genius. In reality, it was rather simple; as Ross's first biographer, Dale Kramer, pointed out, there were only four key elements: *New Yorker* stories were factually correct, clear, casual in tone, and "mildly ironical but paternal" in attitude toward New York. (He might have added a fifth: they were usually humorous, too.) Perhaps Ross's real genius had been in getting the copy to match the concept, and now it was paying off. At the end of 1928, *The New Yorker* announced its first profitable year (income of $287,000 on revenues of $1.77 million). Circulation sailed past seventy thousand, well beyond the fifty thousand Ross had always said would be the optimal size. A grateful board of directors gave Ross a ten-thousand-dollar bonus for conceiving and successfully executing the magazine.

Yet all the while, Ross's staff was having a collective nervous breakdown. His own marriage was failing. So was Thurber's. So was that of *The New Yorker*'s glamour couple, Peter Arno and Lois Long, whose breakup was especially ugly. Two tempestuous people who liked their alcohol, Arno and Long had high-profile rows that sometimes turned violent. Marcia Davenport, who often wrote Long's departments when she was away, recalls, "Occasionally she would come into the office with a bruise or black eye and reply if sympathetically asked what had happened, 'Oh, I ran into a door in the dark,' or 'I was in a taxi accident.'" On one dreadful occasion that was splashed all over the tabloids, Arno sustained a gashed cheek that police said Long administered with a well-aimed glass powder case. Arno moved out, and they were divorced shortly thereafter.

More tragic was the death of Gibbs's first wife, Elizabeth, in late March of 1930. Elizabeth Gibbs, twenty-two, who had married Gibbs just eight months earlier, was a promotion writer for *The New Yorker*, good at her job and popular with coworkers. Gibbs told investigators that his wife had been obsessed with a play the two of them had seen a few days before, *Death Takes a Holiday*, a mystical fairy-tale drama that culminates when the lovestruck heroine walks away with Death, who has been masquerading as a prince. Gibbs and his wife were in their apartment discussing the play after lunch that day when, after he momentarily excused himself, Elizabeth calmly walked into the bedroom and threw herself from a window. Some have speculated that Elizabeth was a frustrated writer and that the jittery, ever-insecure Gibbs had suppressed her ambition; Ingersoll said the two had argued about this the night before. In any event, the devastated Gibbs called Mrs. Angell, who rushed over and found him moaning repeatedly, "I never should have left the room." She rescued him from the clutches of the suspicious police, persuading them that if they didn't let Gibbs go "he would be the next suicide."

Throughout this whole period, however, the drama that genuinely captivated the staff—it was, after all, unfolding literally in front of them—was the burgeoning romance between Katharine Angell and Andy White.

Katharine Sergeant and Ernest Angell were wed in 1915, but by the time she came to *The New Yorker* she had been miserable in her marriage for several years. Ernest, a brilliant lawyer who would become a leading figure in the American Civil Liberties Union, had returned from service in World War I France with a decidedly "modern" view of philandering, and his trysting grew more flagrant and intolerable for Katharine, who also had two children and her own aspirations to look after.

E. B. White, seven years younger than Mrs. Angell, had always liked and respected her, but sometime in late 1927, it appears, his admiration turned into serious flirtation. In January the magazine published a White love poem, "Notes from a Desk Calendar," wherein one office worker contemplates his infatuation with another. Katharine must have approved the poem and certainly took its meaning. At this point, though, White couldn't have been too ardent, for soon he had a new pursuit, one of the magazine's young secretaries.

By the next spring, however, Andy had refocused his affections on Katharine, sending her billets-doux via his *New Yorker* verse and F.P.A.'s "Conning Tower." Then in June the three members of this triangle played out a scene worthy of Hollywood—they all set sail for France. Not together, of course: Ernest and Katharine presumably were going to repair their marriage, though Ernest also intended to look up an old flame from the war; White, on a different liner, was going for a surreptitious rendezvous with Katharine. Indeed, they met in Paris, where he took her canoeing on the Seine, and then moved on to the romantic venues of St.-Tropez and the island of Corsica. Their Mediterranean idyll was as wonderful as it sounds.

But idylls end, and back in the States, returned to reality, Katharine and Andy began thinking better of the affair. She was riddled by guilt, while he wrestled with his fear of commitment. Realizing matters were apt to come to a bad end, they agreed to stop seeing each other outside the office. They were desperately trying to do the right thing—and they were miserable. Soon their colleagues were again taking note of their ardent glances in the hall, or a poignant, clandestine moment on the fire escape at dusk.

In February of 1929, Katharine and Ernest had a bad quarrel, during which he slapped her to the floor. She walked out, having come to the conclusion that divorce, ghastly as it was, afforded the only way out. She made the necessary arrangements, and on May 11 White and Ross put her on a train bound for Reno. There she would spend the next three months establishing Nevada residency in order to obtain a divorce.

Katharine was despondent, alone, racked by guilt. Ernest's family, as well as her own sisters, wrote her urging her to forgo divorce. She didn't know what she would do when she got back; she didn't even know *if* she wanted to come back. In her feverish mind *The New Yorker* was now "poison"; she persuaded herself that the magazine had been "an escape from the life I didn't like."

White was in no better shape. He had not promised Katharine marriage, and in truth he still didn't know what he wanted. Indeed, much apprehension and many misunderstandings passed between them as they corresponded during this anxious hiatus. Perhaps transferring his anxiety, White too became disenchanted with *The New Yorker,* or at least the many demands Ross had come to put on him. Feeling pressed and alone, he bailed out that summer for a favorite retreat in the Canadian woods. In July, in a letter to Ross, he wrote to say things would have to be different when he came back:

> On account of the fact that *The New Yorker* has a tendency to make me morose and surly, the farther I stay away the better. I appreciate very much your extraordinary capacity to endure, and in fact cope with, my somewhat vengeful attitude about *The New Yorker* and my crafty habit of slipping away for long intervals. . . . Next to yourself and maybe one or two others, I probably have as tender a feeling for your magazine as anybody. For me it isn't a complete life, though.

Ross was bending over backward to accommodate these two distraught people, who by now were not just valued colleagues but good friends. Other editors and writers scrambled to fill their intimidating voids; as White suggested, coping was something Ross was always able, albeit loath, to do. But especially in view of his own domestic nightmare and exhaustion (that July he made the first of several trips to recharge at the Austin Riggs sanatorium in Stockbridge, Massachusetts—"when I went to the bughouse," he liked to say), not to mention the staff's other emotional crises, he can be forgiven for feeling like a man drowning in a sea of melodrama. "I have an anguished letter from Ross that sounds as though he could only hang on three days longer," Andy wrote, rather too lightheartedly, to Katharine. "He takes things too hard."

That August, finally, the newly free Katharine returned to start reassembling her life. The following month, White returned from Canada. On November 13, a Wednesday, they drove quietly to a little town fifty miles north of New York City and were married in a Presbyterian church. They told no one, not even Ross, and were back at work the next day. That Friday the world learned of the marriage in Walter Winchell's gossip column. In time, all was right again with the world and *The New Yorker*.

As if to prove it, the Whites' marriage coincided with the publication of a book cowritten by Andy and Thurber, entitled *Is Sex Necessary? Or Why You Feel the Way You Do*. It was a parody of the many clinical books on sex that had recently appeared on the market, and it was a big hit. The most astonishing aspect of the book was the illustrations by Thurber. Suddenly he was being hailed as an artist for drawings just like the curious, amorphous, tossed-off doodles that littered his office and turned up on the bathroom walls. Not for the first or last time, Ross was flabbergasted.

Is Sex Necessary? appeared nine days after the stock market crash, the first shudder of the Great Depression. By coincidence, that October *The New Yorker* had announced that henceforth it would be publishing two editions: one for New York City (as a vehicle for those advertisers who wanted to reach only that audience), and one for national distribution. It seemed that despite Ross's best intentions the old lady in Dubuque was devouring the magazine.

On the face of it, the timing could scarcely have been worse, but in fact the announcement merely presaged one of the remarkable paradoxes of the Thirties: while the Depression ravaged so much, including many of Ross's competitors, *The New Yorker* would flourish.

CHAPTER 7

A CESSPOOL
OF LOYALTIES

AFTER HIS DIVORCE, ROSS MOVED INTO AN APARTMENT ON EAST Fifty-seventh Street that he shared with a burly, genial man named Edward McNamara. Once upon a time (for his was a fairy-tale career) McNamara had been on the police department in Paterson, N.J. But he possessed a fine, robust baritone, and billed as "the Singing Cop" he eventually managed to sing his way off the force and into vaudeville, then the legitimate stage and movies. He became a great favorite of the Round Table, where Ross got to know him, and of show-business types in general. His famous friends ranged from Enrico Caruso, who gave him occasional pointers on voice, to James Cagney, who in turn became chummy with Ross.

All his working life, Ross found it useful to compartmentalize his various selves: editor, husband, father, reluctant celebrity. As a rule he did not bring his personal problems to work, and conversely when he was away from the magazine he welcomed the chance to talk about matters other than *The New Yorker*. He had some intimates at work—Hawley Truax, for instance, was a lifelong companion and confidant—but his true cronies, the people he fished with, drank with, or just palled around with, tended not to be from the magazine, or journalists at all. They were people like McNamara (who, fortunately for Ross, was also a good cook), photographer Alfred Pach, vaudeville comedy partners Joe Cook and Dave Chasen, and, later, New York mayor William O'Dwyer. A particularly good friend was a private detective, Ray Schindler, with whom Ross engaged in innumerable practical jokes—such as the time Ross stole from a bookstore a little metal placard that read "This property is under the protection of the Schindler Detective Agency" and mounted it conspicuously in his own office. When Schindler saw it, he reciprocated by taking a bathmat from the New Yorker Hotel and putting it in his own bathroom. When Ross, in his turn, noticed this, he got some stationery from the hotel and wrote Schindler a letter from the "House Detective," demanding the mat's return. For Ross, a man with no real hobbies or avocations, such byplay served as a kind of safety valve for the pressures of his work and gave him as much simple pleasure as almost anything in his life.

Ross was, in fact, always most comfortable around other men, whether hatching pranks or just talking shop over a late-night Scotch. He loved women, respected them, admired them, enjoyed their company, but, as he said himself many times, he never understood them. He found them mystifying, inherently and sometimes purposefully so, and he would prove to have a very hard time living with them. Perhaps it was inevitable: as a child he grew up in the rough environment of hard-rock mining; he came of age in the exclusively male world of tramp reporting; then he joined the army and went to war. He didn't even have a sister to mitigate his masculine take on the world. "Harold, of all the men I've known, was most essentially a man's man," says Clifton Fadiman, who was *The New Yorker*'s book reviewer from the early Thirties to the early Forties. "I think he was happiest in a bar, with other men. He of course liked women and married three of them, but I don't think he ever really understood them. Marriage was probably not his natural state. His natural state was talking with guys at a bar or at dinner. He was very male—*very* male."

Each of those three marriages came to a bad end, and it may be more than coincidental that all three wives remarried happily the next time around. As utterly charming as Ross could be with a date or even a casual female acquaintance at a cocktail party, he could be that hard on a spouse. If this seems odd, it was nonetheless consistent with Ross's erratic, almost schizophrenic behavior where women were concerned—one of the most pronounced dichotomies in a life and personality fairly brimming with them.

This particular contradiction can be explained a little more readily than some of the others. At heart a nineteenth-century man, Ross had predictably Victorian attitudes about sexuality, virtue, and women's roles. Yet at a still-impressionable age he tumbled into Jazz Age New York, a time and a place where those traditional attitudes and roles were being pitched out like so much bad bathtub gin. The man who emerged could appreciate the modern woman, all right, but more so intellectually than emotionally. Thus the challenge of an independent, spirited woman might bring out the best in Ross the paramour but the worst in Ross the husband. Likewise, he could profit enormously from the recent arrival of clever and ambitious women in the workplace (he simply could not have pulled off *The New Yorker* as we know it without the likes of Jane Grant, Katharine Angell, Lois Long, Dorothy Parker, Janet Flanner, and Helen Hokinson); yet it would be many years before he was wholly comfortable with the idea of women reporters—or even women secretaries, for that matter. Women belonged on a pedestal, he believed—to be venerated, yes, but also to be kept an eye on.

Even so, and as hard as it was for many of his male friends to conceive, Ross was immensely attractive to many women. Some found a certain handsomeness in the rugged, rubbery face and its odd commingling of features. For most, though, his appeal was wrapped up in intangibles. Harold Ross was strong, impish, intelligent, unorthodox in appearance, a great talker, and, it should not be forgotten, a man of no small influence—a rare convergence of qualities that add up to a powerful personal magnetism. Many who knew him well attest that Ross was that singular person one noticed the moment he walked into a crowded room, a characteristic all the more impressive for his utter lack of pretense. Albert Hubbell, a longtime *New Yorker* artist and writer, says it was the same kind of charismatic force that he had seen in James Joyce, whom Hubbell knew when he lived in Paris as a young man.

(Ross was not unaware of his attractive qualities, even if they didn't always carry the day. Once, on a fishing trip with some friends and a grizzled fishing guide, he was holding forth on why different trout are to be found in the East than in the West; it all had something to do with the Continental Divide, Ross maintained. "Just as he gained cruising altitude in this discourse," recalled Nunnally Johnson, who was present, "the guide looked at him with contempt and said, 'Bullshit.' I never saw a man so taken aback. 'But goddammit,' Ross kept saying later, 'I'm recognized by everybody as one of the finest conversationalists since Oscar Wilde. So how the hell

On a Coney Island excursion, Ross, center, is flanked by Constance Collier, Noel Coward, Marc Connelly and Jed Harris. *(Courtesy of the Dramatists Guild Fund)*

does this son of a bitch get off saying "Bullshit" to me!' " Added Johnson, "I have no explanation for this.")

Women who knew Ross mention other qualities when discussing him. For one thing, in their company he was courtly, unfailingly gracious, less noisy, and never profane. Unlike many men, when he talked with a woman (that is, a woman not his wife), he listened carefully and was genuinely interested in what she had to say. "He had a wonderful kind of embracing quality," said longtime *New Yorker* theater critic Edith Oliver. "When he was talking to you, it was to *you*." Others recall his naturalness and lack of guile. "He was bluff and funny and famous. He was *very* masculine," said Daphne Hellman Shih, who socialized regularly with Ross when she was married to *New Yorker* writer Geoffrey Hellman. "You had the sense that he was absolutely sure of himself; whether he was or he wasn't, you had that sense. But in a very comfortable way. He wasn't arrogant."

Then there was that charm, which, when it suited, Ross could switch on like an incandescent lamp. Climbing into a taxi one evening with a date, he asked where she wanted to have dinner. "Oh, I don't know. You choose some nice place," she said. He asked several more times, and each time she demurred. Suddenly Ross hit on the solution; he instructed their driver, "Follow that taxi ahead of you."

But if there was charm, there was sometimes its flip side, gaucherie. More than a few stories were told of how Ross's dating etiquette failed him, especially in his younger, wilder years, and especially when he was trying to make a pass. In such instances, he was known to employ an awkward grope, or a sudden and startling lunge *d'amour*, demonstrating all the suavity of an old Aspen prospector. A lady friend of Ingersoll's said that once at dinner Ross even chased her around their table, until she collapsed into laughter at the absurdity of the situation.

Indeed, in the magazine's salad days, Ross's various romantic misadventures made for reliable water-cooler fodder. Sally Benson, one of his favorite writers, described a particularly loopy evening when he escorted her to a party given by book publisher Bennett Cerf:

Ross sent me a thing that was in the shape of a corsage, but it was two-and-a-half feet wide with ribbons dripping from it and forget-me-nots trailing from the ribbons. I couldn't wear it, and it was heavy to carry. Every time I set it down, Ross would shout at me that I was supposed to wear it.

There was a big heavy man, drunk, who kept asking everybody where Adam Gimbel was. And Ross pushed me forward and said, "Here's *Mrs.* Adam Gimbel." And the man threw me back on the couch—I was off center on account of the bouquet—and shook me. "Where's Adam? Where is he? Where's old Adam? Get him over here!"

Then Ross crashed a party next door—a party of wholesalers. And he took me in to them and told them I was the greatest handkerchief designer in the world, and they offered me thirty thousand dollars a year, starting the next day, if I'd sign on with them. They wanted to know if I had any ideas . . . if I could just throw one at them . . . so they could see. I asked if anyone had ever thought of putting Mickey Mouse on a handkerchief and they lost interest in us.

On a later occasion, when Ross was between his second and third marriages, St. Clair McKelway, then *The New Yorker*'s managing editor for Fact, dropped by his office to discuss an upcoming story by A. J. Liebling. McKelway couldn't help noticing that Ross was fidgeting uncomfortably in his chair, and after a while he asked what was wrong. "They ought to have covers, wooden or metal covers of some kind, around the goddamn radiators," Ross blurted. McKelway was confused by this. What radiators? he asked. Here? "Good God, no," said Ross. "At the Ritz. I had this dame in bed and it got cold so I got up and walked over to the window to shut it. I had to lean over to shut the window and my you-know-what dangled down on this red-hot radiator. Feels like a second-degree burn, for Christ's sake. Now this piece of Liebling's here . . ."

After his divorce, Ross wasted little time capitalizing on his freedom. Quite the bachelor, he became a fixture at Broadway openings,

Park Avenue soirees, and glittery Saturday nights at the Mayfair Club. He was especially partial to actresses, not just for their beauty but for their glamour. No chorines for him; he squired leading ladies, such as Madge Kennedy, who was starring in his friend Noel Coward's comedy *Private Lives.*

The truth is, the Colorado miner's son had always been stagestruck, and now he took full advantage of his proximity to the show business set. Ross could be counted on to dish the latest back-stage gossip, and he moved comfortably in an ever-broader circle of celebrity friends: cocktails with good friend Beatrice Lillie, dinner at the Stork Club with Fred and Adele Astaire, the occasional game of softball (after croquet, surely his most taxing recreational pursuit) with Ed Sullivan, Billy Rose, and Harpo Marx. Weekends might be spent in Oyster Bay or the Hamptons. This was a side of their editor

Ross shares some cake with Humphrey Bogart, James Cagney and Paul Kelly, but judging from his inscription on the photo–"This is Priscilla Lane!!!"– it was the beautiful actress who made the biggest impression on him.
(Courtesy of Patricia Ross Honcoop)

that his *New Yorker* associates seldom encountered. One sees it, however, in the child's scrapbook that Ross's daughter, Patricia, kept of her father. There, pasted onto black construction-paper pages beside the assorted letters, World War I memorabilia, and faded photographs of long-dead relatives, are snapshots of Ross and his marquee acquaintances—here having cake with Humphrey Bogart and the ravishing Priscilla Lane, there posing with Cagney ("From one pretty one to another. Jim," the actor inscribed). There is a boyhood still of Clifton Webb ("Same to you") and a note from Coward, dated February 1929, that begins playfully, "Yes, dear Ross. I always have been and always will be your Valentine."

In 1930 Ross moved out on his own, and up, to 277 Park Avenue. Ironically, several years later he would be sent packing for allegedly violating a lease provision against having "persons of the opposite

Cagney's note reads, "From one pretty one to another."
(Courtesy of Patricia Ross Honcoop)

sex" visiting overnight. But for now he was happy to be rubbing shoulders with his readership, and he spent five thousand dollars to have the apartment professionally decorated and furnished. At about this same time one of his favorite companions was a very young Ginger Rogers. That fall, at age nineteen, she landed the starring role in the Gershwins' hit musical *Girl Crazy*. Ross already socialized with her mother, Lela, who had deftly steered her daughter's career through vaudeville and a handful of small movie roles. Ross, now thirty-seven, came around more and more, and, as Ginger wrote in her memoirs, Lela soon realized that he "had a mighty big crush" on her daughter. Some of their mutual friends warned Lela that Ross's intentions might be less than honorable, but she wasn't worried. "Her instincts, as usual, were right," Ginger said. "Harold always behaved properly. Whatever his inclinations really may have been, I had no romantic feelings about him whatsoever; he was my pal and I welcomed his company."

Those inclinations almost certainly were romantic, at least at first, said Ginger's cousin Phyllis Cerf Wagner, who was also close to Ross. When he saw that romance wasn't in the cards, however, he and Ginger fell into a comfortable friendship. They genuinely enjoyed each other's company and were together often, whether at cocktail parties, where he introduced her to the day's leading theatrical and literary names, or simply sitting around playing backgammon. Both of them had come from the heartland and were by nature down-to-earth, and Ginger found him gentlemanly, amusing, and unpredictable. One Sunday morning Ross called to invite her to the circus with him and Coward. After taking in the spectacle from front-row seats, they went backstage to feed the elephants. Ross had bought twelve bags of peanuts, and one of the more mischievous beasts grabbed his eyeglasses with her trunk and held them aloft for ransom.

In the summer of 1931, Ross joined Lela and Ginger on a cross-country train trip to California. He was taking a vacation and eventually was to meet up with Woollcott, who was returning from a cruise, in San Francisco; Ginger was bound for Hollywood to resume

Ginger Rogers in
the early Thirties.
(AP/Wide World)

her burgeoning movie career. Shortly after they got under way, Ross announced that two surprise guests would be joining them for dinner, Alfred Lunt and Lynn Fontanne. The opportunity to meet the legendary Lunts thrilled Ginger, but also intimidated her. The conversation stuttered until Alfred allowed that he and his wife were heading west to shoot a movie for MGM. What little film the Lunts had done heretofore had been in the medium's primitive infancy, and they were apprehensive about how it had changed. Ross piped up, "You know, Ginger is also on her way to make three films for Pathé." Ginger was mortified at his implicit equation of the proletarian Pathé with the prestigious MGM, but Ross pressed on: "Ginger has made a number of films in New York City, so she's really a movie veteran." With this discovery, the Lunts began peppering her with questions—about directors, production techniques, how to be made up to best effect for the camera. The tables were turned—the acting novice was instructing the acting legends—and suddenly Ginger realized what her friend had been up to. "Harold knew what he was doing," she wrote.

In Hollywood, Ross took Ginger to more parties, and made more introductions: to Charlie Chaplin, Douglas Fairbanks, Norma Talmadge, Zasu Pitts, Groucho Marx. Ross always professed a jaundiced view of the Golden State ("People in California live in a world of rumors, dreams, and superstition, because newspapers out there don't print much news," he once informed Rebecca West), and of Hollywood in particular. He considered the early motion pictures more gimmick than art form, so much so that, uncharacteristically for him, he goaded his reviewers to rough them up. One of these, John McCarten, became especially notorious in Hollywood, which only made Ross happier, for the studios were constantly seducing his most promising writers. It would take him a long time to accept the hypothesis that writers can be motivated by mammon as well as by art, and for years he regarded the studio moguls as the lowest rung on the food chain. (It perturbed him that Darryl F. Zanuck never seemed to remember who he was, so when he got the chance he always misspelled the producer's name "Zanick.")

But in truth Ross loved California, especially since he had so many transplanted friends there, and he visited often. On one such occasion, Harpo Marx recalled, he was awakened at his apartment at the Garden of Allah in the wee hours by the sound of dice being shaken; it was Ross outside his window, backgammon cup in hand, ready to play. "We had quite a long session, and every hour or so he would bellow, 'Where are all those Hollywood beauties I've heard so much about?'" Harpo later told Groucho. "Unbeknownst to him, I finally arranged with the local madam to send over three of her more presentables. But when they arrived, he furiously handed each girl twenty bucks and said, 'Go home, girls, I'm on a triple blitz!'"

As such high jinks make plain, Ross was enjoying the last great blowout of his life, playing as ferociously as a child racing nightfall. Having grown up far too fast, he stubbornly clung to a piece of the little boy within. To a great extent the responsibilities of marriage, and then starting a business, had caused him to repress his boyish impulses, but with bachelorhood, and with *The New Yorker* up and running, he was free to indulge them. To his ulcerous regret, he was drinking too hard and eating too well, and routinely staying out till the wee hours. His mother disapproved of this tomcat behavior, and when she stayed with him in New York, as she often did in the early Thirties, he was reduced to making preposterous excuses for his nocturnal comings and goings. After one party, when he found her waiting up, he explained that he was on his way out at ten-thirty when suddenly the host bolted the doors and declared, "Nobody is going to leave this house until one-thirty."

Bad alibis notwithstanding, these relatively carefree days were among Ross's happiest. Never again would he have quite the same freedom, much less the stamina, to prowl the city however he wished. Consider the memorable evening he spent in the company of his friend Stanley Walker, storied city editor of *The New York Herald Tribune,* and the New York Police Department vice squad. Over dinner Walker casually mentioned that in a few hours he would be riding along when the cops raided a notorious clip joint. "Instantly he was on the alert, the smell of battle smoke in his nostrils," Walker wrote. Ross invited himself along, and sometime after three in the morning they drove up to their destination, a basement dive on West Forty-sixth not far from Ross's old co-op. "The detectives and I went first, crashing the door," Walker said, "and then the detectives gave the half-dozen thugs and pimps a terrible going over, and then wrecked the joint and threw all the furniture into the street. It was a horrible and bloody sight, and Ross was tickled. He laughed through most of the festivities." Since it was too late for Walker to catch a train home to Great Neck, he went back to Ross's apartment. "Of course, Ross and I . . . and the cops had been drinking steadily (my booze) all night, and we were pretty fagged out. It was a good night's work for society, and it had all made Ross very happy."

———

BUSY SOWING THESE LAST WILD OATS, ROSS WAS SLOW TO NOTICE that for almost everyone else the party was over. For millions of

Americans, the Depression meant anything from discomfiture to destitution, but he was not among them. He never would be faced with the prospect of selling pencils on street corners, and neither, by and large, would his readers. Had they been more profoundly touched, doubtless *The New Yorker* would have been quicker to recognize the hard times. As it was, the magazine would be criticized, and not without cause, for more or less sitting out the Depression. Especially through the early Thirties, it tended to treat hard times as more a nuisance—an inconvenience, really, on a par with balky automobiles or feckless valets—than the catastrophe it was. The magazine wielded its blasé attitude like a shield. Just after the stock-market crash, this was how Benchley began a Wayward Press column: "There was a slight benefit accruing to the stock-market unpleasantness of last week—oh, very well, then, there wasn't. You don't have to get so sore."

In fairness, it must be said that the harshest criticism of *The New Yorker*'s stance was not contemporaneous but came long after the fact—that is, from the perspective of what *The New Yorker* became rather than what it was at the time. A few critics even imputed to Ross a measure of personal callousness that, on reflection, seems unwarranted. He came to see the pain around him and was not without compassion; time and again in his professional life he demonstrated genuine concern for the common man, and in a fight his instinct was always to side with the underdog. But there were editorial reasons, right or wrong, behind his reluctance to confront the bad times in the pages of *The New Yorker*.

For starters, the Depression, of all the century's now-familiar shocks, was the first to occur on *The New Yorker*'s watch. The magazine, not yet five years old when Wall Street collapsed and only just out of the red, still lacked confidence, most especially where grave matters were concerned. Neither Ross nor anyone on his staff had any grasp of global economics; it was bound to be the case that for a while the magazine would be at least as naïve as the Hoover administration.

More significant, Ross was determined to keep politics out of his magazine. He might profile political personalities and monitor the shifting political tides, but he was adamant that *The New Yorker* proffer no agenda of its own. It was first and foremost a humor magazine, and in its early years he was fond of saying, with a trace of condescension (to him "important" was a euphemism for "dull"), "Let's let the other magazines be important." At this juncture, virtually nothing in the magazine was really serious; the cultural and press criticism was far more whimsical than analytical, and what sober matters Markey and Ross's other journalists took up were still being treated casually and ironically. Later Talk veteran Russell Maloney would write that until the Hitler menace became too ominous to ignore, the magazine's editorial stand "was simple and, theoretically, not impossible to put into action. *The New Yorker* was on record as being against the use of poisonous spray on fruit, and against the trend in automobile design which narrows the driver's field of vision by lowering the front seat."

In other words, it wasn't merely the Depression that was largely ignored, but the New Deal, the Spanish Civil War, racial upheavals, and most other major developments of the day. William Shawn, who joined *The New Yorker* in the early years of the Depression, explained the then-prevailing attitude this way: "In our inattention [to the Depression] we were being completely true to ourselves at that time—in those days the people who worked for the magazine were actually proud of being apolitical and socially detached."

As Ross had conceived it, this wasn't his job. The whole point of *The New Yorker* was to give people a laugh and a lift, and in the Thirties this seemed more important than ever. He had worked hard to gather about him the best cartoonists, as well as the greatest collection of humorists in the land—White, Thurber, Gibbs, Benchley, Parker, Frank Sullivan, S. J. Perelman, and Clarence Day, not to mention such specialists as Ring Lardner, who for the last year of his life, while bedridden with illness, produced a delightful radio column for the magazine. It was their work that in the first half of the Thirties formed its bread and butter, and in fact *The New Yorker* of that vintage probably hewed closer to Ross's 1924 prospectus and initial vision than any other incarnation. He was thrilled and honored to be able to publish talent of that caliber.

Besides, Ross was always confident that where society at large was concerned, the magazine's conscience, White, would say anything that needed saying. And indeed, as White looked about him, increasingly his conscience was troubled. His commentaries on the national despair became more frequent, and more bold, especially as the crisis deepened and Herbert Hoover's policies revealed themselves to be ineffectual. In early 1932, for instance, White was moved to write:

We walked over to Union Square the other morning to dry out our soul in the sun, and sat a while with the dismal on the benches— the men who were thinking, and waiting. (We ourselves were only waiting.) Before leaving the Square, we read the motto on the monument, a quotation from Thomas Jefferson: "How little do my countrymen know what precious blessings they are in possession of. . . ." Uneasily we glanced around at our countrymen. The only precious blessing most of them were in possession of was the cup of coffee they had recently got from the relief shanty nearby. In such graven words, it seemed to us, the disconsolate must taste the ultimate bile.

At about this same time *The New Yorker*'s cartoonists were unsheathing their pens too, lacerating government policymakers and defrocked tycoons with equal gusto. (Conservative in his personal finances as well as in his politics, Ross had little sympathy for those who were ruined by what he regarded as foolish stock-market speculation. Though many of his high-flying friends lost huge sums in the 1929 crash, what little money he then had was still tied up in *The New Yorker*.) And eventually some recognizable victims of the times, such as Erskine Caldwell's beaten-down characters, turned up in the prose as well. Yet on the whole these remained tiny islands in a *New Yorker* sea of privilege and prosperity. This was especially so when one factored in the advertisements, which remained relentlessly upscale, aimed at people whose decisions involved their next vacation rather than their next meal.

Perhaps Ross believed that by poking fun at anyone and everyone, the lecherous old poop as well as his dizzy scullery maid, *The New*

Yorker inoculated itself against charges of insufficient concern. Yet as the Depression wore on and its human toll mounted, this detachment increasingly came off as hard-hearted, the usual focus on pigeon roosts and potholes less good-natured than strangely cold.

The critic Dwight Macdonald, who years later joined *The New Yorker* himself, smartly articulated this view in 1937 when he chastised the magazine in the *Partisan Review*. "In the class war *The New Yorker* is ostentatiously neutral. It makes fun of subway guards and of men-about-town, of dowagers and laundresses, of shop-girls and debutantes. . . . *The New Yorker's* position in the class war, however, is not so simple as its editors would have us believe. Its neutrality is itself a form of upper-class display, since only the economically secure can afford such Jovian aloofness from the common struggle. In times like these there is something monstrously inhuman in the deliberate cultivation of the trivial."

Given his innate sensitivity and his experience with Comment, White might have concurred. He too had been increasingly disturbed by the disparity between the worlds of *The New Yorker* and the average New Yorker. This nagging sense of guilt was one of the causes of his second serious bout of discontent with the magazine, which in turn led, in the summer of 1937, to his only separation (albeit a temporary one) from it. A quarter century later White's guilt was still there. As he told a friend in 1963, "*The New Yorker* was, of course, a child of the Depression, and when everybody else was foundering we were running free, and I still feel that I escaped the hard times undeservedly and will always go unacquainted with the facts of life."

There is no evidence that Ross himself ever experienced this level of anxiety, but to the extent that *The New Yorker's* laggard response to this national crisis was a mistake, it was one he would never make again.

On the business side *The New Yorker* was never seriously threatened by the Depression, managing a profit even in its bleakest years. The only period of genuine worry was the nervous election year of 1932, when the magazine shrank enough (it ran to a meager forty-eight pages in the dead summer months) for Ross to squeal, revenue fell off sixteen percent, and circulation slipped from 121,000 to 113,000 (the only real interruption of growth in Ross's stewardship). In the wake of this scare, the magazine cut salaries across the board by ten percent in February 1933; the cut was restored in early 1934. The election of Roosevelt was good for *The New Yorker,* primarily because of Repeal. By late 1933, beer and liquor advertisements began dribbling in, and by 1934 they amounted to a veritable torrent of found revenue. The depressed price of paper helped the magazine's bottom line, and its city edition turned out to be a godsend at a time when magazines relying exclusively on national ads were badly squeezed. While *The New Yorker* profited, its competitors fell, one by one, to the wayside. Crowninshield's *Vanity Fair* was subsumed into a sister publication, *Vogue,* in 1936. The same year, Henry Luce bought *Life*'s nameplate in order to launch his splashy new picture magazine. Old *Life*'s emaciated subscriber list went to *Judge,* but it didn't help; it too succumbed in 1939.

———

PERHAPS BECAUSE OF THE TIMES, OR PERHAPS SIMPLY BECAUSE HE WAS maturing, Ross was becoming much less cavalier in his handling of personnel. By the early Thirties, *The New Yorker* was a dream destination for many newspaper reporters and editors, owing not only to its editorial freedom and excellence but to its financial vitality. It was during this time that a young Boston newspaperman, Charles Morton, who had sold the magazine several casuals, was summoned to New York to talk to Ross about a job. They had arranged to meet at the magazine on a Sunday evening, and Morton was so anxious that he walked around outside for thirty minutes until it was time to go up.

Beyond the night watchman, it appeared that the only other person in the building was Ross. The *New Yorker* offices were cramped and stark; an unwitting visitor might have assumed that the many cubicles housed accountants or actuaries but for the telltale artistic flourishes, such as the huge Thurber characters looming on the walls.

Along one corridor, for instance, he had drawn a life-size man walking along without a care in the world. Just around the corner, however, a life-size woman was waiting for him with a club in her hand.

Ross was friendly, garrulous, persuasive. As usual, his approach to the job candidate was to evoke sympathy for himself. All evidence to the contrary, he whined about his inadequate staff and moaned about being unable to cover certain subjects for lack of the right reporter. He was expert at making a recruit feel he was the only person in the world who could steer this foundering ship free of the shoals. Sure enough, before long Morton was compelled to reassure Ross that things would be all right. "I was chattering away about what I felt to be the magazine's virtues and how various weaknesses might be shored up when I noticed Ross eyeing me intently. . . . 'Goddammit,' he said, 'let *me* talk.' "

He wanted geniuses, Ross told Morton. He had three—White, Thurber and Gibbs; they could do anything—but he was always on the lookout for another. Maybe Morton was it—though the odds, Ross was quick to add, were against it. They would see during a three-month trial. The excitable young man was so intoxicated at the mere suggestion of genius that he failed to detect the inherent warning in these words. Ross also insisted that Morton obtain a leave of absence from his Boston newspaper first. "Ross was firm about the leave," Morton would write. "He knew a great deal more about himself and his wants than I did. He was not running a school in which promising young men were brought along and promoted; neither was he hiring anyone as an encouragement."

The confident Morton thought this precaution surely unnecessary. He didn't know it yet, but Ross was looking out for him. The editor knew how difficult an adjustment *The New Yorker* was for most newspaper people; he had seen it dozens, maybe even hundreds, of times. "He did not wish to uproot a Massachusetts family and a man with a job and cast them adrift in New York at the darkest point of the Depression," Morton said later.

In fact, things didn't work out, as Morton struggled with the magazine's unique reporting and writing demands. One Thursday, with his probation nearly over, Bernard Bergman, then managing editor, walked up and said, "Mr. Ross thinks you should plan to go back to Boston when your three months are up." Mortified but not really surprised, Morton decided that under the circumstances it would be best if he cleared out immediately rather than hang around as an object of pity, "the failure who would not leave." He asked an office boy to settle up his pay, said a few good-byes, then returned to his boardinghouse to pack. A few hours later the office boy came by in a panic. "Ross had just told him that by leaving on Thursday instead of finishing the week I was beating *The New Yorker* out of two days' pay, and if I did not return the money, Ross was going to take it out of the office boy's pay." The misunderstanding only deepened Morton's humiliation ("I was leaving not only as an incompetent but also as untrustworthy, if not downright dishonest"), but eventually it was cleared up.

Outwardly, Ross seemed to be maturing too, or at least he was trying harder to look the part of the editor of a sophisticated magazine. He had yet to forgo his high-top, lace-up shoes, but he was wearing a better cut of suit (invariably dark) and had begun combing his hair back. This last amounted to a hopeless exercise, however, not only because the grand pompadour was beyond taming (it always seemed on the verge of springing back upright), but because he was constantly mussing it; one of his nervous tics was scratching his head, usually reaching across the scalp with his right hand to attack the left side. Just as rigorously he was cultivating other idiosyncrasies. He forbade whistling in the halls and discouraged staffers from speaking to him in the elevators (not to be antisocial, but because when he was identified as the editor of *The New Yorker,* invariably his fellow passengers turned out to be closet writers or cartoonists). For a large and vital man, he had a notoriously limp handshake. Then there was a curious manifestation of his shyness or self-consciousness: when he came to work, he tended to trudge straight into his office without a word, virtually oblivious to anyone who might happen to be around, as if hoping that his arrival might go undetected. But once there, he was "in," ready to circulate, chatty enough to tell a colleague all about last night's dinner with Benchley at "21." In so doing, said James M. Cain, who preceded Bergman in an unhappy stint as managing editor, Ross would punctuate his story with hands that somehow managed to be animated and lifeless all at once. "They droop off his wrists like dead things," Cain remembered, "all the fingers hanging separately, and seeming to have grown twice as long. There is something about them as final as the undertaker's patent pulley that lowers the coffin down in the ground. After they get it in you might as well go home. There ain't no more after that."

Of course it's altogether possible that lifeless fingers and limp handshakes were only Ross's subliminal way of conveying how taxing his job was—work, these slack limbs seemed to say, that sapped the last measure of his energy. If so, the gesture was not completely hyperbolic. Editing a weekly magazine in Ross's aggressive fashion was extraordinarily time-consuming and nerve-racking, with hundreds of moving parts to account for and potential disasters to sidestep. If done well, the work was also invisible; a good editor could nurse along a story or picture for months but leave no evidence of his involvement in the finished product. Fortunately two rare memos from May 1931, wherein Ross spelled out shortcomings in two consecutive issues, demonstrate how his editorial mind was turning at this time. The critiques are also worth excerpting as concrete proof that his fabled reputation for "sharpshooting"—that is, editorial nitpicking—was no exaggeration:

Notes on the Issue of May 2, 1931

GOINGS ON: Theatre: Blurb on "Vinegar Tree" misleading. Does it mean "renewing whatever comes along handy?" or "renewing whatever old love comes along handy?"

Art: Peggy Bacon is not an American Hogarth. Not the same sort of thing at all. Very misleading.

Opera: The Bluehill Troupe. What are they? Amateur or Pro? Aida. What company gives? Not mentioned.

Sports (Wrestling): Landos vs. Szabo wasn't Landos vs. Szabo but probably shift to Steele was announced too late for correction. (Racing): Maybe Pimlico Preakness and trains should have been listed considering that it is listed under "On the Air."

TALK OF THE TOWN: "Mercury" personality piece very questionable. Much too old. Sure to get letters from people who knew him once saying he's been dead for two years. "Sir Walter" a type anecdote. Very old. "Outposts"—George Gray Barnard still working? Pretty flat department on whole.

Page 21: Auslander poem "Excavations in Ur" pretty trite, the kind of stuff for the *Ladies Home Journal,* not us. Brubaker item about Mr. Coolidge laughing off suggestion that he become Speaker of the House is about three weeks late. Alfonso item faces end of Sullivan's Alfonso piece. Did Brubaker mean to be funny when he said Prajadhipok is "King of *Persia*"?

The Oarsmen: Lines 6–7 "attention should be drawn to New Haven and Yale," meaning New London and Yale? Otherwise redundant. Department good on the whole.

Feminine Fashions: Are all hats (French models) mentioned in "And in New York" to be had only at Saks-Fifth Avenue? If not, why not mention other places? A little development of themes like this, instead of stopping with one retailer, would help the department.

As to Men: Why mention Tripler's particularly for soft tab ready-to-wear collars? These can be had anywhere.

The Current Cinema: A little slipshod in spots. For instance, "Gunmen appear in both *Dude Ranch* and *Gun Smoke,* in both cases by some coincidence moved from their urban haunts to the wilds of the West, and in both cases they are bettered—bested, I should say, even—by the honest ranch folk. In *Dude Ranch* Jack Oakie does most of the besting—" But Jack Oakie doesn't represent the "honest ranch folk." He's a traveling actor.

Horse Shows and Hunts: A pretty poor department. Hard to follow what horses he's talking about, and what shows or events they were in. Covering of Maryland Hunt, very inadequate. It was the event of the week in this field.

Books: Still no fiction being reviewed. Best sellers neglected.

Also some books of special interest to *New Yorker* readers—*Orange Valley* by Howard Baker, for instance. Think continuation of blurbing Thurber's and Gibbs' books inadvisable. Lincoln Steffens *Autobiography* not yet noticed.

Notes on the Issue of May 9, 1931

TALK OF THE TOWN: 1st Comment piece: Model Brassiere Company is not "topmost tenant"—only one of several on 41st floor; not eleven hundred feet up—less than five hundred. Last Comment piece: On X-ray photographs—pretty thin and very old. Better to have killed. "Planet's Rival": Never possible to see Venus in daylight with street telescope. "Extant": A pretty trite and pretty thin anecdote. "Ex-Queen": The Queen of Spain was not Princess Ena, but Victoria Eugenie. Three out of first four pieces of Talk, about money.

Page 22: Drawing of ship not so good in midst of text about "My Dream Ship."

Art Galleries: Is Eilshemius an established painter?

The Oarsmen: Department continues good.

On and Off the Avenue: Valuable write-up of Hattie Carnegie. Mention of Frida Mueller, "an enthusiastic reader writes in to say," sounds as if Long had not investigated. That seems like bad policy—seems to imply that maybe other things haven't been either. Misleading to reader.

Motors: We've laid it on a little thick about Marmon. Had a full write-up of this same car last winter. Same dope about it.

Books: Still no fiction reviewed. I think this department is a little dull and longwinded and gives too much space to rather heavy books. Should review more books at briefer length.

The critiques are vintage Ross: they range all over the magazine's landscape, reveal a remarkable catholicity of knowledge, and raise questions of fact, tone, balance, and credibility. (As can be seen, Ross would no more unduly promote his staffers' books than he would take a reader's word for a shopping tip.) They also underscore what its editor was trying to accomplish with his *New Yorker*—a journal he insisted be at once amusing, informed, up-to-date, and completely trustworthy—and by now he had largely succeeded.

The critiques also remind us just how much the magazine was a direct extension of the man. If there had been an organization chart—a *New Yorker* document that never was, since titles there have traditionally been as transitory and useful as pixie dust—it would have resembled not the conventional pyramid but a wagon wheel, with Ross at the hub and spokes shooting off in every direction. Nothing, from major Profile to tiniest Newsbreak, went into the magazine without his approval. It remained difficult for him to artic- ulate his intentions and standards; instead, he demonstrated them, by trial and error, in the magazine itself, and gradually a collective understanding of *New Yorker* material emerged. Those people who couldn't decipher his wishes were largely gone, most carrying with them an impression of Ross as an impossible lunatic. The people who were left understood him perfectly and formed a hard, protective core around him. (Many of these people considered Ross impossible too, but less a lunatic than an inspired eccentric.) By now this core, besides the Whites, Thurber, Gibbs, Rea Irvin, and Rogers Whitaker, would have to include such *New Yorker* stalwarts as Talk writers Geoffrey Hellman, the stylish chronicler of old-line New York, and Charles Cooke, the first Our Man Stanley; two of Gibbs's old school chums, Hobart Weekes, who would become the magazine's maven for style and grammar, and the colorful Fred Packard, who succeeded Whitaker in running the checking department; and such key staff as the temperamental but brilliant Carmine Peppe, who oversaw the magazine's layout and makeup operations, and the tyrannical Daise Terry, who presided over a cowed clerical staff.

Like Ross, these people put *The New Yorker* ahead of all other con- siderations, even personal ones. Back in 1929, when White suddenly dropped from sight (on the spur of the moment he had decided to intercept Katharine on her train trip to Reno), a panicked Ross com- pelled Thurber to tell him where his friend had gone. White was hurt by this because he had sworn Thurber to secrecy. Ross subsequently tried to explain to him that Thurber had squealed only out of a larger loyalty to *The New Yorker*. Replied White, "*The New Yorker* is a cesspool of loyalties."

A further testament to Ross's editorial core and the magazine's underlying stability was the fact that by this time it had rendered the Jesus, ostensibly the editor's second-in-command, more or less superfluous. This was fortunate, for since Ingersoll's withdrawal the Jesus Parade had become more like a stampede. The problem was that in his heart Ross, like his fellow Irishman Yeats, believed the center couldn't hold. He had tried his best to impose "order," with labyrinthine routings of manuscripts, Rube Goldberg pay structures, and increasingly complex editing fail-safes. (These forays at times achieved comic proportions: Once, a huge, color-coded bulletin board was erected to help an incoming Jesus keep track of the magazine's many moving parts. Ross was crushed to learn that the new man was color-blind.) But the editor continued to insist that only an effective junior executive could give him true peace of mind.

Of course the reality of the situation was that between Ross's own firm direction and the quality control exerted by highly capable lieutenants like Mrs. White, Whitaker and Weekes, the Jesus position had become that of a glorified traffic cop. With a surpassing logic, one of Ross's Jesus candidates in fact *was* a traffic cop, a man who in a previous life oversaw traffic control for the N.Y.P.D. His was an exceedingly short stay, *New Yorker* gridlock apparently proving even more intractable than Manhattan's.

Yet Ross persisted, his search as mystifying as it was relentless. At a party one night, Jane Grant overheard him talking nonsense to his latest genius. Afterward she asked him what he had been doing. "It built him up, made him think he was smarter than me," Ross explained. "If he couldn't see through what I was saying, he's just a damned fool and I might as well know it first as last."

Ross auditioned friends and strangers; "he brings them back from lunch," said Ingersoll; "he cables for them." Some he liked well enough personally but fired anyway, but most he considered "horse's rosettes." In his desperation he even tried to push the job onto Gibbs, whose general opinion of the magazine's managing editors was that they were "pinheads." Over dinner Ross drank heavily, and Gibbs walked him home. "We got to Park Avenue and before I could stop him he weaved right out into the traffic. It was like one of those old Harold Lloyd movies, with cars practically snipping the buttons off his fly, and I never thought I'd see him alive again. We were both full of love and admiration because he'd offered me such a beautiful job and I'd had enough sense to decline it."

Others were caught less awares. According to *New Yorker* lore, when a naïve Ogden Nash accepted Ross's offer near the end of 1930, he became the twenty-fifth Jesus in six years. There simply is no way of knowing if this count is accurate—for one thing, to be considered a Jesus one did not necessarily need to be the managing editor, merely the administrative point man of the moment—but it is undisputably true that by then Ross had churned through a lot of them. Nash was a decent, amiable young man who had recently sold *The New Yorker* a few poems, but Ross somehow got the impression that because Nash frequented speakeasies, he was just the kind of "sophisticate" the editor desired at the helm. It was a fiasco that lasted less than three months.

At the time, Ross was still prone to jeremiads, and the resident Jesus usually got the full brunt. People who knew the editor well had come to intuit which of these hysterical outbursts were for effect and which were the genuine lamentations of a latter-day Sisyphus. A new Jesus, however, was likely to be bewildered, as Nash clearly was. In a letter to his girlfriend, later his wife, he described a typical Ross performance: "The day at the office was quiet enough, if you except Ross's usual blow-up. Ross, who made *The New Yorker* what it is, and who really is a genius, is probably the strangest man in the world. . . . His expression is always that of a man who has just swallowed a bug. . . . Once a day at least he calls you into his office and says, 'This magazine is going to hell.' He never varies the phrase. Then he says, 'We haven't got any organization. I'm licked. We've got too many geniuses around and nobody to take any responsibility.' He has smoked five cigarettes while saying that. Then he takes a drink of water, prowls up and down, cries 'My God!' loudly and rapidly, and you go out and try to do some work."

As he had with Thurber, Ross quickly freed Nash to pursue his true gift, which was splendid light verse, and on came the twenty-sixth Jesus, James M. Cain. He was not yet the acclaimed author of such period thrillers as *The Postman Always Rings Twice* and *Double Indemnity*; those were a few years off. In early 1931 he was an out-of-work editorial writer, *The New York World* having just been sold out from under him, and his buddy Morris Markey brought him to Ross's attention.

Cain's Gethsemane, as he later called it, lasted all of nine months. A tall, serious man, he had several strikes against him: he was not a natural administrator, he had the daily newspaperman's difficulty adjusting to the magazine's long lead times, and he considered much of *The New Yorker*'s content overly frivolous. All these might have been overcome, however, but for the fact that he and Ross, like Ingersoll and Ross, were temperamentally unsuited. As a dinner companion, Cain found Ross delightful and gregarious, but as a boss he was vexing, inconsistent, and interfering. Ross constantly told him he wanted him to "organize" the place, but when Cain fired an incompetent secretary and hired another at thirteen more dollars a week, Ross was stupefied. He contravened his own rules by cutting special deals with certain writers, sometimes without telling Cain, and he resisted Cain's efforts to make the magazine's pay structure more logical and equitable. Eventually Cain was convinced that wittingly or no, Ross actually relished the administrative chaos he professed to hate. Within months Cain "was about as miserable a human being as I have ever encountered," said Bernard Bergman. As it happened, Hollywood had been enticing him all along, and in November 1931 he yielded.

In Cain's estimation Ross was a great but flawed editor, and his admiration for both the man and the magazine grew through the years, especially as *The New Yorker* matured into a more serious and substantial journal. When he left, Cain framed and bequeathed to Bergman (number twenty-seven) a memo that Ross had hastily

James M. Cain. *(Culver Pictures)*

typed and clipped to a rejected manuscript; it read simply, "What is the signigifance of it all?" Bergman kept it for the rest of his life.

Bergman would experience many of the same frustrations as his predecessor had, but he lasted a relative eternity: two years. He considered his greatest contribution persuading the gifted Alva Johnston to join the staff (though there were other major additions on his watch to the cultural and reporting staff, among them St. Clair McKelway, book critic Clifton Fadiman, and a quiet young Talk reporter, recently arrived from Chicago, named William Shawn). Bergman's biggest regret by far was having to fire John O'Hara.

This occurred in late 1931. Ross, at Gibbs's urging and against his better judgment (he was forever uneasy about O'Hara, who he felt should stick to fiction), had agreed to try O'Hara as a Talk writer, on a "drawing account" of seventy-five dollars a week. This was in effect an advance against the purchase of pieces for the magazine; unfortunately for O'Hara, Ross killed every item he turned in. Bergman had approved the Talk items and thought them satisfactory, and Ross offered no explanations for his animus. After four weeks of this, the editor abruptly told Bergman, "O'Hara's in us for three hundred dollars. He won't do. Fire him before we're in him for more." Bergman tried to dissuade him, but, failing, finally had to break the bad news to O'Hara. For all his efforts on the writer's behalf, it was Bergman, not Ross, against whom O'Hara nursed one of his famous grudges for years.

What exactly brought Bergman and Ross to a parting of the ways in 1933 isn't clear, although there are indications it involved office politics. Apparently Bergman had a dicey relationship with Mrs. White; he told her biographer, Linda H. Davis, that his counterpart for fiction could be duplicitous and had worked to undermine his position with Ross. Years after he left *The New Yorker*, Bergman wrote to Thurber, "You, I believe, had warned me that Mrs. White was spreading the story that I had hired my mistress as my secretary. So silly I laughed it off. A big mistake to laugh Mrs. White off." Whether or not Mrs. White spread such a rumor, or whether it had anything to do with Bergman's leave-taking, is anyone's guess, but it certainly was the case that the young magazine, like most small organizations, was a cauldron of rumor (a pot the mischievous Thurber especially enjoyed stirring) and petty politics, and Mrs. White could more than hold her own.

Other nonentities drifted in and out until the arrival of the next major figure, Stanley Walker, whom Ross had wooed for years. He would prove to be one of the most influential figures in the early history of *The New Yorker*, although, ironically, not for anything he did while actually working at the magazine. In fact, the laconic Texan and the manic Coloradan never quite managed to get on the same wavelength—like Cain, Walker chafed at the bureaucracy of the place, "the endless memos, the buck-passing"—and he left the magazine, amicably and under his own power, after only a year. However, his groundbreaking work at the *Herald Tribune*, where Walker had championed a freer, more literary approach to news writing, had deeply impressed Ross and helped shape his own views. Beyond this, at the *Herald* Walker had cultivated the likes of Johnston, McKelway, Joseph Mitchell, Joel Sayre, John Lardner, and Sanderson Vanderbilt. All these men, in their turn, came to work for, and flourished at, *The New Yorker.*

After Walker came Ik (pronounced Ike) Shuman, a man with a head for business but whose editorial capabilities were widely suspect. Ross was true to form: "In the beginning, he kept on saying 'Shuman knows how to handle that,'" Gibbs recalled, "and before you knew it, he was saying 'Let's see how he fucks this one up.'" Though a short-lived Jesus, Shuman remained an important figure at *The New Yorker* for eight years, as an administrator and the editorial side's liaison with the business office. He even sat for a while on the company's board of directors before Ross essentially shoved him off the train.

Shuman's chief crime was becoming too cozy with his business-side counterparts, which was the surest way to kindle Ross's suspicions—and once you were suspect, you were on borrowed time. (Conversely, once you had his trust, you had it forever.) Over the years, the editor had nurtured a heartfelt disdain for the commercial side of the operation. It was more than an outgrowth of his antipathy to Fleischmann. Ross resented the business side's necessity, and he questioned its efficiency. To illustrate the latter point, he liked to tell a story from the magazine's earliest days. Ross had become friendly with department store magnate Bernard Gimbel and elicited from him a lucrative advertising contract from Saks. Not long after, he and Gimbel were at the Ritz when they spotted the Saks advertising manager and *The New Yorker*'s advertising director, Ray Bowen, across the room having lunch. "We laughed about which one was picking up the check," Ross said, "but also about what in Christ's name they had to talk about. The whole goddamn thing had been settled and signed without either of them knowing anything about it. They [Bowen and his salesmen] are nothing but a bunch of messenger boys."

The plain fact is that Ross simply disliked advertising and any-

thing associated with it. He hated to be beholden to anything or anyone, whether Philip Morris, Helena Rubinstein, or Raoul Fleischmann. His World War I experience at *The Stars and Stripes* had
spoiled him. There, because of a unique set of circumstances (army
sponsorship, captive readership, and finite advertising space), the
paper literally rationed ads. It limited not only their size and number
but their claims, and certain categories—liquor, patent medicines,
political material—were rejected outright. For Ross, if a publication
had to run ads at all, it should at least be as discretionary as *The Stars
and Stripes*. It galled him that in its first few years *The New Yorker* of
necessity had to accept virtually anything that came along.

Ross was also disturbed at his lack of control where contributors
were concerned. Advertisers could and did ring up *New Yorker* artists
for illustrations. Likewise, some of his better-known contributing
writers, most notably Woollcott, were making lucrative endorsements for products that turned around and advertised in *The New
Yorker*.

But on a more fundamental level, Ross despised advertising
because he considered most of it inherently dishonest, and he no
more wanted dishonest or shabby advertising in *The New Yorker* than
he wanted dishonest or error-ridden editorial copy. He realized this
level of integrity was not entirely possible, but the magazine might at
least sift out the ads whose claims were demonstrably untrue.
Unfortunately, his was an age when ad claims were even more
brazen than they are today; Lucky Strikes boasted they were easy on
your throat, Camels helped your digestion, and Viceroys kept your
teeth "pearly white." A particularly egregious offender, it seemed to
Ross, was Fleischmann's Yeast, whose tacky advertisements, unsurprisingly, had been a *New Yorker* staple from the beginning. Its ads
featured testimonials from real people about the many salutary
health benefits (more energy, cleaner skin, happier intestines) they
derived from regular digestion of yeast. Ross was dubious of these
health claims and was repulsed by the ads, which sometimes featured
diagrams of the alimentary tract. (He was so squeamish that he hated
references to any bodily function in his magazine.) When feeling

particularly frisky, Ross liked to call up society matrons, posing as a representative of Fleischmann's Yeast. He would inquire whether they used his product, and if so, he would ask whether they would be willing to endorse it for one thousand dollars. If they agreed, he would say, "Fine. We ask you only to declare that before using our yeast your face was a mass of blotches and unseemly pimples." This usually ended the conversation.

By 1930, there was so much advertising coming into *The New Yorker* that Ross felt confident enough to lecture the business side about ad standards. That March, he fired off a remarkable and incendiary memo to general manager Eugene Spaulding, although the real target undoubtedly was Fleischmann. Ross had been provoked by the appearance of yet another Woollcott endorsement, this one in collaboration with artist John Held, Jr. Ralph Ingersoll, who cited the memo as one of the inspirations for his ad-less newspaper *PM,* called it "the most succinct and accurate statement of Ross's attitude toward business in general and advertising in particular" that he ever saw. It is revealing not just for its obvious principle and passion, but for the moral terms Ross invokes to make his case. Misleading ads are "lies" and "palpable lies"; the magazine has "offended" in the past, but "it is never too late to reform." *New Yorker* integrity, it seems, was about as close as Ross ever came to a religious conviction:

Well, I am as bitter as ever about some of the advertising we have been carrying, and since the situation has recently led to embarrassing complications, I think we ought to do something definite about it. I propose as follows: That we establish a rule that we will not use any endorsement advertising containing a palpable lie, or a statement we are morally certain is a lie.

The Fleischmann Yeast advertising is certainly hocus-pocus. I haven't read it much lately, but I assume that the statements made therein are more or less true—certainly they are such as cannot be, without pretty thorough investigation, branded as untrue. I don't like the tone of these advertisements, but would say (speaking offhandedly) that we should continue to use them. Such advertisements as those run by the Lux people are, however, palpable lies. So are the Simmons Beds. The recent endorsement of coffee by the Messrs. Held and Woollcott, both contributors to this magazine, are also lies.

We were very much embarrassed by the appearance of the Held and Woollcott endorsement. We have been rather severe with the newer and less widely known contributors, being strict with them even in the matter of the use of their drawings in advertisements appearing in the magazine. This is possible with the newer people because they are inclined to trust us and accept our advice, and have grown up with us in an atmosphere which has inculcated in them some sense of truth, honesty, dignity and integrity. Our viewpoint has not been so readily impressed upon certain money-grabbing writers and artists who were established before *The New Yorker* was started. A few recent examples, such as the Lux stuff and the Held-Woollcott endorsement, have seriously embarrassed our policy.

Obviously, the thing for us to do is to attack the matter at its roots, by making it a rule not to print advertising which we know of our own knowledge to be untrue, or which we are morally certain is untrue. That would be a simple, clear-cut rule. I urge that we adopt it. If it is not adopted we will, editorially, have to deal in our own way with contributors who offend, but we haven't much face left if our own management isn't with us.

I urge this policy not as an idealistic measure in any way. I may be idealistic in it, but I would point out also that it is not good business to print palpable lies. It is not bright to do so. Our readers, or the readers we hope to hold and to get for *The New Yorker,* are intelligent enough to know that this stuff is the bunk. We are being shortsighted in running it. We have an opportunity to live honestly. We have also the great privilege now of being in a position to lead the advertising industry. For Christ's sake let us no longer pussyfoot. Let us be really honest, and not just slick. I think that in our present prosperous condition we could afford to suffer even a temporary small loss in revenue to keep our own conscience clear. Moreover, it is never too late to reform. We have offended often in the past, but that is no reason why we shouldn't institute a reform now. We can at least stop being cheap.

P.S. I am not certain about this, but I am of the opinion that the *New York Times*—a great monument to simple integrity—will not run this stuff.

It would take several more years before Ross was able to stamp out all the endorsements by his own contributors, and he never ceased crusading against ads that he considered tasteless, misleading, or merely "inappropriate" to *The New Yorker*. Over the decades, the magazine would cause more commotion on Madison Avenue for ads it wouldn't print—for deodorants, laxatives, vitamins, mortuaries, and most famously, beginning in the mid-Sixties, cigarettes—than for the ones it did. Indeed, the story was perpetuated that Ross, and later Shawn, had a veto power over ads. Like so many *New Yorker* stories, this was somewhat fanciful. Both editors insisted on screening suspect ads, and neither was bashful about raising objections. However, neither had an outright veto; what they did wield, rather, was the ultimate club: the implicit (or sometimes in Ross's case explicit) threat of resigning if their wishes were ignored. For this rea-son—and, it must be added, out of genuine deference to Ross and Shawn's sensibilities—the business side always weighed seriously editorial objections to ads, and usually agreed. Usually, but not invariably. *The New Yorker* ran many ads Ross didn't like, and he waged the fight until the day he died.

Of course the advertising side picked its share of bones with Ross, too. If Lois Long trumpeted something at Macy's, for instance, other stores were sure to howl. The same was true with apartments, cars, or any other goods Ross's writers saw fit to discuss. If a dustup proved serious enough, as Cain recalled, "then at last there is a *conference*" at which Fleischmann, the business staff, Ross, and his current Jesus would huddle to talk it out.

Cain paints a memorable picture of what happened next. "The front office boys, one by each, explain why it has to be done thus and such way, in words of one syllable, so Ross can get it through his notoriously thick head—or perhaps not thick head, as they see it, but wacky head, a head not born for the intricacies and subtleties and futilities of business. To all this Ross listens with obvious pain, but some sick imitation of a smile pasted on his face, for in spite of a notion to the contrary he does have some impulses toward courtesy, and doesn't like to hurt feelings." Ross patiently hears everyone out, after which there is a long, uncomfortable silence, so that Fleischmann and the others start to wonder if he has even been paying attention. Then, slowly, the editor begins to talk. "He announces, not in the like-to-speak-on-the-motion way the others have done, but in a flat, definitive tone, like a P.E. rector beginning 'I am the Resurrection and the Life.' Presently he says: 'So this is the way we're going to do it.' He explains the way. He explains the reasons. They're solid, cogent reasons, that take account of pesky business angles the businessmen don't appear to have thought of. It's wholly different from their way, but before he gets done all of them know it's the right way and the only way. He finishes, then gets up and goes out, with no fare-thee-well of any kind: too preoccupied. All sit looking at each other, then somebody looks at his watch. Fleischmann looks relieved, as though at last it's settled with less fuss than might have been expected, considering Ross. And yet there is a look on his face that makes you wonder how much fun he gets out of publishing this, what is supposed to be his magazine, but apparently is whatever Ross decrees it to be, after which it makes still more money."

———

AFTER ENOUGH SUCH SCENES, THE INEVITABLE ROSS STORIES, heretofore confined to the intramural Round Table–journalism-Broadway circles, began finding wider, but just as appreciative, audiences. A mythos about this vulgar, gat-toothed Merlin, the mad genius of Forty-fifth Street, was starting to build in earnest.

Then in the summer of 1934, the world at large was introduced to Ross. A splashy eighteen-page article in *Fortune* magazine drew back the curtain, really for the first time, on *The New Yorker* operation. The effect of the piece, written anonymously by Ralph Ingersoll, was to partly explain and partly enhance the burgeoning Ross legend.

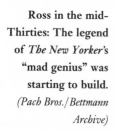

Ross in the mid-Thirties: The legend of *The New Yorker*'s "mad genius" was starting to build.
(Pach Bros./Bettmann Archive)

By this time Ingersoll was managing editor of *Fortune,* the follow-up brainchild of *Time* founder Henry Luce. His agents had begun wooing Ingersoll in late 1929, offering to double his pay, and the following summer he opted to go. He delayed breaking the news to Ross for fear of another violent scene, or at the very least reproach. Instead Ross listened sullenly to Ingersoll's reasons for leaving, not saying a word. At last Ingersoll asked, "Well?" Ross simply sighed and said, "Hell, Ingersoll, *Fortune* was invented for you to edit." After another protracted pause, he added, "G'bye."

In the *Fortune* article Ingersoll discussed Ross's background, personal quirks, unorthodox management style, and editorial acumen at great length, and detailed the contributions of Ross's top editors, writers, and artists, as well as Fleischmann, John Hanrahan, and other key business executives. There were many facts and figures about the magazine's rocky start-up and current balance sheet (this was, after all, *Fortune*), and an assessment of how it was weathering the Depression. Ingersoll gently chided the magazine for not being more egalitarian, but in general the article was flattering and positive.

This was not how it was construed in the *New Yorker* rabbit warrens, where there was great consternation. Apparently the magazine that made an art form out of poking into other people's business was itself rather thin-skinned. Ross had to deal with the fallout for weeks. For instance, he had to hose off an incensed Gluyas Williams, who, the article said (inaccurately), generated none of his own cartoon ideas. Far more upsetting to the staff, however, were Ingersoll's printed guesses, generally high, about their annual salaries. Ross himself was compelled to post a note saying, "It is not true that I get $40,000 a year." In the following week's Comment, White wrote this single line, "The editor of *Fortune* gets $30-a-week and carfare," an observation that surely baffled countless *New Yorker* readers. There was much talk of retaliation, such as a full-blown parody of *Fortune* or *Time*. Ross rejected these but ultimately did authorize a Profile of Luce, which, when it appeared in November 1936, drew the first serious blood in the escalating feud between *Time* and *The New Yorker*.

For the moment, however, Ross had more serious things to worry about than trading spitballs with Harry Luce. For one thing, his mother had recently died. The previous November Ida Ross had broken her leg in a fall, and she never really recovered. At the time she was living in the small town of Hillsdale, New York, a few hours north of the city, looked after by her dead husband's relatives. Ross saw his mother often in her last years, usually stopping on his way to or from the Saratoga area, where he liked to relax with his cousin and boyhood friend Wesley Gilson, now an executive with the Niagara Mohawk electric utility, or with Frank Sullivan. After his father's death in 1925, he had tried to board his mother with relatives, knowing how much she hated New York, but Ida proved to be difficult and bossy, and she moved around quite a bit until settling down in Hillsdale a year or two before her death. She was buried there in a small country cemetery, which Ross visited every year.

Fortunately there were happier diversions in 1934 as well. Early that year Ross was introduced to a beautiful and mysterious Frenchwoman half his age. Her name was Marie Françoise Elie, but Ross always called her Frances.

Born in southern France in 1911, Frances came to Canada when she was nine to live with an aunt in Montreal. She took a trip to New York in June 1932, and that September married a man named William Pierce Clark. The young couple moved about a great deal, living in New Mexico and Florida before returning to New York, but after little more than a year they were divorced.

Mutual acquaintances introduced Frances to Ross. She knew very little English when they met, but being stylish and French, she was a vision to a confirmed Francophile like Ross, and he was captivated instantly. For her part, the young woman apparently was charmed by the solicitous affections of this successful older man.

In other words, the two had practically nothing in common, as they would later discover to their regret. But as Patricia Ross points

Frances Ross.
*(New Yorker
Collection, New York
Public Library)*

out, in that more innocent time something as trivial as incompatibility seldom kept people from the altar. After a whirlwind courtship,
they were secretly wed on May 16.

Hard as Ross had fallen, romance hadn't swept him away entirely:
continuing to feel the financial headaches of his divorce from Jane,
he had Frances sign a prenuptial agreement. Still, there was every
indication that by now Ross was more than ready to exchange a
singing cop for *une demoiselle charmante.*

CHAPTER 8

FLEISCHMANN

RAOUL HERBERT FLEISCHMANN WAS BORN IN AUGUST 1885 IN THE SPA resort of Ischl, in the Austrian Alps. He was the sixth and last child of Louis Fleischmann, a career army officer, and his high-spirited Viennese wife, Wilhelmine. The Fleischmanns had resettled in America a decade earlier; Raoul's rather dramatic arrival came as the family was on summer holiday in the homeland. Still, there was something fitting about Raoul's being born on the Continent, for he would grow up to become a gentleman very much in the Old World European manner: genteel, immaculately groomed and tailored, well-spoken, fluent in three languages, and with an ease about money that can come only from growing up with it. Raoul Fleischmann didn't drive; he motored. Had his family never left Vienna, he might have been an accomplished boulevardier.

But after much persuading Louis did leave, the last in the large Fleischmann clan to do so. Two brothers, Max and Carl, had blazed the trail for the rest, having come to America shortly after the

Civil War to exploit a specific business opportunity. The brothers owned the foreign rights to an Austrian patent for making compressed yeast, and they knew that much of the yeast produced across the United States was unreliable. They set up a manufacturing business in Brooklyn, then aggressively and methodically expanded west, buying out or undercutting the smaller domestic yeast-makers. Their consolidation efforts were so successful that by the turn of the century Fleischmann's Yeast Company, now based in Cincinnati, was the top producer in America, well on its way to spawning several generations of millionaires.

Louis Fleischmann was not directly involved in the yeast business, though a small stake in it provided him a very handsome income, about sixty thousand dollars a year as Raoul was growing up. To promote its product, the family established the Fleischmann Vienna Model Bakery at the 1876 Centennial in Philadelphia. The restaurant proved such a success that it was transplanted to Tenth Street and Broadway in New York, and the family prevailed on Louis to run it. Though the café was popular, Louis was unhappy and eventually gave it up, but not before leaving a small mark on American culture. To underscore the fresh-baked quality of his bread, each evening Louis gave away the restaurant's unused loaves to passersby. Word of these handouts got around, and thus was born the concept of the "breadline."

Louis went on to establish a bakery at Eighty-first Street and East End Avenue. It wasn't a huge success, but it provided an adequate income—which was fortunate, for around this time a family feud over control of Fleischmann's Yeast resulted in the severing of Louis's financial ties to the company. As a boy Raoul was more interested in the old livery horses stabled at the bakery than in the business itself, but after college (one year at Princeton, three at Williams) he dutifully went into the family operation. By 1910 he was running the place, and in 1911 he merged the company with eighteen other New York bakeries to form the General Baking Company, whose first real success came with the introduction of Bond Bread. The twenty-six-year-old Fleischmann managed General's two plants, making a comfortable ten thousand dollars a year at a job that he considered important, if somewhat tedious. In later life, after he had made his own fortune in publishing, he enjoyed referring to himself as "the honest baker."

For all the privilege in his upbringing, and as much as he loved his family, Raoul grew up with strong feelings of disconnection. He and his siblings were not intimate; one older brother was remote, another killed himself, and his sisters, it seemed, were always in Europe. He was probably closest to his flamboyant cousin Julius, Carl's son, who came to run Fleischmann's Yeast and whose death in 1925 so unsettled Raoul. A more fundamental rootlessness, and one that tormented him all his life, involved his heritage. The Fleischmanns were Jews, but Raoul's parents went to great lengths to camouflage this fact, if not expunge it altogether, even to the point of baptizing Raoul and his brothers and sisters as Catholics. "We never went to Sunday school; we never went to church; we certainly never went to any temple, and I did not know what I was," Fleischmann would write near the end of his life in his private history of the family. "Why they gave up the Jewish religion, I have no idea, and they did it in the most sloppy, unworthy way. They just let the whole subject of religion drop out of their lives, and we children were presumably required to make up our own minds."

This denial of heritage by a prosperous family might be understood in light of Austria's virulent anti-Semitism, yet in the family, and within Raoul himself, it caused no end of confusion and conflict. As he acknowledged, "This whole subject is a mess in my life . . . and is one of the few facts that reflects very little credit upon my parents." His emotional discomfort with his Jewishness at times verged on disdain, it seems; on more than one occasion acquaintances were taken aback to hear the usually gracious Fleischmann utter an anti-Semitic slur. When Ross approached the publisher about stopping advertisements in *The New Yorker* by restricted hotels and resorts, Fleischmann, whose extended family had built so many summer homes in one part of the Catskills that a nearby village was renamed Fleischmann, is reported to have replied that the ads were actually a

Raoul Fleischmann and son Peter, circa 1930. *(Walter Scottshinn)*

service "because then the Jewish clientele knows forthrightly where they are not made comfortable." Eventually he relented, and in 1942 all restricted advertising was banned from the magazine.

Raoul Fleischmann was a short man, elegant, good company, with twinkling blue eyes and a touch of noblesse oblige. He was a person of habit. His lunchtime regime, for instance, seldom varied: two Beefeater martinis straight up, a dozen oysters on the half shell, and ice cream. He never lost his love of gambling and horses, interests that neatly converged in his passion for Thoroughbred racing. As a businessman he was neither a screamer nor a backslapper. He was firm but effectively low key with the business-side people, who genuinely liked and respected him. His office door literally was always open to them, and anyone dropping by could count on finding him in his suit coat, never in shirtsleeves. If he was not as creative as Ross, he was intelligent and, more important, shrewd. Where Ross was a doubtful poker player because his face forever betrayed his hand,

Fleischmann was a good one because he was unflappable. He also tended to keep his own counsel. At the outset of *The New Yorker,* when he knew nothing about magazine publishing, he never let on; instead, he learned as he went. And the more he learned, the more he relished this life he had fallen into, a business about as far away from the predictable, prosaic world of baking as could be imagined. He was always as proud of *The New Yorker* as Ross was, if not more so.

Certainly Fleischmann had earned the right. Having been lulled into the enterprise back in 1924 on the understanding that his total contribution would be twenty-five thousand dollars, Fleischmann actually spent over the next three years the better part of his total net worth, some seven hundred thousand dollars. (Of that total, a hundred thousand came from his wife, Ruth, who had considerable independent means.) Week after week he wrote personal checks to cover the magazine's bills. At first he took back more stock in exchange, but when his stake reached fifty percent—Ross's never exceeded his original ten percent—Fleischmann stopped increasing his equity, and the last half of his investment amounted to loans that he prayed his magazine might one day be in a position to repay. It was never Fleischmann's intention to accumulate a huge personal stake in *The New Yorker*—with subsequent splits he let his share fall back to thirty-five percent—and over the years he was fairly liberal in bestowing stock on business-side executives. (A handful of key editorial employees—but only a handful, such as the Whites—received stock too.)

How was it, then, that this affable man, who was either too foolish or too sentimental to let *The New Yorker* die, came to earn the "mortal antipathy" of his partner, Harold Ross, the kind of gut-level disdain that Fleischmann himself described as "a hatred which is almost an obsession"? In the beginning, certainly, anyone could see that the shaggy Ross and the suave Fleischmann were unlikely associates, but how did it happen that they wound up like two antagonists in a knife fight, lashed together at the wrist against their will? That they could go without speaking for years, referring to one another as "that son of a bitch"? That twenty years after they began, Ross would protest being "robbed" by "Fleischmann et al., [who] hogged everything they could hog, which was practically everything there was"?

Looking back on it, their relationship can be charted like a plunging trendline, with several especially nasty clashes serving as the plot points. In general, though, their differences could always be reduced to one question: Where should the money go? According to Peter Fleischmann, who succeeded Raoul as publisher of *The New Yorker,* "My father used to say that he and Ross always got along well until they began making money, and that's when the trouble started."

———

A *NEW YORKER* HALLMARK, FROM THE MAGAZINE'S EARLIEST DAYS, HAS been the extraordinary separation of business from editorial—what staffers on both sides have always called church and state. The concept transcended editorial independence to include physical separation: in their first home and their second (in 1935 *The New Yorker* moved to its better-known address, 25 West Forty-third Street), the business and editorial employees were on different floors, kept apart, with fraternizing regarded more like trespassing. This philosophy dates from the beginning, that brief but crucial time when the two men were truly "equal" partners, even financially. Of course Ross would have insisted on complete editorial freedom, and Fleischmann, not yet knowing the ways of meddling publishers, would have concurred. Rather quickly they established "the ground rules," as William Shawn explained it years later: "The publisher was to have the overall responsibility for the business, and the editor was to have the responsibility for the magazine," a neat and not insignificant distinction. The editor had full control of the editorial product, staff, and operation—that is to say, what the magazine *was*—without interference from the business side. The publisher's job was to find the revenue and pay the bills. Should he become dissatisfied with the performance of the editor, as part of his "overall responsibility" the publisher theoretically could remove him. Of course, at *The New Yorker* this would always prove to be a little trickier in practice than in theory.

Still, this was their "understanding," and to his credit, even when Fleischmann came to appreciate just how extraordinary was the freedom that Ross had demanded and got, he very seldom attempted to traduce it. The minor qualification is necessary because inevitably there were exceptions. In the late Twenties, for instance, he coerced Ross into accepting one of his close friends, Arthur Samuels, as the magazine's Jesus. Ross couldn't abide Samuels, especially after he filled his office with pricey rugs and other lavish furnishings, in stark contrast to the editor's own spartan, linoleum-lined accommodations. Ross fired him by telegram just as he was returning from a long European vacation. After Samuels bawled him out for this cheap gesture, Ross sheepishly admitted to a friend, "I did a thing no decent man would have done."

Then there were invariable fights about editorial material bound to offend squeamish advertisers. Fleischmann was particularly acrimonious on the occasion in 1934 when Ross ran a casual spoofing a series of Camel ads, wherein attractive housewives testified to the calming property of the cigarettes (Says Mrs. Phyllis L. Potter, Montclair, New Jersey: "I can smoke Camels freely without a hint of jumpy nerves!"). As if the piece wouldn't invite enough trouble on its own, due to an oversight it was printed right next to one of the ads it was lampooning.

In the main, however, Fleischmann showed stunning self-restraint with the editorial side, considering that essentially he owned *The New Yorker*. He read and enjoyed the magazine like everyone else— after it came off the press. He didn't ask to see stories ahead of time, and he reserved his opinions afterward so as not to sway the editorial department, either consciously or unconsciously, with his likes and dislikes. He even honored, at times to his irritation, the physical segregation. In 1943, when Edmund Wilson joined the staff of *The New Yorker* as the chief book reviewer, he had heard about this famous division of business from editorial, but being familiar with publishing he had his doubts. Then Fleischmann invited him to lunch and arranged to meet him in the building's lobby. "I was sorry not to come to your office," the publisher explained, "but you know the situation here." As Wilson would subsequently observe, "It was a little like a Russian grand duke in exile."

This, then, was the backdrop, largely Ross-imposed, to the three-decade relationship between *New Yorker* editor and publisher: Go about your business, and leave me to go about mine. It was truly a liberating philosophy for a magazine, and it made for a vigorous, uninhibited product. On the other hand this segregation, with its inherent suspicions and implicit distrust, tended to undermine any fragile bond that might once have existed between Ross and Fleischmann.

As mentioned previously, Ross's resentment of Fleischmann really began at the beginning, in 1925, when the latter sought to repair the damage from Ross's poker debacle, and the editor's guilt only swelled as Fleischmann's bank account drained. Their relationship was exacerbated by the appearance of John Hanrahan, just as future issues would exacerbate it: the allocation of dividends, staff pay, the direction of the company's board, and, ultimately, the extent to which Fleischmann had profited, and Ross had not, from *The New Yorker*'s phenomenal success. Over the years, as in most personal feuds, Ross's antagonism took on a life of its own, out of all proportion to its ostensible causes. Within a few years of the magazine's start, intermediaries were required to conduct any serious business between Ross and Fleischmann. Their mutual friend Hawley Truax, a businessman-scholar (and a man who never spent a dollar when a dime would do), performed this delicate task informally until 1942, when he joined the magazine's employ and gave over his career to keeping the peace at *The New Yorker*.

Personalities aside, Fleischmann's biggest problem, plain and simple, was that he was the embodiment of the magazine's business side. Ross's disdain was evident in the smallest details: he labeled a folder that bulged with ongoing problems and disputes, largely with the business side, his "Hell File." He forever complained that the magazine's sales effort was token (the salesmen themselves were "ad-takers" or "plugs"), its circulation strategy misguided, its promotional materials insipid and wasteful. For twenty-six years he argued that there was a better way to advance the cause of *The New Yorker:* simply put the money into editorial. Ross firmly believed the magazine sold itself; no doubt it did to a point, but Fleischmann was enough of a businessman to know that even free ice cream doesn't sell itself. Still, for the most part he suffered in silence, considering Ross's invective the price to be paid for his golden editorial touch. "Harold just had a great distaste for business people, or anybody who was not creative," Fleischmann explained. "For creative people he had the greatest respect, but the business office was made up of people who did 'chores' (which was one of his favorite words involving our labors) and we were beneath contempt."

———

IN TRUTH, THE SEEDS OF DEEPEST DISCORD BETWEEN THE TWO MEN were planted in 1929, and at first they had nothing whatever to do with Raoul Fleischmann.

When Ross and Jane Grant were working out the details of their divorce, the independent Jane was uninterested in conventional alimony; besides, Ross was practically broke. On the other hand, she was concerned for her long-term security, especially given her parlous health, and she was intent on deriving some dividend from her hard work and personal sacrifice in behalf of *The New Yorker.* After some negotiation, then, the divorcing couple came up with a creative and, at the time, a win-win solution. Ross put four hundred and fifty shares of his charter F-R Publishing Corporation stock into a trust for Jane. She would receive all dividends from the stock up to ten thousand dollars a year. In the event that the dividends fell short of ten thousand dollars, Ross would pay the difference. (To further protect her, he took out a fifty-thousand-dollar life insurance policy on himself, with Jane the beneficiary.)

This arrangement caused Ross no real hardship for the first few years, as the magazine repaid most of its robust earnings to shareholders. With the deepening of the Depression, however, Fleischmann made an important decision that inadvertently would cost Ross dearly. The publisher decided it would be prudent for *The New*

Yorker to build up over several years a large cash reserve, a kind of corporate rainy-day fund. To accomplish this, of course, the company had to cut back its dividend, so suddenly Ross found himself writing Jane big checks every quarter. The "Jane Grant agreement," as it was known to one and all within the *New Yorker* hierarchy—for it was something virtually everyone had to deal with, in one way or another—became an unending nightmare for the editor, looming over every financial decision he made for almost twenty years.

As with so many aspects of his character, Ross was wildly contradictory where money was concerned. On the one hand, he had a sophisticated grasp of finance and meticulously tracked the performances of dozens of stocks and bonds in his portfolio. On the other, he could be so cavalier as to walk around Manhattan with blank checks peeking out from his coat pockets, or sign over his power of attorney to a secretary and promptly forget about it for years. He used to say, "I only want enough money to live on," by which he actually meant enough to live *comfortably* on: to be able to afford a nice home and car, domestic help, good Broadway tickets; to have the wherewithal to play poker all night or take off for Colorado or California without worrying how to pay for it. Beyond this, money was basically a nuisance, something that required him to spend his precious time with lawyers and accountants instead of writers and editors. To him, money was more significant in terms of what it represented, and where Fleischmann was concerned, increasingly it came to represent inequity, certainly, and even perhaps iniquity. The way Ross saw it, he was working sixty-hour weeks to ensure the excellence of *The New Yorker*, but for all his trouble he was struggling to stay afloat financially, while Fleischmann and his associates (or as the editor put it, his "stooges," his "ring of stupid fumblers") pulled in much more of the proceeds.

Still, by itself Ross's running debt to Jane Grant was not at first a crippling burden, even allowing for a Park Avenue address, the travel, the dinners at "21," and the sometimes extravagant gambling debts. In the early Thirties he was generally earning more than thirty thousand dollars a year in total compensation (salary and bonuses), and he still held several thousand shares of increasingly valuable F-R stock. When the "Jane Grant agreement" was piled atop his many other financial obligations, however, it all became too much. For years he had been providing for his widowed mother. No sooner did she pass away than he remarried and acquired another big apartment to furnish. No sooner had he married than the happy couple was expecting. Most ominously, the Internal Revenue Service had its hooks into him for several thousand dollars (which he disputed) in back taxes over his *New Yorker* stock, the opening skirmish in what would be a deleterious twenty-year war with the tax man. Partly because of his tax woes, Ross, who always before had harangued employees who fled the city for the bucolic 'burbs, was even contemplating a move to Connecticut, which had no state income tax. Yet a house would mean still another financial burden.

The upshot was that by the summer of 1934, Ross was strapped for cash. He turned to his only real asset, his stock. A part of him was reluctant to sell, because of the exigent circumstances and because he was convinced the stock's value would keep rising. On the other hand, he had been thinking about divesting for some time anyway because he had a nagging sense that somehow, even subconsciously, his editorial judgments were subject to compromise if he had to worry about their potential impact on *The New Yorker*'s bottom line. That would be an intolerable encumbrance. He had given the same reason for quitting the company's board of directors shortly after *The New Yorker* started. He wanted to be free to do what he pleased, including criticizing the company's business practices. It scarcely needs saying that he exercised this freedom liberally.

Since Ross regarded Fleischmann as the chief source of his predicament, he wielded the stock sale like a club. That August— ironically, at the very time he was sweeping up behind the nettlesome *Fortune* story—he sold the bulk of his stock to Time Inc.

Ross knew that Fleischmann would have bought back his stock in an instant, especially if the alternative was seeing it go to a rival publisher, and particularly if that publisher was Henry Luce. But Fleischmann, vacationing in Europe at the time, didn't have the chance because Ross didn't tell him. According to Ralph Ingersoll, who quietly helped swing the deal, the whole affair was coming on the heels of some recent indignity or other, with the editor ranting about not wanting to own stock in "Fleischmann's company" and taking pains to make sure the transaction was kept secret.

Ross started the process by asking a Wall Street friend, Philip Boyer, to shop the stock discreetly. Boyer, in turn, approached the well-connected Ingersoll for the names of prospective buyers. Ingersoll apprised Time's corporate officers, suggesting that a happy opportunity had just presented itself. With that, the treasurer of Time, Charles Stillman, arranged to have lunch with Ross and talk things over; before dessert he had agreed to purchase 2,190 shares for $104,000, or $47.50 a share. (The stock split two months later.) Out of curiosity, Stillman asked Ross why he wanted to part with the stock. The editor reiterated his vague discomfort with having a financial stake in his own magazine, but later Stillman said he did not find this overly convincing.

Time bought Ross's stock not with any mischief in mind but because it regarded *The New Yorker* as a sound investment. Luce, in fact, was not even involved in the transaction. Nonetheless, before long word was racing around *The New Yorker* offices that the dreaded Luce had acquired a big chunk of their stock (the identity of the turncoat was as yet a mystery, though not for long). Takeover rumors flew. Juicier still was the speculation that Luce intended to make a wedding present of *The New Yorker* to his fiancée, the glamorous Clare Boothe, then managing editor of *Vanity Fair*.

Not only did the dire predictions fail to materialize, but the following year Ross had Boyer approach Time again about the possibility of buying up the rest of his F-R holdings. By this point Time was on the verge of adopting a policy against investing in other publications, so Stillman passed and Ross sold the stock elsewhere. In 1936, Time sold its F-R stock at a handsome profit. Eventually Fleischmann was able to reacquire the rogue stock, still irate at having lost it in the first place.

Again Ross told Boyer (as he would later tell many of his colleagues, including Thurber, St. Clair McKelway, and Ik Shuman) that he wanted to divest in order to safeguard his editorial independence. Though his financial dilemma was a factor, there is no question that Ross's ethical impulses were genuine, as they were completely consistent with his lifelong management views and conduct. By the early Forties the founder of *The New Yorker* held just eighty-six shares, out of a total of eighty-five thousand outstanding, in his own company, and by 1948 he held none at all. Ross's divestiture may or may not have been unprecedented for an editor-entrepreneur, but it bespoke a remarkable professional ethic at a time when the prevailing scruple was perhaps better typified by Frank Crowninshield, who was known to buy a painting he liked, then publicize the artist in *Vanity Fair* to drive up the value of his investment.

Yet it must be said that Ross had one other important motivation for selling his stock in 1934 and 1935: fear. For Fleischmann had just committed *New Yorker* money to an enterprise that Ross was convinced would come to a bad end, and to his everlasting dismay he was right. As Ross told Katharine White long after the fact, "I got onto the *Stage* thing enough to know that it was a near-disaster and sold most of my stock then, thank God, or my ruin would have been complete."

The "*Stage* thing" was Fleischmann's sub rosa decision to underwrite a magazine that turned out to be, in essence, a direct competitor to *The New Yorker*. When *Stage* finally blew up and Ross learned the full extent of *The New Yorker*'s support, "his resentment was almost boundless," Fleischmann admitted. This was the breach, he said, that "was never healed."

To understand how Fleischmann got himself into such a bizarre predicament, it must be remembered that in the Thirties he not only was infatuated with publishing but had won big on his first try. The gambler in him was tempted to roll again. At the same time, the businessman in him believed a little diversification might be wise; *The New Yorker* was going fine, yes, but how long could an upscale magazine expect to prosper in a depression economy? So he was open to reasonable-sounding propositions. Before there was a *Newsweek*, for instance, James M. Cain seriously interested Fleischmann in starting up a competitor to *Time*. Cain wanted Mencken to edit it; when Mencken flatly refused, that was that. In 1935, F-R bought a stake in Condé Nast, which not only published *Vanity Fair* and *Vogue* but operated printing plants that produced, among other magazines, *The New Yorker*. At about this same time, his old friend and consultant John Hanrahan asked Fleischmann to help underwrite a new publication, *Stage*, and Fleischmann agreed.

A big, glossy book, *Stage* at first meant to focus almost exclusively on theater, which is probably why Fleischmann didn't think it would compete directly with *The New Yorker*. But to Ross it was clear from the start that Hanrahan was aiming for the same readers (and perhaps more important, the same advertisers) as *The New Yorker*. He also had no confidence in Hanrahan and believed that focusing on such a narrow subject as theater, especially in a bad economy, doomed *Stage* from the start. Indeed, it didn't take Hanrahan long to recast the struggling publication more broadly as the magazine for "after-dark" entertainment, and to make it even more imitative of *The New Yorker*. Hanrahan wasn't subtle in his copycat intentions: *Stage* employed drawn covers, tried (and failed) to achieve a similar sense of off-hand elegance, and ran a knockoff of *The New Yorker*'s Goings On calendar. Most galling of all to Ross, *Stage* was paying better money to *New Yorker* contributors for lesser work, and he was in effect subsidizing it.

Ross was apoplectic over the situation. He despised everything about *Stage*. He hated Hanrahan, hated the fact that free ads for *Stage* regularly ran in *The New Yorker*, hated that his contributors were being diverted as if to a bawdy house. *Stage* was a "preposterous enterprise," Ross told Fleischmann. "I could understand your spending money to put it out of business; I cannot understand your spending one cent to support it." Nonetheless, the publisher stuck with Hanrahan as stubbornly as he had stuck with Ross ten years before. The only difference was that this time the money was not really his own to spend, but *The New Yorker*'s.

Fleischmann was able to do as he pleased since his board of directors was largely filled with friends, Hanrahan among them, and was most perfunctory. For several years Ross was largely kept in the dark about the extent of *The New Yorker*'s subsidization of *Stage*. This was not unusual; he was always complaining about a lack of financial information, though the situation was largely his own doing because he tended to scold business-side denizens who interrupted him with their tiny problems. Still, he surmised that the total outlay was into the high six figures, and climbing. Then in April 1938, when he saw annual report figures and became alarmed over what a drag *Stage* was becoming on his magazine, he prevailed on Fleischmann for a complete accounting. A day or two later Fleischmann complied, and Ross got the whole unpleasant picture: Hanrahan was into *The New Yorker* for nearly a million dollars, and Ross's own magazine actually owned thirty-six percent of *Stage*. The loans supposedly were secured by Hanrahan's shares in *The New Yorker*, but his equity was nowhere close to covering *The New Yorker*'s investment.

The next day Ross rampaged into the office. "I'm not going to work myself to death so we can lose money in a magazine that competes with us," Ross told Shuman. "I'm going to tell Fleischmann he has to get *The New Yorker* out of *Stage*."

The editor sat down, pulled his typewriter close, and started banging. When he was through he gave the one-page document to Shuman to read, then to ferry personally to Fleischmann. It was a Tuesday afternoon, and the memo was an ultimatum.

Said Ross, "Unless, before 5 p.m. Friday of this week, I have your written promise that you will stop the financial contributions to *Stage* . . . I shall terminate my services with the F-R Publishing Corporation with the closing of the present issue of *The New Yorker*. You are requested to consider this communication as notice to that effect."

Ross's threat to quit was nothing new. He employed the tactic so often, over transgressions large and small, that it became a kind of intramural *New Yorker* sport. McKelway recalled that after his first year as managing editor, he was hoping for an increase in pay; Ross sprang into action, dashing off a note to Fleischmann insisting on a three-thousand-dollar raise for McKelway. "If this demand is not met, I quit," Ross wrote. He showed the note to McKelway and said with a grin, "How will that do?" McKelway replied that as touched as he was by the gesture, the matter certainly wasn't important enough for Ross to quit over. "Ah, nuts to them," Ross said. McKelway got the raise.

The difference this time was that Ross's threat was in deadly earnest.

There was no word from Fleischmann that Wednesday, or on Thursday morning. At this point, with Ross looking grim and the atmosphere growing more ominous by the hour, Shuman took it on himself to intervene. He rode over to Fleischmann's Park Avenue apartment, where he found the publisher nursing a cold but otherwise sanguine. Shuman asked him what he intended to do. The publisher replied that this time he had decided to accept Ross's resignation. He even had a successor in mind, Arthur Krock of *The New York Times*.

Shuman was not altogether surprised. Tactfully he tried to point out that as capable as Krock was, bringing in any new editor amounted to taking a huge risk with *The New Yorker*, whereas Ross, for all his aggravations, was a proven success.

Fleischmann frowned. "Ross is so bad mannered," he said.

This was scarcely news to Shuman, who arguably endured more tongue-lashings from Ross than any other person in his employ. Still, for the sake of *The New Yorker* he pressed Ross's case, and in time the logic of his argument carried the day. Swallowing hard, Fleischmann relented: he would withdraw from *Stage* immediately. "Tell Harold he's won again," Fleischmann said. The note to Ross came the next day.

Even taking into account Hanrahan's stock, which reverted to *The New Yorker*, the *Stage* debacle cost the magazine about $750,000. There was never a full airing to the stockholders, and Fleischmann, while conceding and regretting the "unsound investment," never really explained it. The fallout from this unhappy episode did have a profound effect on the onetime gambler, however, as it transformed him into one of the most conservative publishers in New York. In later years, when *The New Yorker* was awash in cash, Fleischmann would be teased about his stodgy accounting practices and his preference for Treasury notes over acquisitions and other glitzy investments. The lesson of *Stage* had been a sobering one.

A few weeks later, perhaps emboldened by his successful ultimatum, and having lost what shred of confidence he still had in the magazine's management, Ross once again raised the specter of resignation. He told Fleischmann that his financial picture had become so clouded that he would have to leave *The New Yorker* unless his compensation was improved substantially. He blamed Fleischmann's business decisions, which he said had weakened *The New Yorker* and thereby substantially enhanced Ross's indebtedness to his first wife. "I . . . find myself in what I must candidly call my late forties with my finances depleted to a point where I have no confidence in keeping up with my obligations," he said. "Hence, something must be done." He added helpfully that he was considering other "opportunities," which no doubt referred to his proposed detective magazine; unknown to Fleischmann, he was exploring its feasibility and costs more seriously now than at any other time.

Apparently Fleischmann's first reaction was to approach Andy and Katharine White about replacing Ross as coeditors. They thought it over for a few days but then told Fleischmann that because of their loyalty to Ross the idea was out of the question.

Stymied again, Fleischmann put together an attractive package for Ross that, at least for the time being, placated his demanding counterpart. His salary was set at thirty thousand dollars, but he was given a fifteen-thousand-dollar annual expense account. He and his wife would get at least two company-paid trips a year "to Florida, California or Europe or to such other places . . . where the type of subscribers, to which *The New Yorker* caters, or writes about, are accustomed to congregate." He was also free to work out of his new home in north Stamford, Connecticut, rather than the office, as often as he wished.

With this amelioration Fleischmann ducked another Ross bullet, but he would face yet one more serious consequence from the *Stage* episode—an all-out *New Yorker* civil war.

The *Stage* loss had decimated *The New Yorker*'s cash position just as war was breaking out in Europe. Advertising for European travel, as well as luxury items generally, eroded quickly. The magazine's revenues flattened and profits shrank. In 1942, which would prove to be its worst financial year of the war, *The New Yorker* made only $107,000 on sales of $2.5 million, the thinnest margin since it had started making money back in 1927.

Such were the glum realities when the company's board met early in 1942. The F-R dividend had been moribund at $1.50 per share for several years, but now the directors, pessimistic about the immediate future, voted to pass it altogether. For increasingly disgruntled secondary shareholders, this act was the final straw. For all his affability, in their view Fleischmann had been far too cavalier with the company's money; more to the point, he wasn't moving aggressively enough to find new revenue or to cut expenses. A number of the stockholders banded together to take aim at the publisher's handsome head. The insurgents were led by Jane Grant and Fleischmann's now ex-wife, Ruth, who held the second-largest block of shares. (Upon hearing that Ruth Fleischmann had married *Country Life* editor and publisher Peter Vischer in 1937, Ross dryly reported to E. B. White that he was working harder than ever since "we have another little mouth to feed.")

Jane and the Vischers lined up another shareholder, lawyer Lloyd Paul Stryker, to lead an informal investigation into Fleischmann's management and to pursue any subsequent legal action or negotiations. Truax, Stryker's brother-in-law, joined in, as did several other small shareholders. A few demurred, however; Katharine and E. B. White especially were offended by the revolt and feared it would undermine the magazine.

Ross initially stayed out of the fight, pointing out that he had only a few shares left; besides, the interests of the editor and the shareholders "weren't exactly parallel." Nonetheless, he made it clear that he sympathized completely with the Grant-Vischer faction. And the more Ross heard of Stryker's findings, the angrier he got; finally, in May, he bluntly informed Fleischmann that he was throwing in with the other side.

Sportsmen: Raoul
Fleischmann, left, and
older brother
Charles. Ross once
said that he would
sooner see *New Yorker*
profits go to the
writers than to the
publisher, "who would
just lose it at the races."
(Bettmann Archive)

The rebellious shareholders threatened to sue Fleischmann for past malfeasance in running *The New Yorker* if he refused to relinquish the chairmanship and otherwise agree to a serious change in the magazine's management. They made a special point of their intention to hold him and Hanrahan personally liable for the *Stage* losses.

It was all very exasperating to the proud Fleischmann, and his initial impulse was to fight. He believed he could beat the malfeasance charge, and so did his lawyers. Yet he also understood that a high-profile court fight would sully him personally and might well devastate *The New Yorker*. In the end he determined that compromise would be best, and in June the two sides commenced what would be painful, protracted negotiations.

During an especially difficult four-hour session in Stryker's Wall Street office, Fleischmann deliberately reviewed, point by point, the opposition's bill of particulars. For a few moments he mulled over their proposed new board of directors. "As I get it, this new board is to be a kind of jury to pass upon the management," Fleischmann said, a defendant's air of resignation in his voice.

That's what this board, or any board, should be, Stryker concurred.

"Well," replied Fleischmann, "let's look over [it] and see whether I am getting a fair jury."

After months of haggling, an agreement was reached early in 1943. The board was trimmed, and only two of Fleischmann's aides— Eugene Spaulding and Raymond Bowen—remained, a face-saving gesture to the humbled publisher. Ross rejoined the board. Fleischmann was forced to vote his shares with the board's majority for five years, while Ross's job was assured for the same length of time (he had the option of renewing it in one-year contracts). Fleischmann remained president, but was joined by Truax and Stryker on an executive committee that would make all the key management decisions. Truax officially joined the company as treasurer—or, more accurately, as on-site referee.

It was a near-complete repudiation of Fleischmann, who was stripped of most of his power and all of his independence. He managed to accept it with the good grace that was his hallmark, and years later he would reassert his authority over the board and the magazine. Yet the *New Yorker* civil war had wrung any lingering innocence from the enterprise and unquestionably took a good bit of the joy out of the job for Fleischmann.

There would be more haggling with Ross in the coming years— over staff pay, stock, editorial space, advertising, printing quality, paper quality, health benefits. . . . By now, however, the pattern of Ross and Fleischmann's nonrelationship was firmly entrenched. They merely muddled along with each other, talking through Truax and trying to put the best face on things for the sake of *The New Yorker*. "Ross was a constant irritation that my father kept under control," said Peter Fleischmann.

Irritating as it was, the twenty-six-year standoff between Raoul Fleischmann and Harold Ross proved extraordinarily profitable, in every sense of the word. Had Fleischmann faced a less implacable adversary than Ross, he might well have been tempted to become more involved with editorial, possibly with dire results. Likewise, if Ross had been loosed on the business side, there would have been no one left to carry out his orders. In its delicate, perverse balance, their acrimony ensured that the product was editorially peerless, which the business side adroitly exploited. True enough, there was real principle behind *The New Yorker*'s vaunted separation of business and editorial. Yet that high wall also proved convenient for two neighbors who eventually couldn't stand the sight of each other.

———

FOR ALL THE CORPORATE INTRIGUE, ROSS WAS MAKING A REAL EFFORT to bring some order to his personal life, a settling down with beneficial results that carried over into the office. If he was just as nervous as ever, and certainly just as driven, he was keeping his passions under tighter control. He was much less the hysterical force of legend; now he was content to dash off a tart memo rather than dress someone down in the middle of the office. Writers and editors who came to *The New Yorker* in the middle to late Thirties describe a Ross with virtually none of the manic attributes that amazed and cowed their counterparts from the middle and late Twenties. There were various reasons for this sea change beyond the natural maturation that usually attends aging. Whenever Ross checked into Riggs or other clinics for rest, his doctors preached the virtues of delegating one's problems, and thereby one's stress, and at long last he was getting comfortable with this . . . sort of. (Once at Riggs, as part of the occupational therapy, Ross built a table; he was so proud of it, Frank Sullivan said, that friends didn't have the heart to tell him that no two legs were the same length.)

Meanwhile, Ross's troublesome stomach was persuading him to curb his drinking. He still took in the occasional party, such as the jazz bashes that E. J. Kahn, Jr., and his roommate, Bruce Bliven, Jr., regularly hosted in the late Thirties (with William Shawn on the piano, always playing in the key of C). He could also still be found at a few favorite hangouts, like Bleeck's and the Coffee House. But his drinking was definitely tapering off, and before long he would give it up altogether.

By far the biggest change in Ross's life, however, was that he became a family man. An unorthodox family man, to be sure, but a family man nevertheless.

Shortly after their low-key wedding Ross and Frances moved into a new apartment on East Thirty-sixth Street, which they had professionally decorated, again at no small expense. Junior Treadwell, Woollcott's valet, saw Ross's spiffy new digs while helping out at a party there. To the unamused Aleck he reported back, "It makes [your] place look like a shit house."

Acquaintances recall the young Frances as charming and gracious, though clearly the pairing with Ross was an odd one. "She was a simple, beautiful, and warm-hearted person, totally unsuited to Ross," Katharine White noted, "but she was likable, decent, and very much the lady." Frances was still not wholly comfortable with English—for some time she had Ross read over all her correspondence before mailing it—and she was neither temperamentally nor linguistically up to his rambling, esoteric conversations. She loved to be out on the town, to shop, and to travel, but she was less at home with other of the national pastimes. As part of his effort to Americanize his French bride, Ross, accompanied by Gibbs and another friend, took her to a Dodgers game at Ebbets Field. No great baseball fan himself, Ross got them box seats right on the first-base line. Unfortunately, Gibbs reported, no fewer than five foul balls pelted their box that afternoon, and Frances decided that "the primary purpose of baseball was to kill the customers."

Frances became pregnant shortly after the marriage ("Conceived in an absent-minded moment, no doubt," offered one *New Yorker* wag), and on March 17, 1935—St. Patrick's Day—delivered a daughter, named Patricia in honor of the occasion. Ross acceded to Frances's request that the girl be baptized Catholic, and a ceremony at St. Patrick's Cathedral was arranged. The only problem was that he had already asked Woollcott to be the godfather, and now he had to take back the invitation since Aleck wasn't of the faith. Another good friend, Frank Sullivan, gladly stood in for the disappointed Woollcott, but the Town Crier was not to be denied altogether. As Sullivan recalled it, at one point in the service the priest asked the godparents to place their hands on each branch of a Y-shaped candle. "As I reached to do so, a hand followed by an arm slid past me from the rear and the hand joined my hand on the candle," Sullivan said. "Need I say that the hand was Aleck's. . . . [He] got in on the baptism in spite of the Church, and I don't suppose Patricia was any the less effectively baptized because of his alien touch."

That September, Ross and Frances bought an acre of land in north Stamford, a scenic, wooded parcel along the Rippowam River. The next year they bought ten adjoining acres, property abutting that of Mount Rushmore sculptor Gutzon Borglum and the Merritt Parkway. That fall they began constructing a large home, and in April 1937 they moved in.

Eighteen years in New York City had made Ross thoroughly

The doting father cradles newborn Patricia, 1935.
(Pach Bros./Courtesy of Patricia Ross Honcoop)

urban, and he would always maintain a residence of some kind in the city, but he loved the serene beauty of his country retreat. Here there was space enough for a man to read galley proofs in utter quiet, or to stroll about the grounds shooting at crows, offending no one save the birds. His combination bedroom-study overlooked the river, and he often worked there late into the night, the rat-tat-tat of his typewriter reverberating through the house.

The Stamford home had been designed with entertaining in mind, and it was common for Ross to have friends out for the weekend. Favorite activities included swimming, badminton, croquet, backgammon, and of course conversation. Lela and Ginger Rogers were frequent guests, and on one occasion Ross asked his friend Bennett Cerf, then still one of New York's most eligible bachelors, to come along to help entertain Lela's young niece, Phyllis. The two hit it off so well that a year later they were married in a service presided over by Mayor Fiorello La Guardia. Matchmaker and best man Ross turned up with a big rifle, the same weapon he trained on the crows, to ensure that Cerf didn't back out.

Astonishing as it was for many of his friends to behold, fatherhood also agreed with Ross. He doted on Patty from her first days till his last, and as the only child of an only child she developed a particularly close bond with him. If he was not as discreet with his language around his daughter as he was with other females—Patty was always told that her first spoken word was "goddammit"—he was in almost every other way a concerned and solicitous parent. He took special interest in her education and intellectual development. For instance, he knew that Patty was intelligent, but when she seemed slow to learn he had her examined by specialists. His instincts were correct, though he never learned the real reason for Patty's classroom trouble: years later, she was diagnosed as dyslexic.

Complete domestic happiness, alas, continued to elude Ross. There was never any fundamental rapport between him and his young wife, and it didn't help that there were parts of his life that he apparently preferred to keep to himself. A case in point was his relationship with certain writers, such as Clarence Day. Ross was in the habit of dropping by the apartment of the bedridden writer during the last few years of his life; Day suffered from a crippling form of arthritis and died in late 1935. The two men would talk for hours, often trading stories about their colorful fathers. Ross, of course, had helped make Day's famous by printing his many "Life with Father" stories. Day's wife, Peg, recalls that one afternoon Ross came by, looking glum, with Frances in tow. Peg pulled the young woman aside and asked what was wrong. "Ross didn't want me to come," Frances said.

Sometimes the experiences Ross *did* wish to share were just as confounding. According to Patricia, her mother was flummoxed, as most wives would be, when her husband invited her along to chat with some local prostitutes. Ross was intrigued by what made people tick—hence his fixation with detective magazines—and over his years of roving he had come to know hundreds of what he called "fallen women." He was genuinely more curious about their lives than their wares, but Frances neither shared nor understood the compulsion.

Before long Ross's second marriage was going the way of the first, a reality that by late 1938 and early 1939 was obvious, if not surprising, to friends. The tension was compounded by a swirl of rumors regarding Frances's pre-Ross pedigree and alleged affairs; doubtless these were spawned, at least in part, by her foreign birth, by the age differential, and by the fact that Frances's brief, mysterious first marriage was not supposed to be common knowledge. A prime source of this upsetting gossip, it turned out, was Woollcott, who never liked Frances—the feeling definitely was mutual—and who was on the outs with Ross early in 1939 after *The New Yorker* published a bittersweet three-part Profile of him (title: "Big Nemo") written by Gibbs.

Quite young at this time, Patricia recalls no pivotal arguments or hysterical scenes between her mother and father. She remembers only how one summer day in 1939 they simply disappeared, not to return for some time. Later she learned that they had gone to Reno to obtain a divorce. Even in Nevada at that time grounds had to be proven, so Frances's complaint accused Ross of "extreme cruelty," alleging that he often stayed out late drinking, and on other occasions was rude to her friends, all of which caused her emotional distress. No doubt there was some truth in the charges, but again—as in Ross's divorce from Jane—everyone knew how to play his or her part. The divorce was decreed on August 26, a Saturday morning. Ross's prenuptial agreement with Frances was annulled, but it didn't matter. That afternoon, Frances drove to Carson City—to get married.

The groom was another Harold—Harold Wilkinson, though he was known to one and all as Tim. An Englishman, Wilkinson was a genial, wealthy Shell Oil executive. He and Ross got on famously from the start, which made the shared custody of Patty much more amicable than it might have been. "He is a man of substance," Ross told Rebecca West, "and it was a thousand to one that she would marry a bum."

———

JUST BEFORE THEIR MARRIAGE BEGAN UNRAVELING, IN THE SUMMER of 1938, Ross took Frances back to Europe for an extended vacation. This was to be something of the grand tour, with stops in England, Scotland, France, and Switzerland. He was most keen to show Frances the World War I battlefields and the Paris of his *Stars and Stripes* years, but anticipating this, she thwarted him. As Frank Sullivan recalled it, "The second they got into the Gare du Nord, or whatever, she popped into Mainbochers with [traveling companion] Sophie Gimbel and didn't come out until four days later, just in time to take the train to Cherbourg. So poor Ross had to go see Noter [sic] Dame alone."

Since he was to be away two months, Ross signed over the power of attorney for his securities to his private secretary, Harold Winney. It was merely a precaution, against the chance that one of his various accounts or trusts would require emergency attention. He already relied on Winney to administer his personal banking and checking anyway, so after he signed the papers he promptly forgot about it. It was the costliest mistake—financially speaking, at least—of his life.

Quiet and mousy, Harold Winney was the very incarnation, some thought, of the Thurber Man. He was also efficient and, most of all, discreet. He had come to *The New Yorker* in 1930 and for half a dozen years had served Ross well and faithfully, not only with his personal finances but in the most sensitive kinds of office matters. As mentioned earlier, it was no easy thing to earn Ross's trust, but once a person had it, he had it for keeps.

Unbeknownst to Ross, Winney had already started his defalcations, albeit on a small scale. Once the timid secretary discovered how little attention his boss paid to bank statements and the like, it was all too easy for him to forge the distinctive "H. W. Ross" scrawl and write himself several checks for cash. As these involved only a few hundred dollars here and there, Ross never noticed. He wrote such checks himself all the time.

By signing over power of attorney for his securities, however, Ross practically invited an escalation of the thefts. Beginning in 1939, Winney grew ever more bold, dipping in and out of Ross's accounts, selling some stock here, transferring some there to keep things outwardly in balance to the editor's unwary eye. A secret gambler, Winney lost much of the money at the track. A homosexual, he lavished increasingly expensive presents on his men friends. Upon Roosevelt's reelection in 1940, Winney threw a champagne party at a suite in the Astor Hotel. Later Ross remarked that he had been by the Astor several times that night. "I was hit on the head by my own champagne corks," he complained in amazement.

Then in 1941 Winney tapped a new source: he began drawing advances on Ross's salary. He could pull off this audacious trick because it was not uncommon for his boss to take advances, and because Ross had his checks deposited directly into the Guaranty Trust Company, where he banked. Of course he also relied on Winney to keep track of these accounts.

As it was, only a chance conversation finally unmasked Winney. That July, just before Ik Shuman was to leave town on vacation, Fleischmann pulled him aside and casually inquired whether Ross was hard up for cash. Shuman was taken aback by the question; he didn't think Ross was particularly pressed, and he asked why Fleischmann thought he was. The publisher replied that the editor had already drawn his salary through that December.

Shuman reported back to Ross, who said no, he believed he was extended only a few months. He called in Winney for an explanation, and the secretary assured him that the advance was only through September. This satisfied Ross, but a few weeks later, when Shuman returned from his vacation, he had Ross's payroll records pulled. Fleischmann had been right; the editor was withdrawn through the end of the year.

Again Ross summoned Winney. Under questioning his secretary admitted that December was correct after all, then launched into an obfuscatory "explanation." A baffled Ross finally waved him off and said the hell with it, he'd stop by the bank tomorrow and find out for himself what was going on.

With that Winney left the office for his Brooklyn apartment. There he scribbled a note, went into the kitchen, turned on the four gas jets on the stove, lay down on the floor, and died. He was thirty-seven.

Friends and colleagues were astounded that Ross could be so thoroughly swindled by his own secretary, but everything about the situation played into Winney's thieving hands. Ross's finances were tremendously complicated, yet he didn't want to be bothered by them. Unexpected revenue was beginning to stream in from the restaurant that he had underwritten for his friend Dave Chasen, and yet there were always gambling losses going out. Moreover, because of his position, Winney was able to intercept any correspondence that might have tipped off his boss. Mostly, however, Winney's crimes were possible because Ross was capable of spectacular inattention. Several years later the editor tried to explain this phenomenon to Stryker: "As I have said, and as few people understand, I get so engrossed in my editorial duties that I slip up in personal matters and, in effect, need a guardian. Anybody—Winney included—can take advantage of me when my eye is off the ball as it necessarily is here." Even in this calamity he managed to make *The New Yorker* culpable.

The money meant less to Ross than the egregious breach of trust, and his initial response to Winney's death was pity. Sitting in the Ritz bar that afternoon with Sullivan, a dazed Ross kept muttering, "The little bastard, why didn't he *say* something to me about it? I wouldn't have thrown him into jail." The next day he told McKelway, "The poor son of a bitch. Christ, if I'd known he was in the hole I could have helped him out." (He couldn't help adding, "Of course he was always at opening nights with a friend—I might have known.")

For days detectives buzzed about the office, trying to make sure Winney's death was really a suicide (it was) and to piece together exactly what had happened. Meanwhile, Ross asked one of his own sleuths, reporter Eugene Kinkead, to assess the full monetary damage. Right away it became clear that the embezzlement was much greater than first believed, and the editor's sympathy turned to anger.

In his mortification, Ross initially insisted that the swindle was only in the ten-thousand-dollar range. Later, *New Yorker* staffers were told it was more like seventeen thousand. Ross's damage control was so effective that for years, whenever people brought up the strange case of Harold Winney, these were the numbers they cited. But the truth was that over six years, Harold Winney actually stole more than seventy thousand dollars.

Faced with so staggering a loss, Ross transferred his rage from the dead man to Guaranty Trust, "which recently allowed me to be forged out of all my worldly cash and securities." He retained Stryker to press the bank for restitution, but expected nothing to come of it. For its part, the Guaranty searched for ways it might legally reimburse Ross, a valued client; yet because he had allowed himself to be victimized, there was nothing to be done.

No matter; Ross never forgave the bank, and in fact conducted something of a one-man vendetta against it. A few years after the Winney swindle, Ross's then-secretary, Harriet Walden, caught the bank in a one-cent discrepancy in his checking statement. She was inclined to overlook the penny, but Ross seized on it. He taunted the bank for weeks about its carelessness and demanded a written apology. The day he got it, he was as happy as she had ever seen him, Mrs. Walden said.

It took more than two years to unsnarl the insurance and estate questions that resulted from Winney's crimes and suicide. Ross did finally receive one reimbursement check—for $3,705.15.

———

"ANY AMERICAN CAN BE TAKEN FOR SEVENTEEN THOUSAND OR TWENTY thousand dollars," Thurber duly noted, "but it takes a really great eccentric to be robbed of seventy-one thousand dollars right under his busy nose." Ross's financial eccentricity transcended mere myopia to include some unorthodox investments, made with eyes wide open. A Colorado relative got him to sink money into an unproductive gold mine, for instance, and he lost thousands of dollars speculating in a company that produced an automatic spray-painting gun—a good idea that, sadly, outpaced the technology.

Harold Ross was the kind of man who could argue for hours against paying a certain writer an extra twenty bucks, on principle, for a Profile, then turn around and give the man a hundred dollars from his own pocket if he happened to be down on his luck. His personal generosity was expansive and legendary. Perhaps it was simple justice, then, that with all his bad financial tidings, he would realize a windfall where he never expected it, from a personal loan to a hard-pressed friend.

Ross came to know the personable Dave Chasen through the comedian's partner, Joe Cook, who was a great friend and fellow prankster (thanks to Cook's wide travels, Ross amassed one of America's great collections of Gideon Bibles). In the Twenties Cook and Chasen were one of the most popular comedy teams in vaudeville, the red-mopped, Ukraine-born Chasen playing foil to the rollicking Cook. Performing was Chasen's first love; his second was cooking. He regularly put on lavish backstage feeds—his specialties were barbecued spareribs and chili—for cast members and lucky guests. For years friends urged him to start his own restaurant; Ross went further, pledging his financial support if Chasen ever became serious about the idea.

When the talkies killed vaudeville and Parkinson's disease ended

Cook's career, the orphaned Chasen headed for Hollywood in the vain hope of breaking into motion pictures. Ross was so worried about him that he quietly encouraged some producers to hire Chasen, but it didn't help. Nearly broke and utterly discouraged, his career languishing, Chasen started thinking again about that restaurant and wired Ross.

Ross responded with $3,500 and got another friend, stockbroker Daniel Silberberg, to pitch in a smaller amount. It was enough for Chasen to acquire a plain stucco building on Beverly Boulevard in Beverly Hills—where the restaurant still stands today—and start pulling together his new business. There, in December 1936, he opened Chasen's Southern Barbecue. The menu wasn't auspicious—chili, barbecue and burgers were virtually the only offerings—and neither were the surroundings. Six tables and a chili counter were crammed into the tiny dining room. Chasen was so strapped that a friend, the director Frank Capra, brought his own silverware from home for the place settings, and the proprietor did everything, from the cooking to the dishwashing.

Still, the good food, cheap prices, and celebrity clientele—charter regulars included Capra, Cagney, Benchley, W. C. Fields, Frank Morgan, and Pat O'Brien—were customer magnets. Chasen's took off almost from the start. The Hollywood crowd made the little chili parlor a kind of boys' club; hanging out in the back room, they could get a massage, play cards, or guzzle Dave's thirty-five-cent drinks. The indefatigable Chasen fired off increasingly rosy progress reports to his benefactor. Ross was delighted but dispatched his old pal McNamara to keep an eye on matters anyway.

While it was common knowledge that Ross had staked Chasen, few people knew the extent of his enthusiasm and personal involvement. The reverse of his inattentive side was the astonishing zeal he mustered when he became interested in something, and he was intensely interested in helping make Chasen's a success. He bought out Silberberg and kept sending Chasen money for expansion. The man who James M. Cain marveled was treated like "the king of England" at "21" had firm opinions about eating and eateries. Chasen welcomed Ross's input on literally every aspect of the restaurant, from his assessment of glassware breakage to his critique of the menu (entrées *and* typos). Ross looked for prospective headwaiters. He sent instructions for the proper way to smoke a turkey ("take a fresh turkey and soak it in brine for three days . . .") and to mix an intoxicating drink from his San Francisco days, a pisco punch. When World War II made good Scotch almost impossible to get, it was Ross who pulled strings with Joseph Kennedy to take care of Chasen's.

In those first years Ross put some twenty thousand dollars into the operation, and he watched with paternal pride as Chasen, with hard work, splendid food, and showmanship, turned it into one of the great restaurants of the world, a favorite of movie stars and presidents. Magazine editors liked it too, and whenever Ross was in California he held court there with his friends from the old days—Benchley, Mankiewicz, Nunnally Johnson, Dorothy Parker, the Marx boys. At Chasen's, he was treated less like a king than like a god.

When visiting California Ross often held court at Dave Chasen's restaurant. Here he is joined by Chasen, left, and Nunnally Johnson. *(Courtesy of Chasen's)*

For his faith and perseverance, Ross got back more than ten times his investment in Chasen's. He made so much money, in fact, that it started to bother him. He began to think he was taking advantage of Chasen the way that he perceived Fleischmann had taken advantage of him. Thus in the late Forties he and Chasen worked out an arrangement wherein Ross began to back out of the enterprise; by 1953, ownership of the restaurant was to revert entirely to the people who had made it a success, Chasen and his family. As it happened, Ross's death in 1951 hastened that transition.

Until the day it closed in 1995, upstairs at Chasen's could be found The New Yorker Room, an intimate space used for private parties and special occasions. The walls were paneled in rich, dark wood and decorated with Manhattan scenes and original Thurber drawings. Hanging prominently at the head of the room was an oil portrait of Harold Ross, looking for all the world like a man who can't believe his luck.

CHAPTER 9

LIFE ON A LIMB

IN MORE THAN FIFTY-FIVE YEARS AT *THE NEW YORKER,* THE VERSATILE Philip Hamburger has performed many duties, and for a brief while he was even part-time movie critic. One day he saw Gloria Swanson in *Sunset Boulevard* and was not exactly moved to superlatives. As he recalled, "I wrote, 'This is a pretentious slice of Roquefort,' and I turned in the review."

A short while later, an anxious Ross came by, running his hands through his hair in customary distress, the very picture of the man who always said that when he wrote his autobiography he would call it *My Life on a Limb.* "Goddammit, Hamburger, what are you trying to do to me? This is a movie everyone is raving about. They say it's going to win the Academy Award. And you call it Roquefort!"

Now it was Hamburger's turn to be anxious, but he had an intuition. "Have you seen it?" he asked the editor.

"Yeah, I saw it," Ross replied. "It was a piece of shit."

The review ran, with cheese.

It's a hard thing to say what an editor is, much less explain what makes one great. In the narrowest sense, editors lay twitchy hands on someone else's work, fixing it, patching it, polishing it, and generally trying to keep it upright. In the broadest sense, however, they set the agenda, standards, and tone for a publication. They hire and fire; they pick stories, and the writers to go with them. They must have enough ego to confidently steer talented people, but the will to subordinate it. They must assuage prima donnas, compel laggards, and sober up drunks. Equal parts shaman and showman, they must have an unwavering vision for their publication, convey it to a staff, and then sell it to the great yawning public. For these reasons and many others, editing a magazine is not a job suited to the faint or uncertain, and it is enormously difficult to do well. Harold Ross arguably did it better than anyone who went before him, and not a few people would say anyone since.

How to explain such a feat from a frontier lad with a tenth-grade education? It wasn't merely that Ross had the kind of mischievous mind that drove him to scour a newly published atlas for mistakes; or that he insisted writers not arouse a reader's curiosity without satisfying it; or that he was so passionate about grammar that he read Fowler's four daunting pages on the distinctions between "which" and "that" for his own amusement. And certainly it wasn't just luck, though there was some of that, too. Ross's *New Yorker* represented an almost magical confluence of an idea, a time, and a place, arriving just after New York emerged as a world city, yet before the pervasive presence of television: that brief window when an erudite little "comic paper" could be a major cultural force in a way that is unthinkable now. It was also a time when young and gifted practitioners of the fictive, factual, comic, and illustrative arts seemed to be everywhere, waiting only for a passerby to pluck them up. Ross himself often reinforced this impression of *The New Yorker* as a phenomenon of editorial serendipity. "I was the luckiest son of a bitch alive when I started it," Ross told George Jean Nathan. "Magazines are about eighty-five per cent luck. All an editor can do is have a net handy to grab any talent that comes along, and maybe cast a little bread on the waters."

If Nathan knew better than to swallow this whole, less knowing people didn't. Many figured Ross must be the luckiest fisherman around, while others spoke of the roughneck with the miraculous "genius for finding talent" as if he were an idiot savant. This genius, as E. B. White observed, was really a "diligence in looking at everything that comes in—every picture, every manuscript. [Ross] also believes that talent attracts talent: you get talent if you publish a good magazine, you get tripe if you publish tripe."

And talent, the editor understood, was the key. He never stopped searching for it or, once he had found it, nurturing it. On that point Fleischmann had been absolutely correct: Ross had a respect for creative people that bordered on veneration; everyone else, himself included, was meant to be in their service. Needless to say, this was an attitude that writers and artists didn't come across every day. Once they understood Ross's mystical, unwavering faith in them, they were free to validate it. He championed them even if he didn't always grasp their ideas—say, in the case of a Lewis Mumford or an Edmund Wilson—or was uncomfortable with their linguistic invention, as he sometimes was with Vladimir Nabokov. As William Shawn once put it, "By being hospitable to the best, and expecting the best, he often received the best." Ross operated his *New Yorker* less as a magazine than as a kind of great laboratory where associates were encouraged to pursue individual projects, yet in that pursuit advanced a common cause. His laboratory was invigorating, even intoxicating.

Why? Primarily because the editor encouraged people to write or draw what they wanted, the way they wanted (within a certain *New Yorker* framework of "good taste," to be sure); all Ross desired, he seemed to say, was to help them find their rightful audience. With certain favorites—White, Thurber, Benchley, Arno, Arthur Kober, Gluyas Williams, Charles Addams, to name only a few—he was not above wheedling or begging for new material. To his intimate Frank Sullivan, not a letter passed that didn't include the line "Write me some pieces" or increasingly adamant variations thereon—"Write me some pieces, goddammit," or "GODDAMMIT, WRITE SOME PIECES!" To a writer, an editor like this was almost too good to be true.

Besides his faith, Ross gave his people strength and the comforting knowledge that he would always be there for them, whether this meant troubleshooting a complicated Profile or covering an emergency hospital bill. It was the kind of unending commitment that probably cost Ross any real chance at a stable home life, but he had long ago, and consciously, made this trade-off.

Add to this Ross's intrinsic understanding that writers and artists are different from other people and must be treated—tolerated, he would more likely harrumph—as such. He believed that the same unique vantage point that made creative people insightful could also render them vulnerable, impractical, and maddeningly unreliable. ("I wish I were a writer and could take a summer off," he told Geoffrey Hellman just before the writer boarded an ocean liner for Europe.) Ross's style had less to do with coddling his people—"If you can't be original at least be interesting," more than one chastened writer heard him say—than with protecting them. "I . . . think he thought that people with talent didn't in general know enough to come in out of the rain," said William Maxwell, "and he was trying to hold an umbrella over them."

If so, the canopy was high and wide, for there were so many to shelter and so much to protect them from: bruised advertisers, irate Profile subjects, hostile theater producers, carpetbagging book publishers. From the time in the Twenties when Ross told a clothing retailer to go ahead and pull its *New Yorker* advertising—Marcia Davenport had written that the shop's models were "ill groomed"—he stood squarely behind his writers and seemed immune to intimidation. Edmund Wilson, hardly an unqualified fan of Ross (he considered the editor anti-intellectual, which was true, and something of a philistine, which wasn't), nonetheless hailed that integrity. "When publishers wrote complaining about me, he would simply hand me the letters and tell me to pay no attention," Wilson wrote. "His independence and refusal to be blackmailed or bullied was one of his most admirable qualities."

Even the occasional priest and nun bounced off Ross's protective shield. Whenever he said "I live the life of a hunted animal"—and he often did—he was bemoaning occupational hazards like spot visitations from the profanity watchdogs of the Holy Name Society. The irony was that Ross so disliked seeing blue language in *The New Yorker* ("This is a family magazine, goddammit") that he expunged the great majority of his spirited staff's "hells," "damns," and "bastards" long before they hit print. Those profanities that made it, however, were there because they were essential to a given story, and in such cases no amount of protesting could budge him. (He devised an effective Holy Name defense; as he explained to an appreciative Mencken, whenever the society's delegations turned up in the lobby looking for the man in charge, he sent out the brilliantly troubled Kip Orr, "who looks at them with a bleary eye and exudes a stale whiskey odor.")

Ross's protective impulse reached beyond the office directly into the lives of his staff and contributors. He pioneered the then-heretical idea of reassigning the rights to a story or artwork to its creator once it had appeared in the magazine (not to mention handling the copyright paperwork and helping contributors find secondary markets for their work). Beyond this, he endlessly hectored book publishers for their alleged exploitation of his writers. This kind of gesture naturally merged with his personal generosity, about which literally every senior *New Yorker* writer has a story. He secured a larger apartment for Hamburger's expanding family ("I saw your wife on the street today. For Christ's sake, she's pregnant"). When Emily Hahn returned from China, he secretly brought in her mother from Chicago to surprise her at the pier. During World War II, when Ross's secretary feared that something had happened to her brother, an intelligence officer serving in Burma, Ross used his military contacts to learn that the young man was fine. During and after the war, he sent relief packages of food and scarce sundries to Rebecca West and Mollie Panter-Downes in England, and to Janet Flanner in France. He paid for Russell Maloney's funeral long after the writer had left *The New Yorker,* and he gave an office boy twenty dollars to buy a new raincoat. He routinely bought pieces he had no intention of publishing to help out struggling writers, and kept his old friend F.P.A. on the magazine's payroll (scouring the *Congressional Record* for

Newsbreak material) when, in the columnist's final years, his career hit the skids. To the chagrin of the business side, Ross carried dozens of writers who were hopelessly in debt to the magazine, and forgave some of their obligations altogether.

For this kind of loyalty and respect, Ross was more than repaid in kind. Other places, most conspicuously Time Inc., paid better, but they offered nothing like this kind of paternal attention from the top. "I think the attraction was that you knew it was the best magazine being published," explained John Bainbridge. "I had friends working at *Time,* and they were taking holidays and living in nice places and not worrying so much about the rent. We were worrying about the rent most of the time. But we were sustained by the fact that we were not writing for Henry Luce. We were writing for Harold Ross."

Given literally hundreds of staff members and contributors to tend, Ross did a considerable amount of his shepherding by correspondence. This was especially true in the late Thirties, when so many of his key people departed New York City—the Whites having left for Maine and a farm, Thurber for Connecticut and fame—and later, during the war, when his staff scattered to the far reaches of the globe. In his *New Yorker* tenure Ross wrote tens of thousands of letters, not just tossed-off notes or memos but long, involved, impassioned models of the epistolary art.

Examining this trove, one cannot help but appreciate the staggering amount of his time Ross devoted to his sensitive, skittish charges—time spent kvetching, scheming, explaining, and long-distance hand-holding. More than this, though, one instantly grasps the other great weapon in Ross's management arsenal: his expansive, infectious humor, often as not employed at his own expense. It turns up everywhere—for instance in his scribbled postscript to a 1943 letter to Samuel Hopkins Adams, after the editor was profiled in *Harper's:* "I didn't read [it]. The hell with it. E. B. White said it was the dullest document of the year and I don't want to get bored by myself." Or in this friendly admonition to Arthur Kober: "Several of you writers . . . have had passing reference to me as dynamic, boisterous, mad, violent, impatient and so on, when everyone whom I ever associated with knows that I am one of the longest-suffering and pleasantest and, at heart, quietest men alive today, a sort of gentile Christ. I had a straight flush the other night that gave me a momentary lift, but only momentary. . . ."

Other random samples from the Ross files:

When Margaret Case Harriman once turned up unexpectedly in the Midwest, Ross professed amazement at the range of her wanderings. "For instance, what in God's name were you doing in the Hotel Mayflower, fifty rooms, European plan, Fireproof, Ralph G. Lorenz, manager, Plymouth, Mich.? Don't answer; regard the question as rhetorical. It's all too sordid, probably."

In 1947, in a letter to Nunnally Johnson, Ross explained how he ferreted out a case of mistaken identity involving *New Yorker* writer Joseph Mitchell: "I could have asked Joe Mitchell himself, of course, but I am a trained newspaperman and don't get my dope in any such half-baked way as that. After going as far as I could with my office inquiries, I then referred to *Who's Who.* There I find that Doris Stevens is married (2nd) to Jonathan Mitchell, not Joseph, and I find that Jonathan was b. Portland, Maine, 1895, worked on the *New York World,* and wrote a book, *Goosesteps to Peace,* 1931. Not only is the first name different, but it would be contrary to the nature of our Mitchell to write a book called *Goosesteps to Peace.*"

One day after the war, during a writing sabbatical from the magazine, Maxwell ran into Ross on the street at about one in the afternoon. Ross asked what he was doing in town, and Maxwell said he had tickets for a show—neglecting to mention that the performance was in the evening. Ross assumed Maxwell meant a matinee, and this bothered him; he told a coworker that he had been under the impression that only women attended matinees. Maxwell later straightened him out, and Ross wrote back: "I am enormously relieved to learn that you didn't go to a matinee of those shows. I don't like the feeling that I know men who go to shows in the afternoon. It's worse than smoking reefers and, I believe, practically the same as subsisting on the fruits of fallen women."

In a letter to White, Ross addressed his shortcomings: "I am not

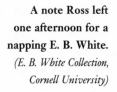

A note Ross left
one afternoon for a
napping E. B. White.
*(E. B. White Collection,
Cornell University)*

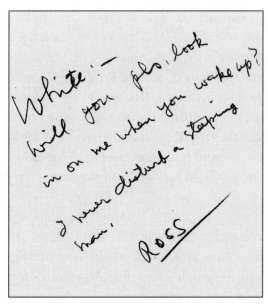

God. . . . The realization of this came slowly and hard some years ago, but I have swallowed it by now. I am merely an angel in the Lord's vineyard."

Ross often referred to himself as "an old double-standard boy" when it came to profanity. As if to prove it, he once returned a reworked story to Frank Sullivan, using the occasion to admonish Sullivan, John O'Hara, and others to "stop writing letters to me full of [profanities] because they are apt to be read by pure young girls around this office, and I don't want them corrupted." Then, returning to Sullivan's story, he added, "Don't hesitate to complain if you think I've fucked up this piece."

In the early Forties, Ross got so far behind in his payments to Jane Grant that he became embroiled in a series of increasingly sharp exchanges with her law firm, Chadbourne, Wallace, Parke & Whiteside. One day in exasperation he wrote, "Long life to the legal profession! In just about ten years you boys will have this country so thoroughly tied up that it can't turn a wheel, and then everybody will just go gracefully out of business." He signed the letter H. W. Ross, of "Ross, Ross, Ross, Ross & Ross."

The personality that shines through these letters explains why to the editor of *The New Yorker* humor was not merely a pleasing adjunct to the magazine but a part of its core. Even in preparing otherwise "straight" stories, Ross's writers were not to lose sight of this. As Thurber noted, "He didn't like his facts bare and stark; he wanted them accompanied by comedy—you unwrapped the laugh and there was the fact, or maybe vice versa." In his long career no single thing discouraged Ross more than having to watch the Depression, Fascism, and the Cold War drain all the humor out of the world.

———

ROGER ANGELL, THE DISTINGUISHED BASEBALL WRITER AND LONG-time *New Yorker* fiction editor, remembers having lunch one day with Ross not long after Angell had returned from the war and published his first few pieces in the magazine. The conversation was proceeding agreeably when suddenly Ross asked, "What about this Hemingway? Is he any good?"

Angell smiled, thinking he was being teased. Hemingway had been his literary hero in college, Angell recalls, "and at the time everyone knew he was the number-one writer in the world." But looking at his companion he could see the editor was quite sincere in his question. Ross might have his own opinion of Hemingway (he did, and it was decidedly mixed), but at this moment his curiosity had overtaken his doubts, and he was genuinely interested in a different and younger perspective.

In fact, when discussing the essential Ross, one always returns to his bristling curiosity. *New Yorker* editors were constantly struck by the scope and arcana of his knowledge, from the vagaries of plumbing to the sex life of the eel, and when Ross didn't know something he wanted to find out. In his play *Season in the Sun*, Wolcott Gibbs only slightly exaggerates this quality when, in the closing moments, a character explicitly based on Ross is seen hungrily reading the encyclopedia entry for "hurricane" even as the real thing bears down on him. (Gibbs once tried to help remedy Ross's ignorance of the classics by dragging him to a production of Shakespeare's *Henry IV*,

Part II. The experiment was a dismal failure. It was bad enough when Ross saw that there were two different characters named Bardolph, but when Rumour opened the play with a long speech describing, as Gibbs said, "what *isn't* going to happen," it was all too much. "What kind of writer would put in a dame like that just to fuck me up?" the editor asked.)

Ross's lack of a formal education bothered him for years and contributed to his natural insecurity, though in the end he came around to the idea that it was probably just as well. Had he been better educated, chances are that he would have been much less curious, or perhaps less willing to ask the kinds of blunt questions that accounted for so much of *The New Yorker*'s admirable clarity. Consider his famous query "Is Moby Dick the whale or the man?" There is no doubt he asked it, though there is considerable disagreement among *New Yorker* people about whether he was serious or only having a bit of fun. But the point is that it doesn't matter, because it was precisely the kind of question he *would* have asked if he didn't know the answer. He never worried about egg on his face, never pretended to know something if he didn't.

On the other hand, to take the reverse side of the "Moby Dick" argument, Ross often pretended *not* to know something when in fact he did. He made it his business to be informed about a good deal more than he let on, be it a writer's rocky marriage, Europolitics, or maybe even Herman Melville. Yet by occasionally "presenting himself" (Shawn's phrase) to the world as a bit of a rube, Ross could use his rusticity to great advantage. Playing the Colorado hayseed, a dim fellow who needed things explained to him in one- and two-syllable words, he might elicit from a writer that perfect word to clarify a muddy sentence, or the right fact to finish an incomplete thought. Likewise, he was aware that bedroom humor was too easy and unworthy of *The New Yorker.* By eschewing it, ostensibly on the grounds that it offended his prudish sensibilities, he kept his writers and artists striving for more honest and therefore satisfying kinds of humor. Of course, the fact that many of these same writers and artists blithely failed to see what he was doing also suited Ross; sometimes it was simply more efficient, and easier on the digestion, to get his way playing the philistine than to engage in philosophical arguments over every disputed comma or brushstroke.

Besides, those who chose to explain Ross chiefly in terms of his alleged ignorance and curmudgeonly pose discredited all his other fundamental qualities. Ostensibly he may not have been what one might imagine as the editor of *The New Yorker*. Then again, countless people said that a single conversation with him revealed a mind so keen, a curiosity so expansive, and a humor so droll that afterward it was hard to imagine anyone *but* Ross editing the magazine. Some contemporaries likened him to Twain and Mencken, others to Sandburg and Frost, all of whom flashed a genius grounded in, and resonating with, the American experience. Or as Peter De Vries put it, Ross, like those other men of letters, reminds one that "America's great contribution is not plastics but quarter-sawed oak."

———

HAROLD ROSS COMES TO WORK. HE WALKS STOOPED FORWARD, AS IF leaning into a strong wind. Slung over his shoulder is a manuscript-stuffed bag looking rather like a mail pouch, a long leather strap laced to his wrist so as not to leave behind by accident his precious cargo in trains or taxis—which he once did when he carried a conventional briefcase. A Parliament is stuck to his lower lip (inevitably described as pendulous) as if he has glued it there. Shambling along in a loose-fitting topcoat, battered homburg pulled down on his head, he calls to mind not so much a savvy New York editor as Willy Loman. He passes his secretary, Harriet Walden, and his longtime assistant and aide-de-camp, Louis Forster. He does not say hello; he does not say anything. Ross was not a "Have a nice day" kind of person, and in any case there will be time enough later for conversation.

Inside his large, airy office, tucked into a corner of the nineteenth floor, he drops his coat onto the dingy linoleum. Clearly at a magazine that has always maintained—insisted on—a full quota of eccentrics, the founding editor established the tone. (White remembered one particular elevator operator there, a nervous young man who had obtained the job through his sister, a *New Yorker* secretary.

One day he confided to office manager Daise Terry that he continually heard little voices in his ear. "What do the voices say?" she asked. Said the elevator man, "They keep saying, 'Drop the sons of bitches.' ")

On a credenza in Ross's office are some dictionaries, on his desk a few manuscripts and some freshly sharpened pencils—a clerk has replaced the chewed ones from the day before—as well as the glass of cream and ulcer medication, Amphojel, that Mrs. Walden has left for him. He drinks this unpleasant cocktail at regular intervals through the day, and if anyone is in the room at the time he is apt to raise the glass, grimace, and say, "To your health!" In places paint is peeling from the walls. By way of furnishings, there are some Thurber drawings, the bewigged head of Sterling Finny, and a large, ugly poster of an Oriental nude that Mrs. Walden would later throw out one day when she could no longer abide it. In his previous office, on Forty-fifth Street, Ross had displayed the opera hat that Rudolph Valentino was wearing the night in 1926 that he collapsed and died. (Charlie MacArthur is said to have pilfered it from a collector and presented it to Ross with much fanfare, but a few years later it was lost in one of Ross's many domestic moves.)

Sitting in an old-fashioned wood-and-leather steno chair of daintier issue than one would imagine for a man of Ross's size, the editor begins his office routine. He dives into the waiting pile of correspondence and interoffice memos, reading them over quickly, now and then crumpling one and tossing it to the floor. At day's end Mrs. Walden will sort through this detritus to retrieve those letters requiring action or filing. Then he moves on to letters and memos of his own, pounding at his black typewriter in the way he learned as a boy reporter, his two index fingers firing like pistons. Formal correspondence he usually drafts himself and then edits before having it retyped, but personal notes, such as the story compliments he lavished on writers, he is apt to pass on as written, X-outs and all. Since he tends not to look at his hands when he types, he has been known to compose a whole note having started off on the wrong keys, leaving Mrs. Walden to unscramble it like a cryptographer.

After an hour or two of this, Ross might typically go on to a more enjoyable pursuit, reading manuscripts or galley proofs of stories. He will read and approve virtually everything that goes into the magazine, and as he reads he concentrates so intensely that he won't notice a person entering the room. Lost in thought, he clucks his tongue through that signature gap in his front teeth.

Ross is often on the telephone, though unless a call is from a friend the conversation will likely be a perfunctory one. (He didn't like his time wasted, and didn't suffer fools. Patricia Ross recalls once seeing her father trapped in a telephone conversation he clearly had no use for. After pacing for twenty minutes he put down the receiver and left the room. A few moments later he came back, picked up the phone and said, "Oh, are you still there? I had to go to the bathroom—I've got diarrhea.")

Editors drift in and out through the day. (After one unsatisfying conference, Ross stared into the distance and said with a sigh, "I'm surrounded by a bunch of 'no' men.") If it is Tuesday, his entire afternoon will be given over to the art meeting, where cartoons and cover illustrations are examined and culled. If it's Thursday, he will work late into the night while the editors start buttoning up the next issue. If it's Friday, he will sit down with Forster and go over all the sundry management matters that require his attention. (In contrast to Ross's personal life, at work his follow-up was unrelenting, and he relied on Forster to keep him organized. At the time Forster was not only Ross's executive assistant but his "A issue" editor—that is, the magazine's chief scheduler and production traffic cop—and also assumed many of the administrative duties that Shuman had handled. As such, he was one of those unseen but indispensable people, like Hobart Weekes and Eleanor Gould Packard, *The New Yorker*'s chief copy editor for nearly fifty years, who kept the magazine steaming along week after week.)

Otherwise, toward day's end Ross might decide to roam the eighteenth floor, where staff writers could be found stuffed into cubbies with just enough room for two average-size human beings, one beat-up sofa, and some secondhand desks. Ross would be drawn by the siren sound of typing; finding a writer at home, he would poke his head in to exchange jokes, kick around story ideas, or simply to "let people in on things," as one veteran staffer put it (pointedly contrasting this to Shawn's close-to-the-vest style). He practiced "management by walking around" long before anyone thought to call it that.

For the most part, however, writers encountered Ross in the "proofs." Galley proofs are typeset, working versions of stories that a magazine intends to publish. Once a manuscript had been deemed far enough along at *The New Yorker*, it would be typeset in long, one-column galleys. Copies of these proofs then were distributed around the office so that the serious editing might commence.

Armed with his proof, Ross set about to construct what was known as his query sheet. This was his primary weapon in the never-ending battle for clarity, as well as the source of countless anecdotes about him. His query sheet was a long, amazing list, sometimes two pages, sometimes eight or more, of questions, comments, sermonettes, and flights of fancy that came to him as he read a story. Each entry was numbered to correspond to his marked-up proof. His queries delighted some writers and outraged a few, but in any event they reveal, perhaps better than anything beyond the actual 1,399 issues of *The New Yorker* that he produced, his editing mind at work. (See Appendix III, page 447.)

When going over these long proofs, which Ross at times described as "coiling up around me like hissing snakes," he reacted to the material in a manner opposite that of most casual readers: on a literal level first and then on an emotional level. Things needed to make sense to him. He was the kind of man who, while enjoying E. B. White's children's classic *Stuart Little*, could complain to the author that he should have had the protagonist adopted rather than "born" into the Little family, since everyone knows a human couple cannot conceive a mouse. He didn't like to be surprised, which is one reason he couldn't abide what *New Yorker* editors called "indirection." That is, as Shawn once explained, it bothered Ross to have a character remove his hat if it had not already been established that he was wearing a hat. And to the extent possible, he liked to have everyday verities observed. Going over a John Cheever story that unfolded over the course of a long day, he suggested that the characters had better be sitting down to a meal soon.

This, then, was the Ross that writers found in their proofs. There were almost audible snorts when he came to a far-fetched passage: "Bushwah," he might write, or "Nuts." Other times he could be painfully dry. Bainbridge says that about the worst thing one could incur on a proof was the dreaded "Oh"; this might happen when a writer had reached for what he considered a supremely subtle irony or artful flourish, only to elicit from Ross "Oh." It was in the proofs that writers bumped up against his linguistic preferences and prejudices, such as his campaign against the use of words like "pretty" and "little" as limp adverbs—she was "pretty tired," he was "a little perplexed"—rather than as the perfectly good adjectives that God and Ida Ross intended them to be.

Often a query conveyed equal measures of inspiration and exasperation. When reading over John Hersey's account of John F. Kennedy and the wreck of the PT-109, Ross stopped when Hersey said Kennedy managed to get a coconut to some natives, on which he "wrote a message." "With *what*, for God's sakes?" Ross demanded. "Blood?" Or if a writer dropped a surprise character into a story, deus ex machina, Ross was famously known to wonder, "Who he?"

All *New Yorker* writers quickly became accustomed to Ross's sharpshooting. Most appreciated it, regarding it as an inimitable expression of his care and concern for their work—and by extension, for them. During the editing of her story "The Groves of Academe," Mary McCarthy told Katharine White, "I think Ross is wonderful. . . . I hated to concede it, but, as I say in the note, he is really right about the peppermint—you can hold it in your mouth but not properly suck it." Others were less benign. A. J. Liebling, for one, never quite became reconciled to such microscopic examination, considering most—though certainly not all—of Ross's questions trivial or beside the point. After one especially difficult tussle over a proof, Liebling found a sign painter to paint WHO HE? in gold letters on the glass portion of his office door. According to Liebling's close friend Joseph Mitchell, "A few days later one of the elevator operators said that another tenant on that floor had asked him what in the name of God kind of product did the Who He? company put out."

Of course, at times an author's ire was justified. Some of Ross's queries *were* trivial, some were non sequiturs, and some were just plain odd. Every writer had favorite Rossisms. Emily Hahn wrote a story in which two characters were chatting beside a fireplace. Inquired Ross, "Which *side* of the fireplace?" A more widely circulated example was his response to an S. J. Perelman line about "the woman taken in adultery." Asked the editor, "What woman?"

William Maxwell, who sifted through hundreds of Ross's query sheets as a writer and fiction editor, speculates that one reason for Ross's more oddball questions was that he simply read too many proofs too fast. When he read a manuscript—say of a short story that the fiction editors were keen to buy—he invariably raised five or six solid questions that went to the heart of the piece's quality or credibility. But when he was reading proofs, Maxwell says, compiling those query sheets in his stream-of-consciousness fashion, he was of necessity in a rush. Considering that under Ross *The New Yorker* typically ran over one hundred pages a week, and at times upwards of two hundred, the proofs amounted to a bottomless well; a fat issue might present the editor with two thousand column inches to read. Maxwell explained that it was not uncommon for Ross in his haste to misconstrue a statement early in a story, and based on this misstep string along a series of erroneous queries. He once spent hours marking up a Profile as woefully sketchy before realizing he was reading the second part of a two-part piece. Eleanor Gould Packard concurred that Ross would sometimes moan and groan in his queries, then catch himself and type, "Oh, I misread it!" Part of his charm, not to mention his successful management style, was that he would leave the comment there for all to see.

At heart, Ross's queries were a means to an end—his way of insisting that everything in *The New Yorker* be as clear and accurate as possible, that shortcuts be resisted and lazy work discouraged. His editors always knew which of his queries to disregard, which to finesse, and which to take seriously. Besides, in his twenty- or thirty-odd comments on a story, one or two usually would highlight some overlooked problem or otherwise improve the piece. His suggestions might be matters of nuance—altering "we can use a few dollars" to "we can use a few bucks" in Cheever's "The Enormous Radio," for instance, a change the author called "absolutely perfect"—or fact, such as pointing out that a writer really meant "birdshot" when he said "buckshot." And who but Ross would have thought to ask, "Were the Nabokovs a *one*-nutcracker family?" These might seem small matters, but he subscribed strongly to the theory that God, if he existed, was in the details. Yet the big picture was seldom far from view. Hundreds of times, halfway into a story, the editor would pose the awful question that writers are so fearful of asking themselves: "Is this interesting?"

Fortunately for them, Ross was interested in almost everything. He was always scribbling notes on cocktail napkins, menus, or those blank checks he carried around, with last night's anecdote from Toots Shor's or a gee-whiz fact just gleaned from his barber. Not surprisingly, much that piqued his interest found its way into *The New Yorker*, often only after this self-styled "hunch man" had paired up a certain writer with a certain idea. In early 1947 he persuaded his friend Rebecca West to come to the United States to do some pieces; once she was here, he dispatched her to Greenville, South Carolina, where some taxi drivers were accused of breaking into a jail and lynching a black man. In only a few weeks' time West turned out a masterly and widely remarked-on series about the town, the trial, and grisly Southern justice.

At about the same time, Ross prevailed on S. N. Behrman to return to London, where he had written some memorable stories during the war. "But Ross," Behrman protested, "I've been. I've done it." Ross persisted. "Write me a cold piece on London," he said. Finally yielding, Behrman would recall, "I went. London was indeed cold. The resulting piece was called 'It's Cold at Lady Windermere's.' It was a singular mission: to register frigidity. Ross's instinct was sound."

This same instinct was at work when Berton Roueché stumbled onto a genre that he would make his own, the medical detective story. Roueché had come to *The New Yorker* from St. Louis in 1944, and began work as a Talk reporter. Eventually he was assigned to write a story about the outbreak of a mysterious illness in Queens. Ross was pleased with the result, saying, "You know, this is kind of like Sherlock Holmes—like a detective story." He suggested that Roueché follow it up with some similar pieces. These ran under a heading Ross devised, "Annals of Medicine," and ultimately Roueché would write more than forty of them.

A 1945 memo to Joseph Mitchell, not untypical of those Ross wrote every day, began by complimenting the writer on a recent triumph, then quickly veered off onto a pigeon tangent:

> I herewith pass the idea [for a story on the pigeons of New York] along for what it is worth, with some sympathy for the idea. I was in the Post Graduate hospital once for a week and all I could do was look out the window at East Side roofs and the pigeon activity was tremendous; gents were always waving fishing poles around scaring the pigeons into the air. I assume this was for exercise, for the pigeons returned as soon as the brandishing was over. [Lawton] Mackall says these fellows are mostly pigeon fanciers, rather than commercial raisers of pigeons, and that some New York pigeons are worth $1,200 for breeding purposes. . . . I suspect that Mackall is getting homing pigeons mixed up with common eating pigeons, but it may be that all the privately owned pigeons in New York are homing pigeons (otherwise, why would they stay home all the time?). Maybe homing pigeons are as good eating pigeons as any others.

Lynchings, the cold in London, medical mysteries, pigeon pedigree: facts of all kinds not only intrigued Ross but moved him ever ahead as he consumed them, like a lumbering farm combine. It was no accident that the journalistic portions of the magazine (Talk, Profiles, Letters, Reporter at Large pieces, reviews, etc.) were termed Fact; they predominated, and clearly were Ross's passion. In his heart, he never stopped being a newspaperman. He strove to make

The New Yorker as current as possible, and he dreaded the few days between the magazine's close and its appearance on the newsstand for fear that the interim might make it seem stale. Indeed, Friday was his favorite day of the workweek because this was when Talk, the timeliest department of the magazine, was put together. While he read everything that went into the magazine, he took a personal interest in Talk, doing much of the hands-on editing and rewrite work himself.

It was not merely the department's currency that made Talk Ross's favorite. Probably more than any other part of the magazine, it embodied what Ross was trying to achieve with *The New Yorker* generally. The stories were brief; they were anonymous and were propelled by their factual content; they lent themselves to humor; and at their best, just for a moment they pulled back the curtain on some hitherto little-known aspect or colorful denizen of metropolitan New York. They were, in a word, distillations, which took the very best kind of reporting and writing. Philip Hamburger, a Talk writer for many years, remembers happily sitting down with the editor to go over material line by line, occasionally to hear Ross utter a useful piece of advice, such as the time he said, "Never go cosmic on me, Hamburger."

———

SINCE HE USUALLY FOUND HIMSELF IN FRONT OF OLD TYPEWRITERS, Berton Roueché was in the habit of putting an apostrophe where the accent is supposed to go in his last name, so that it looked like this: Roueche'. After about a year of seeing this, Ross suddenly turned up one day at the writer's door. "I'm getting sick and tired of this apostrophe after your name," he said. "I'm sending in a typewriter man to put an accent key on your typewriter." And he did. Though everyone understood that the apostrophe was nothing more than a typographical accommodation, to Ross "Roueche' " was patently incorrect, and he could no more abide it than he would a pebble in his shoe.

Every aspect of *New Yorker* editing followed from this kind of perfection fixation—perfection being a commodity, Russell Maloney once observed, that Ross thought belonged to him, like his watch or hat. When asked, the editor was inclined to attribute the magazine's zeal for accuracy to its publication of Newsbreaks—people who live in glass houses, and all that—but his perfectionism was a more satisfactory explanation. The same went for the magazine's aggressive approach to grammar and punctuation, for *New Yorker* editors took their cues, after all, from a man who could hold forth for hours on the application of the serial comma. A British professor once asked Thurber why *New Yorker* editors placed a comma in the sentence, "After dinner, the men went into the living room." "I could explain that one, all right," Thurber said. "I wrote back that this particular comma was Ross's way of giving the men time to push back their chairs and stand up."

There were two distinct levels of editing at *The New Yorker*: the macro (story selection and assignment, rewriting, working with authors, etc.) and the more famous—or infamous, some would say—micro (the rigorous fact-checking, copy-editing, and proofreading procedures, with various redundancies and fail-safes meant to keep inaccuracies and typographical gremlins at bay).

In late 1936, Ross took a huge step toward working out the macro side of the equation when, after a decade of consternation, trial and error, he finally brought the Jesus parade to a halt. Heretofore his organization problems stemmed from the fact that while his mind's eye always conjured managing editors who could do it all (including, should it ever become possible, assume his job), his experience was that they could usually do about half. Those who could edit couldn't administer, and vice versa. Among other complications, this situation kept fiction editors like Mrs. White and Gibbs working on journalistic pieces, on which they had next to no expertise. After Stanley Walker's disappointing washout, and after Ik Shuman rapidly demonstrated that his strength was in numbers, not words, in desperation the editor turned to a bright but junior member of the staff. St. Clair McKelway was not only a superior reporter and writer but was already spending half his time editing Fact pieces when Ross asked him to be managing editor.

McKelway agreed to take the job on two conditions. First, he was willing to do it for only three years; second, he wanted Ross to reorganize, by establishing a clear demarcation between fiction and nonfiction. Under this setup, McKelway would be responsible for all the journalism, Mrs. White the fiction, art, and poetry, and no longer would either side involve itself in the affairs of the other. Ross agreed to both conditions. Beyond this, he gave Shuman all the administrative business that had saddled previous Jesuses. With McKelway's prodding, he finally had hit on a logical solution to his most vexing management problem. As his assistants, McKelway took two of Ross's most promising young editors, Sanderson Vanderbilt (who, while not one of *the* Vanderbilts, nonetheless found it a most useful surname for a working journalist in New York) and the quietly confident William Shawn.

Only thirty-one when he was named managing editor, McKelway already was well on his way to becoming one of the most accomplished and colorful figures in *New Yorker* history. Son of a prominent Southern family that had produced both notable journalists and ministers, he had just returned to the *Herald Tribune* after five years in the Orient when Ross recruited him in 1933. Unlike so many other newspaper practitioners, he immediately understood what the editor was trying to do with *The New Yorker,* and he quickly began turning out stories that reflected his personality: graceful, unhurried, stylish, and sparkling with what Shawn would later call "the lightest of light touches." On the streets of New York and among his *New Yorker* colleagues, the tall, well-dressed McKelway cut a dashing figure. In the late Thirties, sitting down over drinks to review John Bainbridge's early job performance, he had only one criticism: "Be more debonair." McKelway was the kind of fellow who could marry and divorce five times, yet remain good friends with all his ex-wives.

He was also, as it happens, an eccentric of the first rank, courtesy of severe manic-depressive illness that worsened over the years. He used to say his personality could fragment itself into twelve different "heads." If this condition made his behavior occasionally bewildering, it only served to increase his colleagues' esteem and affection for

The dapper St. Clair McKelway, standing at right, was managing editor for Fact for three years. He once told one of his reporters to "be more debonair." Here he attends a party with Wolcott Gibbs, seated, and Alan Campbell, husband of Dorothy Parker. *(UPI/Bettmann)*

him, even as it added whole chapters to *New Yorker* lore. It was McKelway who, while serving as an Air Force information officer in the Pacific during World War II, somehow persuaded himself that Admiral Chester Nimitz was a traitor and fired off a telegram to the War Department saying so. This earned Nimitz an apology from the Air Force and McKelway a trip stateside for safekeeping. Years later, while traveling in his ancestral Scotland, McKelway became convinced he had stumbled onto a diabolical Soviet plot to kidnap President Eisenhower, Queen Elizabeth, and Prince Philip. Such was his unique talent that when the manic-depressive episodes passed, he was able to write about these adventures in psychosis with great style and humor for the magazine.

With a clearer division of labor in place, the entire editing system at *The New Yorker* became more coherent. Which is not to suggest the gauntlet was any the less formidable. From the start *The New Yorker* scrutinized, debated, and poked at its stories more than any other publication in America. Its procedures reveal so much about Ross and his magazine that they warrant some examination.

Everything began with the acceptance of a piece. Fact stories usually were pursued only after the idea had been approved by the Fact editor and/or by Ross. Authorized Profiles and other specific story ideas were "reserved" by individual reporters in a fat book; they could reside there untouched for years, but other writers knew to steer clear. A reporter, by now usually someone on *The New Yorker* staff rather than a contributor, would work directly with his "assigning" editor—at the time this would be McKelway, Shawn, or Vanderbilt, and later such editors as Gardner Botsford. Once the main reporting was done and a writer had produced a first draft, the two would sit down and begin working on the manuscript line by line, agreeing on strengths and probing it for weaknesses.

On the fiction side, stories were considered only upon submission, even by the biggest names or regular contributors. (One reason *The New Yorker* published so little F. Scott Fitzgerald—a handful of poems and casuals—was that he wanted a commitment before writing, and the magazine declined to make an exception for him.) Of course, unlike new writers, whose manuscripts were appraised by a first reader, the O'Haras, Kobers, and Bensons had regular editors too—Mrs. White, Gibbs, or Maxwell, and later Gus Lobrano, Rogers Whitaker, and Roger Angell—and their stories got prompt consideration. In any case, several editors read a submitted story and offered their opinions before a decision was made to buy or reject.

From this point, whether a piece was fiction or nonfiction, the editing and production process was more or less the same (though often corners were cut when material was being hustled into the magazine). Once a piece was set up in proof, copies went to the assigning editor, a copy editor (who read it scrupulously for grammar, spelling, and general sense), and the fact checkers. A fact checker was expected to do what the name implied—check every verifiable assertion of fact. A Profile or lengthy Reporter at Large might well take a week to check, involving long hours in the library, calls to embassies, or even conversations with the subject of the story. On the other hand, checking the "facts" in a short story—for instance, if a writer casually referred to traffic on Forty-third Street, it had better be running west rather than east—might take only a few hours.

Once all these marked-up proofs came back, a collator put them onto a single master proof. This was what the assigning editor then used to do the final editing on the story, and this was when the process could get considerably more interesting. Depending on the editor and author involved (or more important, depending on the latter's sensitivities), an editor might go over the story in person, on the phone, or by mail, and he might or might not show the writer the proof—which, after all, could be a disheartening document. Resolving obvious factual errors and misspellings was no problem, but subjective matters—questions of cuts, suggested rewordings, punctuation, profanity—were often much thornier. Louis Forster vividly recalled one occasion when John O'Hara dropped by to go over a short story with Gibbs. The two men were devoted friends—O'Hara named his fictional hometown Gibbsville—but when the writer was drinking, friendship was no protection from his temper. Forster, whose office was just across the hall, began to notice their voices rising, then becoming more animated, until suddenly there was a veritable explosion: "Gibbs, you're *fucking* my story!" With that, O'Hara stormed out.

However, this contretemps was the exception. *New Yorker* editors, whose job was dealing with delicate egos, strove to make the editing process more collaborative than adversarial. They were tactful with writers, even deferential, and their preferences were always couched as suggestions; *The New Yorker* never demanded. Still, these suggestions could be most firm, and the writer who wanted to see his story actually published in *The New Yorker* discounted them at his peril.

It didn't take *The New Yorker* many years, then, to develop a reputation for supreme finickiness among writers, many of whom likened its editing to a pasteurization process. At times even a venerated elder like E. B. White tired of the compulsive fiddling and said it helped bring about a "sameness of sound" from otherwise disparate voices. "Commas in *The New Yorker* fall with the precision of knives in a circus act," he once said, "outlining the victim."

This kind of talk invariably upset Ross, who had created the system for his own peace of mind and with the best of intentions, yet who knew full well that in their zeal to scrub out the copy stains his editors sometimes got carried away. It was not a subject he addressed often, but in 1945 he went into it at some length in a letter to Marjorie Kinnan Rawlings, one of whose stories, "Miriam's Houses," had just emerged from this treatment. As Ross explained it, while he and his editors did raise many points,

> what [we] do is query . . . for in the long run the story is the author's and is run over the author's signature, and if the author wants to retain some bad grammar or some ambiguity, or even print two or three words upside down, we let them do it if the story is good enough to get by with the defects, or what we consider the defects. We've got to accept or reject what the author wants in the long run, in toto. We do put up a hell of an argument about details sometimes, though, and occasionally we have to hand back a story we think we have bought because the author won't yield on points we consider important. (The worse the writer is, the more argument; that is the rule. There are a vast number of writers around who can't write. They get by through diligence, application, and various other qualities that are not primarily literary.) . . .
>
> The only great argument I have against writers, generally speaking, is that many of them deny the function of an editor, and I claim editors are important. For one thing, an editor is a good trial horse; the writer can use him to see if a story and its various elements register as he or she thinks they register. . . . For another thing, editors perform a technical function in small matters that I suspect writers shouldn't concern themselves with overmuch. I think writers, or most writers, ought to let editors backstop the small, more or less technical points. The trouble with our querying system is that it sometimes makes writers self-conscious; they get

to thinking—oh, Christ, three or four people are going to pick flaws in this—and they freeze up. . . . Most of the writers think we are helpful at times, if a nuisance generally. We are unquestionably captious and careless frequently and occasionally we suggest changes for the mere sake of change, or for a peculiar personal feeling, but we try not to cram our theories, little or big, down writers' throats.

Different writers took different views on the magazine's editing regimen. O'Hara, obviously, could be violent on the subject, and yet when he *wasn't* drinking he accepted editing well. James M. Cain, having become intimately familiar with the magazine's rigmarole, politely declined Gibbs's invitation to submit some stories not long after he left: "I am gradually starving to death, but I think on the whole I would rather be dead." John Cheever complained of repeated efforts to cut his story endings, and Emily Hahn said that the fact-checking tried her patience. Edmund Wilson, as usual, had especially strong feelings. In a screed to Katharine White, he asserted that "the editors are so afraid of anything that is unusual, that is not expected, that they put a premium on insipidity and banality. I find, in the case of my own articles, that if I ever coin a phrase or strike off a picturesque metaphor, somebody always objects."

On the other hand, care breeds care. Irwin Shaw said that more endings *should* be lopped off, and H. L. Mencken lauded *The New Yorker's* scrutiny as "something that deserves high praise in this careless world." In fact, it appears Ross's own assessment was about right. Of the nearly two dozen veteran *New Yorker* writers interviewed for this book, the great majority said that for all the occasional, inevitable irritations, they found the magazine's editing process reassuring and believed it improved their work.

However loudly or quietly the questions in a given story were resolved, it was then reset into a revised proof. This meant that the piece theoretically was ready to appear whenever it was needed— which, given *The New Yorker's* "Be prepared" motto, could mean right away or a year from now. Material might be scheduled three or four weeks ahead, but typically a given issue's lineup wasn't firm until that very week. The issue in progress was called A issue, one week out was B issue, two weeks out was C issue, and so on; the issue just gone to press was X issue. With so many moving parts and so many Ross rules to follow—e.g., no more than one talking-animal cartoon per issue; the first cartoon in the magazine must have a caption; the theater and film columns could not run adjacent to each other—production of the magazine involved intricate choreography. *The New Yorker's* wheezing, septuagenarian couriers were familiar sights on the New Haven rail line as they lugged manuscripts, proofs, artwork, and pasted-up pages back and forth between the office and the Condé Nast printing plant in Greenwich, Connecticut. As an issue's deadlines descended, coordination was so close that any small slip could create havoc. Gardner Botsford said he once inadvertently brought the magazine to a dead halt the night before it went to press when he mislaid the London Letter by the water cooler.

Except for Woollcott's one-page Shouts and Murmurs column, *New Yorker* pieces were never cut to fit a page. Since they had already been edited to what was considered their rightful length, it was up to the magazine's makeup wizards to build the pages around them. This they did by juggling cartoons, dropping in the distinctive "spot" illustrations (five thousand of which were kept ready for use), and filling in column endings with Newsbreaks. Once a page was ready to go to the printing plant, a page proof was pulled, and the story would be read again. It was not until a final proof was initialed by a designated proofreader that it was deemed all right to print.

In other words, between the time an author turned in a manuscript and the time it appeared in *The New Yorker,* a piece might be scoured fifteen or twenty times by six or eight different people, all in the name of perfection. However, perfection is not only an elusive target but a maddening one, and the editing wars helped spark off some of the magazine's more legendary animosities, such as that between two charter *New Yorker* characters, Rogers Whitaker and Fred Packard. The tart-tongued Whitaker, so charming to pet writers or his many performer friends, could be a bully with his underlings. In the magazine's early years, one of these was Packard, a bon vivant and man of considerable charm, who himself would go on to run the checking department for many years. When he was still working for "Popsie," Packard once threw out some important galley proofs by mistake, and Whitaker made him wade through the building's filthy trash bin to retrieve them. At another time, when Packard had missed a mistake in a story, Whitaker had him memorize the galley proof on which it had appeared, then repeat it aloud to him. Little wonder then that through the years, as each man cultivated countless friends and admirers, Whitaker and Packard would never have a kind word for each other.

Former *New Yorker* checkers, who are, by and large, a fastidious lot, discuss their work with great pride, and certainly they were aware how much solace Ross derived from their labors. Still, this only increased the pressure on them to be right. Every mistake that wiggled into *The New Yorker* was investigated to see how it had occurred, and if it was a factual error that had slipped past a checker, he was generally held to be more at fault than the writer who made the mistake in the first place.

Therefore the checkers would go to storied lengths to get a fact right. William Mangold, who succeeded Forster as A issue editor, first came to *The New Yorker* as a checker, and he recollected one especially memorable assignment from Ross. Dwight Eisenhower, then U.S. Army chief of staff, was about to become president of Columbia, and Ross believed that the head of the university, founded as Kings College by the British two centuries earlier, was supposed to be a High Episcopalian. No one around seemed to know the general's religion, so Ross asked Mangold to find out.

Mangold scoured every conceivable source, but turned up nothing except a passing mention in the *Daily News* that Ike had grown up belonging to a small sect in Abilene, Kansas, known as the River Brethren. Ross had never heard of the sect and yelled, "The *Daily News*! We can't go with something like that on the word of the *Daily News*!" He told Mangold to call Eisenhower's staff in Washington. A helpful aide there made some inquiries, but he too came up empty.

When Mangold, a bit desperate by now, pressed him, the aide asked why the information was so important, and Mangold replied that the editor of *The New Yorker* needed to know. At that the aide excused himself, and a few moments later Ike himself got on the line: "Son, what can I do for you?" Startled, Mangold nonetheless blurted out that he was trying to learn whether as a boy the general had belonged to a sect called the River Brethren. Said Eisenhower, "That's right." Mangold thanked him and reported back to *his* commanding officer, who was never more tickled than when he got his information straight from the horse's mouth.

But at other times Ross followed his fixation for facts right out the window. E. J. Kahn told of an occasion during World War II when he cabled a dispatch on deadline from the South Pacific. The story had to do with how Japanese bombing raids were driving American troops into the jungle, where mosquitoes fed on them, so Kahn made a passing reference to the nefarious alliance between the "Japs and the mosquitoes." Somehow in transmission "Japs" became "waps." Kahn was incommunicado, so back in New York his editor decided "waps and mosquitoes" must be "wasps and mosquitoes." Seeing this, Ross was thrown, though not for long. He had his fact checkers contact entomologists at the Museum of Natural History, who decided, based on the evidence, that Kahn had stumbled onto a rare strain of wasps long thought vanished. Not only did "wasps" make the magazine; so did several lines explaining their remarkable resurrection.

———

IN 1934, MCKELWAY WAS WRITING WHAT HE INTENDED TO BE A single-part Profile of dancer Bill Robinson, and in the course of the piece he made a glancing reference to Harlem. As Ross read the proof, something about the offhand mention struck him as inadequate; "What is Harlem?" he queried. As McKelway later explained, "Ross didn't mean he didn't know what Harlem was, or that anybody else didn't know, but that an offhand reference to such an interesting place shouldn't be made in such a piece." His editor having cracked open the door, McKelway responded with an extended essay on Harlem, as well as what the neighborhood meant to Robinson, and he to the neighborhood. The result was that a one-part Profile became a much richer two-parter.

Reading the Profile Ross was flabbergasted, though pleased, at what his small remark had wrought. Still, he couldn't help himself from muttering in mock dismay, "Jesus Christ, two parts on a coon." His attitudes toward race were no more or less contrary than any other aspect of his makeup. A product of the nineteenth-century West and a man of coarse language anyway, he casually used the pedestrian slurs of the day, especially for blacks and homosexuals. Yet his social conscience was strong, considerably more advanced than one might have expected from the son of a Colorado prospector.

Whatever his views, they were of no real consequence to him or his magazine—which was, after all, still being put out by mostly middle-class whites for mostly middle- and upper-class whites—until 1942, when a highly charged letter, composed in haste and given scant thought, blew up in his face.

In the fall of 1941, the state of Connecticut was proposing to create a public picnic area along the Merritt Parkway adjacent to Ross's property. Ross and nearby homeowners took a dim view of the project, and when the neighborhood association decided to file a protest he was quick to do his part. He dashed off a letter to Governor Robert Hurley, addressing him "in a state of considerable panic and alarm" and describing the ramifications of the park in the kind of hysterical terms that his staff members knew well but that gave the uninitiated pause.

Ross began by explaining that he and his neighbors had worked hard for their property, yet already had experienced many headaches—litter, petty theft, vandalism, and skinny-dipping strangers in the river—because of the parkway. If the proposed park was meant only for Stamford residents, Ross said, he might understand it, but opening it to all

is just inviting Harlem and the Bronx, New York City, up to Stamford to spend the day. I do not mean to be undemocratic, but by God, you couldn't choose a more alarming bunch of people anywhere in the world. The parkway has put Stamford within thirty or forty minutes of the northern sections of New York City, and Stamford is sitting on a keg of dynamite as it is. . . . Stamford is on the verge of becoming the playground of the Borough of the Bronx and the dark, mysterious, malodorous stretches of Harlem, without doing anything further, and why the State of Connecticut should gleefully go out of its way to complicate the situation, I don't know.

Ross strongly urged Hurley to reconsider, closing, "I write in sheer terror."

There the matter lay dormant, a private complaint between a citizen (albeit an influential one) and his governor, until the following spring. That May, *The New Yorker* published the Gibbs-written Profile of Ralph Ingersoll, who had moved on from *Fortune* to help midwife *Life* and, in 1940, founded the legendary New York newspaper *PM*. The Profile, flattering enough in Gibbs's backhanded way, nonetheless gleefully needled Ingersoll for his hypochondria and his gift for overachievement (it was titled "A Very Active Type Man"), and allowed Ross to get in some anonymous digs at his former lieutenant. A few weeks later, *PM* acquired the ammunition with which to return fire. The Stamford newspaper had got hold of Ross's letter to Hurley, and *PM* decided to reprint it. Ingersoll himself was preoccupied with his draft board at the time; better than most he understood Ross's hyperbolic rhetoric, and he didn't consider Ross in any way racist, but he also did not want to interfere with his editors (who may still have been smarting from Ross's great line "*PM* is put out by a bunch of young fogies"). When the letter hit New York, to be reprised again in the other major papers and newsmagazines, all hell broke loose.

Calling Ross a "grandee," Bronx Borough President James J. Lyons suggested that the editor might get a better view of normal American life if he spent more time mingling with the good people of Harlem and the Bronx. "There are thousands of those who love and practice the democratic ideals that are now suffering in internment camps, while your ilk sit in Ivory Towers with a superiority complex." Walter Winchell, who was feuding with *The New Yorker* anyway over an unflattering Profile, similarly castigated Ross in his NBC Radio broadcast. Letters poured in, some supporting Ross but most accusing him of prejudice against blacks and Jews.

Ross publicly acknowledged that parts of his letter were thoughtless and overblown. He tried to explain, rather lamely, that he had not meant to slight the Jewish or black communities; his concern about the park was that it would draw crowds, period, and since the Bronx and Harlem are New York's northernmost neighborhoods, he assumed this was where the crowds would come from. He told Lyons that "*The New Yorker . . .* if you'll pardon my saying so, has an outstanding record for supporting democracy, decency, and tolerance, and even of tolerating such obstreperous phenomena of the age as flag-waving politicians."

Though outwardly defiant, Ross was stunned—and genuinely chastened—by the furor. "I was certainly indiscreet in my remarks," he admitted privately to Frank Sullivan, "and I'll never send another letter off without reading it carefully—to a governor." He added that he certainly had nothing against Jews, but had written the letter "the day after I had a run-in with four carloads of flashy and slick coons, the bad boys, in sports clothes and yellow roadsters with convertible tops. But that was long before the war and the gasoline shortage, etc., and the matter would have been dead if it hadn't been for my pals on *PM.*" (The park, by the way, was not built.)

The charge of anti-Semitism can be dispensed with summarily, as it was simply untrue. From his brave coverage of the Leo Frank trial to his position on restricted resort ads to his protests of anti-Semitism in other publications, Ross's convictions were strong and consistent. More to the point, consider Ross's associations: the cofounder of *The New Yorker* was Jewish, as were dozens of Ross's top staff writers and contributors and hundreds of his friends. He was even made an honorary member (Ross being a common Jewish surname) of a Jewish men's club.

Similarly, if Ross casually referred to homosexuals as "fairies" and "pansies," the fact was that over the years he had dozens of gay and lesbian friends and staff members and, for his time, was rather sophis-

ticated in his outlook on the subject. Their well-known sexual orien-
tations, for instance, in no way eclipsed Ross's respect and affection
for John Mosher, an early film critic and longtime first reader for *The
New Yorker,* or for Paris correspondent Janet Flanner.

Much trickier to sort through are Ross's personal attitudes toward
blacks. From the few instances the subject even arises in his correspondence, one almost gets the sense that he regarded blacks (Asians,
too, for that matter) as less inferior to whites than simply different
from them. If on the one hand he allowed that "coons are either
funny or dangerous" or remarked that a certain person wrote "like an
educated Negro," elsewhere he observed that in his experience
blacks were much more adept at new languages than whites. Indeed,
it appears that Ross considered racial differences a fundamental fact
of life, and he had little patience with those who, in his view, pretended otherwise. In a 1948 letter to Emily Hahn, he wrote, "I meet
many modern Abraham Lincolns these days, who have freed the colored race all over again. Their activities consist mostly of entertaining the Negroes in their homes. That doesn't convince me at all. The
test comes when Negroes entertain the white folks in their homes,
and the white folks go. Most of the activity seems to me straight, self-
conscious patronization of the colored folk—or dangerously close to
being simply that—and moreover, I think the colored folk feel it."

Richard Rovere ran into the same sentiment in Ross's comments
on an early Letter from Washington. As Rovere recalled in his book
Arrivals and Departures, the letter's subject was a report on segregation
in the District of Columbia, and Rovere obviously was sympathetic
to the idea that it should be eradicated. In going over the piece with
a nervous William Shawn, he spotted Ross's queries nearby and
asked if he might see them. In the notes the editor maintained that
the race issue was much more complex than Rovere realized, and
that the writer "plainly doesn't know what he's talking about.... This
is damned foolish stuff, and altogether too much of it is getting into
the magazine. I don't know about the rest of you, but I'm saying right
now that if the Oak Room [of the Algonquin] goes black, I'm clearing out. I suppose we've got to print this, but I hereby file a protest. I

don't see why this magazine has to draw every Abraham Lincoln in New York."

The tirade had so abashed Shawn that he hadn't wanted to show Rovere these notes. Haltingly, he tried to explain: for all Ross's fine qualities, he told Rovere, the man had some blind spots, and "on the Negro question . . . he did not share the enlightened view." In the meantime, Ross himself had thought better of the remarks; he was waiting for Rovere as the writer left Shawn's office, and he apologized. "Jesus, I've got nothing against Negroes," he said. "I guess your piece was all right, Rovere. Just hit me at a bad moment. I hope you don't mind my talking this way."

Rovere told Ross, as he had Shawn, that there was nothing to apologize for, because what the writer had fixed on was Ross's remark, "I suppose we've got to print this." At that moment, Rovere would recall,

> my admiration for Ross was . . . almost limitless. The man clearly despised what I had written for his magazine. He thought it was nonsense. To a degree, he regarded me as an enemy of his values. Yet the article was factually accurate, reasonably well written, and a serious piece of reporting by a man he had asked to cover Washington, and that, for Ross, was that.

Therein, as always, resides the heart of the Ross paradox: He might say or feel one thing, but what did he do in the magazine? And there, whether it was a Rovere Letter or a Dorothy Parker short story (such as "Arrangement in Black and White") or a forceful E. B. White Comment on a black boardinghouse, *New Yorker* writers could attack intolerance because they were *New Yorker* writers. It is significant that with the exception of John Hersey's "Hiroshima," probably the Fact story Ross was proudest of printing was Rebecca West's powerful account of the Greenville lynching. He was pleased that so many Southern newspapers had excerpted or otherwise used it to examine the despicable practice, and he was quick to credit her upon learning that in 1947—West's story had appeared that spring—

Rebecca West
became one of Ross's
favorite reporters and
a good friend.
(UPI/Bettmann)

there was only one reported lynching in all the South. "I think probably your piece was a strong influence against lynchings," he told her. "I think the South has got self-conscious about them and that it has gained a certain amount of enlightenment—or anyhow, restraint."

Those people who saw Ross up close and knew him best—Shawn, Sullivan, the Whites—were well acquainted with his imperfections. Yet they also knew that as an editor, invariably he rose above them. During the Cold War, when this conservative man found himself publishing a magazine with a decidedly liberal, even leftish, cast to it, he wasn't always happy about it. But he believed his loyalty was to his people, not to his own ideologies. "He was a man following a dream," Andy White once said of Ross's single-mindedness and integrity, "and that was good enough for me."

CHAPTER 10

SKIRMISHES

PRINTING THE TRUTH HAS ITS COSTS, AND SOMETIMES THESE include personal relationships. Sooner or later anyone who ever came to work for Harold Ross heard him declare that a journalist cannot afford to have friends. No doubt this must have struck some of his recruits as disingenuous, for Ross seemed to know more people than anyone else in New York. While it was true that his acquaintanceship was vast, probably in the thousands, it was just as true that he had very few intimates, and through the years *New Yorker* articles had indeed whittled at that trifling number. A man whose nature was to shy away from confrontations came to find them an inescapable part of his job.

Crossing swords was never more painful for Ross than in the case of a friend and colleague he once described as being "built like the first joint of your thumb," Alexander Woollcott. The decades have dimmed Woollcott's star considerably, in large part because he was really less an author than a raconteur, albeit a good one. His single great creation, in fact, was Alexander Woollcott, and between the wars this was one of the most influential and omnipresent characters in American culture. In that primeval age before television or celebrity magazines, he was one of the great gatekeepers of fame, hard to miss and even harder to ignore.

And hard to take. Many people simply dismissed Woollcott as a blowhard and bully, with a mean streak as wide as his cummerbund. Even friends suffered his derision. "Hello, repulsive," he might greet a colleague dropping by his East Side apartment-cum-salon, known everywhere as Wit's End. Yet hundreds did like him—loved him, in fact. "You know, I was Aleck's dearest friend," the actress Ruth Gordon told a startled audience of five hundred at Woollcott's memorial service, then added, "And so, I suspect, were all of you." These were the ones who ignored Woollcott's defense-mechanism arrogance, treasured his wit, shared his many enthusiasms, and found that beneath the wattles lurked a man of surprising sentiment and compassion, to whom personal loyalty was the paramount virtue.

The editor of *The New Yorker* was well acquainted with both Woollcotts. "He was a friend," Ross recalled, "who demanded much and would pull you apart if you didn't watch out." For Ross, as for so many others, the Woollcottian trials were worth his bracing company, and for years he was as close to Aleck as he was to anyone—including, perhaps, Jane Grant. After all, his debt to Woollcott was incalculable. In France Aleck had been one of the first to detect greatness in the tumbledown private. In New York he was something of a mentor, seeing to it that the reticent Ross met the right people. He introduced the editor to his future wife, and he helped hatch the idea for what would become *The New Yorker*. Then for nearly six years he provided one of the magazine's most popular columns, Shouts and Murmurs, the kind of feature that helped the magazine cement its bond with discerning readers. To Ross these obligations more than offset Aleck's occasional insults and tantrums. Besides, loyalty was as important to Ross as it was to Woollcott, so when Aleck unilaterally severed their friendship after he was profiled in *The New Yorker*, as much as Ross tried to pretend it didn't hurt, it did.

Woollcott had stopped writing Shouts and Murmurs by a sort of mutual consent at the end of 1934. Both he and Ross had wearied of the wrangling over the off-color and tired nature of the column, not to mention the fact that Woollcott continued to endorse almost any product that would meet his price. Woollcott was also interested in pursuing other careers—including, remarkably for a former drama critic, an acting career. "All the time [Woollcott] wrote for us he was a trial—something of a nuisance and an embarrassment," Ross told Samuel Hopkins Adams. "That was just at the time he was getting drunk with power. He did the page for us, radio broadcasts, pages for other magazines, personal appearances, and Christ knows what." Even so, both men took it for granted that at some point Woollcott would resume the column, and they went so far as to negotiate a pay raise and other matters. In the meantime, however, Woollcott simply became too busy and too big, less a journalist than a celebrity whose opinion on the best current reading was sought out by Franklin Roosevelt. Rather than return to *The New Yorker,* he instead began a regular page with the much larger *Reader's Digest,* and his fame spread wider still.

It was this ubiquitous Woollcott that Gibbs, in late 1938, suggested profiling. Ross was reluctant. The subject was uncomfortably close to him, and he could well imagine the sting of Woollcott's retribution if the story was even remotely complete. On the other hand, he felt Woollcott had gotten too big for even his roomy britches, and there was no denying that he was an obvious Profile candidate. Not that Gibbs set out with the intention of carving up Woollcott. He had a certain respect for Aleck's malicious charm and genius for self-promotion; it would be a challenge to capture in print so complex a beast. Ross at last acceded, and the resulting Profile leaned heavily on his many (unattributed) stories about Aleck.

The Profile was in three parts; Woollcott, who had cooperated fully, was given Gibbs's preliminary draft to review. As he would later in writing about Ralph Ingersoll and his peccadilloes, Gibbs focused more than he might have on Aleck's grotesqueries and petulance, but on the whole the Profile was fair, somewhat flattering—

Alexander Woollcott:
The "Town Crier"
would break with his
longtime friend over
a *New Yorker* Profile.
(Brown Brothers)

there was much about Aleck's philanthropy, for instance—and quite funny. Woollcott examined the draft carefully and pronounced himself satisfied. "With certain reservations," he telegraphed Gibbs, "you have made me very happy."

The "certain reservations" involved a handful of anecdotes that Woollcott hoped could, and doubtless would, be deleted from the final version. One related an embarrassing but harmless hoax played on Woollcott during his "Town Crier" radio career. The other was more serious. It involved a buddy of Ross's and Woollcott's from *The Stars and Stripes,* Seth Bailey. Bailey, called Sergeant Quirt in the Profile, was an amiable ne'er-do-well, and after the war he prevailed on the kindnesses of his old comrades, especially Aleck, who let him move in for a time and gave him pocket money. Bailey drifted west, only to land in San Quentin for having counterfeited traveler's checks and Southern Pacific paychecks. A stunned Woollcott was so sure of Bailey's innocence that he rashly pledged to redeem any check provably traceable to his friend. Confronted with fraudulent drafts totaling thousands of dollars, he had to withdraw his offer.

Woollcott continued to aid Bailey after his release. By 1939, however, the wayward friend had reformed and landed a job, with Ross's help, at the *Chicago American.* Woollcott saw no need to dredge up this tawdry business, believing it subjected an army pal to ridicule and, worse, might jeopardize Bailey's job if it became known that he was the counterfeiter in the story. Ross and Gibbs, however, considered the anecdote revealing of Woollcott, and they were confident that their use of a pseudonym protected Bailey. Just to be certain, Ross contacted Bailey's editor in Chicago, who knew the whole story, to determine what would happen were Bailey unmasked. "Nothing would happen," the editor told Ross. "What is one more ex-convict on the *Chicago American?*" Woollcott was not appeased.

When the Profile, with anecdotes intact, appeared in March and April of 1939, various Woollcott friends were outraged and suggested that he should be too. His earlier sunny opinion notwithstanding, Aleck now took grave offense. "To me you are no longer a faithless friend," he wrote to Ross. "To me you are dead. Hoping and believing I will soon be the same, I remain, Your quondam crony, A. Woollcott."

To Woollcott, using the Bailey story amounted to a personal betrayal of the worst kind, and he always insisted that this was his sole provocation in breaking with his friend. Ross had his doubts—he thought that Woollcott actually was more embarrassed by having to relive the radio hoax—but he was never sure. Whatever the real reason behind the estrangement, it bruised and confused Ross, and he badly wanted to patch things up. Shortly after the blowup Frank Sullivan was with him at "21" when someone mentioned that Woollcott was upstairs playing cribbage with Moss Hart. Ross decided to try a reconciliation; Sullivan thought it a bad idea, especially given that Ross was well into his cups by then, but he tagged along. "He was rebuffed as man has never been rebuffed," Sullivan reported to E. B. White. "It was embarrassing. Aleck refused to shake hands with him and asked him to leave before he really started to tear loose on him."

The standoff continued for three years until Woollcott, having taken ill and convinced he was near death, proffered a truce. From his sickbed in Vermont he sent along this vintage sweet-and-sour message to Ross:

> I've tried by tender and conscientious nursing to keep my grudge against you alive, but I find it has died on me. In the matter of that chuckle-headed pathetically unsuccessful lawbreaker Sergeant Bailey, I still think that you were incredibly cruel in intention and a liar after the event; but it dawns on me a little late that, like most people I know, I, too, have been both cruel and dishonest at one time or another in my life. Anyway, what of it?

The gesture bucked up Ross considerably, and he would have liked nothing more than to accept Aleck's invitation to Vermont. By then, however, the United States had entered World War II, which meant that he was frantically trying to keep *The New Yorker* going in the face of massive staff defections to the war effort. Then he himself was hospitalized for ulcer flare-ups. Eventually Woollcott effected a miraculous recovery—and promptly withdrew his peace offering.

Ross and Aleck never saw each other again. In January 1943, Woollcott, star of an extraordinary and lifelong melodrama, managed one of the most theatrical exits in show-business history. Fifteen minutes into a live panel discussion on CBS Radio—the subject was "Is Germany Incurable?" and Woollcott had just allowed that Germany deserved Hitler the same way Chicago deserved the *Chicago Tribune*—Aleck scribbled a note to the moderator that he was feeling sick, then collapsed at his microphone of a massive heart attack. He died later that night.

———

FOR THE MOST PART, ONLY THE OLD ALGONQUIN COGNOSCENTI knew or cared about the Ross-Woollcott spat. All New York heard about a later incident, however, when *The New Yorker* gored Walter Winchell, and the powerful gossip columnist extracted his revenge on Ross.

Ross was never dazzled by power the way he was by glamour. There were powerful people he admired, but only if he discerned character behind the clout. As a rule, he enjoyed keeping the mighty humble, as J. Edgar Hoover discovered one Friday evening at the Stork Club. There Ross was dining with Lela Rogers and her niece Phyllis Fraser before the three headed up to Stamford for the weekend. Suddenly in walked the FBI director and his sidekick, Clyde Tolson. Lela often accompanied Hoover when he was in New York, and seeing her, he walked over to inquire about getting together sometime that weekend. Lela said she couldn't because she was going to be out of town. Hoover's curiosity was piqued. Where? he asked. Before she could reply, Ross interjected, "You're a flatfoot, find her."

Ross was not a crusading editor, really, yet let someone swell up with self-importance—whether Hoover, Henry Luce, Thomas Dewey, or even his old friend Woollcott—and he was compelled to put in the needle. Certainly he considered Walter Winchell's ego ripe for pricking. He was especially intolerant of Winchell and his ilk because New York's gossip columnists were wildly inaccurate and unconcerned whose reputations they sullied with their sniggering innuendo. In social settings Ross appreciated his gossip as much as the next person—some said more so—yet in general he tried to keep it out of *The New Yorker*. In any case, a writer was to stop at the subject's bedroom door. "A man has a right to a private life," Ross often held.

So when McKelway, freshly liberated from the managing editor's job, proposed a full-scale examination of Winchell and his modus operandi, Ross gave the go-ahead, though he couldn't know at the time that the Profile would balloon into a six-part demolition of the *Mirror*'s popular and influential columnist.

A longtime fan of *The New Yorker,* Winchell was so thrilled at the prospect of being a Profile subject that he not only cooperated fully with McKelway but made sure his friends did too. He anxiously awaited the series, which finally appeared in June and July of 1940.

For McKelway, happy to be writing again instead of editing, the Profile was a masterwork; for Winchell it was a month-and-a-half-long root canal. The columnist was stunned at McKelway's disdainful tone, and incensed at his characterization of Winchell as a vain ex-vaudevillian and not especially talented purveyor of dirt and innuendo.

A young, recently arrived John Bainbridge had helped research the Profile and was responsible for its most devastating indictment. Winchell's three-dot gossip column generated some nine thousand items a year; this staggering volume alone would have precluded Winchell from checking them for accuracy even if he had been so inclined, which he wasn't. With the help of his wife, Bainbridge dissected the five Monday columns Winchell had written that April. His assignment was to check the veracity of as many of the items as was humanly possible. As McKelway had suspected, the arithmetic was more than unflattering; it was appalling. There were 239 specific items, of which 108 were "blind" and therefore unverifiable. Of the remaining 131 that could be checked, Bainbridge found that 54 were wholly inaccurate, 24 were partly inaccurate, and 53 were accurate. "In other words," McKelway summed up, "Winchell was not quite half right in the month of April."

In his anger and embarrassment, Winchell immediately set out to get even. He exhumed and printed any goofy tale that he could find out about McKelway or Ross. He reported to *Mirror* readers that Ross didn't wear undershorts. Seeing this, Ross immediately removed the pair he had on and mailed them to Winchell. On another occasion, the columnist repeated what he had told a waiter who asked where he might find the editor of *The New Yorker:* "He always sits with his back to the check."

Then in September, Ross, who, it will be remembered, had brokered the romance in the first place, attended an engagement party for Bennett Cerf and Phyllis Fraser at the Stork Club. The nightclub's proprietor was Sherman Billingsley, but its king was Winchell, who used it as his de facto office. The party was in full swing when Winchell spotted Ross and demanded that he be bounced. The next day the editor posted this note on *The New Yorker* bulletin board:

> In the interests of avoiding possible embarrassment, I would report that I was kicked out of the Stork Club last night, or asked not

Heroic Sculpture of a Great Expulsion Act

After the Fall:
Stage magazine's
rendering of
Walter Winchell
expelling Ross
from the
Stork Club.
(By Willi Noell)

WILLI NOELL 40

SHOWING MR. WALTER WINCHELL AS THE AVENGING ANGEL EXPELLING UNDESIRABLE ELEMENTS FROM THE STORK CLUB

41

to come in again (suavely), because the sight of me causes distress to Mr. Billingsley, the proprietor—something I'm doing my best to take in my stride. It's because of the Winchell pieces. I don't know to what extent Mr. Billingsley's aversion extends into this organization, but it certainly includes McKelway.

The spat amused more than it annoyed Ross. Winchell, on the contrary, never forgave or forgot. His wrath extended even to Ross's associates; he once went so far as to try to have Mayor O'Dwyer banned from the Stork Club. He continued to print random digs at Ross until the editor's death, and even beyond. When the city's other newspapers reported that upwards of a thousand people had attended Ross's funeral, Winchell questioned the estimate, allowing as how there weren't half that many people in New York sad to see the editor go.

WHEN MOVED BY RIGHTEOUS INDIGNATION, ROSS COULD SUMMON the fire of an Old Testament prophet, a trait to which virtually every book publisher in New York could attest from unhappy experience. Many, like Random House's Cerf, were old friends of his, but as a magazine editor Ross deplored what he regarded as their chiseling attitude toward writers, not to mention their habit of cherry-picking new talent that *The New Yorker* had gone to the time and expense of cultivating. Ross's files are full of incendiary examples. When Brendan Gill was uncomplimentary about John O'Hara's *A Rage to Live* in a *New Yorker* review, O'Hara, mortified at being roughed up in his own magazine, coerced Cerf into demanding Gill's dismissal. Ross's reply began, "Dear Bennett: You are incapable of ratiocination," and concluded, "You are my natural enemy." In a wide-ranging squabble with Viking's Marshall Best, Ross said, "I herewith swear a small oath to make a junior crusade of doing what I can to protect our rights and those of our authors, who in my mature opinion have in quite a number of instances been subject to unholy gypping and exploitation by you book publishers." Ross conceded that his passion sprang partly from guilt over *The New Yorker's* notoriously low pay in its first ten or fifteen years, but it also reflected his genuine outrage that a monolithic industry was taking unfair advantage of his writers. So persistent was he that his efforts were formally recognized by the Authors Guild.

Yet Ross hardly restricted his professional animus to book publishers. The two other magazine men who in the Twenties, along with Ross, revolutionized the industry, DeWitt Wallace of *Reader's Digest* and Henry Luce of *Time,* came in for their licks too, if for quite different reasons.

Ross had a certain grudging admiration for Wallace, whose little "digest" of reprinted and condensed articles, started out of his garage apartment in 1922, became one of the all-time American success stories. But he despised the *Digest* and its many clones ("They have a selection of all stuff written for all time, whereas poor bastards getting out a magazine like *The New Yorker* have to run what's written that week," Ross told Thurber), disliked their amputative approach to literature, and was dismayed that Wallace's largess had wooed away Woollcott.

Moreover, Ross was positively acrimonious upon discovering in 1936 that *The New Yorker* had been virtually giving away its reprint rights, at least compared with other magazines. Up to then, the *Digest* had been reprinting a great deal of the magazine's material, especially its humor and Talk pieces, for only eighteen hundred dollars a year. Shortly after Ik Shuman arrived at the magazine, he learned that other publications, while contributing far less to the *Digest* than *The New Yorker*, were nonetheless getting fifteen or twenty thousand dollars a year for their reprint rights. An angry Ross immediately instructed Shuman to renegotiate *The New Yorker*'s deal, so he invited Wallace to come down for a chat.

As he was being led to Shuman's office, Wallace looked about him with just a touch of awe. "This is the first time I've ever been in *The New Yorker*," he said. "I've always dealt with a young lady [Daise Terry] in the hall." After agreeing to raise his rates to a more appropriate level, he volunteered that he would gladly have done so sooner "but nobody seemed interested in talking to me."

Shuman and Wallace became quite friendly, and one day the latter asked if he might meet the elusive Mr. Ross. Shuman said certainly, and a lunch was arranged at the Ritz. When Ross walked in he greeted Wallace with his limp handshake and said, "Well, boss, how do you like our work for you? Are we working hard enough?"

The renegotiated contract placated Ross for a while; besides, the *Digest*'s handsome fees augmented the earnings of many *New Yorker* writers, so he was under substantial pressure to continue the arrangement. Throughout, however, he was very troubled by a development that was common knowledge in publishing circles but otherwise a secret. Beginning in the early Thirties, the *Digest* had gotten into the habit of planting stories in other magazines in order to reprint them later. The way it worked was that the *Digest* covered a magazine's fee and the writer's expenses for an agreed-upon story. In effect the magazine got a free story, and the *Digest*, increasingly influential and ambitious, got to print material more to its liking. This under-the-table practice had become so accepted and widespread that by the early Forties fully half or more of the *Digest*'s contents were stories of its own origination.

To Ross, the practice was both dangerous—one magazine should not be setting so wide an agenda—and dishonest. *The New Yorker* was one of the few major magazines that would not permit the plants. But neither did it protest them—at least in public.

In 1943, however, the *Digest* committed what, to Ross, was mortal sin: it made a serious play for E. B. White. That spring, in the wake of Woollcott's death, Wallace opened his checkbook in hopes of convincing White to take over Aleck's popular feature in the *Digest*. As if this weren't galling enough, it came just as Ross was desperately trying to persuade Andy to return to *The New Yorker* after his five-year hiatus with *Harper's*. As it turned out, Ross needn't have worried; White thought as little of the *Digest* as the editor did, and he agreed to come back and resume Comment. Ross's relief was as palpable as his delight in seeing a writer actually turn his back on *Digest* money. "You are a man who should not be digested," he told White; "hydrochloric acid should never be applied."

Perhaps it was White's act of defiance that gave Ross the courage to do what he had long contemplated: make a complete break with *Reader's Digest*. The decision was not made lightly; he knew how upsetting and costly it would be for some contributors, particularly the prolific Thurber, whose only serious disagreements with Ross invariably were about money. Nonetheless, that December he notified the *Digest* privately that it could no longer reprint *New Yorker* articles. Then he enlisted White's help in drafting a letter of explanation to the staff and contributors, which was dated February 9, 1944, and was widely reprinted in newspapers and magazines a few days later.

The letter detailed and decried the *Digest*'s practice of planting articles. "The effect of this (apart from spreading a lot of money around) is that the *Digest* is beginning to generate a considerable fraction of the contents of American magazines. This gives us the creeps, as does any centralization of genius." If it desires to publish original articles, the letter said, the *Digest* should do so openly. "*The New Yorker,* furthermore, has never been particularly impressed with the *Digest*'s capsule theory of life and its assumption that any piece of writing can be improved by extracting every seventh word, like a tooth. . . . Mostly, however, we object to the *Digest*'s indirect creative function, which is a threat to the free flow of ideas and to the independent spirit." The letter was signed simply, "The Editors."

The New Yorker's declaration of independence from the *Digest,* as well as its exposure of what Ross termed the "reprint myth," sparked a furor within the publishing community, as well as a great deal of publicity that painted Ross as something of a publishing paragon and Wallace as rather less so. The *Digest* offered no apologies for planting stories, but the practice died out as its client magazines, like remorseful alcoholics, swore off.

There was one curious postscript to the controversy. Not long after the uproar, a *New Yorker* story *was* reprinted in *Reader's Digest*—Hersey's piece about John Kennedy and the PT-109. Well aware of Ross's antipathy toward the *Digest,* yet not privy to the story behind the story, Hersey assumed that Kennedy's powerful father must somehow have muscled Ross into submission. The truth, as usual, was more involved.

When the Navy became aware of the PT-109 story, it recognized its tremendous public-relations value and began pressing Ross to yield it up to a larger national magazine. Joseph Kennedy was also keen on seeing it appear specifically in the populist *Digest,* anticipating correctly how useful it would be in helping launch his son's political career. *The New Yorker,* of course, wanted to keep the story for itself, not only because, as Ross contended, it "was morally ours," but because William Shawn had made such a point of having the talented Hersey in the magazine. Still, Ross was definitely beginning to feel squeezed, and now there was the further complication that the *Digest* was offering to pay two thousand dollars more for the story than *The New Yorker,* with the extra money to go to the widow of one of the men in Kennedy's crew. Under the circumstances, and after much anguished give-and-take on the nineteenth floor, the editor decided to violate his own decree, the ink still fresh on it, and permit the *Digest* to reprint the story—but only with an accompanying note saying that it did so at the Navy's behest. Ross even offered to make good the widow's two thousand dollars if the *Digest* backed out, which it didn't. The compromise mollified everyone except perhaps Ross, and even he could take some comfort in knowing that Chasen's would never run out of good Scotch.

In 1945, Bainbridge produced for *The New Yorker* an unblinking five-part series on DeWitt Wallace's pint-size dynamo, material that he subsequently turned into a book entitled *Little Wonder, or the Reader's Digest and How It Grew*. Ross had played no part in originating or steering the series, Bainbridge said, but took undisguised pleasure in seeing the weekly discomfiture it caused the people up in Pleasantville. Afterward, he gave Bainbridge a five-thousand-dollar bonus.

———

IF THERE WAS ONE PUBLICATION THAT PAINED ROSS MORE THAN *Reader's Digest*, it was *Time*. As in the former case, his gripe had less to do with the man behind the magazine, Henry Luce, than with the magazine itself. *The New Yorker* and *Time*, so antithetical in everything from editorial approach to corporate culture to audience, had been sniping at each other ever since their shared infancy on Forty-fifth Street, but this wasn't why Ross so disliked *Time*. He was put off by its recklessness, its appetite for scandal, and its obvious biases, but most of all he deplored its repeated crimes against the mother tongue.

Time's house idiom, the phenomenon then known as Timestyle, has long since vanished from the publication, but in the Twenties and Thirties it was as much a part of the magazine as its red border. Timestyle was marked by tortured, attention-getting syntax and bizarre neologisms, usually formed by fusing two words into an awkward one; hence, in *Time* someone who worked for Luce would be a "Timeployee." Cofounder Briton Hadden had devised the style to give the magazine some pizzazz when it did little more than regurgitate newspaper stories, but by now its peculiar conventions were as fixed and conspicuous as dandelions.

The first major escalation in the feud was *Fortune*'s 1934 story on *The New Yorker*, which Ross considered something of a betrayal of confidences by Ralph Ingersoll. The editor rejected various proposed counterpunches until the fall of 1936, when the impending launch of another Luce enterprise, the picture-oriented *Life*, provided a handy pretext. *The New Yorker* assigned Gibbs to write a Profile of Luce that would, in the process, send up *Time*. To secure Luce's cooperation, the great man was approached as if it were to be a straight Profile. Since Gibbs's misanthropy was well known at Time Inc., his involvement was kept top secret; Luce and Ingersoll were informed that McKelway would be the lead reporter. The suspicious Ingersoll still advised Luce to decline, but his employer took the enlightened position that one journalist had an obligation to cooperate with another; besides, like Winchell four years later, the unsuspecting subject was flattered by the gesture. His only stipulation was that Ross extend to him the same courtesy that Ingersoll had extended to *The New Yorker* in 1934—the opportunity to look over a draft of the story in order to correct factual errors and discuss serious differences of opinion. Ross agreed.

Since Gibbs was as yet unaccustomed to factual pieces, he was fed his information—from McKelway, who interviewed Luce several times, and from a small battalion of other reporters who were busy accumulating the kinds of details that, when piled up, lent chiaroscuro to a *New Yorker* portrait. Eugene Kinkead, for example, managed to wangle his way into Luce's old apartment, then being sublet, to discover that it was not the modest four- or five-room dwelling Luce had described to McKelway but an immodest fifteen-room, five-bath palace.

As promised, Gibbs's caustic first draft was sent over to *Time* for review. The response was swift and hot. Luce, who had a humor deficiency anyway—Gibbs had noted this prominently in the story—was predictably unamused. Ingersoll, feeling suckered by his former playmates, was incensed. He rang up McKelway and pressed for an immediate meeting to thrash matters out. Ross already had dinner plans, it turned out, so he invited the *Time* men to come over to his apartment on East Thirty-sixth later that evening.

Luce and Ingersoll arrived around eleven. Ross was seconded not by Gibbs but by McKelway. Coming into the living room, Luce spotted the dapper McKelway, walked straight over to him, and said in a thin whine, "It's not true that I have no sense of humor." Later McKelway would tell Thurber, "I thought it was one of the most humorless remarks I'd ever heard."

Ross broke out the liquor and the shouting started almost immediately. McKelway and Ingersoll grew so tipsy that they nearly came to blows. As for the principals, the furious Luce grappled with his stammer while Ross purpled the air with his profanity.

At first Luce focused on the inaccuracy of this and that "fact" in the Profile, such as Gibbs's claim that the average Timeployee took home $45.67802 a week. Ross reminded his counterpart that this was, after all, a parody, and that no one would take such a preposterous figure seriously (Gibbs had arrived at the meaningless figure by typing the numbers sequentially). Eventually it became clear that what most disturbed Luce was not the details but the virulent tone of the piece. At one point he muttered, "There's not a single kind word about me in the whole Profile."

"That's what you get for being a baby tycoon," Ross answered.

Later, still fighting his stammer, Luce yelled, "Goddammit, Ross, this whole goddamn piece is ma ... ma ... *malicious,* and you know it!"

Ross hesitated for a long moment, then said, "You've put your finger on it, Luce. I believe in malice."

The carnival summit bumped along this way until three in the morning. In the end, Ross agreed only to review and evaluate Luce's various concerns with Gibbs and his key editors, including the Whites. This he did the next day. Afterward, Gibbs made some slight adjustments, but for the most part the Profile was left intact. A few days later, having promised to report back to Luce, Ross composed a remarkable letter—five single-spaced pages—that as usual said as much about the writer as it did about the recipient:

I assume it is up to me to make certain explanations; at any rate I do so, to clear my conscience, with which I always struggle to keep current. . . .

I was astonished to realize the other night that you are apparently unconscious of the notorious reputation *Time* and *Fortune* have for crassness in description, for cruelty and scandal-monging and insult. I say frankly but really in a not unfriendly spirit, that you are in a hell of a position to ask anything. . . .

Ross went on to explain, point by point, the group's review of Luce's complaints, and why they were leaving in such details as the fifteen rooms ("You are offering the place for rent as a fifteen-room apartment, a pretty state of affairs if it isn't true"), Ingersoll's hypochondria ("One of our investigators reported that the second drawer on the left-hand side of Ingersoll's desk contains twenty-eight bottles, phials, boxes, etc. of remedies"), and Luce's purported political ambitions. Then he moved on to a cutting personal observation:

After our talk the other night I asked at least ten people about *Time* and, to my amazement, found them bitter, in varying degrees, in their attitude. You are generally regarded as being mean as hell and frequently scurrilous. Two Jewish gentlemen were at dinner with me last night and, upon mention of *Time,* one of them charged that you are anti-Semitic, and asked the other if he didn't think so too. The other fellow said he'd read *Time* a lot and he didn't think you were anti-Semitic especially; you were just anti-everything, he said—anti-Semitic, anti-Italian, anti-Scandinavian, anti-black-widow spider. "It is just their pose," he said.

Still in high dudgeon, Ross closed the letter "Sincerely yours, Harold Wallace Ross—Small man . . . furious . . . mad . . . without taste"—all being adjectives that Luce publications had variously used to describe him through the years.

As for the Profile itself, which appeared November 28, 1936, it is probably Gibbs's single best-known piece of work, and with good reason. Gibbs was a parodist without contemporary peer, and six decades after the fact, the Luce Profile remains a supreme example of the parodist's art, pointed and hilarious, if a tad more wicked than it really needed to be. It is laced with sardonic little touches (Gibbs's footnote comment on one of *Time's* rare disappointing financial years: "Hmm"), and the dead-on send-up of Timestyle convolutions is merciless. An example:

> "Great word! Great word!" would crow Hadden, coming upon "snaggle-toothed," "pig-faced." Appearing already were such maddening coagulations as "cinemaddict," "radiator." Appearing also were first gratuitous invasions of privacy. Always mentioned as William Randolph Hearst's "great & good friend" was Cinemactress Marion Davies, stressed was the bastardy of Ramsay MacDonald, the "cozy hospitality" of Mae West. Backward ran sentences until reeled the mind.

After Gibbs touched on Luce's empire-building ambitions and supposed interest in the White House, he concluded the Profile this way:

> Certainly to be taken with seriousness is Luce at thirty-nine, his fellowmen already informed up to their ears, the shadow of his enterprises long across the land, his future plans impossible to imagine, staggering to contemplate. Where it all will end, knows God!

Of course Luce survived the spoof, though Gibbs's thrust proved fatal to Timestyle, which began to recede almost immediately. "Nobody over there could go on writing in that style after reading [Gibbs's] piece," McKelway noted. Certainly the Profile added a few years' worth of fuel, were any needed, to the sometimes funny, sometimes silly feud between *Time* and Tilley.

Indeed, in 1938 Ingersoll slipped the name of Eustace Tilley into *Time's* masthead, apparently with the intention of dropping it later and announcing that the old gent had been fired. He withdrew the name when Corey Ford, who had invented Tilley in *The New Yorker*'s 1925 "Making of a Magazine" series, threatened to sue. For its part, *The New Yorker* never tired of lampooning *Life*. Just before the war, in a play on the popular "Life Goes to a Party" feature, *The New Yorker* produced "Life Goes to the Collapse of Western Civilization." In 1938, *The New Yorker* answered *Life*'s much-talked-about "The Birth of a Baby" photo feature with E. B. White's cartoon send-up, "The Birth of an Adult." One aspect of *Life* that Ross especially hated was the great length the erstwhile family magazine would go to print cheesecake photos. In the summer of 1951, while he was literally preoccupied with the matter of his own life and death, he was nonetheless exasperated enough to scribble this note to White: "*Life* does story on the placid and historic Thames and finds nude sunbathers on its banks. This must be the *fifty-eighth* way of working in naked women."

It must be said that long before then *Life* had given Ross a reason

With a few deft strokes, artist Al Hirschfeld "doodled" Ross into Joseph Stalin for *Life* **magazine in 1937. The editor was not amused.** (© *Al Hirschfeld; The Margo Feiden Galleries Ltd., New York*)

for maintaining a grudge. In August 1937, less than a year after the Luce Profile, *Life* published a series of "photo-doodles" in which, with only a few deft strokes of the brush, the great caricaturist Al Hirschfeld transformed certain famous people into other famous people. He doodled Winston Churchill into W. C. Fields, Gertrude Stein into Albert Einstein . . . and Harold Ross into a very credible Joseph Stalin. The juxtaposition was very funny, but this time it was Ross who was caught without his sense of humor. However, recalling the episode more than half a century later, Hirschfeld still laughed about it. The nonpareil illustrator of Broadway greats would seem to have been a natural contributor for *The New Yorker,* but after the Stalin doodle he learned from friends at the magazine that "Ross was so furious he said I'd never be in *The New Yorker.*" And at least while Ross was alive, he never was.

The *Time–New Yorker* feud limped along in this intramural way for years, finally expiring of its own pointlessness. The memories, though, remained vivid. Years after he was abraded in *The New Yorker,* Luce was at Rollins College in Florida to make a speech, and while there he dropped in on a class in contemporary biography. The students were discussing Henry Luce, and their text was the Gibbs Profile. It was all too maddening for the once-baby tycoon. He turned to a traveling companion and exploded, "Is this thing going to be engraved on my tombstone?"

The answer, after a fashion, was yes.

WORDS AND
PICTURES

AN IRONIC ASPECT OF THE LUCE PROFILE WAS THAT EVEN AS EARLY AS 1936, if there was an American magazine as ripe for parody as *Time* it was *The New Yorker*. Its characteristic mannerisms and voice were becoming so familiar and successful that eventually Ross's magazine would be more widely copied—and parodied—than any other periodical in the world. By the late Thirties, *The New Yorker* had managed to metamorphose from an unprepossessing comic sheet into an articulate diary of a great city, just as in the postwar period it would become something of a diary for the nation (and in time, with William Shawn at the height of his power, for the world).

Haul down one of the fat bound volumes from those years and flip to any issue; the formula is as recognizable as it is reassuring. Here is February 26, 1938: A charming Hokinson cover depicts two wealthy tykes under the reproachful eye of their chauffeur pulling pies from little windowed cubbyholes at the Automat. Inside are cartoons from Thurber, Arno, Whitney Darrow, Jr., Sydney Hoff, Garrett Price,

Barbara Shermund, and Gardner Rea. A Talk story on the New York Badminton Club indulges two Ross passions at once, facts and nostalgia (oldest organization of its kind in the world; gentlemen competitors are expected to remove their hats but not their coats). The critics were in a rare uniform good mood: Benchley praised T. S. Eliot's *Murder in the Cathedral,* Fadiman was enchanted by Thomas Mann's *Joseph in Egypt,* Mumford acclaimed the thoughtful, progressive design of new housing projects in Harlem and Williamsburg, and Robert A. Simon commended the week's offerings at the Met. There were dispatches on racing from Hialeah and fashion from Paris. There was a Kay Boyle short story and humor from Frank Sullivan. The Profile was an A. J. Liebling classic called "Tummler," about a small-time hustler, Hymie Katz, who is addicted to opening nightclubs. Beyond its irresistible subject, the story celebrates the New York patois that always captivated Liebling. (" 'Hymie is a tummler,' the boys at the I. & Y. say. 'Hymie is a man what knows to get a dollar.' ") The full-page ads are for Tiffany, Henri Bendel, Guerlain, Lincoln automobiles, and the Bermuda tourist board.

One also finds a handful of E. B. White's Newsbreaks and their still-familiar headings, such as "Raised Eyebrow Department," "Wind on Capitol Hill," and "How's That Again? Department." In fact, about the only thing that the February 26 issue didn't have going for it was White himself. Having tired of New York and *The New Yorker,* requiring new challenges of himself, White had forsaken Comment in August 1937, and in early 1938 decided to move full-time to Maine, where he and Katharine had summered for years. He also kicked off a new monthly column for *Harper's,* called "One Man's Meat." Unlike Comment, "Meat" was a signed personal essay, which meant that White could deal more forthrightly with the sober issues of the day than was possible in *The New Yorker.* Just losing White's services was enough to depress Ross, but making it incalculably worse was that Andy had had the temerity to take his wife with him. The move to Maine amounted to an incredible sacrifice on Katharine's part; unlike Andy, she loved her job and loved New

York, or at least their tranquil, sunny apartment in Turtle Bay Gardens, a unique collection of brownstone homes on Forty-eighth and Forty-ninth streets between Second and Third avenues, with a vast common courtyard. Andy, however, was determined to go, and though he sometimes might wonder about Katharine's priorities as she lay in bed engulfed by manuscripts and *New Yorker* proofs, her loyalty to her husband would always transcend that to her boss.

For Ross, getting out *The New Yorker* without the Whites was like trying to walk deprived of legs. To keep her own sanity and to help Ross keep his, Katharine agreed to continue editing fiction part-time, and to perform sundry other duties, such as reading and critiquing the just-published issue. Ross, however, had come to rely on both Whites so intimately—which is to say, in person—over a dozen years that continuing the association by mail was a genuine hardship. For her part, Katharine was intent on doing a thorough job even at her long remove, and she missed the gossip, the give-and-take of the office, and the comforting sense of being in on things. So to stay informed, she did what came naturally—she relied on Ross. But as he was already feeling overwhelmed, this new demand was too much, and he made no effort to hide his irritation. "As to your sharpshooting of the issues . . . I say do it your way," he wrote to Katharine in 1939. "I deplore your way, but since you can't do it another way, I'll settle on it. One of the earliest and most distressing discoveries I have made in administering an office (after my fashion) is that a piece of paper won't go two ways. Your report has to go twenty-four ways, including back to you in instances where you ask outright questions. I make one exception to swallowing your method. I won't be responsible for answering personal questions asked by you in the body of a report. These are so preposterously unfair that I'll stand on that. If you want to know who P.W.W., the author of the Court Games Dept., is, it's up to you to put the question on a separate piece of paper and send it in here *not personally addressed to me.* It is unfair to bother me with such things. . . . (P.W.W. is [Philip W.] Wrenn, but that's the last time I tell you.)"

Ross was no less frustrated about Andy's defection. With White out of the picture, the daunting task of producing Comment fell mostly to Gibbs. What seemed to come so easily to White came so hard to Gibbs that the responsibility only tweaked his propensity to drink, which only made Ross more nervous. Comment, being opinion, was the one part of *The New Yorker* he had never been altogether comfortable with anyway—"I never did know how to lead off the magazine," he was often heard to mutter—but he had been entirely comfortable with White. Now White was gone. He continued to edit Newsbreaks from Maine, but apparently both Gibbs and Ross were counting on him to submit some Comment and miscellany. Evidently they had underestimated White's need for a clean break. Not long after Andy left, an anxious Gibbs told him, "I think it's a crime that you should be out of this book altogether, and wish to God you'd write something—verse, casuals, fables, anything at all. I thought you were going to do some more fables, and so did Ross, who often speaks about it, with his fingers in his hair. 'He just sails around in some goddamn boat,' he says. I think you would find this pitiful if you could hear him."

As discouraging as the Whites' departure was, Ross could at least be cheered by one happy development that distinguished *The New Yorker* of the late Thirties. This was the explosion of reporting talent at the magazine, and the growing prominence of their journalism. These new voices belonged to young writers, most with newspaper experience but all with freer, more interpretive writing styles than was typical of the dailies. They drew on the fiction techniques of narrative, character development, shading, and irony to tell their stories—stories that just happened to be true. Their so-called literary journalism was a hybrid of a very high order.

Ross loved news, considering it his specialty, and had come to be very choosy about his reporters. For every one he hired, he passed on ten others because he could not countenance sloppy reporting or a lazy imagination. He especially had no use for reporters who talked a good game but who fell down at the typewriter. Anyone starting to explain a good story in person to Ross as often as not was cut off with, "Get it on paper." No sooner had he promoted St. Clair

McKelway, who knew a thing or two about getting it on paper, than Ross told him, "We've got to have more journalism." Thus charged, McKelway in his three years built a breathtaking roster of reporters.

A. J. Liebling had been at *The New Yorker* about a year by then, but he was struggling and had yet to see a byline; it was McKelway who made a magazine writer out of him. McKelway lassoed Liebling's good friend and colleague from the *World-Telegram,* Joseph Mitchell, who already had sold Ross a few freelance pieces. McKelway hired Sanderson Vanderbilt, Jack Alexander, and the acclaimed *Times* reporter Meyer Berger. He hired E. J. Kahn, Jr., and Brendan Gill after Katharine White had bought casuals from them and called them to McKelway's attention. He hired a promising recruit just out of the Columbia School of Journalism, Philip Hamburger. (In typical *New Yorker* fashion, after Hamburger turned in some sample Talk stories to McKelway, the editor mumbled something unintelligible and dismissed the young job candidate. Hamburger assumed he had washed out until McKelway rang him up a few days later to say, "Where are you?" "What do you mean?" said Hamburger. Said McKelway, "I hired you last week.") McKelway also recruited David Lardner, the precocious twenty-year-old son of Ross's old crony Ring, and John Bainbridge, who a few years later was helping McKelway torpedo Winchell. (Other notable contributors to *The New Yorker*'s journalism of this time were freelance reporter Richard O. Boyer, who wrote dozens of incisive Profiles, and Emily Hahn, who was sending back from the Far East not only delightful short stories but also news dispatches.)

At Ross's *New Yorker,* journalists tended to arrive in distinct waves that paralleled larger developments at the magazine. The first wave comprised those reporters present at the creation, or nearly so: Janet Flanner, Morris Markey, Lois Long, Murdock Pemberton, Geoffrey Hellman, Niven Busch, Charles Cooke, Alva Johnston. The second belonged to the early Thirties, when *The New Yorker* was growing more prosperous and ambitious: reporters McKelway, Eugene Kinkead, William Shawn, and Margaret Case Harriman (daughter of Algonquin owner Frank Case and a specialist in show-business

Profiles), and the critics Lewis Mumford (who covered art and, with Ross's imprimatur, produced the first substantive architectural criticism in America) and Clifton Fadiman (who, while not as entertaining as Dorothy Parker—who was?—gave the magazine's book department some sorely needed depth and its first real credibility within the publishing community). Liebling, Mitchell, et al. were the third wave. The fourth wave rolled in during World War II, when so many experienced reporters were serving in the armed forces or otherwise in government, or were working abroad for *The New Yorker.* Newcomers to the magazine at this time included some remarkable women who finally erased Ross's suspicion of female reporters—Andy Logan and Lillian Ross (no relation)—as well as Berton Roueché and Richard Rovere, critic Edmund Wilson (he replaced Fadiman on books at the end of 1943), and celebrated contributors Rebecca West and John Hersey.

However, it was the third wave, the class of the late Thirties, that probably did the most to advance the innovative, literate reportage that became a *New Yorker* trademark. They set the standard for all the great *New Yorker* reporters who followed, as well as the so-called New Journalists of the Sixties. (Some of these later lights seemed to think they were creating a new art form, but the truth is that they were still playing stickball and delivering newspapers when *The New Yorker* was perfecting "literary journalism.")

Of course these *New Yorker* writers didn't exactly invent the form either. They had a godfather in New York's own Stephen Crane, and in Europe, as Lillian Ross and others have noted before, the tradition can be traced back to Turgenev and Defoe. One also cannot discount the profound influence on Ross of the romantic war correspondents of his youth, such as Richard Harding Davis. Indeed, Ross's great achievement with literary journalism, just as with Talk, or with Newsbreaks, or even with Profiles, was less a matter of invention than of reinvention—that is, reviving a moribund form, giving it a metropolitan slant, then polishing it to a high gloss.

For many people, the great *New Yorker* reporting tradition was epitomized by a pair of Joes: A. J. (for Abbott Joseph) Liebling and

Joseph Mitchell, two close friends who could not have come from more dissimilar backgrounds. Liebling, son of an immigrant Jewish furrier and his wife, was born on Manhattan's Upper East Side, while Mitchell was the scion of an old North Carolina planter family, whose father was not pleased to see him forsake tobacco for the typewriter. But New York brought them together in their many shared passions—for newspapers, for literature, for good food expertly prepared, and for the city's abiding parade of characters. Each man was a peerless stylist. Liebling could usually be found smack in the middle of his stories, which he told with virtuosic gusto. By contrast, Mitchell stood outside his tales, the observer who misses no remark, and spun his pieces out in immaculate, understated prose. Together, they introduced *New Yorker* readers to a grittier side of the city than they were accustomed to, either in their lives or in their magazine. Liebling and Mitchell inhabited the city's wharves and fish markets, its smoky boxing halls and greasy "beefsteaks," which were gluttonous political feeds. Their subjects were Liebling's tummler, his pugs and pols, Jacob and Lee Shubert, the vainglorious Roy Howard; and Mitchell's gypsies, his high-steel Indians, the denizens of McSorley's Wonderful Saloon, and Joe Gould, the enigmatic and erratic compiler of an "oral history of our time." Liebling would come back to the office and write in self-satisfying torrents. Mitchell, on the other hand, was deliberate when he wrote, meticulously assembling his stories with infinite patience. (McKelway, in fact, said he was able to persuade Mitchell to come to *The New Yorker* only by promising him a salary instead of the drawing account that other reporters got. The mere idea of a draw "terrified him," McKelway would recall, "as indeed it should have.")

Liebling would have done well to take a cue from his cautious friend. He went into the hole as soon as he joined *The New Yorker* and never climbed out in more than twenty-five years there. This was partly attributable to his rocky start at the magazine. It took him several years to figure out how to go from glib but straightforward newspaper stories to the more complex demands of longer pieces. This deficiency, in fact, nearly derailed his first major *New Yorker*

Friends and intrepid reporters, Joseph Mitchell, left, and A. J. Liebling helped establish the *New Yorker* tradition of "literary journalism."
(Lillian Ross; from the collection of Philip Hamburger)

effort, a debunking Profile of a charismatic Harlem evangelist known as Father Divine. Always a first-rate reporter, Liebling had amassed terrific material for his exposé, but his various drafts were shapeless, hopeless blobs; he seemed to be writing less a *New Yorker* Profile than a "million-word book on comparative religion," he said. Desperate, Ross called in McKelway for a consultation. The latter imposed some organization on the material and rewrote much of it, though he left large chunks just as Liebling had written them. The result was an extraordinary multipart Profile that carried the bylines of both.

Despite Ross's constant admonitions against straying too far beyond the Hudson River, in the early Thirties *The New Yorker* inevitably had expanded the scope of Profiles to such national and international figures as Lindbergh, Einstein, Stravinsky, and FDR. Ross had been more successful in keeping the approach to Profiles broad and relatively brief—brushstrokes still showing, as it were— which was his original intent, but this was changing too. By the middle and late Thirties, the Profiles, as well as the magazine's reporting generally, were becoming more muscular and multifaceted. Even more significant, they were exhibiting a sharper point of view from the writer, as McKelway and Liebling demonstrated in their study of Father Divine. This is how they began the second part of the Profile, entitled "Who Is This King of Glory?":

George Baker, who by a process of multiple birth had become The Messenger and then Major J. Devine, was born a fourth time, and then a fifth time, almost as soon as he established himself in Sayville, Long Island, in 1919. He became Rev. J. Divine, dropping the military title and adopting a vowel which gave the name a supernatural significance. Then almost immediately afterward he became Father Divine (God). He has been God ever since. A few weeks ago his disciples in Harlem stretched a streamer of black-and-gold silk across the throne of Heaven, the headquarters of the cult, on West 115th Street, with the blaring legend:

FATHER DIVINE IS DEAN OF THE UNIVERSE

But that is rank hyperbole. The promotion to Dean of the Universe is simply a gratuitous expression of the enthusiasm of his followers and does not represent a formal rebirth. Neither in the early years in Sayville nor in the later years in Harlem has Father Divine ever hinted that he considers himself to be anything more than God.

Having persevered to see Father Divine actually in print, Liebling was at last on his way to becoming a magazine writer, and his work would truly come into its own a few years later under William Shawn, McKelway's eventual replacement as the top nonfiction editor. For Joseph Mitchell, the transition from newspaper to magazine was less traumatic. He is a great talker, spinning out thoughts and stories in long, looping sentences gilded with his Carolina accent. More to the point, he is a great listener, and whenever possible he prefers to let his characters carry along their stories in their own words. Here is Mitchell on Mazie, a no-nonsense lady with the proverbial heart of gold who spent her days and nights selling tickets at a dime picture show near the Bowery:

> On her walk, Mazie usually tries to steer clear of other well-known nocturnal Bowery characters. Among these are the Widow Woman and the Crybaby. The Crybaby is an old mission bum who sits on the curb for hours with his feet in the gutter, sobbing brokenly. Once Mazie nudged him on the shoulder and asked, "What's the matter with you?" "I committed the unforgivable sin," he said. Mazie asked him what the sin consisted of, and he began a theological description of it which she didn't understand and which she interrupted after a few minutes, remarking, "Hell, Crybaby, you didn't commit no sin. You just prob'ly got the stomach ulsters."

Ross, who had spent so many of his own reporting years profitably working the wrong side of the tracks, appreciated Mitchell's fascination with New York's underbelly, but he worried about it too. Once he told Mitchell, "You know, you write about a pretty depressing people. You're a pretty gloomy guy." Then he added thoughtfully, "Of course, I'm no goddamn little ray of sunshine myself."

Mitchell and Liebling were not the only reporters, as is sometimes assumed, transfiguring New York street life into *New Yorker* prose. In 1935, for instance, Meyer Berger used a Profile on the doyenne of Brooklyn's Irish mafia, Anna Lonergan, to examine the violent world of the waterfront—a world not without its comic ironies.

> Back in the twenties, every time there was a killing in Irishtown, the newspapers would label it "dock war murder," but Anna Lonergan says that was a lot of journalistic prittle-prattle. When Jim Gillen was killed on Jay Street in 1921, for example, his death was attributed to dock trouble, but the motive was something entirely different. Wild Bill Lovett killed Gillen for pulling a cat's tail. "Bill always hated to see anyone hurt a animal," Anna says.

If Mitchell, Liebling and Berger were operating in neighborhood nooks and crannies, other reporters, most notably Flanner, were taking *The New Yorker* into the world's presidential palaces and glitter domes. Flanner had quietly undergone a metamorphosis as remarkable as that of the magazine itself. Her style, in personal letters as well as Letters from Paris, was always elegantly iconoclastic, a touch rococo. At times editors had to deal with her obscurities—one of them called it simply a matter of "unknotting" her—but over the years it became clear that few reporters were her match for intellect, wit, or sheer power of observation. With the encouragement of both Ross and Mrs. White, Flanner had gradually branched out into broader pieces: some Letters from London, for instance, Profiles of such cross-cultural figures as soprano Lily Pons and couturiere Elsa Schiaparelli, and a richly detailed two-part examination of England's Queen Mary. It had also been impossible for Flanner to ignore the political winds whipping up all about her, particularly after the bloody Paris riots of 1934. As Genêt's Paris columns inevitably contained more politics, Ross offered no objection, which she correctly took as his sanction.

Yet in their new boldness, the occasional misstep served as a reminder that both *The New Yorker* and Flanner were working uncharted territory. In early 1936, she wrote an ambitious three-part Profile of Adolf Hitler entitled simply "Führer." Thoroughly researched and handsomely written, the piece was indicting in its way, as Flanner found the man as repugnant as his politics—in fact indistinguishable from them. Yet in her strenuous effort to remain detached, as Ross would want her to be, there was an odd bloodlessness about the Profile; her understatement had the unwanted effect of almost trivializing the horror of Hitler's racial views and already murderous behavior. Some *New Yorker* patrons mistook Flanner's reluctance to be overtly censorious of Nazism for sympathy. The author was said to have been startled upon learning that in Berlin many considered the piece positive.

———

IN HIS OTHERWISE CATHOLIC PROSPECTUS FOR *THE NEW YORKER*, ROSS made no mention of fiction per se, only a pledge, near the end, to publish "prose and verse, short and long, humorous, satirical and miscellaneous"—what might be called the kitchen-sink clause. The editor liked fiction, supported and encouraged it, and had an intuitive sense of what was good and what wasn't. But it didn't touch his soul the way factual writing did, didn't move him in the same way it obviously moved William Shawn, who as a young man thought he might write fiction for a living. This is one reason serious fiction was slow to develop in *The New Yorker*, probably the last major piece of the formula to fall into place. In the beginning it simply was not a Ross priority.

This also helps answer the nagging question of why some of the major names of between-the-wars literature—Hemingway, Fitzgerald, Wolfe, Dos Passos, Sinclair Lewis, and others—were in the magazine infrequently or not at all. There were other reasons, of course, chief among them that when *The New Yorker* was founded there were dozens of magazines competing for top fiction, many paying substantially more than Ross could afford. There was no logical reason for a Scott Fitzgerald to submit to an upstart when he could make so much more money at *Collier's* or *The Saturday Evening Post.* Ross said as much himself in 1929, when he made a halfhearted pitch for more material from Fitzgerald: "You wouldn't get rich doing it," he wrote, "but it ought to give you satisfaction." Likewise, Ross, a now-and-then fishing companion of Hemingway's, years later admitted to the writer's wife that "in the early days I never went after him because we didn't pay anything." By the time *The New Yorker* was so well-off that money wasn't the obstacle, its preferences and idiosyncrasies were so apparent that one cannot conceive of certain writers—Faulkner, say—bending themselves to fit in.

There was also the simple fact that big names never mattered a thing to Ross. He said so himself many times and made it plain in his magazine. *New Yorker* articles were signed at the end, rather than the beginning, to play up the writing and play down the writer. A spare index steered readers to standing departments but gave no clue about what they said, and it didn't mention the issue's fiction at all. The cover offered no promotional come-ons or gave any other hint as to what was inside. In this way the editor cultivated a sense of weekly discovery among his readers, letting them stroll through the magazine as if through an inviting wood, to come across their own pleasant finds—a Perelman here, a Steig there, a Thurber seemingly everywhere.

Ross had nothing per se against marquee names—if they could write—but out of necessity *The New Yorker*'s editors for years had been discovering and developing their own authors, and they liked it that way. Once he decided that fiction did have a place in the magazine, in fact, Ross insisted that Mrs. White, and later her successor, Gustave Lobrano, not only keep lists of promising young writers but stay in touch with them, read their developing work, and encourage them. In the process, Ross's *New Yorker*, more than any other magazine at the time, managed to incubate and sustain a whole generation of American writers. This was not necessarily the editors' intent, merely a happy by-product of their tastes and passion for cultivating talent.

Another thing that must be remembered about early *New Yorker* fiction is that it wasn't "*New Yorker* fiction" at all—or at least the kind of story that came to be the stereotype. For well over a decade, *New Yorker* short stories were almost without exception brief, humorous, and/or carefree enough to waft away on a decent breeze. They were White and Gibbs stories. More notably they were Thurber stories: already by 1933 the Columbus expatriate had rendered his hometown so memorably in such stories as "The Night the Bed Fell" and "The Night the Ghost Got In" that when he collected them in *My Life and Hard Times,* the book was considered a masterwork, and still is. But plenty of other humorists were working alongside Ross's Big Three, including Benchley, Parker, Sullivan, Joel Sayre, and, beginning in 1930, the virtuosic S. J. Perelman. Meanwhile, some of their contemporaries were turning out highly successful serials. Clarence Day's father first turned up in 1933, and Arthur Kober's Bronx family, the Grosses, followed in 1934. There were the Mr. Pan pieces of Emily Hahn, Richard Lockridge's Mr. and Mrs. North, and Leo Rosten's memorable H*Y*M*A*N K*A*P*L*A*N, working hard to master night-school English with his fellow immigrants. Outside this mold, certainly, were the stories of Kay Boyle and John O'Hara, yet even O'Hara's early fiction was lighter and extremely brief—a column and a half at most—fitting nicely into Ross's "casual" concept. It was the Harold Ross of these formative years whom Katharine White was referring to when, rejecting a submission from Gertrude Stein, she told Alice B. Toklas that she was not allowed to buy anything her boss didn't understand.

However, anyone who ever doubted Ross's capacity to grow need look no further than the dramatic evolution of *New Yorker* fiction. Not that Ross was looking for change, exactly; he might have been content to publish "Life with Father" stories until the day he died. But he didn't have the chance. As the Depression wore on, as Communism and Fascism spread and another European war began to look inevitable, the world became less amusing to the Thurbers, Parkers and Sullivans. They wondered whether their funny little stories weren't trivial, even impertinent, in light of the pestilential times. As a friend, Ross could appreciate their reticence and understand their waning enthusiasm, but as an editor, he found the situation maddening. He would repeat his conviction that anxious times are when people need humor most, but he simply received less and less of it. This dearth provided the first real opening for a new kind of writer, one keen to convey cultural angst, especially as seen through the urban and suburban experience. Mrs. White was intrigued by this emerging work, and if Ross had his qualms, he wasn't interfering, either.

So it was only in the late Thirties that what would become known as "the *New Yorker* short story" was actually starting to turn up in the magazine with any regularity. This was the relatively plot-free, mood-intense, character-driven story—or as Jerome Weidman once heard a sarcastic Somerset Maugham describe it, "Ah yes, those wonderful *New Yorker* stories which always end when the hero goes away, but he doesn't really go away, does he?" Years later Maugham told Weidman that he had moderated his contempt for such stories; it seemed that after inexplicable years of rejection, *The New Yorker* had actually purchased one of his. (Maugham probably never knew why, but his "breakthrough" resulted chiefly from lucky timing. For some reason Gus Lobrano had an aversion to Maugham and had rejected his every submission. However, Lobrano was away on vacation when Maugham sent in "The Romantic Young Lady." All the other editors liked the story, so they bought it and ran it. Lobrano was not pleased, and it was the only Maugham story *The New Yorker* ever ran.)

This new kind of short story was a backlash against its ornate, artificially plotted ancestor. Relying heavily on dialogue, it was more naturalistic, more slice-of-life, and like the world itself, it was more somber, enigmatic, and sometimes violent. Its writers had come of age during the Depression, experiencing little or none of the postwar gaiety of Ross's generation, and their struggle just to survive was often palpable in their prose.

One of those in the vanguard of the new *New Yorker* fiction was a boyish John Cheever, who was nearly starving to death in a three-dollar-a-week Greenwich Village flat when Malcolm Cowley, then a subeditor at *The New Republic,* took an interest in him. He encouraged Cheever to try his hand at short stories and then sent a batch of them to Katharine White. *The New Yorker* started running them in 1935. Another new voice belonged to Irwin Shaw, who considered his startling three-thousand-word "Sailor Off the Bremen," published in 1939, the first long and politically serious piece of fiction to appear in *The New Yorker.* At about this same time O'Hara was producing his entertaining letters from that wise guy "Pal Joey" (a particular favorite of Ross's), and John McNulty was beginning his classic, darkly comic Third Avenue sketches. Edward Newhouse started appearing after he was plucked from the magazine's slush pile. Dorothy Parker's tales turned darker and more overtly political. And Jerome Weidman could move from the amiable Lower East Side color of Harry Bogen and *I Can Get It for You Wholesale* to a 1938 piece, "I Thought About This Girl," a troubling, affecting tale of a Polish emigrée who must suddenly give up the bakery job that has given her so much satisfaction because "my mother wrote me it isn't right . . . to work for Jews."

This last, as it happened, was that rare *New Yorker* story that even

John Cheever.
(UPI/Bettmann)

brushed up against what was internally referred to as "the Jewish question." This was one of a handful of themes that in general Ross considered unsuitable for *The New Yorker.* Homosexuality was another taboo, as was cancer, and other subjects, like promiscuity, had to be treated with supreme delicacy if they were discussed at all. Wolcott Gibbs conveyed a sense of the ground rules in an illuminating and droll tract that he called "Theory and Practice of Editing *New Yorker* Articles." Written sometime around 1937 at the behest of Katharine White, who was constantly trying out new editors, "Theory" is a specific enumeration of *New Yorker* do's and don'ts and was a working document. (See Appendix II, page 442.) In point nineteen, Gibbs counsels, "Drunkenness and adultery present problems. As far as I can tell, writers must not be allowed to imply that they admire either of these things, or have enjoyed them personally, although they are legitimate enough when pointing a moral or adorning a sufficiently grim story. They are nothing to be lighthearted about. '*The New Yorker* cannot endorse adultery.' Harold Ross vs. Sally Benson. Don't bother about this one. In the end it is a matter between Mr. Ross and his God. Homosexuality, on the other hand, is definitely out as humor, and dubious, in any case."

Ross was squeamish on these subjects less on personal or moral grounds than on those of taste and general *New Yorker* propriety, in much the same way that he was always on patrol against sexual double entendres (which, in fairness, pranksters like Thurber and O'Hara constantly tried to slip by him). When Frank Sullivan wanted to call a story "The Lay of the Land," Ross balked on the grounds that it sounded faintly obscene, and Sullivan reproved him thusly: "All I can say is that any man who can read a double meaning into the word 'land' is a fit subject for a psychoanalyst."

The final entry on Gibbs's list contained this observation: "Try to preserve an author's style if he is an author and has a style." Gibbs the editor heeded his own advice, and as a parodist he was expert at fixing up lame copy in a voice identical with the writer's. He could not fall back on some *New Yorker* house style or sound, even had he wanted to, because such a concept did not exist in the way it did at *Time*. For the fiction editors, the integrity of the individual writer's voice was paramount, and whenever critics chided the magazine for somehow imposing a "*New Yorker* style" on writers, Ross, Mrs. White, and Gibbs invariably bridled. They pointed out, reasonably enough, that a magazine managing to accommodate writers as diverse as Clarence Day and J. D. Salinger, or Sally Benson and Mary McCarthy, or Shirley Jackson and Ruth McKenney, could not be guilty of perpetuating any one type of story.

On the other hand, there is no question that even allowing for this laudable multiplicity of voices, Ross's magazine did propagate something that can fairly, if ambiguously, be called *New Yorker* style—a phenomenon marked by similarities not only in theme but in internal cadence and form. Various *New Yorker* writers agree about this, and they offer various reasons for it. Taken together, these help explain what should have been, on its face, a contradiction—different writers, yet similar sounds.

Much of it had to do with what *New Yorker* stories *weren't*. As indicated above, they tended not to be about sex, and especially not about promiscuity or what was considered sexual deviance. They weren't profanity-ridden. They weren't elliptical or overly impressionistic; under Ross's firm influence, fiction editors preferred that stories be straightforward in the telling. Nor were they ambiguous, at least in terms of the action. Ross did not want to be tricked or make his readers labor too hard to understand what was going on.

Almost invariably the stories were briskly paced. Because *New Yorker* fiction under Ross was relatively brief, they moved ahead sentence by sentence rather than paragraph by paragraph, and long passages devoted to mood or setting, much less to secondary action, were excised as waste motion. In William Maxwell's phrase, this "elimination of superfluities" naturally accounted for a similarity in pace. Also, regardless of the author, these stories, in their subtleties and understatement, somehow maintained that consistent *New Yorker* attitude to the world. Finally, of course, the popularity of the genre fed on itself; after watching the proliferation for years, Katharine White herself began to be wary of what she came to characterize as the "slight, tiny, mood story." Hundreds of the stories were anthologized, many by the magazine itself, eventually helping to cement in the public mind the "*New Yorker* story" as a literary category.

Whether the label is fair or not is beside the point. What matters is that this naturalistic fiction marked a major turning point in the development of the form—the difference, as it were, between rhymed verse and blank verse. It also made possible the even more original voices that would emerge in the magazine under Shawn's liberalizing influence—McCarthy, Updike, Barthelme, and many more.

No one, including Ross, planned all this to happen at *The New Yorker*, but neither was it an accident. At Ross's insistence and following Mrs. White's lead, the magazine's fiction editors maintained deep and long-standing relationships with their writers that transcended the work. They paid attention to the seemingly little things that matter so much to writers—quick responses to their stories, for example, and even more important, prompt payment (definitely *not* the industry norm). They made it their business to keep up with authors' families, their health problems, their drinking (if they drank to excess, as far too many did), and their writing blocks. The editors solicited stories on the one hand, and yet at least every other letter to a writer was a rejection, but usually one couched in yet another solicitation, and as much encouragement as the editors could muster.

This kind of shepherding was an art form in itself, and over the years Katharine White proved a master at it. For one thing, while she was capable of great tact, she was tough-minded and not someone to be underestimated or patronized. When she nearly died from complications giving birth to her and Andy's son Joel, a nurse whispered in her ear, "Do you want to say a little prayer, dearie?" Katharine roused herself to reply, "Certainly not." She could be just as blunt with Ross, especially in situations where she found him mulish and wrongheaded, as in his sporadic forays against serious poetry in the magazine. (Ross sometimes had days when he woke up and simply couldn't believe that he was printing deliberately ambiguous material in *The New Yorker*.) If he didn't try to eliminate poetry altogether, he might try to dismiss his marvelous critic, Louise Bogan, or propose to pay poets based on how wide their verse happened to be set. In such cases, Katharine, who almost singlehandedly had built up serious poetry in the magazine, would passionately argue to Ross why it was important, remind him how lucky he was to have Bogan, and deride his pay proposals as "absurd" gestures designed to make *The New Yorker* a "laughingstock" in literary circles. That was usually enough to get Ross to back down—until the next time.

But if she was fearless, Katharine White found it much less easy to be openly warm. With her austere manner and her influential position as one of the original disciples, she was an intimidating figure to many subordinates. Helen Stark, who came to *The New Yorker* in 1945 as an assistant librarian (and stayed forty-seven years, the last twenty-two as head librarian), at first considered Mrs. White aloof and was somewhat cowed by her. Then one day, shortly after she had given birth to her son, Mrs. Stark was pleasantly surprised to receive "the most beautiful letter" of congratulations from Mrs. White. The gesture forever changed her opinion of the editor.

The incident is significant, not only for its sentiment but for the manner in which it was conveyed. Perhaps fittingly for an editor, Katharine White best related to others through the written word.

Emotions and feelings she was uncomfortable expressing face-to-face came quite naturally in her letters, which were warm, passionate, concerned, and nurturing. Her collected papers are full of examples, from four decades of long-distance relationships with writers from James Thurber to John Updike. Not every *New Yorker* writer found her easy to work with, preferring Gibbs or Maxwell or, later, Gus Lobrano or Robert Henderson, but those who did were devoted to her.

This excerpt from a letter to Clarence Day is typical of Mrs. White's approach in that it manages to transmit concern, rejection, and affection—not to mention a dash of personal news, and the company line—all at once:

> You are one of the people that I want to see the most of all, both as a friend and as a contributor, and I promise to be there by hook or crook before very long to discuss the whole plan for the Father series....
>
> In the meantime I have to tell you the bad news that the final decision on "Father Expects Every Tree to Do Its Duty" is a "no" just because the theme of this story is really too much like "Father and Old Mother Earth." The essential idea of both of them is Father disciplining nature. As you know, I had thought the two might be combined and we could pay you for the extra work so that you would not suffer, but you didn't want that and the scheme fell by the boards.... I do feel that the first page of "Father Expects Every Tree..." could be part of another Father piece for us.... Do think it over in the midst of your wrath. If you are too cross with me I shall weep, so don't be. As an editor, one has to steel one's self in sending unpleasant news to contributors, especially after three months of country calm and a month of illness when no such tasks came up.
>
> Much love to you and I will see you soon.

When it became apparent that the Whites would be leaving New York for good, Katharine began the melancholy search for her replacement. As it turned out, she didn't have to look far, finding him in Lobrano, one of her husband's closest friends. Lobrano came to *The New Yorker* around the end of 1937 from *Town and Country*, where he had been an assistant editor and unhappy. Katharine tried him out on fiction, and he demonstrated quickly that he was a natural, blessed with impeccable taste, a strong sense of style, and a sharp but guarded wit. Lobrano took on more responsibility as Katharine withdrew, and in 1941 Ross formally named him to succeed her as managing editor for fiction.

Born in 1902, Gustave Stubbs Lobrano came from an old New Orleans family—he could trace his lineage back five generations to a pirate confederate of Jean Laffite's—and in the Southern manner he was gracious and soft-spoken, a man whose placid demeanor belied an inner intensity. He went to Cornell, where he studied liberal arts and law simultaneously. He trailed White there by several years but got to know him by working on the campus newspaper, and after college they shared a Greenwich Village apartment. They also shared a love of writing, and the two quiet men became lifelong friends. After his marriage, however, Lobrano moved upstate and worked for seven years at his in-laws' travel agency. Eventually, with White's help, he got back to New York, first at *Town and Country*, then at *The New Yorker*, where he would at last be doing what he considered serious editing.

Lobrano's way of relating to his writers was precisely the opposite of Mrs. White's. He was great personal friends with many of them, including Cheever, Shaw, Newhouse, Perelman, and Salinger, and he often had them to his suburban Westchester home for dinner, or to play tennis or badminton. (Tall, graceful, and that rarity at *The New Yorker*, a staff member who was even remotely athletic, Lobrano enjoyed sports and outdoors activity of all kinds, especially golf and fishing.) What few letters he wrote to his contributors were most perfunctory; unlike Mrs. White, he tended to convey more intimate concerns in person. It was his habit, for instance, to get writers together in groups for lunch. In such settings Lobrano, less a talker than a practiced listener, not only learned what might be bothering his contributors but at the same time inculcated in them a sense of *The New Yorker* as an extended family. This approach also demonstrated what an effective buffer he was for Ross, whose aggressive queries and gruff demeanor now and again were known to put off a writer.

Eventually a low-key but distinct friction would arise between Lobrano and Mrs. White. This was the perhaps inevitable consequence of her on-again, off-again presence at the magazine (not only mutually frustrating but, it should be remembered, Andy's doing), and her continued special relationship with Ross, which, for all the editor's respect for Lobrano, no one could possibly supplant. For the moment, however, Lobrano was glad to be there, and Mrs. White was glad to have him.

If their temperaments and styles differed, the magazine's various fiction editors were together in one respect; they shared Ross's reverence for the written word, and his respect for writers. In his auto-

Gustave S. Lobrano.
(By Ray Shorr for Mademoiselle: ©1952, 1980 by Condé Nast Publications, Inc. Courtesy of Dorothy Lobrano Guth)

biography, *Praying for Rain*, Jerome Weidman recalled his maiden *New Yorker* editorial conference, with Gibbs, after the magazine had purchased his first story, which Weidman had titled "Chutzbah." At the top of Gibbs's long list of discussion points was a question about the title.

"The copy department feels it should be spelled with a *p*," Gibbs said.

"They're wrong," insisted the nervous young author.

Gibbs asked how he could be so sure of the pronunciation. Because that's the way his mother pronounced it, Weidman replied.

When they had worked their way through the rest of Gibbs's list, all that was left was the business of the title. "The copy department gets a bit sticky about these things," Gibbs said. "Is there any chance you might change your mind?"

"No," Weidman said. "My mother would disapprove."

Gibbs gave him a sharp look, then smiled and extended his hand. "Nice meeting you," he said. "Come in again soon."

———

PERHAPS WHAT HAROLD ROSS MISSED MOST ABOUT THE OLD *STARS AND Stripes* days was that he never lost a minute's sleep over how much to pay writers. Corporals got corporal's pay, doughboys got satisfaction for their doggerel, and it was all decided by the War Department anyway. At *The New Yorker*, on the other hand, he never spent a day that wasn't somehow darkened by the vulgar subject of money.

This being so, there was a wisp of irony in the fact that of all his writers at *The New Yorker*, Ross was probably closest socially to Geoffrey Hellman, who was the single most persistent staffer in ragging Ross for money. However incidental a meeting, however trivial a memo, Hellman couldn't resist injecting a plea or a harangue. He was not without cause; he had started at the magazine back when Ross was still paying out mostly in promises and sermons, and Hellman feared he might never earn a respectable salary if he stayed there. One night in 1936, he cornered Fleischmann at a party and raised his favorite subject. The publisher looked at him evenly and told him that as much as his editors thought of him, sometimes they considered him a tiresome nuisance—"a horse's ass," in fact.

This was all the confirmation Hellman needed, if any, that his future lay elsewhere, and he jumped to Luce's new baby, *Life*, the picture magazine endlessly patronized by Ross and *The New Yorker*, for a handsome increase in pay. Though acutely aware that for Hellman the core issue was money, Ross was never told of the catalyzing conversation with Fleischmann. He and Hellman remained on friendly terms; Hellman even sent over some of *Time*'s distinctive, powder-blue memo pads, which Ross delighted in using to communicate with his wayward friend (and thereby perpetuate their little joke on Luce). Besides, they both knew that *Life* was no place for a writer, especially one of Hellman's metropolitan interests and nuanced style, and within two years Ross happily welcomed him back.

Twenty years later Hellman and Fleischmann were attending another party, this time a banquet at the Waldorf. As they chatted amiably over their martinis, Fleischmann suddenly mentioned that he had always regretted something he had said to Hellman many years before. Hellman stopped him short and told him to think no more about it.

Beyond their pride in being a part of *The New Yorker*, about the only thing the magazine's fiction and nonfiction writers had in common, at least for the first fifteen or twenty years, was dissatisfaction with their pay, which ranged from the merely inadequate to the execrable. In its later years *The New Yorker*'s rates would become among the highest in the business, but through adolescence its penury was almost a point of pride. As John Bainbridge said, "People [were] working for what I should say was about eighty percent kudos and twenty percent cash."

In the beginning the men who ran *The New Yorker* were cheap because they had to be. Later on they were cheap because they just were. Revered as he might be on the editorial floors for his intellect and bonhomie, Hawley Truax was a notorious tightwad. (A legendary but true story is told of the time a panhandler asked Truax to spare some change for a meal. Suspecting what the man really wanted was a drink, Truax gave him no money but reached into his pocket and handed over the wrapped sandwich he had planned to eat for lunch.) Fleischmann, who could be so generous to business-side employees—certain key people were even given low-interest company loans to buy their homes—thought that the sheer privilege of being published in *The New Yorker* should satisfy the editorial side. And for years Ross was impulsively cheap, too. "Ross . . . would no more have thought of offering a writer money than of offering a horse an ice-cream soda," Liebling would write. The editor's attitude derived partly from the exigencies of the magazine's early years, partly from his own meager upbringing, and partly from his honest conviction that a touch of hunger was not a bad thing for a contributor.

But unlike the other *New Yorker* principals, Ross eventually underwent a Saul-like conversion on the question of pay, admitting to Thurber in 1945, "I have been a party to robbing [writers], for I unquestionably sat around this joint for years and didn't see that authors were done right by." Perhaps it was the years of being beaten on by Hellman and Thurber (and O'Hara and Ingersoll and Benson and Cain and Cheever and Liebling and Gill and . . .) that sparked his conscience. Perhaps it was his own personal money woes, or the high-priced Hollywood competition. Or perhaps he saw it merely as another way to unnerve his nemesis on the seventeenth floor. ("The magazine is having a slight boom now," Ross told White in the spring of 1943, "and I'd rather have contributors getting it than Fleischmann, who would just lose it at the races.") Whatever his motivations—and no doubt they included all of the foregoing—by the late Thirties Ross had upgraded editorial pay considerably, and in the mid-Forties, when the profits really started rolling in, he fought incessantly to push much of it to the writers, in higher drawing accounts, better piece rates, and bonuses. He also took the progressive view of insisting on regular cost-of-living adjustments for writers to help protect what pay they *did* get.

But in the bad old days, *The New Yorker* was so cheap that it refused to advance a hundred dollars to Sally Benson, one of its most popular writers and so prolific that she used a pseudonym, Esther Evarts, for lesser, back-of-the-book stories. Hers was scarcely the first or last complaint on this score. O'Hara, so strapped in his salad days that even the most token gestures elated him ("A dollar bonus on each casual—nice!" he wrote Ross in 1934), eventually came to develop what one staff member described as "an endless sense of grievance" against the magazine—the chief grievance, naturally, being money. In 1948, during one of his spells of feeling unloved and taken for granted (with some justification; Ross tended to be more suspicious than appreciative of O'Hara, whose characters were always toying with the magazine's morality code), the writer abruptly demanded that *The New Yorker* should pay him several hundred dollars for any submission, whether it was accepted for publication or not. Even had Ross been inclined to agree to that extraordinary arrangement, which he wasn't, it would have presented an expensive dilemma, for O'Hara could bat out a workmanlike short story in an afternoon. Instead, the editor sent O'Hara an inexpensive gold watch, picked up at a Third Avenue pawnshop, on which he had had inscribed, "For John O'Hara from *The New Yorker* 25 West 43rd Street BR 9-8200, With Love and Admiration."

Forever linked as he was with *The New Yorker*—he would sell Ross more than two hundred stories—O'Hara did not work for the magazine. Like all fiction writers he was a contributor, an independent agent, living from sale to sale. This can be the most nervous kind of existence, not just for young writers of unmade reputations but also for established names with growing children and onerous mortgages. John Cheever and some of *The New Yorker*'s other fiction stars came to resent the fact that their journalistic counterparts were considered employees and received those reassuring weekly checks. A few even pushed Ross, unsuccessfully, for their own version of a drawing account.

The Fact writers, of course, would have begged Cheever's pardon; since that draw represented not salary but rather an ever-mounting, open-ended debt, it was anything but reassuring. Here is how the

John O'Hara wanted
payment for every story
he submitted. He got a
used watch instead.
(Culver Pictures)

account worked. Say a *New Yorker* staff reporter was drawing $125 a week, which would have been common in the late Thirties or early Forties. He might sell Ross a Profile for $1,000 and a handful of Talk items for $250, which theoretically wiped out ten weeks of obligation. Ross had devised the system in the early days of the magazine as a way to spur productivity while trying to mitigate a writer's financial insecurity. As usual with his pay systems, however, it had the opposite effect. Most reporters considered the draw insidious and anxiety-inducing, a form of indentured servitude. (Richard Rovere said it took him six years to get into the black with Ross.) To stay afloat, a writer not only had to maintain steady productivity but to continue generating ideas that touched Ross's fancy—neither circumstance being one of life's sure shots. A *New Yorker* writer staring at a blank sheet of paper in his typewriter might appear to be concentrating, but he really was listening to that insistent meter in his head ticking away.

On the fiction side, contributors generally signed a "first-reading agreement" under which, in exchange for one hundred dollars a year, *The New Yorker* got first crack at any of their stories. Pay was based on length but also on quality: acquiring editors were supposed to "grade" the stories for relative merit: A, A–, B, C, and so on (though Maxwell, for one, says he nearly always graded a story A, and nobody ever complained).

Ross was constantly tinkering with pay rates to motivate and steer writers. His main goal was restraining length—he despaired watching his once-beloved casuals gradually interred by ever-longer "short" stories. But he also paid to encourage productivity, such as offering a twenty-five percent bonus to writers who sold the magazine six stories in a given year. He even used inducements to modulate the tone of the magazine. For instance, for years he was in the habit of paying more for so-called "highlife" stories than "lowlife" ones, but the work of Liebling and Mitchell defied such facile classification. Mitchell once recalled how the editor went about reconciling the Mazie Profile. "Ross said, 'I'll tell you what we'll do. You've got Fannie Hurst in [the piece]. She's highlife. That makes it a "highlife lowlife." ' And then he put another classification in, that if it was 'humorous highlife' it got a certain amount, but if it was a 'humorous highlife lowlife,' that was as high as you could get."

Calculations like this explain why *New Yorker* writers through the years have invariably characterized their compensation as "byzantine." Staffers could scarcely understand their own pay, much less anyone else's—which was another, albeit ulterior, goal of the system, since Ross was petrified that employees might actually compare paychecks.

This sheepish "explanatory" letter to Frank Sullivan, apparently from the mid-Thirties, suggests the typical convolution of a new Ross system, as well as the sorry track record of its many forerunners:

I must write you in connection with this check, which you probably will see instantly is not as big as you have been getting, although the story is of a very unusual degree of excellence. It's one of the best by anyone in a long while, in fact. We have a new and revolutionary scheme for payments, an explanation of which is now being mimeographed. . . . Briefly, the plan is to pay somewhat more per word (in your case twenty cents) than we have been paying for all pieces under 1,200 words in length and for the first 1,200 words of pieces that run longer than that. Then, after 1,200, [we] pay half the word rate. This, we hope, will accomplish several things, one of which is to make it profitable for writers to do quite short pieces—a few hundred words—or to encourage them to do it anyway. The flat word rate didn't encourage them. The flat price per piece didn't. The fact is that both *dis*couraged them. . . .

Although, perhaps unfortunately, your first check under the new system is a little smaller than your flat price check would have been (this piece being a short one—just over 1,200 words), an average (of the past) sized piece would have been as much, or greater. We have gone over all our writers, and especially you, I will say, and found that there would have been no suffering of loss except in a few cases of long-winded persons that ought to be choked off anyhow, probably. You won't lose, on the basis of past performance, and if you write some short pieces, goddammit, you'll profit to a considerable extent and can buy more Pennsylvania R.R. stock. For instance, you'd get eighty dollars for four hundred words, the length of some of the best things you used to do in your good old newspaper days, and haven't done since. One hundred dollars for five hundred words. Think of it!

As usual, this particular scheme was doomed. Writers being writers, they disregarded the "brevity premium" and simply wrote longer stories to compensate for what they had lost vis-à-vis the old system. When he wasn't on the warpath himself over pay, Thurber tended to regard Ross's elaborate formulas with bemusement, and as just one more incarnation of his fixation on systems. "It's Ross's old wall-tearing-down urge taking a new form," he told Katharine White in 1938 after the editor had unveiled his latest calculus. "It's a variant of the old red and green tab system, it makes up for there being no more Greta Palmers to fire, no Ingersoll to harry, no Talk passing system to bother about. Remember the famous 'White passes to Levick who passes to Bergman who passes to Ross who passes to Hellman, second down and fifteen to go'?"

———

PAYMENT CLASSIFICATIONS DIDN'T STOP WITH THE WRITERS. FOR A while Ross tried them with the artists too. His original intention toward establishing a relative pay scale was to rank artists as either A, B, or C, but such judgments quickly got out of hand. According to one hierarchical rating sheet—undated, but from the Forties—Ross considered two of his finest, Charles Addams and Mary Petty, "AAA." At "AA" were Thurber, George Price, Whitney Darrow, and many others. "A" artists were Carl Rose, Sam Cobean, Otto Soglow, etc. There were a handful of "B" names, a "C," and even a few luckless souls who were deemed by Ross to be "D" artists, whatever this meant.

Then there was a "special" category that Ross reserved for a trio of his franchise artists, implying that they were above ranking. These three, whom Ross tried to have represented somehow in every issue, were Helen Hokinson, Gluyas Williams, and Peter Arno. In September 1936, Arno published one of his most memorable cartoons, in which he depicted two elderly, affluent couples beckoning some friends to join them at the movies. The caption read, "Come along. We're going to the Trans-Lux to hiss Roosevelt."

Whenever readers have encountered *New Yorker* editors through the years, whether in Ross's time or today, more often than not they ask about the cartoons and the artists. What is Steinberg like? (A brilliant recluse.) Was Addams as mischievous as his delectably macabre cartoons suggest? (Yes.) But mostly what people want to know is, how do *New Yorker* artists come up with their clever ideas?

In the case of the Arno drawing, the cartoon actually began with a man named Richard McCallister and an evening at the movies. He had just settled into his seat when the customary newsreel began to roll and the jut-jawed image of FDR flickered across the screen. Suddenly McCallister heard a hissing sound. At first he thought it must be a radiator, but as he looked about he was appalled to see that the hissing actually was coming from some well-dressed patrons. McCallister sent in the idea to the *New Yorker*'s art editors, who passed it on to Arno, who realized it perfectly.

("Trans-Lux" was one of more than five thousand cartoon ideas that McCallister sold *The New Yorker* in more than fifty years, enough to provide him a very handsome living.)

Especially in the beginning, *The New Yorker* relied on writers and gagmen for the great bulk of its cartoon ideas. Ross then turned to his stable of extraordinary draftsmen and -women—classically trained artists like Rea Irvin, Ralph Barton, Alice Harvey, and Perry Barlow—to bring the ideas to life. After they were done, editors like the Whites, Thurber and Gibbs (and later Lobrano and James

(By Peter Arno; © 1936, 1964 The New Yorker Magazine, Inc.)

"Come along. We're going to the Trans-Lux to hiss Roosevelt."

Geraghty) would look over the marriage of word and picture to see if it could be sharper yet. The process was always intended to be collaborative. In 1934, when Ingersoll's *Fortune* piece suggested that Gluyas Williams drew no original ideas, the bruised artist informed Mrs. White that henceforth he would draw none *but* his own. Panicked by this, Ross told Williams, "This magazine is run on ideas. . . . My God, a very large percentage of the contents of *The New Yorker*, drawings and text, are based on the ideas originating with the staff and suggested to writers. . . . The one thing that has made *The New Yorker* successful is that it is a collaborative effort, switching ideas back and forth to find the man best adapted to doing them, and I hope to high heaven that you aren't going to be discouraged into not being willing to work collaboratively."

A well-known example of Ross's philosophy in action was the occasion when Carl Rose drew a cartoon of a fencer taking off his opponent's head, with a caption reading "Touché!" Ross loved the concept but found Rose's rendering, with its lifelike figures, disturbing. He asked if Thurber might try the same idea. "Thurber's people have no blood," he said. "You can put their heads back on and they're as good as new." Thurber turned it into one of his best-known drawings.

(For the most part Thurber, whose first cartoons appeared in *The New Yorker* in early 1932, worked from his own ideas. Rea Irvin deplored his drawings, offended by the amateurish quality that helped make them so appealing to nonartists. Indeed, it took Ross himself several years to be won over; to him, seeing Thurber acclaimed as an artist was akin to finding out that the dim lad next door was a chess prodigy. Once convinced, though, he became Thurber's biggest champion, to the point where he tried to recycle the artist's old cartoons when blindness halted his drawing. Even so, he constantly needled Thurber about how his artistic popularity was a fad perpetuated mainly by the British. "Well, if it's a fad it's lasted quite a while," Thurber once snapped back. "Don't be impatient," Ross replied, "give it time.")

Most of the early *New Yorker*'s top artists collaborated to some extent. Arno relied almost exclusively on outside ideas, and Hokinson did much of her best work after teaming up with writer James Reid Parker. Still, dealing with creative egos was a touchy business, and friction was not uncommon—especially in cases when, as sometimes happened, artists learned that the editors had farmed out the same idea to several of them in a kind of underhanded contest. Inevitably, many of the magazine's artists became as self-conscious as Williams and began to rely more and more on their own ideas for drawings. While some critics have argued—Ross among them, at times—that this trend resulted in less-funny ideas and less-satisfying pictures, it also inspired many artists whose work was uniquely and inextricably influenced by their personalities, like Addams, Steig and Steinberg.

Arno, whose drawings of lecherous old men and lascivious young women were marked by bold lines and a wicked sense of humor, was almost certainly the best-known artist of the Ross era. He was also one of the most self-centered. Albert Hubbell, who during World War II acted briefly as the magazine's art editor, remembered taking some cartoon ideas over to Arno's Park Avenue apartment early one afternoon. A creature of the night, the artist was still in his silk dressing gown. He went into the kitchen to fix himself a thick hamburger—without offering Hubbell one—then settled down to hear the ideas. One that Hubbell liked and pitched hard involved a billiard table, but in no time Arno was frowning. It turned out that Ross paid him a substantial bonus for full-page cartoons, which presupposed vertical concepts, so a billiard table was altogether too lateral to even consider. "Wait a minute, Hubb, wait a minute," Arno said. "Let's go for those pages."

Whether the drawings were vertical or horizontal, the ideas self-generated or supplied, all of them went through the same rigorous development process, which culminated in the Tuesday afternoon art meeting, a venerable *New Yorker* tradition. The purpose of the meeting was to cull proposed cover illustrations, judge hundreds of cartoon ideas and works in progress, okay anything ready to run, and come up with suggestions for those pictures still in need of fixing. The meeting began promptly at two o'clock—Ross encouraged lunchtime sobriety on Tuesdays—and took place in a small conference room. Usually there were six participants: Ross; Daise Terry, who recorded approvals, rejections and suggestions; Rea Irvin; Geraghty, who came aboard as art editor in 1939; Mrs. White (later replaced by Lobrano, as the broad "fiction" bailiwick traditionally included art); and an art clerk. The clerk, usually a young man, had the job of organizing the art to be presented, preparing the room (everyone had pencil and pad, an ashtray, and knitting needles, which the editors used to point out details on the drawings without smudging them), and displaying the cartoons during the meeting. Otherwise he was to be as unobtrusive as the furniture. A conspicuous exception was Truman Capote, who as a teenager worked for several years as a *New Yorker* clerk. He was known to hide drawings he didn't like or cluck his tongue when he disagreed with the group, at least until Ross insisted he keep his tart views to himself.

Curiously, for fifteen years *The New Yorker*'s art director virtually never worked directly with the artists. Ross believed they might resent a colleague's telling them how to draw, so from the outset Irvin was more consultant than manager. A nonartist—first Gibbs, then Maxwell—had always sat in on the art meeting, with the thankless task of reporting back the group's criticisms to the artists. Upon his arrival as art editor, Geraghty—another nonartist—changed this, becoming the cartoonists' and cover artists' direct liaison to the magazine.

Even if James Geraghty had known nothing whatever about art, Ross would have been predisposed to like him. Not only did he share Ross's Irish wit and temperament, but he came from the West—born in Washington state—and had even worked in the lead mines of Idaho. But Geraghty *did* know art. His passion for fine drawing was complemented by a perfectionist streak and a strong intuitive sense of what worked—qualities that *New Yorker* artists immediately recognized and respected. He was also a whiz with captions. It was his writing ability, in fact, that got him to *The New Yorker* in the first place, albeit through the back door. In New York he had been a radio gag writer and for several years had successfully submitted cartoon

Though not an artist himself, James Geraghty had a highly developed aesthetic sense.
(Courtesy of Mrs. James Geraghty)

ideas to Arno. It was Maxwell who brought him to the attention of Ross, who hired Geraghty in spite of his thin résumé. Years later Geraghty asked Maxwell what he had seen in him. "You looked like a gentleman," Maxwell said, "and I wanted to leave."

Geraghty would have to prove himself to the artists, certainly, but perhaps his most daunting challenge was winning over the formidable Daise Terry. In addition to being the office manager, Miss Terry functioned as the secretary of the art department, and she had firm ideas about how it should be run. After he had hired Geraghty, Ross took the new man around to see her. "Miss Terry, I want you to meet James Geraghty, who will be taking over the artists," Ross said. "Mr. Geraghty, meet Miss Terry." Then throwing his hands high in the air, like a referee kicking off a boxing match, the editor exclaimed, "And may the best man win!"

If Geraghty's good taste and discerning eye were apparent right away, he had some management shortcomings to overcome. In his early years he could be abrupt and abrasive with some of the artists, who felt he rode roughshod over them. However, his tenor mellowed as his confidence increased, and many of those same bruised artists became his devoted, lifelong friends. Geraghty helped his cause by being a fierce, passionate advocate for the artists, something they had never had at the magazine before. They saw he could often make Ross come around to his way of thinking; they also appreciated his creativity and hard work on captions, and his enthusiasm for their aesthetic. He was known to approve some ideas simply because he knew they would make elegant drawings. Recalled Dana Fradon, "He would come back and say, 'Dana, now make it beautiful.'"

Sadly, there was one artist Geraghty would never convert. His relationship with Rea Irvin would always be his most ticklish problem, for by the time Geraghty arrived at *The New Yorker*, Ross had little use for the older man. He was routinely rejecting Irvin's drawings, a situation the artist only exacerbated by circumventing the routine and not bothering to get his ideas approved before he drew them up. Irvin still came in every Tuesday, yet he often dozed through the art meetings, rousing only if something by Gluyas Williams turned up on the board. He was feeling eased out, his turf traduced; yet as a *New Yorker* founding father he was to be accorded respect. Even though Irvin's real complaint lay with Ross, to his mind the villain was Geraghty, and the tension between the two never completely dissipated.

This friction notwithstanding, lovers of *New Yorker* cartoons might consider sitting in on the art meeting a dream job. But with hundreds of submissions to plow through each week, including partially formed (and some deformed) ideas, it was much more business than pleasure. It took a cold eye and, given that the meetings could last three hours or more, an iron posterior. The editors moved through the drawings quickly and deliberately, pausing only over those that were particularly good or that showed promise. Ross would dispatch inferior submissions by the wave of his hand, by growling "Get it out of here!" or even "Cut your throat!" if he deemed a picture especially offensive. An obvious joke might be dismissed with the comment "Bird rock"—art-meeting shorthand since the day a drawing turned up that showed a seagull on a rock, and one man telling another, "They call it 'Bird Rock.'"

Ross was attentive to every detail. He brought to the art the same sharpshooting instincts he did to stories, and the same kinds of eccentricities. Though they were cartoons, verisimilitude mattered. As Geraghty noted, "Ross approached drawings in the mood of those quasi-educational drawings that appeared in the *Book of Knowledge.* 'What is wrong with this picture? The artist has made twenty mistakes. See if you can find them.'" In Ross's cartoon universe, houses were supposed to face the road; doors theoretically had to be able to swing unobstructed; lamps were expected to have cords (though some of Ross's favorite artists had dispensation to conceal them beneath a rug). He became notorious for insisting that it be clear which character in a cartoon was speaking, especially if they were animals. If the artists took these quibbles and crotchets seriously—and they did—some also teased him about them. Once when he was peeved at Ross, Clarence Day, who also drew cartoons, sent the editor a drawing of a naked man with a conspicuously flaccid penis. Ross drew an arrow to the offending appendage and scribbled a note: "Delete." Day returned it with a note of his own: "Delete what?"

As much as Ross prized cartoons, he spent little time with the artists themselves because the few he had known well tended to lead even more complicated lives than the writers. In 1931, he was overcome with sadness and guilt when one of *The New Yorker*'s charter artists, Ralph Barton, killed himself (his wife, Carlotta, had left him for Eugene O'Neill). Ross was sad because Barton was a good friend and talented contributor; he was guilty because Barton had told him he intended to kill himself, and Ross didn't believe him.

Like the fiction writers, the artists were not employees per se but contributors, and most worked out of their homes (eventually forming something of a ghetto in western Connecticut). When Ross had lunch at the Algonquin with some artists one day in 1942, it was the

"Oh, speak up, George! Stop mumbling!"

The dark genius
of Charles Addams,
one of Ross's
favorite artists, is
evident in this
cartoon from 1941.
*(By Chas. Addams;
© 1941,1969 The New
Yorker Magazine, Inc.)*

first time he had ever met Charles Addams, even though the artist
had been contributing since 1933. William Steig seldom saw Ross;
Mischa Richter met him once. Arthur Getz, who began appearing in
The New Yorker in 1935, never did meet him. If Ross occasionally
interjected himself into important matters of state—say, those times
when Arno stopped drawing in pique over his pay—for the most part
he was content to let Geraghty run his own shop.

But once in a while Ross did involve himself in special art projects,
and on these occasions his enthusiasm crackled through his correspondence. For instance, he was swept away by Thurber's classic
"Our New Natural History" series of 1945 and 1946, a catalogue of
flora and fauna that could exist only in the creator's fervid imagination. As Thurber biographer Burton Bernstein has pointed out, Ross
was so caught up in the series that when Thurber's store of usable

puns and clichés ran low, he was quick to suggest entries of his own, such as the Lazy Susan and the Blue Funk. Before the series even began appearing, however, the editor was well into the spirit of it:

> The checking of the names in your Natural History series has revealed that only one name is a real name, the one Rea Irvin happened to know about: there is an actual fish called the pout.
>
> You have a bird called a shriek. In real life there is a bird called a shriker and also one called a shrike. I should think the approximation here does not matter.
>
> There is a bee called a lapidary, but you have drawn an animal.
>
> You have a clock tick. There is, of course, a tick. No matter, I say. There is a bird called a ragamuffin. You have drawn a ragamuffin plant. No real conflict.

In similar spirit Ross conducted a long "covert" correspondence with Gluyas Williams leading up to the publication of his splendid "Wedding" portfolio in June of 1948. (The actual title of the twelve-page spread was "Mr. and Mrs. Melvin Davison Watts Request the Honour of . . .") Williams was the artistic equivalent of E. B. White, in that to Ross (and to thousands of fans) he simply could do no wrong. He drew with immaculate line and infinite detail, qualities displayed to maximum advantage in his large panels for "The Wedding" and other notable projects, like his "Industrial Crises" series. Williams could pack dozens of characters into these drawings, each with his own expression of bemusement, confusion, or ennui. Once Ross decided to run the sixteen "Wedding" drawings in a single issue, he determined to keep the whole project a secret, and thereby jumped into it like an enthusiastic child with a new decoder ring. As Williams himself said later, these clandestine letters not only reveal how much Ross cared about art, but suggest how much fun the artists had working for him, "and how much constant stimulation one got from him."

Ross loved the "Wedding" drawings from the first day he saw

them. As with all things he loved, his first impulse was to engage in a little sharpshooting:

> You don't think the father looks too old in two or three of the drawings, do you? You might take a look at that. I had a fleeting impression he looked older in some than in others. The biggest laugh for me in the series so far is the bride's father. He's a wonder. All the characters are pretty wonderful, though. The bridegroom runs the father a close second.

Eventually Ross decided it would dilute the impact of the "Wedding" series to break it up. He also believed running it as a package would give readers a nice lift in advance of what he correctly anticipated would be an anxious and heated season of politics:

> I am writing this at home, in a conspiratorial manner. We held a solemn session—three or four of us—the other day and decided that—what the hell?—the only thing to do with the wedding series is run it all at once, and this we will do unless you disapprove. . . . The more we have looked at the pictures, the more wonderful they have seemed, and the greater has seemed the crime of separating them.
>
> Please let me know whether or not you approve of our plan. . . . But *do not write me at the office*, for we want to keep this project secret, if we can. The columnists are always telling what we are going to print, and with considerable accuracy, and we'd just as soon they didn't take the edge off this surprise.

The editors managed to keep the project under wraps, and with days left before publication, the only remaining snag was Williams's insistence on calling the post-wedding reception a "breakfast." This baffled Ross—the wedding, after all, was an afternoon affair—but he was not a man for jumping to conclusions. For a ruling the magazine prevailed on Emily Post, a Ross acquaintance ever since the evening he found himself beside her at a formal dinner, palpably anxious in anticipation of reaching for the wrong fork or committing some other

A panel from Gluyas Williams's "Wedding" portfolio. *(By Gluyas Williams; © 1948, 1976 The New Yorker Magazine, Inc.)*

gaffe. He relaxed when he noticed America's arbiter of decorum sweeping the crumbs from her dinner roll into her hand, then popping them into her mouth—just the way he always had. In this letter Ross explains their fact-checking methodology, then prevails on Williams to keep their secret just a while longer:

> I don't know what the hell to make of the gulf between Emily Post and the Boston caterer in the matter of what you call the post-wedding function. We got out Emily's books (or anyhow, one of her books, which was right on a shelf in the checking room) and found that she discusses wedding breakfasts at considerable length but that she doesn't name any hour at which a wedding breakfast ceases to be that. We did that before we called her up. Then, she is quoted to me as having said that she just never heard of such a thing in her life. "Reception" is a better word, doubtless, anyhow, for whatever the caterer says, and whatever Emily might have said, everybody in this office was astonished at the use of "breakfast," and we have a Harvard man and an Oxford man here, too.
>
> Operative KX12 didn't slip up in mailing those proofs from the office. I said nothing whatever in my note that would reveal our

fell plan. I assumed that my secretary (whom I recently acquired and, to tell the truth, do not trust completely) and whoever else saw the communication would think I was just lining up a normal series—if they thought anything. . . . Anyhow, I couldn't bring the batch of proofs home here and mail them, for lack of facilities. The strain of finding a stamp in the rat-nest of my wife's top dressing-table drawer, addressing an ordinary envelope, and slipping out through the kitchen to the mail chute, propping the kitchen door open so that I am not locked out on the landing, is as much as I can take. I would never make a spy. I'd tip over the invisible ink.

From here on I will be completely underground and you won't hear from me unless there is a crisis of some kind, in which case I will probably endeavor to telephone you. If you get a call from Ulysses S. Grant, talking in a low, husky voice, you will know who it is.

PART III

SEASON
IN THE SUN:
1939–1951

CHAPTER 12

WAR

NINETEEN THIRTY-NINE WAS A YEAR OF COLLIDING SENTIMENTS IN New York, and the dichotomy was plain in the pages of Ross's magazine. Like all Americans, New Yorkers were staring at Europe in alarm and disbelief; even for the carefree *New Yorker,* talk of war was hard to avoid. In his Comment paragraphs on Hitler, Gibbs was less a Cassandra than a derisive heckler, and the magazine's cartoonists mocked the Nazis and Fascists in their gaudy raiment in a manner that recalled Ross's lampoon of bedsheet-wearing Klansmen in *Judge* fifteen years earlier. By contrast, the magazine's dispatches from Paris and London were simply grim, more so by the week.

Yet for all this pessimism, optimism was only a train ride away. The 1939 World's Fair, with its seductive vision of a future in shimmering glass and chromium steel, opened to justifiable fanfare in Flushing Meadows, New York. Ross, whom Thurber pegged as the original gee-whiz guy, was as dazzled as anyone else by the Olympian scale, the fresh thinking, the sheer spectacle of it all. He deployed

New Yorker writers and artists as if for battle to cover the exposition: there were covers, Talk stories, and Profiles, even detailed double-page color maps of the fairgrounds. Like millions of other parents, Ross shuttled his child, then all of four years old, out to Queens to show her what kind of world she stood to inherit—assuming there would be a world left for her.

At *The New Yorker* they were adjusting to one other major development in 1939, though one that readers didn't know about and wouldn't have cared about in any case. The quiet, unassuming William Shawn had been named managing editor for Fact. Week by week, story by story, he was taking over the journalistic side of the operation from St. Clair McKelway, who, as agreed to by Ross, was contentedly returning to writing.

If some insiders were a little surprised by Shawn's elevation to what was essentially second-in-command, their reservations had less to do with his editorial skills, which were considerable and well known, than with his utter incongruity with his superior. Where Ross was tall, ruddy-complected, and bristle-headed, Shawn was short (just over five feet five), pinkish pale, and balding. Ross was profane, Shawn punctilious in the extreme. Ross was rowdy, Shawn the picture of calm, a man who moved deliberately and never spoke above a stage whisper, as if conserving his strength for some unforeseen contingency. Ross was a footloose, social animal, Shawn a stay-at-home who seemed intimidated by the technology of modern convenience (his many phobias included riding in automatic elevators or in underground trains).

Shawn was so decorous that no one, including Ross, ever wanted to hurt his feelings, which is one reason he usually got his way. The only other employee who could even approach him for courtesy was Truax. Of these two colleagues Ross once observed, only half kidding, that "when Hawley and Shawn try to go through a door together, *nobody* gets through."

The contrast between the two men was so pronounced, in fact, that it was easy to miss how at a more fundamental level they were soulmates. Each of them lived for *The New Yorker.* Each prized good

writing, was a fiend for punctuation and accuracy, and preferred the spotlight to be on his writers rather than himself. And each had a passion for discovery; if such a thing was possible, Shawn was even more voraciously curious than Ross. Many people said of him that he simply could not be bored.

Most important, Shawn's will was the daunting equal of Ross's. Someone meeting him for the first time might have taken him for meek, even mousy, but those at the magazine knew that beneath the facade there was steel. Especially where the editorial department's welfare was concerned, Shawn could be even more hardheaded than his mentor, as Raoul Fleischmann was uniquely positioned to testify. In early 1961, a full nine years after Shawn had succeeded Ross as editor of the magazine, the publisher enlisted Katharine White's help in persuading "that little devil—pardon me, little angel" to publish a table of contents in the magazine. "I haven't been an astonishingly influential man since our inception," Fleischmann admitted to Katharine. "Heaven knows I didn't have any influence over Ross, and I can't say I have any over Bill Shawn. I go good with elderly messengers." (A table of contents didn't appear in *The New Yorker* until 1969, the year Fleischmann died.)

William Shawn began life as William Chon. He was born in Chicago in 1907 to a well-to-do family of Russian Jewish origin. Thinking he might be a writer, he changed his surname early in his career: Shawn sounded more writerly, and could not be taken, like Chon, for an Oriental name. Shawn's father, Benjamin, ran a successful cutlery store called the Jack Knife Shop. His sensitive son's interests ran more to music and literature, and the young man attended the Harvard School for Boys, a college preparatory school on Chicago's South Side. But after two years at the University of Michigan, Shawn gave in to his wanderlust and headed for a more agreeable climate. He spent a few months as a newspaper reporter in tiny Las Vegas, New Mexico, then returned to Chicago as Midwest editor for the International Illustrated News, a Hearst photo service. In 1928, he married Cecille Lyon, a feature writer (and later editor) for the *Chicago Daily News*. Then, just before the Depression, Hearst closed its Chicago office and Shawn was out of a job. Cecille managed a leave of absence and the newlyweds sailed for Europe and a belated honeymoon. They wound up staying the better part of a year, Shawn picking up odd jobs playing piano in Paris nightclubs. He was an excellent jazz pianist and wrote some music for small theatrical groups. He enjoyed composing so much that he considered doing it for a living, only to find that composers were paid even less than writers. Besides, with no formal training, he thought himself only a capable amateur.

Back in the States, Shawn did freelance work for the Chicago papers and even published some short fiction in the Sunday supplements under pseudonyms. By now, however, New York was exerting a strong pull on him. From the time he was first exposed to *The New Yorker* a few years after its inception, he had been enchanted by the magazine. Its literate style, understatement, and progressive approach to news all appealed to his own sense of how journalism should be produced. Almost immediately he aspired to work there, and in 1932 he got his chance. Through her newspaper contacts, Cecille Shawn arranged to have an interview with one of Ross's lieutenants at *The New Yorker,* Don Wharton, who was in need of freelance reporters for Talk. When he invited her to give it a try, she mentioned that her husband was a reporter too; might he help? Wharton replied that he didn't care who did the reporting as long as it was done right.

Shawn took to the assignment with enthusiasm, if little initial profit. He would dig up information for Talk stories, turning over great piles of notes to E. B. White, James Thurber, or whoever happened to be handling rewrite that week. In return he got all of two dollars for every typeset inch of story that resulted. If a story didn't run, he didn't get paid. "It was practically starvation," Shawn would say years later, but it was also opportunity, and he was shrewd enough to embrace it. His big break came courtesy of Alva Johnston, for whom he sometimes did legwork. The writer found Shawn to be so thorough and scrupulous that he commended him to Ross. Praise from his star Johnston was high praise indeed, and Ross hired Shawn for the Talk staff in 1933.

A department where writers worked anonymously would seem to have been a natural fit for Shawn, whose reticence even then was almost painful. Yet it turned out that shyness wasn't his only problem as a writer. Gifted as he might be, and he *was* gifted, Shawn was incapable of satisfying his own high standards. In more than half a century at the magazine, the only identifiable piece (it was signed "W.S.") Shawn ever wrote was a 1936 short story called "The Catastrophe." This was a fanciful, amusing tale of how a meteor destroys greater New York, after which the rest of the world shrugs and goes about its business. Shawn didn't like "Catastrophe," and despite the entreaties of his colleagues to compose more pieces like it, he never did.

Almost from the start it was evident to his editors that Shawn was more comfortable generating ideas than reporting or writing them, and in 1935 Ross obliged him by putting him in charge of compiling ideas for Talk, Comment, Profiles, and other nonfiction pieces. For this, Shawn not only drew on his own sources and observations but scoured the daily newspapers, press releases, and other correspondence that came into the office. He carefully typed up a synopsis of every idea, and each week he would march into the news meeting with a sheaf of these stuffed under his arm. The ideas were debated, and those deemed worth pursuing were parceled out to reporters. The idea job not only accentuated Shawn's creative streak but forced him to become quickly attuned to what Ross was looking for in *New Yorker* pieces. He responded with the kind of efficient, organized approach that the editor always marveled at on those rare occasions when he saw it. Little by little Ross brought Shawn along as an editor, inviting him to sit in on story conferences, then easing him into the actual editing of stories. To Shawn, fifteen years his junior, Ross was a strong role model, even a father figure, and the younger editor soaked in everything.

As was the case with Gibbs and both the Whites, Shawn's professional experience prior to *The New Yorker* was virtually nil. Yet Ross could clearly see promise in Shawn's creativity, in his intellectual range, and in his astonishing capacity to work, which rivaled his own. In 1936 Ross approved his promotion as McKelway's assistant, whereupon Shawn took on even more responsibility, including editing Comment from time to time. In a letter to White in the summer of 1936, Ross noted of Shawn that "he's bright, by all indications." Still, to a degree he remained something of an enigma to the editor. This shy, abstemious young man was the antithesis of the hard-bitten, hard-drinking, boisterous editor of Ross's experience, and his reserve could be almost unnerving.

No doubt this was why Ross had some initial reservations about promoting Shawn again when McKelway's job came open. *New Yorker* lore has it that his first reaction to the suggestion that he name Shawn managing editor was "Dismiss it from your minds." Even if the story is accurate—and McKelway, who was pushing for Shawn, never indicated that Ross's reluctance was truly serious—the editor's innate confidence in the younger man overcame any lingering uncertainty. Ironically, that famous reserve of Shawn's turned out to be a useful quality for Ross, for right away it was clear that theirs was

William Shawn:
Despite a gentle mien,
there was nothing
timid about his will.
(Hilde Hubbuck)

a near-perfect match of temperaments—Ross the manic worrier backstopped by the efficient, unflappable Shawn, a person who not only had exquisite editing sensibilities but could get things done. Indeed, long after Ross had given up as hopeless his search for a Miracle Man, one had fallen into his lap.

Ross let his new managing editor run his department as he saw fit, but given his passion for the Fact side of the operation, he and Shawn worked virtually in harness. Shawn not only shared Ross's taste in stories but enthusiastically embraced Ross's creed that if an editor edited for himself first, readers would follow. Moreover, since Shawn's interests encompassed the world, he was well poised to broaden even further what *The New Yorker* considered its editorial purview—an impulse that was about to come in very handy.

Still, there were differences to be resolved. One of the biggest was in their respective attitudes toward written communication. Whereas Ross would dash off a letter or memo at the least provocation, Shawn had an almost physical aversion to committing anything (especially himself) to paper. In part because of this—Ross again adapting—the two conducted their business mostly in person. As it happened, their offices were as far away from each other as was possible on the same floor, at the points of a horseshoe on nineteen. Yet they consulted with each other every day. Whether they talked for hours or only a few moments, in Shawn's office or in Ross's, they always talked alone, the door closed. In complete candor they could get down to the nitty-gritty of personnel, pay, assignments, and how certain stories were or weren't progressing.

Mostly what they talked about, at least for the next six years, was war.

———

ON A BRIGHT SUNDAY MORNING, JUST HOURS AFTER BRITAIN AND France had declared war on Germany and with the close of the September 9 issue pressing in on him, an uneasy Wolcott Gibbs sat down to reformulate the week's Comment and grope for some perspective. As he gazed out his office window to catch sight of children on their way to skate in the park, or a nonthreatening plane flying low over the Hudson, the idea of the world being pitched into war again seemed not only unreal but beyond explication. Still, summoning his best impression of E. B. White, he made an eloquent job of it, concluding:

> The ten million men who will die are still just an arbitrary figure, an estimate from another war; the children who will be starved or bombed belong to people we can never know; the bombs themselves will fall only on strange names on a map. It will be another day or perhaps another week before we realize fully the implications of what we've read this morning, before the horror is personal and real. As a matter of fact, though, there's no particular hurry. We'll all have plenty of time to get used to war. It's very likely that a good many of us will have all the rest of our lives.

We'll all have plenty of time to get used to war. A tragic and true enough sentiment, to be sure, and yet Ross wondered if he could ever get used to the idea. The fact was, he had seldom been so frustrated. He was desperately trying to figure out the right editorial stance for *The New Yorker* about the war, wondering how he might reconcile his own isolationist sympathies with a growing chorus demanding that the magazine be more aggressive. Moreover, his professional conscience was three hundred and fifty miles away in a boathouse on a Maine cove, writing for another magazine. "Great pressure is being put on me to have *The New Yorker* swing over strong to preparedness and the hop-right-over-and-aid-the-Allies viewpoint," he wrote White in May 1940. "Wish you were here."

Up to that point Ross's magazine had been scrupulously evasive on the question of American intervention. Only a few weeks later, however, when France fell to Hitler, an emotional White wrote a Comment (he still provided items on rare occasions) that for the first time implied that American involvement was not only a military necessity but a moral imperative. "Democracy is now asked to mount its honor and decency on wheels," he wrote, "and to manufacture, with all the electric power at its command, a world which can make all people free and perhaps many people contented." At about the same time, a bulletin went out to *New Yorker* artists reminding them that the hostilities in Europe had rendered much of their work unfunny, and some of it potentially callous. The editors cautioned them to be vigilant, sensitive, and, perhaps above all, flexible. The reality of war was setting in even on Forty-third Street.

White's Comment on the fall of France was one of his few contributions during the long prelude to American entry into the war. Ross's political opinions from this period are known chiefly because he was carrying on an anguished correspondence with White—not as one concerned friend exchanging views on current events with another, but to beg his estranged writer, in increasingly desperate and coercive terms, to send in some Comment to relieve the flagging Gibbs (who was never really at ease with the subject of politics anyway, and particularly the politics of mass destruction). But even Ross's threat to discontinue Comment, no doubt perceived as the hollow gesture it was, failed to move White.

Their letters invariably waded into politics because White favored a more aggressive American response in support of the Allies, while the conservative Ross had grave misgivings, both about intervention as policy and about *The New Yorker*'s thumping the tub in any event. The editor's letters reveal a man clearly wrestling with himself. The carnage he had witnessed in World War I remained vivid for him, and he could not bring himself to condone another American military adventure except as a last resort. He remained cynical about some interventionists' true motives. Though the Anglophile in him prayed for Britain (he told a friend, "My very great fear is that the hell is going to be kicked out of England. Jesus"), he suspected that some people wanted the United States to enter the war essentially to preserve the Empire. If he had little use for the hard-line isolationist rhetoric of Lindbergh and others, whose crowd was taken to task in Comment, he didn't hear anyone—and he was listening hard—making a truly persuasive case for intervention either. As he mulled the issue, he kept *The New Yorker* officially uncommitted. Now that both Ross's parents were dead, about the only people in the world the editor ever felt he had to explain himself to were the Whites, and in a June 1941 letter to Andy he tried to do so:

> My decision is that we have been doing it right and that we ought to go on as we have been going, call it slacking, call it escapist, call it what you will. I'll be goddamned if I've got the slightest bit of confidence in the opinions and emotions of all the people who have advised me, denounced me, ridiculed me, tried to lead me, etc. Nor have I any in myself. I have been an earnest clutcher for a straw but I haven't got ahold of a straw yet. I doubt if there is any mind on earth that [can] work out a solution to the present situation or tell me what I ought to do, in positive action. I am, therefore, for drifting. After a great deal of thought, I think the thing for American publications to do is follow the President, for better or for worse.... I haven't the confidence in him that a great many of you people have (although he may be just the man for a big philosophical situation such as this), but I don't see anything to do but do as he says from now on.

In this view, Ross added, he had been considerably heartened by a recent conversation with his old friend Robert Sherwood. The playwright was then counseling FDR on public relations, so Ross pulled him aside for some advice of his own. "Much to my astonishment," he said, Sherwood told him that he thought *The New Yorker*'s wait-and-see editorial position was fine, at least for now. The fact was, Sherwood told him, Roosevelt was similarly inclined; he was determined not to commit the United States to war until the time was right. This struck Ross as reasonable behavior, especially for a Democrat.

Whatever misgivings he harbored about *The New Yorker*'s political stance, Ross, this time with Shawn's counsel, was being much more decisive on the question of journalistic coverage. It was already clear there would be no repeat of its performance in the Depression—no feigned ignorance, no smug detachment. By the fall of 1939, the magazine had engaged Mollie Panter-Downes, who lived in Surrey and had contributed some short stories to *The New Yorker*, to provide a regular Letter from London. Panter-Downes, who published her first novel when she was just seventeen, was a writer whose grace and restraint mirrored her personality and lent her wartime dispatches complete authority. All that winter, as Britain braced for attack, and then the following summer and fall, when it staggered through the Blitz, her weekly letters were devoured by American readers, received like reassuring notes from a relative at the front, which in a sense she was. In a manner at once elegant and down-to-earth, Panter-Downes transmitted the anxiety and fear, but also the underlying British resolve, and even—Ross thanking his lucky stars—some of the black humor.

At the same time across the Channel (which, Panter-Downes observed, "has suddenly shrunk in most people's minds to something no bigger than the Thames"), A. J. Liebling was replacing Janet Flanner. "Genêt" left Paris intending to be away a few months and instead wound up exiled in America for more than five years. Flanner had been pressing for home leave for several years, to address her own exhaustion and to see her elderly mother, who was ill in California. Twice before in the previous year she had stayed put at *The New Yorker*'s explicit request; this time, increasingly anxious about the deteriorating situation in France, she was resolved to go. In mid-September 1939, just weeks after German tanks had stormed into Poland and with all of France bracing for the worst, Flanner set off for America.

That October Liebling arrived in Paris in her wake. He was happy enough to be there but somewhat uncharitable about Flanner's leave-taking, writing later that it was hard to conceive of a journalist "coming away from a story just as it broke." Flanner was sensitive to the charge; her intention all along, she maintained, had been to return to France in a matter of months, but Ross wouldn't permit it until her safety could be assured (which was certainly true). Whatever her intent or frame of mind, by the time Flanner actually booked her return passage to Europe in May 1940, the Germans were rolling through Belgium and the voyage was canceled.

Like everyone else in France, Liebling thought the fireworks were about to begin; instead, he would spend the next seven months covering the "Phony War," scrambling in frustration for material he considered meaty enough to send back to *The New Yorker*. But when France did fall in June, it fell shockingly fast. Liebling was chased out of the capital, like the French government itself, to Tours. Eventually he returned to New York for home leave and wrote a two-part reconstruction of the capitulation of Paris, the unthinkable event that, as White noted, finally made the war real for many Americans.

Back home, Liebling was distressed by the general American apathy—including, in his opinion, Ross's—toward the war, and in the summer of 1941 he returned to England. The worst of the Blitz was long past, and to some extent Liebling felt he was spinning his wheels again. Yet in digging up and recounting such stories as the nasty (and generally overlooked) pounding that the northern city of Hull had taken in the Battle of Britain, or the success of the BBC's "V for Victory" campaign, he was serving as a kind of pathfinder for *The New Yorker*'s daring, unorthodox approach to war coverage. It was the "Reporter at Large" concept gone to battle. Ross and Shawn told him to leave the spot skirmishes, press conferences and predictable features to the newspapers; they wanted the untold story, the story behind the story, the story from the average citizen's perspective. As Liebling's biographer, Raymond Sokolov, put it, "In effect, Liebling treated war as if it had been Times Square with bullets. This was exactly the assignment . . . that Ross intended."

Meanwhile, at Ross's urging, Flanner was channeling her own frustration by starting to cover the war long-distance. Debriefing anyone she could find coming out of France—friends, diplomats, American expatriates—she pieced together in December 1940 a portrait of occupation whose chilling headline said it all: "Paris, Germany." The first thing all these witnesses agreed on, Flanner wrote in what must have had special resonance for her, was that "anybody who loved Paris and grieves at its plight is fortunate not to see it now, because Paris would seem hateful." At about this same time, meanwhile, Rebecca West published the first of her occasional reports about the war's impact on her own household in the English countryside. These more intimate pieces would serve as a kind of counterpoint to Panter-Downes's letters, which were meant to sum up the news and sentiment of the nation as a whole.

Throughout 1941, then, with the United States still technically a noncombatant, the war was *The New Yorker*'s dominant theme and its common thread. The magazine had long since abandoned any pretense to its old carefree tone. Domestic Reporter at Large pieces from shipyards, factories, and recruiting stations focused on American preparedness. Gibbs continued to wring his hands in Comment. Finding himself drafted, newly minted private E. J. Kahn, Jr., introduced readers to "The Army Life," an engaging, open-ended series that wound up traversing the war from boot camp to the hellish battle-grounds of the South Pacific.

All the while, Ross continued to search his conscience. By the spring of 1941, he had privately determined that America's entry into the war was inevitable, but as he told E. B. White, he still wasn't sure it was a good thing. "War, after all, is simple. It's black and white," Ross said. "It's peace that is complex."

———

SINCE IT WAS SUNDAY AFTERNOON WHEN THE BULLETINS FROM Pearl Harbor reached the East Coast, the *New Yorker* issue of December 13 was all but locked up. Ross could do little but tear up the Comment page and drop in some spot illustrations with martial themes. Mostly he mobilized the staff to work up war-related stories and art for the following week. They succeeded so well that the December 20 issue might just as well have been called *"The New Yorker* Goes to War." All of Talk, all the major stories, the cartoons, even a few of the poems, dealt in some way with the dastardly Japanese or America's response. It was as if all Ross's earlier reticence had also been destroyed in the sneak attack.

Reflecting the national temper, *The New Yorker* continued in this almost exclusively martial vein for weeks, even months. In time, however, the magazine settled into a more reasonable coexistence with the war, according it preeminence but covering the rest of life too. One could still read about the pennant race, the new books and movies, even stylish getaways that could be reached without burning up a year's ration of gasoline.

The New Yorker's impassioned reaction to Pearl Harbor was not merely Ross making up for lost time; it was also a case of the old reporter responding to the fire bell. Shawn has rightly been given credit for bringing an unprecedented depth to *The New Yorker's* war coverage, and one especially detects his hand in its iconoclastic approach and its willingness to gamble. He was what Ross called a good "hunch man," and when one of his reporters suggested hopping a plane for some remote locale, not really knowing what kind of story he would find there, as often as not Shawn said, "Go." Sometimes, however, it has been implied that without Shawn *The New Yorker* might have slighted the war as it had the Depression, and this contention is wrong. As a patriot and an editor, Ross needed no prodding to put *The New Yorker* squarely behind the war effort once the United States was in it. Unlike the Depression, which was amorphous, hard to understand, and arbitrary in its afflictions, war was a real *story.* It had action, pathos, and interesting, definable characters. It was about elemental forces: good and evil, life and death. In short, it was irresistible to Ross.

Of course it takes storytellers to tell stories, and no sooner was America in the war than the drain on Ross's staff began. The magazine's talent depletion was so deep and inexorable that before long the editor was regarding the global conflict as a personal affront, the result of "something I did to God." Almost every able-bodied man who wasn't drafted enlisted. The *New Yorker* service roster would eventually include such mainstay editors and writers as Geraghty, McKelway, Sanderson Vanderbilt, Rogers Whitaker, Geoffrey Hellman, Ted Cook (an idea man and Ross factotum), Hobart Weekes, Gardner Botsford, E. J. Kahn, Jr., John Cheever, Irwin Shaw, and Edward Newhouse. Ross found himself sending off to war some men even less suited to the military regimen, if this was possible, than he and his old *Stars and Stripes* cohorts had been. McKelway was a sterling case in point. Commissioned an officer in the Army Air Forces, he donned his new uniform one day and headed down to Penn Station and a train bound for his indoctrination. As yet, however, he had not had a single day's military experience. As he strode through the terminal an enlisted man passed and snapped off a salute. Startled, McKelway responded the only way he knew how—with the three-fingered Boy Scout salute.

So many staffers were being called up that Albert Hubbell, acting art editor in Geraghty's absence, was only slightly taken aback when young Truman Capote grandly announced one day that he was through at *The New Yorker*. It seems he too had received his draft notice and was ordered to appear immediately for a physical. So the next morning Hubbell was surprised to find his unlikely clerk puttering around the office as usual. Hubbell asked why Truman wasn't down at the induction center. "I've been," he said. "They rejected me for everything—including the WAACS." (Not long after, Capote would part company with *The New Yorker* anyway. He had infuriated Ross by purporting to represent the magazine at the Bread Loaf Writers' Conference, then offending Robert Frost by walking out of the room while the poet was in the middle of a reading.)

Many of the staffers who were medically ineligible for military service found other ways to contribute. Lobrano, who badly wanted a Navy commission but was rejected for his poor eyesight, secretly worked weekends as a volunteer longshoreman on the Hudson docks. Philip Hamburger, also rejected for bad vision, went to work in the Office of Facts and Figures (later subsumed by the Office of War Information), run by Archibald MacLeish. When he broke the news to Ross, the editor sighed and said, "God bless you, Hamburger, you're going to work for a horse's ass." (Hamburger also recalled that moments later, as he was heading down the hall on his way out, the ever-thoughtful Ik Shuman was suddenly chasing after him shouting, "Youth! Youth! You have a long-distance phone bill outstanding of a dollar forty-one cents.")

Ross wanted to do his fair share for the war effort, but watching this brain drain he grew bitter that *The New Yorker* was unable to wangle any of the draft exemptions that newspapers and other magazines—most conspicuously Luce's—seemed to obtain so effortlessly. He figured that because his magazine published cartoons and had a sense of humor, it wasn't deemed as "essential" to the war effort as those other outlets. So the exodus was unabated, and Ross's paranoia built. At one point he became so panicked at the thought of running low on cartoonists—again, mostly draft-age males—that he arranged to put on "standby" status some of the magazine's earlier artists, like Alice Harvey, who had long since fallen out of the book—and whose hopes, Hubbell said, were raised cruelly by the gesture.

Losing writers and artists was bad enough, but the real affliction was the loss of so many editors—Weekes, Whitaker, Vanderbilt, and the like. This created a special hardship on Ross and Shawn, who were putting out the Fact side of the operation, including the weekend deadline material, more or less by themselves. Both maintained brutal hours all through the war, at least six and usually seven days a week. "I am up to my nipples in hot water," Ross wrote Woollcott in 1942. "This war is much harder on me than the last one." And he admitted to Katharine White, "The magazine is running us; we aren't running it." Cecille Shawn recalls messengers coming by the apartment on Sunday afternoons with stories for her husband to work on. The elderly couriers would sit on a bench in the foyer waiting for Shawn to finish as Cecille plied them with cookies and ginger ale.

Beyond shredding his staff, wartime visited countless ancillary aggravations on Ross and *The New Yorker*. Immediately after Pearl Harbor, advertising fell off dramatically, down twenty-five percent from the previous year. Shortly thereafter the civil war against Fleischmann ensued, consuming huge amounts of Ross's time and psychic energy, as did the Merritt Parkway fiasco. Paper was in short supply; the magazine was forced to use a thin grade of paper, and further rationing was always just around the corner. Staff and resources periodically became so short that several times during the war the editor and publisher seriously considered issuing *The New Yorker* biweekly, at least in the normally dead months of July and August. (Hardships notwithstanding, they could never bring themselves to do it.)

Ross fretted over the military censors—his old *Stars and Stripes*

In this portrait from the early Forties, Ross's thin smile masks the wartime stress. "The magazine is running us," he told Katharine White, "we aren't running it."
(Culver Pictures)

reflexes kicking in—though in fact they proved little problem for *The New Yorker*. He was constantly pulling Washington strings to get his people assigned where they wanted to be, or where *he* wanted them to be—preferably at East Coast desk jobs, where they might conceivably lend *The New Yorker* a hand with some writing or editing on the side. But overseas communications were a recurring nightmare. John Lardner's dispatch from Iwo Jima was missing in action for days until he learned his cable had been refused—by the New Yorker Hotel. ("I guess I will have to start writing for the pulp hotels," Lardner joked.) Radiograms often arrived without punctuation; Ross told Rebecca West that it had taken three editors two full days to figure out that the passage in her cable that said "He left England under our law," which they knew was wrong, should have read, "He left England. Under our law . . ."

Taken together, the pressures were enough to kill Ross—or so it seemed. In the bleak February of 1942, his ulcers kicked up so badly that he went into the hospital for two weeks. For all practical purposes, by this point he had already stopped drinking, and his doctors even persuaded him to give up cigarettes, though only briefly. But he was still working ferociously, and taking on the Nazis, the Japanese, Raoul Fleischmann, and the Bronx borough president all at one time had only made matters worse. The pain in his stomach was so debilitating that he was contemplating surgery. He did not relish the prospect of being cut open, and of missing that much work, and since he respected H. L. Mencken's opinion on medicine, as on so many other subjects, he asked his Baltimore correspondent what he should do. Mencken told him to have the surgery.

Ross might well have followed this advice but for the fact that he was steered instead to the famed Lahey Clinic in Boston. In late July he had an especially bad attack, and he gravitated to the care of an extraordinary specialist there, Dr. Sara Jordan, who preferred to treat ulcers with a combination of medicine and adjustments in diet and lifestyle. A world-renowned gastroenterologist, she considered surgery for ulcers the remedy of last resort, and she didn't think Ross, as much as he was hurting, had yet reached this dire pass. To treat the latest flare-up she pumped him full of medication for three solid weeks—"I have taken it every few minutes," he told Mencken, "through all of the well-known orifices of the body except the ears"—then put the patient on a more general, longer-term regimen. Ross tried his best to follow it—took his pills, watched what he ate, guarded his temper—and the following spring, back at Lahey for a checkup, he was much improved. "I have done everything right but work too hard, and smoke," he reported to Mencken. "Otherwise, I have been like Christ in my simplicity and patience."

Ross was completely won over by Dr. Jordan, who became a good friend, and by her techniques, and he proselytized for Lahey to anyone who complained to him of so much as a stomachache. Even though he didn't really like Boston itself, through the years he would come back often for routine checkups or treatment, and colleagues teased him about the veritable apothecary that went everywhere he did. But with Dr. Jordan's help he finally had his ulcers under something like control, and he always credited her with pulling him through the most stressful period of his life.

Which is not to suggest that Ross had forsaken worry. In letters to the Whites that were progressively bleaker, he wailed and moaned constantly. In one meandering note to Katharine he actually used the phrase "Life is hell here" twice in the same paragraph. He badly wanted and needed *The New Yorker*'s First Couple back at the magazine and was not above sprinkling a little guilt on them if it would help do the trick. Finally, in the spring of 1943, he got his first really good news since the start of the war: White was giving up "One Man's Meat" for *Harper's*, and he and Katharine would return to New York and *The New Yorker*. For some five years White had been able to see through most of Ross's ploys and stiff-arm most of his lunges, but the editor had made one point that the writer found hard to argue with: at this critical juncture in history, with perspectives sometimes changing literally by the hour, the fresh forum of *The New Yorker*'s weekly Comment would be infinitely more useful to White than the monthly column in *Harper's*. Besides, there had always been an implicit understanding among the three of them that if a time came when the magazine was truly in a jam, the Whites, *New Yorker* family that they were, would be there for him. Now was that time. "The giants have come down from the hills!" a sarcastic Russell Maloney proclaimed upon their return, but there is no doubt that it was one of the most satisfying days of Ross's professional life.

The Whites found that wartime had made the office a very different place than they remembered. White told his brother, "*The New Yorker* is a worse madhouse than ever now, on account of the departure of everybody for the wars, leaving only the senile, the psychoneurotic, the maimed, the halt, and the goofy to get out the magazine. There is hardly a hormone left in the place." This last was probably an oblique, if biologically inaccurate, reference to the most conspicuous change at *The New Yorker*; women were everywhere, doing everything from clerking to Talk reporting, filling roles that heretofore had been almost exclusively male. It was not a development that Ross had been happy about. "Nobody knows what war is unless he goes through [one] in a magazine with lady editorial assistants," Ross told Frank Sullivan. It wasn't merely a question of trust for Ross; with more women around, "hanky-panky" was sure to follow, and in no time the office would be a festering "hot love hole." With all his other troubles, he simply didn't have the energy to play summer camp director, keeping the boys and girls at shouting distance from one another. As usual, he adapted—though in this instance *The New Yorker*, like all American businesses during the war, had little choice—and for his trouble was amply rewarded. Wartime reporting hires like Andy Logan, Lillian Ross, Roseanne Smith and Scottie Fitzgerald Lanahan (daughter of F. Scott and Zelda) quickly demonstrated to his satisfaction that the practice of good journalism had nothing to do with gender after all. He even took on a woman in one of the magazine's most sensitive positions, that of his private secretary. In 1944, when it became apparent that the incumbent, William Walden, was about to be lost to the Army, Ross inquired whether he had any ideas for a replacement. Walden asked if Ross might consider his wife, Harriet. The editor knew Mrs. Walden had no secretarial skills at the time, but he also knew that the family, which had a small child, could use the money, so all he asked was, "Is she active?" He needn't have worried. Harriet Walden was a hard-working and valued confidante to Ross for four years, until she left to have another child. On her last night, Ross walked into the small anteroom where she sat, took off his battered hat, bowed deeply, and said, "You're a loss to American industry, Mrs. Walden."

THOUGH HE HAD BEEN IN NO HURRY FOR THE UNITED STATES TO enter the war, once the country was committed Ross suspected the fighting would be relatively quick and the casualties modest, at least by World War I standards. By January of 1943, he already had artists working on "victory" covers. One can appreciate that he did not want to be caught unprepared, but even allowing for long-range planning, this kind of optimism was unjustified, and evaporated quickly.

Happily, Ross was a far more astute assessor of editorial than military capability. As he and Shawn saw it, the world, through no fault of their own, had become *The New Yorker*'s beat. Now they were overseeing the most penetrating and literate reporting of the war. Dispatches arrived from all points of the globe, written from every conceivable angle, stories whose only common denominator was that they were interesting and impeccably told. *New Yorker* readers learned what it was like to be in a sealed troop transport in the Mediterranean, aboard a battleship off Saipan, and in the Plexiglas nose of a B-17. Sometimes these pieces were written from the point of view of the combatants, sometimes that of the correspondents themselves. Their settings ranged from London bomb shelters to a Pennsylvania bomb factory, the characters from Marshal Pétain to the mayor of a Sicilian village who had migrated back to the island from Philadelphia. Nor were they confined to text. Navy ensign Saul Steinberg—Ross had used his pull to get the Romanian-born artist naturalized and into the service—contributed Reporter-like portfolios from outposts in China and India.

Beyond being inventive and informative, *The New Yorker*'s war articles had real power. The magazine's writers, like the men and women they covered, were young, brave, and completely committed to the cause, which infused their work with energy and passion, and because they were on the scene for the most part, they conveyed authority. The best *New Yorker* war pieces had the full-bodied, three-dimensional quality of literature, with none of the stale whiff of accounts reconstructed from military briefings. They dealt with real people caught in dreadful, exhilarating, even amusing circumstances. After John Lardner went ashore with the Allies at Anzio, he sent back a report about life in the middle of this dangerous and claustrophobic beachhead and related how his British hosts drafted him for a delicate mission:

> There was a certain amount of wine to be had from a merchant who slid back into the deserted village of Nettunia shortly after we landed and unearthed his stock, which the Germans had failed to find. In connection with it I had my most discouraging experience since the night twelve small Arab boys conspired, with sensational success, to pick my pocket of five hundred dollars in Algiers. Captain Mason wanted wine because other units on the beachhead had wine and he felt he owed it to us. Besides, there was little water to spare from washing and cooking, and the field-ration, or "compo," tea was poor stuff. He loaded two vast, empty demijohns into the back seat of a jeep. These vessels were laced stoutly in straw and each accommodated sixty litres. I drove the jeep into town, because the deal was one that had to be made through American channels, in an American beachhead area. Negotiations were concluded for twenty-four hundred lire, or twenty-four dollars, cash down. I tipped the loaders three Chelsea, or front-line, cigarettes apiece and drove back with a high heart. Ten yards from home I hit a sharp ditch in the yard, which caused the starboard demijohn to disintegrate with a noise like the crack of a rifle. The floor of the jeep was immediately four inches deep in wine, and the tipple of the country shot through gaps in the sides like a cataract. The other correspondents and the enlisted men came out of our farmhouse and stood around in a circle, taking a lively interest in the plight of four fat, white earthworms beside the car, who stiff-

ened, after stubborn resistance, and passed out. Captain Mason also appeared, and I cast an uneasy glance at him. The captain looked things over silently. The wine supply was close to his heart, but there was something about my position, apparently, which put him in mind of Harry the Horse or Nicely Nicely, if not both, for he scratched his chin and burst out laughing. "This is one of the droll episodes of the war," he announced. He then supervised the unloading of the remaining demijohn, taking care to see that I kept some distance away from the operation.

A different kind of personal note suffused "Cross-Channel Trip," Liebling's masterly three-part account of the invasion of Normandy and one of the best examples of *The New Yorker*'s approach to the war. In it, Liebling whittled down the almost unimaginably large D-Day operation to human perspective—that of the men aboard his LCIL (for Landing Craft, Infantry, Large), a floating box that would dump upwards of five hundred men onto the beach. As it happened, Liebling's ship was one of the first to go in at Omaha Beach, and his brisk, understated account was punctuated by the kind of detail the newspapers usually didn't go in for—like how the deck of the LCIL turned sticky with a mixture of blood and condensed milk when fragments from a German shell simultaneously hit several crewmen and some stray boxes of rations. But Liebling was equally effective when dealing with the fearful quiet. The entire first installment, in fact, was given over to stage-setting. He introduced the four-man complement of officers, then his motley shipmates, waiting for days to sail and warding off the dread by playing cards and engaging in nervous banter. At one point he discussed the ship's coxswain, a long-legged Coast Guardsman from Mississippi whom Liebling had befriended because the fellow aspired to be a newspaperman after the war. Liebling knew the young man, as the coxswain, would be the first one off the craft as it landed. His perilous job would be to run a guideline from the ship to shore and anchor it; this was what the other soldiers would follow. "I asked the boy what he was going to wear when he went into the water with the line," Liebling wrote, "and he said just swimming trunks and a tin hat. He said he was a fair swimmer."

In the second part, the invasion got under way, and within hours the LCIL was heading straight into the beach under withering enemy fire. Rather than trying to paint the whole apocalyptic picture, Liebling instead stuck to the frantic action immediately around him. Just as its last soldier was away, the LCIL took a shell, and with it the aforementioned casualties. Retreating to its staging area, the ship unloaded its wounded and awaited further instruction:

> As the hours went by and we weren't ordered to do anything, it became evident that our bit of beach wasn't doing well, for we had expected, after delivering our first load on shore, to be employed in ferrying other troops from transports to the beach, which the beach-battalion boys and engineers would in the meantime have been helping to clear. Other LCILs of our flotilla were also lying idle. We saw one of them being towed, and then we saw her capsize. Three others, we heard, were lying up on one strip of beach, burned. Landing craft are reckoned expendable. [Lieutenant] Rigg came down from the bridge and, seeing me, said, "The beach is closed to LCILs now. Only small boats going in. Wish they'd thought of that earlier. We lost three good men."
>
> "Which three?" I asked. "I know about Rocky and Bill."
>
> "The coxswain is gone," Bunny said. I remembered the coxswain, the earnest young fellow who wanted to be a newspaperman. . . .
>
> "Couldn't he get back?" I asked.
>
> "He couldn't get anywhere," Rigg answered. "He had just stepped off the ramp when he disintegrated. He must have stepped right into an H.E. shell. Cox was a good lad. We'd recommended him for officers' school." Rigg walked away for the inevitable cup of coffee, shaking his big tawny head.

The progress of the Allies in the spring of 1944 had only intensified the desire of David Lardner, son of Ring and brother of John, to get overseas somehow. The popular young reporter was capably handling an array of duties for *The New Yorker;* he wrote movie reviews, a sports department, and, after E. J. Kahn was drafted, the Tables for Two column. Turned down for active duty because of his eyesight, he steadily campaigned to go to war as a correspondent, but Ross and Shawn were reluctant. Not only was he especially valuable on *The New Yorker*'s depleted staff, but John had already been in and out of harm's way, and another brother, Jim, had died fighting for the Republican side in the Spanish Civil War. Ross, who had been close to Ring, feared imposing more tragedy on the family. Besides, *The New Yorker* already was using all the battlefield accreditations it was entitled to.

However, Lardner would not be dissuaded, and finally *The New Yorker* reluctantly gave him a leave of absence to enroll with the Office of War Information, with the understanding that if he managed to get credentialed independently, the magazine would use his material. The resourceful Lardner got his combat accreditation in no time, and by early October he had bounded into Luxembourg, a bona fide war correspondent. On October 10 he filed a Letter from Luxembourg, which appeared in *The New Yorker* dated October 21. But on the evening of October 19 Ross's worst fear materialized. Returning from a visit to Aachen, Lardner was riding in a jeep with no running lights which veered off the road and hit a pile of mines that GIs had earlier cleared from the area. The driver was killed instantly in the explosion; Lardner died hours later of a head injury before he could get into surgery.

A despondent Ross called on Gibbs to write a brief obituary. In closing, Gibbs wrote, "We have never printed a paragraph with deeper regret than we print this one." The word "regret," at Thurber's suggestion, was changed to "sorrow," and that was how the notice ran in the issue of October 28. Three years later, when *The New Yorker* published its magnificent anthology of war pieces, the book was dedicated to the memory of David Lardner.

———

BACK IN THE SUMMER OF 1940, ON WHAT WOULD TURN OUT TO BE THE last long getaway before the war consumed him, Ross had spent three weeks out west, visiting Colorado, Salt Lake, and then Los Angeles. At Chasen's one night, Dave Chasen, Nunnally Johnson, Ross, and his companion, a beautiful blonde named Ariane Allen, closed down the restaurant and on a lark decided to go back to Johnson's for a post-midnight swim. "We were no more in the house," wrote Johnson, then a bachelor, "than Miss Allen proposed an evening of utter abandon—nude bathing—and such were her high spirits and my hysteria that in less than a twinkling she and I were splashing around together in the deep end." After a few moments, the two revelers realized that Chasen and Ross hadn't joined them—were, in fact, "pacing up and down, discussing the parsley situation," with Ross clearly not pleased about the high jinks in the pool.

"Both Miss Allen and I were immediately cooled off by the sight of this business consultation and its disapproving implications," Johnson continued, "and so we climbed out of the pool (gallantly I let her go first) and presently all four of us, fully clad, were delving into

Ariane Allen just prior to her marriage to Ross in 1940.
(Pach Bros.)

the matter of parsley. And that little girl—I gasped and turned crimson with shame when I read about it—was presently Mrs. Ross. I had no idea!"

Nearly a year into his second divorce, Ross had found himself another golden beauty half his age, and, as Johnson was so abashed to learn, the vivacious young woman indeed was about to become Ross's fiancée.

Ariane Allen was born and raised in Texas, but her family had since moved to Beverly Hills, where her father dealt in real estate. She attended Barnard College, where she studied drama, and graduated from the University of Texas. In 1938 she left California for New York, hoping to find work on the stage, but by the time she met Ross she had managed to land only bit parts in a few movies and one Broadway play, and was spending more time modeling for artists and magazine illustrators.

Ariane Allen was a friendly and flirtatious woman with a talent for charming men—particularly older men of means, it was said. She also had a tendency to talk all the time, whether or not she had anything to say, yet there was an undeniable sweetness about her, an attractiveness in her fresh, uninhibited manner. In her own way she was just as much at home at "21" or the Trocadero as Ross was. Geoffrey Hellman remembered one evening at El Morocco, when Ross and Ariane were still engaged. Her sister was there, and Hellman rounded out the foursome. Since Ross would sooner be caught in church than on a dance floor, it was left to the accommodating Hellman to partner the Allen girls, by turns, all evening. When he thanked Ross at evening's end, he replied, "Don't thank me, Hellman. Next time I'll give you twenty dollars."

It was another curious pairing for Ross, yet his friends detected that the relationship was more than a flirtation. Sure enough, on November 10, 1940, Ross, in what was by now becoming something of a habit, suddenly and discreetly slipped out of town to get married. This time it was a Sunday afternoon civil ceremony outside Elizabeth, New Jersey. Ross had just turned forty-eight; Ariane was twenty-five.

That Ross felt a certain ambivalence about being a married man again was apparent immediately. That Monday he came to work as usual, and was joined in the elevator by Kip Orr, who had read of the surprise wedding in that morning's paper. When he congratulated Ross, the editor glared at him and said, "Fuck you."

There is no question that Ross cared for Ariane, but given his immutable Victorian streak, it seems likely he married her as much as anything to legitimize their affair. Many of his friends would always regard Jane Grant as Ross's one true love, an intellectual and spiritual match whom he had foolishly pushed away. Still, they generally liked Ariane too, and her affection for him appeared authentic enough. If some considered her a gold digger, or perhaps more accurately what today is called a trophy wife, they tended to point the finger less at her than at him. "No pretty woman like that is to blame when an intelligent man, as ugly as he is brilliant like Ross, takes advantage of his appetite for prettiness and argues her into marrying him," Janet Flanner would say of the unlikely union.

For her part, Jane Grant had gotten on with her personal life too. In 1939 she married an editor at *Fortune*, William Harris, with whom she would later found a nationally respected plant nursery, White Flower Farm. For now, however, she was still trying to cultivate *The New Yorker*, and during the war she came up with a brilliant idea that would prove to have a huge positive impact on the magazine's bottom line.

After the initial panic following Pearl Harbor, the magazine's business stabilized. Revenue had picked up markedly by the spring of 1943 ("Advertisers are running around town looking for a place to put their ads," Ross told White in wonderment); total revenues for that year would climb a whopping thirty-three percent, and in 1944 they topped four million dollars for the first time. Business became *too* good: squeezed by the wartime excess-profits tax and paper rationing, the magazine actually had to take steps to suppress its circulation. In early 1943 it started cutting back on newsstand deliveries, and later it stopped taking new subscriptions. Even so, the numbers built inexorably. Circulation, around 170,000 at the time of Pearl Harbor, would reach 260,000 by the end of 1945.

Jane had been an expert "networker" decades before the concept became popular, and some of her most useful contacts were top military officials. After consulting some of these, she proposed in the spring of 1943 that *The New Yorker* start publishing a "pony," or downsized, version of the magazine for distribution to the armed forces. *Time* and *Newsweek* already were doing it. It would be a terrific promotion for the magazine, she argued, and just might ease their paper problems, which the extra advertising had only made more acute. Fleischmann was cool to the idea (no doubt still smarting from the fact that largely thanks to Jane he had nearly lost his job in the shareholder revolt). Ross had reservations too. He feared it meant more work, and he worried about the appearance of pushing an idea by his ex-wife. But Ik Shuman came to her rescue. He recognized the tremendous possibilities in the idea and persuaded the two principals to give it a try as long as it meant more paper for the magazine. Shuman dealt with the internal details, and Jane took on the military red tape.

The first pony edition appeared in September 1943. It was six by nine inches (achieved by photographically shrinking the magazine's normal pages) and carried no ads. Content ran heavily to cartoons, Talk items, humorous pieces, and war-related features. It began as a monthly, with a circulation of 20,000, distributed free to combat troops and sold at some post exchanges. The pony *New Yorker* (also called the overseas edition) was so popular with servicemen, and demand for it so strong, that the following March it went weekly, and by the end of 1944 its circulation exceeded 150,000, rivaling the readership of its parent.

The pony edition, which went out of business after the war, was a success in every sense. It did ease *The New Yorker*'s paper crunch, generated immense goodwill among the public, and made many fans among the military establishment, which began to view the magazine as vital to the war effort after all. Most important, it exposed *The New Yorker* to hundreds of thousands of new readers, and when they came home, many of them became paying customers. In the two years after the war, the magazine's circulation leapfrogged to 320,000, and the lion's share of these new readers were not New Yorkers.

—

AS THE WAR IN EUROPE PUSHED TOWARD DENOUEMENT, *THE NEW Yorker* seemed to be mounting an invasion of its own. By the end of 1944, Flanner finally got back to her beloved Paris, an occasion that Ross extolled as "a historical moment in journalism," and after a long hiatus the byline Genêt returned to the magazine. Daniel Lang was traversing Italy, and S. N. Behrman was touring London, where he found a grand Mayfair house that had been devastated save for a sumptuous "suspended" drawing room on the third floor. Philip Hamburger got to Milan in time to see Mussolini hanging by his heels in the Piazza Loreto, then filed a report from Hitler's spookily abandoned aerie at Berchtesgaden. By the spring of 1945 even Edmund Wilson was accredited and encamped in Rome. Hamburger, who was staying at the same hotel for a time, suggested one day that they try to attend a noontime audience with the pope. Wilson grumbled but tagged along. At the Vatican, they made their way into a large public room, packed wall to wall with Allied soldiers. Noon came and went with no sign of the pope. Wilson grew impatient, then exasperated, and after about twenty minutes barked loud enough to get the attention of the Swiss Guards, "Where is that goddam pope?"

Meantime, Joel Sayre had crossed the Rhine with the Allied advance in early 1945 and began filing the magazine's first reports out of a reeling Germany. That March, in fact, the magazine gave him a challenging if unorthodox assignment: a long, detailed account of the devastating bombardment of Cologne, the German industrial center and transportation hub. The idea was for Sayre to reconstruct the bombing not from the air, but from the ground: What were the German civilians doing when the bombs fell, where did they flee for safety, who lived, who died?

The New Yorker marked V-E Day with simultaneous Letters from London, Paris, Rome, and Munich, then, like everyone else, focused its attention on the war in the Pacific. Meanwhile, Sayre was finishing his Cologne reporting. It would not be an easy piece to pull off, this anatomy of a bombing, and his uneven work from Germany had

made for plenty of headaches back in New York as it was, but by midsummer he was well into the writing of it.

But in early August the United States dropped atomic bombs on Hiroshima and Nagasaki, Japan. World War II was brought to an unexpectedly abrupt conclusion, and Joel Sayre's Cologne piece was rendered so utterly beside the point that it was shelved.

That fall, the young writer and war correspondent John Hersey headed off to China, having made the unusual arrangement of reporting for both *The New Yorker* and *Life,* which would split his expenses. A year earlier he had appeared for the first time in *The New Yorker* with "Survival," the John Kennedy/PT-109 story that Ross and Shawn had fought so hard to publish. Ironically, *Life* had passed up this story (for reasons the author never learned), but up to this point Hersey had been very much a Luce man—a protégé, in fact, who it was thought might one day run *Time.* Luce was especially fond of Hersey not only for his obvious abilities but because of their parallel life paths: like Luce, Hersey had been born in China; had gone to Hotchkiss and then Yale, where both men were Skull and Bones; and then had done postgraduate work in England. During the war Hersey distinguished himself as a resourceful and courageous correspondent, and produced books about Bataan and Guadalcanal. (Having wound up in the middle of the latter battle, Hersey won a Navy commendation for helping wounded men to safety. He wrote the book *Into the Valley* after his plane crashed at sea—he recovered his notebooks while extricating himself, underwater, from the wreckage.) He was best known, however, for *A Bell for Adano,* his 1944 novel about the U.S. Army's occupation of an Italian village, which had won the Pulitzer Prize.

For all his ties to Luce, Hersey, a committed Democrat, had lately become disenchanted with the conservative publisher. He had also found his PT-109 experience with *New Yorker* editors a pleasant and eye-opening change. In China, he was filing regular stories for Shawn when, at some point early in his stay—it is not clear exactly when or how the idea arose—the editor approached him with an intriguing proposition. Shawn wanted to revive the concept behind the Cologne story but apply it instead to Hiroshima. He was astonished that in all the millions of words being written about the bomb—how and why the decision was made, how the bomb came to be built, whether it should have been dropped at all—what had actually happened in Hiroshima itself, where more than one hundred thousand people were killed and wounded, was being ignored. On March 22, 1946, he cabled Hersey in Shanghai to lobby for the idea. "The more time that passes, the more convinced we are that piece has wonderful possibilities," Shawn said. "No one has even touched it."

The aim was to publish a story to coincide with the first anniversary of the bombing. Before he could get to Japan, however, Hersey needed to finish several other projects. This meant that he didn't arrive until late May, and then could spend only three weeks in the country, first in Tokyo for official interviews and research, then in Hiroshima to find his subjects and interview them.

In late June Hersey arrived back in New York, where he sat down and started writing furiously. Several weeks and some one hundred fifty manuscript pages later, he emerged with a stunning tale whose working title was "Some Events at Hiroshima."

Immediately Ross had a problem. From the outset the story had been intended as a serial, and Hersey wrote it in four distinct parts. This meant that the last three sections led off with something of a recapitulation, as the magazine did with multipart Profiles. But Shawn believed that in this case the interruptions detracted from the powerful narrative, and he had a brainstorm: Why not run it all at once?

Ross too had read the piece and found it to be "one of the most remarkable stories I have ever seen." He agreed with Shawn that it would be even more powerful in a single issue, and Hersey thought so too. But the editor also knew that making such an extraordinary commitment meant that virtually nothing else could appear in that issue. True, it would solve one dilemma: how could *The New Yorker*

John Hersey was a protégé of Henry Luce, but William Shawn worked hard to publish him in *The New Yorker.* *(UPI/Bettmann)*

possibly run cartoons—or *any* lighthearted material, for that matter—in proximity to Armageddon? But the idea smacked of a stunt,
and the magazine did not go in for stunts. Besides, gutting the issue
to run "Hiroshima" amounted to the final capitulation, the ultimate
admission from its editor that his onetime comic sheet was now so
serious and, alas, so respectable that it could comfortably publish the
most sober testament he had ever read.

For a week Ross went back and forth. While he fretted about
"cheating" readers of their familiar features, Shawn countered with
the persuasive argument that *The New Yorker* was in a position to
make a unique statement about this unnerving new atomic age.
"Hersey has written thirty thousand words on the bombing of
Hiroshima (which I can now pronounce in a new and fancy way),
one hell of a story, and we are wondering what to do about it," Ross
admitted to E. B. White, one of the few people he let in on the "top
secret" project. "[Shawn] wants to wake people up and says we are
the people with a chance to do it, and probably the only people that
will do it, if it is done."

Ross was so anxious about breaking faith with readers that late one
evening he pulled down the first issue of *The New Yorker* to remind
himself what he had promised them twenty-one long years before in
his statement of intent. The very first line said "*The New Yorker* starts
with a declaration of serious purpose." Ross read no more, and called
an elated Shawn at home with his decision.

For the next ten days Hersey huddled with the two editors in
Ross's locked office. In going over the manuscript, Ross alone had
more than two hundred queries, most of them substantial. (One that
Hersey was fond of repeating was the editor's quibble with his
description of some bicycles near ground zero as "lopsided." Asked
Ross, "Can something that is two-dimensional be 'lopsided'?" It was
changed to "crumpled.") Hersey wrote and rewrote in near-total
secrecy. Having committed himself to an unprecedented single-story
issue, Ross wanted to make sure that it had maximum impact. With
the exception of one frazzled makeup man, no one at *The New Yorker*
outside Ross's immediate circle knew what was going on until the

last possible minute. The business side was kept in the dark; so were staff writers, who naturally suspected something was up but could only mutter while their own copy went unread.

With all the deliberation and rewriting, Ross overshot the anniversary, but only by a few weeks. The colorful cover of that August 31, 1946, *New Yorker* was a typically upbeat summer scene of people frolicking in a park. As a tipoff and subtle attention-getter, Ross ordered that all newsstand copies of the magazine carry a white band warning readers of the editorial departure. The issue, sixty-eight pages, contained only advertisements, the Goings On calendar, and Hersey's story, which started on the page where on any other week Talk of the Town began. The original title, which Ross had disliked, was shortened simply to "Hiroshima." The piece ran as a Reporter at Large, in four sections, the first of which was entitled "A Noiseless Flash." An editor's note to readers on the first page said: "*The New Yorker* this week devotes its entire editorial space to an article on the almost complete obliteration of a city by one atomic bomb, and what happened to the people of that city. It does so in the conviction that few of us have yet comprehended the all but incredible destructive power of this weapon, and that everyone might well take time to consider the terrible implications of its use."

The story itself was, and remains, a journalistic tour de force. It is the straightforward but extraordinary recounting of how six Hiroshima residents—two doctors, a female factory clerk, a Japanese Protestant minister, a German Catholic priest, and a tailor's widow—survived the atomic blast and its aftermath. The characters are all real, the details true, the horror genuine. Hersey presented their story in a clear, unhysterical tone that only underscored the terror of the experience. By running in one piece, rather than serially, "Hiroshima" had a power that accumulated gradually, by grisly twists and turns. As many observers said then, Hersey, without preaching, made Americans see for the first time that "atomic bomb" was more than a concept; it was human suffering on an apocalyptic scale.

The response to "Hiroshima" was instantaneous and overwhelming. Ross had braced himself for some kind of reaction, most likely unpleasant. After all, the story's very existence was an indictment of the bomb—or at least of its use—and was sure to provoke a political furor, but he could deal with that. Far more terrifying was the prospect of thousands of disgruntled readers storming his office wanting to know where their cartoons were.

His fears proved unwarranted. "Hiroshima" was a sensation. The issue sold out almost instantly, copies being scalped for fifteen and twenty dollars. Broadcasters read from it over the radio. Demand to reprint it came in from newspapers and syndicates around the world (proceeds were donated to Red Cross relief). An instant book was made and snapped up by the Book-of-the-Month Club. Congratulatory letters poured in. Albert Einstein asked for one thousand copies of the issue. Henry Luce, who would never even have entertained the idea of running "Hiroshima," nonetheless was so outraged by what he regarded as Hersey's treachery that he removed his protégé's photograph from Time Inc.'s gallery of honor.

At first Ross was surprised by the impact of "Hiroshima"—"There was never any magazine story in my life that went off like this one," he told Frank Sullivan—then a little embarrassed by the reaction. Finally, as the sheer magnitude of the accomplishment sank in, there was humble gratification. When Irwin Shaw praised him for publishing it, Ross could honestly say, "I don't think I've ever got as much satisfaction out of anything else in my life."

"Hiroshima" ran to 31,347 words, and half a century and the culmination of the Cold War have not diluted their raw power. When John Hersey died in 1993, in marking his passing *The New Yorker* could still suggest that the piece was "the most famous magazine article ever published"—and just possibly the most important.

SQUIRE

WHEN *THE NEW YORKER* TURNED TWENTY YEARS OLD IN FEBRUARY 1945, with the war still on but nearing its end, Comment took note of the occasion. E. B. White wrote the words, but one can virtually hear Ross intoning them: "Twenty years ago this week, *The New Yorker* put out its first issue. Our intentions were innocent and our foresight dim. We armed ourself with a feather for tickling a few chins, and now, twenty years later, we find ourself gingerly holding a glass tube for transfusing blood. Perhaps we should have expected this sort of adventure, but we feel like a man who left his house to go to a Punch-and-Judy show and, by some error in direction, wandered into *Hamlet*."

That June, with victory secured in Europe and imminent in the Pacific—that is, with his responsibility to the war effort (and that is how he viewed it) essentially fulfilled—Ross abruptly resigned from the magazine's board of directors and let it be known that he wanted out of his job, too. This was not one of his rash, garden-variety threats to quit, but the real thing. He wished to cancel his employment contract. Not only was he exhausted, but he remained profoundly unhappy over his compensation and his continuing financial straits in general. Fleischmann and the board had heard this complaint before, yet it seemed that every time they cooked up a way to augment Ross's salary, such as with special stock options or bonuses, tax implications undercut their good intentions. The result was that while *The New Yorker*'s financial future looked as bright as could be in the summer of 1945, Ross's was anything but. He was still fending off the IRS on one flank, and on the other Jane Grant's lawyers, who had dogged him all through the war for back payment. He was bitter at his predicament, and tired of being tired.

Taken by surprise, the magazine's executive committee scrambled to put a new offer in front of Ross. That Fourth of July the editor was in his office trying to catch up on work, and he set down his answer in the form of a letter to Lloyd Paul Stryker. He remained in a state of high agitation and seemed intent on leaving. Saying that he had "long ago renounced the hope of justice," Ross argued that there were two "fundamental flaws" with the board's proposal: "One is that the major owner of *The New Yorker* is a fool and that the venture therefore is built on quicksand. Another is that you envisage another employment contract for me, and I feel that I would be an ass and a traitor to my vow if I signed any such thing. . . . I could not contract to edit *The New Yorker* for two weeks, let alone three years, with the Fleischmann ring of stupid fumblers in the background, in a position to take over at will." He added that the magazine would not have an easy time finding a qualified replacement for him. "This outfit is known as a leper spot throughout the industry."

As Ross was finishing up the letter, Truax wandered in and the editor asked him to read it. Taken aback by its fatalistic and angry tone, Truax prevailed on his friend to let the executive committee keep trying. Ross agreed, but remained resolutely pessimistic. In a postscript, he told Stryker, "If you want to go further with this thing, you will, I warn you, find me very stern, and probably preposterous."

As usual, Ross kept the turmoil from his editorial staff, but the key shareholders all knew about it, and before long apparently most of them had joined in the brainstorming to find a way to placate him. These included not only Stryker and Truax but Peter and Ruth Vischer, and even Jane Grant, whose financial welfare was still bound up with the man who had divorced her sixteen years before. Though she continued to press her ex-husband for every dollar coming to her, she understood his bitterness. "It's downright ridiculous that Ross isn't top dog of an enterprise so entirely his," she wrote in a note intended for Stryker but not sent, adding that she herself resented being a "load of hay" to her former husband. One of Ross's demands was that any renegotiation help resolve his financial obligation to Jane once and for all, and she herself thought this only fair.

By coincidence, at this time Jane was pressing a financial grievance of her own against *The New Yorker*. For conceiving and overseeing the tremendously successful pony edition, she was to receive a percentage of its profits, but these figures were in dispute almost from the start, and she was still wrangling with Fleischmann when Ross's disgruntlement arose. Suddenly it dawned on Ross that he might lump their two situations together. In late October, in an emotional and rather gallant letter to Stryker, he reiterated how much Jane had meant to *The New Yorker*, not just in conceiving the pony edition but in getting Fleischmann to underwrite the magazine in the first place—or, as he elegantly put it, "She got a sucker where I failed, after a long hunt for suckers." He strongly urged that as part of any new deal with him, they clean up her complaints too. Further, he proposed that the company undertake to pay her five thousand dollars a year, guaranteed for life:

> I see no room for argument against this debt, except possibly that it is outlawed, and I do not intend to swallow that. Fleischmann and his group have made millions and Jane Grant has made not one cent. All she has ever got from *The New Yorker* she got from me personally, and I could ill afford it because I, too, had been robbed....
>
> It certainly is to Jane's interest to make such an arrangement. It certainly is to my interest to do so, and rid my mind and nervous

system of my terrifying obligation. And it would seem to me that it is just a dandy opportunity for the corporation to clear its conscience by recognition of this claim, however tardily, and thereby contribute to Jane's self-respect and to my peace of mind.

As Jane was angling for a consultant's position anyway, she supported Ross's proposal, and negotiations resumed. More suggestions were floated and refined. At last, in November 1945, Ross agreed to a new contract that raised his pay to fifty thousand dollars, retained his generous expense account, offered him more stock options, and gave him the right to retire at any time, with three months' notice, as "editor emeritus," at half pay. Soon thereafter the other dominoes dropped. By the end of the year, Jane Grant had a contract as a permanent consultant to Fleischmann, worth $7,500 a year and renewable by her for life. At the same time, in an apparent quid pro quo, the anti-Fleischmann bloc from the 1942 civil war rescinded its demand that the publisher vote his shares with the board, a major step toward his regaining control of the company. Lastly, in February 1946, Jane legally absolved Ross of any further financial obligation to her.

Ross's new contract had one other important provision, which required him to "use his best efforts" to train a successor. Certainly he had no philosophical objection to this idea; from *The New Yorker*'s infancy he had preached to subeditors that a manager wasn't "worth his salt" until he had trained an assistant who could step in for him. He had tried to practice what he preached, and Shawn, Lobrano and Geraghty had clearly demonstrated they could keep the magazine humming when he was away on vacations or in the hospital. Indeed, already there were whispers in publishing circles that the mysterious Shawn was looking like an heir apparent. No one had a higher opinion of him than Ross, who considered him "the hardest-working and most self-sacrificing man I have ever done business with," but he wasn't ready to anoint him just yet. Apparently Ross still considered himself the indispensable man. As he was mulling over his new contract offer, Ross told his personal attorney and friend Julius Baer that "the whole editor emeritus proposition . . . is worthless, because it assumes the continuity of *The New Yorker* pretty much and *The New Yorker* will blow up like a firecracker if I leave. I am so sure of that that I wouldn't gamble five cents against it, or an hour's time."

Even had Ross been ready to designate his heir then and there, Shawn nearly deprived him of the chance. Toward the end of 1946, having done *his* bit for the war effort, he too was entertaining plans to leave *The New Yorker*. According to his wife, Shawn wasn't dissatisfied; he simply figured that if he was ever going to indulge his lifelong desire to be a writer, this was the time. Not exactly overjoyed at this decision, Ross nonetheless acceded to it, and for both their sakes he arranged for Shawn to do some freelance editing for the magazine. In the meantime Shawn's assistant, Sanderson Vanderbilt, would take over Fact. Everyone knew Vanderbilt was a genial fellow and a capable editor, but some writers wondered whether he—or anyone else, for that matter—could step in and do all the things that his boss seemed to do so effortlessly. Yet no one better understood Shawn's itch to write than the writers themselves, so they sent him off in style with an expensive silver tray from Tiffany's that was engraved with the signatures of all his reporters. But in January 1947, not long after the formal presentation of the tray, Vanderbilt, in a bizarre accident, badly scalded himself in the bathtub, and it appeared he would be incapacitated indefinitely. A desperate Ross asked Shawn to stay on, and that was the end of his writing career.

Ross was privately relieved to have Shawn back in command, for there had never been so much work to be done. Manpower was no longer the bugaboo; now it was prosperity, which was swelling the size of the issues. Not long after the Shawn-Vanderbilt flurry, *The New Yorker* reported to its shareholders that 1946 had been another banner year, with profits of six hundred thousand dollars on revenues in excess of six million. At times the magazine had more advertising business than it could handle, since it still couldn't get all the paper it needed. That April the magazine raised its cover price from fifteen to twenty cents, the first newsstand increase in its twenty-two-year history.

———

ON WEEKENDS, WHEN ROSS OFTEN HAD CUSTODY OF PATTY, HE would tell her mother, Frances, that he was taking her to a nice restaurant for lunch. Then father and daughter would head off instead to the Bowery or the Brooklyn docks, or perhaps even a Harlem honky-tonk—to some of those same "dark, mysterious, malodorous stretches" of New York that he had written about in alarm to Governor Hurley.

Ross's purpose in showing his young daughter the city's underside was to make sure that she acquired the kind of education she wouldn't get at boarding school or in the Hamptons. His gravest admonition to her, often repeated, was that she not turn out "snobby," Patricia Ross recalled. "He thought I ought to know what life was really all about." If he was feeling particularly righteous they might even stroll along Wall Street, where he would hold forth about venal people in expensive suits who made lots of money without making any *thing*, except perhaps trouble. (Wall Street was merely a convenient and nicely symbolic backdrop; Ross's disdain for this business "type" transcended stockbrokers to include lawyers, accountants, and a certain magazine publisher whose name began with *F*.)

Patricia Ross remembers those excursions as exhilarating adventures. She had no apprehension about the dirty-ankle venues because her father seemed to know virtually everyone they came across. Even allowing for the tricks of memory, this probably wasn't much of an exaggeration. Like notable New Yorkers from Peter Minuit on, Ross wasn't so much a product of the city as he was the outsider trying to take its measure, awestruck and suspicious simultaneously. In three decades he had traversed it often and met countless of its characters. These were drunks, club owners, waiters, and cops on the beat, and Patty met them all. Her father saw to it that they were part of her upbringing the way the colorful characters of turn-of-the-century Aspen and Salt Lake had been part of his.

Ross was devoted to his daughter, and she to him. The most poignant photograph in her dog-eared scrapbook is a formal portrait of Ross, in silk dressing gown, cradling her as a newborn in his arms.

He is beaming intently at her, and across the bottom of the photo he has scribbled, "Buckwheats to you, Patricia Ross."

Though she lived with her mother and Tim Wilkinson, Patty saw her father often, especially in Stamford. Ross and Frances had an informal and civilized arrangement about Patty's custody, and Ross took her whenever he could—usually on weekends and holidays, and for much of the summer. She prized her time in the country. The big, airy house and parklike setting made for countless hiding places and vivid reveries. For all her father's money problems, he managed over the years to add adjacent parcels to his property, much of it purchased from his neighbor Mrs. Borglum, and in time the estate would grow to 157 acres, most of which would be subdivided after his death.

At Stamford, Ross and Ariane maintained separate bedrooms. His was really a combination bedroom, study, and porch. The room was usually a shambles, furniture piled high with detective magazines, newspapers, and *New Yorker* galleys, floor littered with cigarette butts and wadded-up correspondence—there being no Mrs. Walden there to retrieve what needed saving. His bed was more like a military-style cot, low and extra wide. It was a creation of his own design, friends said, because he was prone to nightmares and thrashed about frightfully.

When in the country, Ross frequently worked in this room until two or three in the morning. He was someone who had to really force himself to concentrate when he read, so the privacy of this room and its general absence of interruptions made it one of his favorite places to work. Patty often would slip in late at night to watch him in silence until she drifted off to sleep on the couch.

Whenever Patty stayed at Stamford, Ross made a point of seeing her off to bed, the time he reserved for their most serious father-daughter talks. Often these were mystifying conversations, like the night he explained to her that she should be "careful" about men. At the time Patty thought he was admonishing her to be nice to her elders, but later on she figured out that it was Ross's way of warning her about the male of the species. At other times he might discuss the merits of hard work, or caution her not to value things more than

Scenes from Stamford: Ross looks over the morning newspaper with Patty, and tries to overcome the family dog's indifference. *(Courtesy of Patricia Ross Honcoop)*

people. He also gave her frequent bedtime pep talks, trying to keep her from becoming discouraged over the bad grades that resulted from her dyslexia; he would remind his daughter that there were two kinds of intelligence, academic and common sense, and that they were equally important.

On the whole, Patty had a cordial relationship with Ariane, and when the child crossed her stepmother, Ariane relied on Ross to discipline her. Like so many divorced fathers, however, Ross was the softest of soft touches, and his halfhearted attempts at correction—"*Please* do what your father tells you, Patty dear"—were resolutely ignored. He could be firm on some matters, like insisting she not swim in a nearby pond for fear of polio, and he was apoplectic when-

Fishing was one of Ross's few recreational pursuits. Here he is on a trip to Colorado. *(Courtesy of Mrs. Milton Greenstein)*

ever he caught Patty and her friends skittering along the roof of the tall house, which they often did. Mostly, though, she did as she pleased and got what she wanted.

When not closeted in his room working, Ross liked to use his time in the country to relax. He enjoyed playing solitaire, or simply walking around the grounds, shooting at crows. He made a point of listening to the news on the radio several times a day but seldom turned it on for music or entertainment programs.

There were always a few servants—a cook, a butler, a handyman-groundskeeper. These faces were constantly changing, but generally they were as eccentric a bunch as those at the magazine. For a while during the war their butler was a dour German named Franz. Patty liked to sneak into his room now and then, especially after she noticed that Franz had tacked up a huge portrait of Hitler on his wall. She doesn't think her father ever made it up to the servants' quarters to see this, though he must have had his suspicions about the butler's sympathies because he used to joke, "Patty, try not to annoy Franz. He's in a bad mood; Germany is losing the war."

Eventually Franz was sent packing, but his employer had no more stomach for firing the hired help than for firing people at *The New Yorker*. Anytime this necessity arose, he became overwhelmed by guilt. Patricia especially remembered the time he decided he had to let go their cook, a man named Jerry, and was feeling even guiltier than usual because the man was a fellow veteran, a former Army cook. Prior to 1942, Ross's cooks needed no special culinary talent because his diet was so bland that all the joy had gone out of this important part of his life. Nothing fried, nothing raw, nothing spicy, no shellfish, no rich sauces. Stewed was good. Dining at "21" one evening with Ross and Frank Sullivan, Corey Ford watched as Ross surveyed the menu in vain for something healthful to order. Trying to be helpful, the waiter said, "How about a nice vegetable dinner?" Ross snapped back, "That is a contradiction in terms." However, once Dr. Sara Jordan took over Ross's care and feeding, she reintroduced many of his favorite foods to his diet—*if* they were precisely, expertly prepared, and this, sadly, was beyond Jerry's mess-hall skills. Hence he would have to go, and that morning, as Patty came to breakfast, her father was already pacing. "When I came in he said, 'I'm sorry, darling, but I have to fire Jerry.'" Then he looked at her, wrinkling his face hopefully. "You don't think you could go in there and casually mention that he might be fired?" Even at her tender age Patty didn't fall for this.

Presiding somehow over this loopy establishment was Ariane. With the war over, she and Ross divided their time between the country house and their apartment at 375 Park Avenue (which they took after spending the first three years of their marriage at the Ritz-Carlton). Ross wasn't exactly wealthy, but with two fashionable addresses and a modicum of servants Ariane found the situation more than comfortable. Two days before they wed, she and Ross entered into a prenuptial agreement, part of which established a trust to provide Ariane a standing expense account. This amounted to five hundred dollars a month, which she could use for personal expenses. She received another two thousand dollars a month to administer the households.

By all accounts Ariane enjoyed spending the money—Ross sometimes referred to her as "my purchasing agent"—and a good bit of it went into interior decoration. Her tastes gravitated strongly to the frilly and white-on-white. At Stamford this impulse was pretty much restricted to her bedroom; otherwise the house was done in early American, the work of a previous decorator. But in the Park Avenue apartment this aesthetic ran riot. There were plush white carpets, walls of mirrored glass, even a white bearskin. People who called there seldom failed to remark on it: The apartment was beautiful, but it was so . . . *white*. If Ross came into the living room wearing his ancient bathrobe, as he sometimes did in casual company, he looked like a walking stain. After seeing him in this bleached environment, S. J. Perelman said that Ross seemed to him "mired like a wounded bird."

Wartime had withered any real social life for husband and wife, so afterward they were both anxious to get back into circulation. Ross was especially happy to resume his poker regimen. He played in two games a week, one for low stakes and one for high. (James Gilson, the son of Ross's friend and cousin Wesley, kibitzed the high-stakes game one evening while visiting the city, and recalled that at times there were thousands of dollars on the table.) Getting back to the West again on vacations, Ross always made a point of sniffing out a game somewhere. He regaled Rebecca West about an evening of "no-limit stud poker with the old-timers in a gambling hall in Reno, Nevada, which is an occupation that gives me more fundamental enjoyment than anything else I know." Players in western games are all authentic and fascinating, Ross asserted, "including the one-armed men, who seem to be numerous. I played in the Reno game last year and there was always a one-armed man in the game, and the same was true this year. In fact, both years, there was a one-armed *Chinaman* in the game, and the one-armed Chinaman who was in the game last year was not the one who was in the game this year." Ross said that the plethora of one-armed men apparently had to do with Reno's being a railroad town, as losing a limb was a common railroad occupational hazard. "That is only a partial explanation, though," he added. "It can't include the Chinamen, for Chinamen don't work on railroads. I'm still baffled by that one."

Given the choice, Ross would always prefer the company of one-armed railroad men over New York society, but owing to his position and marriage he wasn't always given the choice. Photographer Jerome Zerbe captured Ross and Ariane one evening at a fete at the St. Regis, with Ross seated next to Gertrude Lawrence and wearing a party hat that more closely resembles a dunce cap. He put in an occasional appearance at the Plaza's swank Oak Room, where at least two *New Yorker* staffers, according to their own report, were on the receiving end of Ross spitballs. (On one of these occasions, his accomplice was James Cagney.) Then there was a dinner party with the Duke of Windsor, which the editor left early when he "damned well had to catch a train, although it was pointed out later that that was a ruinous social act."

By now Ross was also spending a great deal of his spare time with New York's affable mayor, William O'Dwyer, who took office in January 1946, and with whom Ross struck up a great friendship. This was unusual in that while he had been friendly with countless politicians through the years, he had been really close to only a few. Two

Party animal: Ross is flanked by Ariane, right, and Gertrude Lawrence at the St. Regis during the early Forties. *(© Jerome Zerbe. From a private collection.)*

of these were James Forrestal, an FDR aide who became Secretary of the Navy and then the first Secretary of Defense, and Robert Lovett, who was an Undersecretary of Defense. But he felt a genuine kinship with O'Dwyer. A story used to be told about them that is thought to be true, but even if it is only legend it nicely demonstrates their relationship. Ross got a parking ticket in the city, and having always wondered how these things got done, he asked his friend the mayor whether he could fix it. Certainly, O'Dwyer said. A week or so later, Ross's curiosity got the best of him and he called up the mayor and asked if he had taken care of the ticket. "Nothing to it," O'Dwyer said. "I just paid the fine."

Born in Ireland, O'Dwyer as a young man spent several years training for the priesthood at the Jesuit University of Salamanca. He dropped out and came to America, where he became a cop instead of a priest, worked his way through law school, and rose through the ranks of Brooklyn's Democratic machine. With a little whiskey in him, O'Dwyer could match Ross story for story, and was by most accounts a decent fellow. Ross considered him "a wise and remarkable man" with a populist sense as acute as Roosevelt's. The two men were always at ease in each other's company. O'Dwyer would occasionally drive up to Stamford late at night, unannounced, just to talk. Likewise, Ross often came by Gracie Mansion after work, where the two lonely men would sit on the porch for hours.

O'Dwyer was lonely because he was without a wife (a widower through his first term, he had yet to begin courting the former model who would become the second Mrs. O'Dwyer). Ross was lonely because he still had one.

It was plain from the outset that Ross and Ariane's marriage had been manufactured not in heaven but in some other, nether region. Daphne Hellman Shih, who was close to Ariane, said her friend's charm wore off quickly for Ross, and his irritation with her was palpable early on. "Ross got more and more nervous during those times, I guess because of the ulcers," she said. "He was thoroughly impatient with Ariane. She would be wringing her hands, complaining because she couldn't make the servants do what she wanted, that sort of thing." Patricia Ross said it seemed that her father and Ariane were seldom together, and she never saw any tenderness between them, as she did between her mother and Tim Wilkinson (whose marriage lasted until his death).

In certain ways, Ross tried to be a dutiful husband, even a sweet one. When one of Ariane's young nieces appeared to have serious heart trouble, Ross, clearly touched by her predicament, prevailed on Mencken to arrange for the child to be seen by a top specialist at Johns Hopkins. On the other hand, he loathed most of the adults in Ariane's family—which didn't keep them from coming to Stamford for weeks and months at a stretch. At such times he tried hard not to be overtly rude; he simply ignored them.

The fact was that Ross was never comfortable in a traditional domestic setting, and his marriages were progressively more dysfunctional. One symptom of his fissured relationship with Ariane was what Patricia characterized as their "nightmare" dinner parties. At least once a week Ross would arrive home from work to find to his dismay that Ariane had invited guests to dinner. In such cases his initial reaction often was to refuse to attend altogether, but then he would have a change of heart, don old, mismatched clothing, muss his hair, jut a cigarette from his bottom lip, come down the stairs to startle his guests and feign surprise: "Goddammit, I forgot you were coming over!" At dinner, he might start up a game of solitaire or work on a crossword puzzle right at the table as Ariane's guests conversed. Patricia said she learned to eat fast because invariably this would lead to some kind of scene. If this sometimes astonished first-time guests, regulars like Mrs. Borglum paid them no mind and just kept eating.

Such behavior might have seemed lifted from the latest Moss Hart–George S. Kaufman farce if not for its more disturbing underpinnings. A guest remembers another dinner party, one where O'Dwyer was present but Ariane was not, at which Ross suddenly got angry and turned all his wife's pictures to the wall. In legal papers filed near the end of Ross's life, Ariane charged that things deteriorated to the point where Ross insisted she not speak to him at breakfast; if she had anything important to tell him, she should leave a note on his desk. "There was a standing rule that I could not discuss 'trivia' with him," she said in her suit. "And by his definition 'trivia' consisted of everything I tried to say to him."

By the late Forties the rift was so obvious that the Rosses weren't bothering to hide it from friends. For instance, in the spring of 1948 they stopped in Saratoga, en route to visiting Patty at school, to see Frank Sullivan. The drive was so unpleasant that upon their arrival Ariane announced her intention to seek a divorce, and Ross, noted Sullivan, "had something of the same idea." There were a few trial separations between the two, and some separate vacations. That summer, Ross became upset when Ariane stayed in Europe longer than she had said, and so he took off for the West without her.

Elizabeth Paepcke, the doyenne of Aspen, Colorado, and a friend of Ross's, recalled seeing the couple on several occasions at about this time and thinking that the marriage was clearly tenuous. Ross had come to know Mrs. Paepcke and her industrialist husband, Walter, who together transformed Aspen from mining town to glittering resort community and cultural center. He enjoyed them both, even if he was appalled by some of their notions for Aspen, like a grand Goethe bicentennial festival. "Their gay plans curled my hair into small ringlets," he wrote Elmer Davis. "I knew they were going to stink up the old place. Making Aspen cultural is one of the greatest profanities of modern times." But another part of Ross was proud of Aspen's "discovery" by the rest of the world, and he was a regular visitor in the late Forties. On one such occasion, Mrs. Paepcke recalled, she came across a tipsy Ariane in the bar of the Hotel Jerome, her arm around a cowboy, saying to him, "Thank God we can relax."

———

FOR SOME YEARS WOLCOTT GIBBS HAD UNDERSTUDIED ROBERT Benchley as *The New Yorker*'s drama critic, and in 1940, when the latter quit, he took over the job full-time. Though never one for formal correspondence, Gibbs felt an initial obligation to answer all those readers, thoughtful and otherwise, who wrote in critiquing his critiques. For the first month or so, these replies were polite and somewhat detailed, rebutting the readers point by point. By the second month, the letters were becoming more perfunctory, but were still personal. By the third, he had instructed a clerk to answer all such mail with this note: "Dear Sir [or Madam]: You may be right. Sincerely, Wolcott Gibbs."

Gibbs was a small, thin man who usually had little to say. This wasn't aloofness, merely another congenital case of *New Yorker* shyness. "He was a person who was almost incapable of uttering an opinion without clearing his throat first, which to me is sort of a symptom of insecurity about expressing yourself," said Gibbs's son, Tony, who himself became a *New Yorker* writer and editor. "But he never cleared his throat on the page, as many writers do."

If Gibbs seemed outwardly fragile, in reality he was tough and wiry, not to mention an editor and writer of uncanny range. Ross stood in near awe of him. "Maybe he doesn't like anything," he would say, "but he can do anything." This was not hyperbolic praise. For Ross Gibbs cranked out short stories, Comment, theater criticism, even the occasional controversial Profile, such as the Luce piece or his 1940 surgical strike on Thomas Dewey, then New York's crime-busting district attorney, whom Gibbs portrayed as a smug, nervy wunderkind (John Bainbridge contributed the reporting).

But if Gibbs was Ross's most versatile lieutenant, he was perhaps his most dependable too. He could and did grouse about *The New Yorker,* but unlike Thurber or the Whites, he never left it. Partly this was because he lacked Thurber's confidence and White's need to prove himself outside the magazine, and partly because he never quite got over stumbling onto such good fortune. But his willingness to remain ensconced in that "velvet womb" (Tony Gibbs's phrase) as a "paragrapher for a twenty-cent magazine" (as the autobiographical protagonist in Gibbs's 1950 play *Season in the Sun* put it) fueled his low self-esteem and further darkened his already bleak outlook. Gibbs knew he possessed the kind of talent to make more "serious" literary statements—besides, pesky friends like O'Hara constantly reminded him of it—but he had neither the drive nor the inclination to write the Great American Novel. He didn't think he had anything that "important" to say. Yet this presumed underachievement nagged at him, with the result that he tended to trivialize his *New Yorker* output. This was unfortunate, since producing as much top-quality work, on deadline and in such diverse incarnations, as Gibbs did for thirty years was a towering accomplishment.

Unlike his colleagues, Gibbs never got much farther from Forty-third Street than his oceanside cottage at Fire Island, his refuge on warm weekends. There he would fish, or simply fix a pitcher of cocktails and sit out in the sun and roast. In the summer his skin would turn so brown, and his blond hair and mustache so thoroughly white, that his sparring partner Russell Maloney once quipped that he looked like a photographic negative.

Edmund Wilson described him another way. Gibbs, he said, "glided past like a ghost, and we never spoke. His eyes always seemed to be closed." There was something undeniably ethereal about the man. Before a show, he would shrink far down into his seat, as if to disappear. He was self-conscious about being recognized, but perhaps a touch self-conscious too about what he was doing there. "I've always felt that play criticism was a silly occupation for a grown man," he said.

As a critic, Gibbs did most of his writing at his apartment. When he was composing, he would pace the length of his large bedroom deep in concentration, back and forth, with Lucky Strikes burning in ashtrays at either end of the room. When he typed he used only three fingers, the others having been broken in a nasty Prohibition-era tumble down a flight of stairs. Early each evening he would slip out of his preferred daytime wear, a salmon terry-cloth bathrobe, into a suit (or dinner jacket for a major opening) and head to the theater. When Tony was a very young schoolboy, he was assigned to report to his classmates on what his father did for a living. The boy realized he didn't know, so one evening as his father was preparing to leave he asked him. "Well, think about it for a second," Gibbs replied. "I go out to work at night and I don't come back till after you are in bed.

What do you think I do? I'm a burglar." (This information, dutifully passed along to Tony's class, provoked an irate call to Gibbs from the principal's office.)

His was not an intellectual's approach to criticism. Gibbs was more analytical about plays than Benchley, who never pretended to be anything more than a bemused enthusiast, but he employed his predecessor's straightforward approach: he said what he liked, what he didn't like, and why. Certainly he was more cynical than Benchley, yet in his way just as entertaining. This toss-off about a feeble mid-Forties production is typical of his style:

> *Pretty Little Parlor*, by Claiborne Foster, was the latest of a rather alarming epidemic of plays about domineering women. Clotilde Hilyard drove her husband to drink, was partially responsible for a double drowning, and was mixed up in various crooked railway deals. She may have been a little excessive. Anyway, the play closed after eight performances. I regret this only on behalf of its star, Stella Adler, an actress I'd like to see around more or less permanently.

Gibbs went to a production expecting not to like it, and was seldom disappointed. This was not, as many theater people maintained, because he was inherently incapable of enjoying anything, for when he did admire a production (or even a good performance in a bad production, as with Stella Adler), he said so, often loudly. But he had two qualities that rankled many theater people: high standards and a compulsion to tell the truth. His considerable influence on Broadway derived less from *The New Yorker*'s box-office impact, which was probably middling, than from Gibbs's standing among his fellow critics. Not all his peers liked him—the feeling was mutual—but they knew that he was usually right, and that he didn't settle for dreck. He helped keep them honest.

Since no good deed goes unpunished, Gibbs's acerbic reviews earned him recriminations from roughed-up authors and actors, threats to banish him from certain theaters, and countless feuds with owners and producers, perhaps most notably with that egomaniacal genius Jed Harris. On one occasion the League of New York Theatres formally complained to *The New Yorker* that Gibbs had shown up "unfit" to review a show—that is, drunk. Ross replied that his critic had simply been getting shots for an allergy.

Gibbs's entertaining theater criticism was only one of the reasons why arguably the late Forties represented *The New Yorker* at the zenith of its cultural influence. While print was still a dominant medium, no real rival to Ross's magazine had yet arisen, and television was only beginning to exert its great gravitational pull on the public consciousness. The magazine stood as a unique and powerful beacon. For almost any thinking New Yorker, reading it had become de rigueur; like the Metropolitan Opera, the *Times,* or the New York City Ballet, it had taken its place as a quintessential New York cultural institution. Moreover, outside the city it was a status symbol, the magazine one left on the coffee table to impress the neighbors.

Its name notwithstanding, *The New Yorker*'s impact and interests now reached around the world. Ross may have welcomed his reporters back from the war, but they didn't intend to sit still in New York. Their horizons had been broadened, and with them that of *The New Yorker.* Beyond "Hiroshima," the immediate postwar period generated a trove of marvelous pieces, like Philip Hamburger's dispatch from Argentina on Perón's reputed harboring of Nazis, Flanner's "The Beautiful Spoils," an account of the Third Reich's plunder of European art, as well as reports out of Nuremberg from her, Rebecca West, and Andy Logan. Even as the war receded in the late Forties and early Fifties, *New Yorker* datelines read like the itinerary of a restless—and well-heeled—traveler. Flanner was in Capri, Joseph Wechsberg in Warsaw, Alan Moorehead in Sicily, E. J. Kahn, Jr., in Korea. *New Yorker* reporters were even abroad at home. Richard Rovere established his influential Letter from Washington. Liebling reinvigorated the Wayward Press column and so broadened its scope that he could just as comfortably travel to Chicago to needle the *Tribune*'s Colonel McCormick as work over the miscreants in his own backyard.

At the same time the magazine was watching the powerful new medium of television, and Ross asked Hamburger to devote a standing department to it. (In *The New Yorker*'s fine contrarian critical tradition, one of the first pieces Hamburger wrote trashed the man the rest of America had already embraced as "Mr. Television," Milton Berle.)

Lillian Ross was beginning to work the fertile ground of Hollywood (not to mention writing one of *The New Yorker*'s most riveting pieces from this period, a scandalous—or so many said— Profile of Ernest Hemingway). Rebecca West traveled to South Carolina for her compelling story on a lynching and Southern justice. Even homebody Joseph Mitchell turned footloose, tracking his "high-steel" Mohawks, the Indians who assembled the skeletons of Manhattan's skyscrapers, across the St. Lawrence to their tribal home. In a 1949 lament to W. Averell Harriman, Ross was not entirely kidding when he said, "We may sound provincial to you but we seem like the International Gazette to me. We got started on the wide world during the war and can't quit. Also, the writers got in the habit of traveling. They can always see a story far away, although they can't see one here."

Footloose correspondent: Philip Hamburger interviews Dwight Eisenhower in his Gettysburg, Pennsylvania, office. *(From the collection of Philip Hamburger)*

To a great extent Ross's globe-trotting reporters were only trying to reflect the neurotic new age, and certainly the same was true of his fiction contributors. Once again there were grumbles from some old *New Yorker* hands that the combination of "serious" journalism and "grim" fiction was conspiring to squeeze all the fun out of the magazine. Gibbs said to White in the fall of 1947, "Your sports parable is a very fine piece, though quite a shock since I had an idea humor was supposed to be against the rules around here. The moral climate is against it. Right at this minute there is a son of a bitch down the hall writing a thirty-two-part Profile of Stalin, and somewhere east of the water cooler Liebling is trying to beat a little social consciousness into the Wayward Press department, and somebody else is writing a short story beginning 'Cress Delahanty, who was thirteen years old but looked awful, asked her mother if she could stay all night with her friend Irma in a sump hole.'"

This last was an unsubtle jab at Jessamyn West, who did in fact write a Cress Delahanty story called "The Sump Hole," and who represented a new generation of fiction writers imparting an even starker realism to the pages of the magazine. They were audacious talents: Mary McCarthy (whose 1944 story "The Weeds," at ten thousand words, was easily the longest fiction piece the magazine had run to date), Niccolò Tucci, Jean Stafford, Shirley Hazzard. But none of them was more original than a precocious young man named J. D. Salinger.

Actually, Salinger's *New Yorker* career was nearly aborted before it began. In 1941, when he was just twenty-two and had already collected several rejections from the magazine, Salinger had his first story purchased by *The New Yorker*. Called "A Slight Rebellion Off Madison," it concerned a prep-school runaway, an irresistible young man named Holden Caulfield, who would resurface in *The Catcher in the Rye*. Before "Rebellion" made it into print, however, Pearl Harbor intervened, and with the war on, the editors felt the story would come across as irrelevant and unfunny, so they held it—for five years. It finally appeared in December 1946, in the back of the book. Even there, Salinger's talent jumped off the page, and within several years he was steadily contributing such stories as "A Perfect Day for

Bananafish" (one of the strange Glass-family pieces) and "For Esmé—with Love and Squalor."

Another virtuosic newcomer to *The New Yorker* was the Russian writer Vladimir Nabokov, who was brought to the magazine's attention by Edmund Wilson. He had written some poetry for *The New Yorker,* but his early prose pieces, which began in 1948, took a prodigious amount of work on Katharine White's part. His syntax required some ironing, and he was partial to queer or archaic words that no one recognized. "Edmund Wilson once explained this . . . by saying I must remember that Nabokov learned most of his English vocabulary by studying the Unabridged Oxford English Dictionary," Mrs. White noted years later. This was just the sort of thing that exasperated Ross, and when he heard that Nabokov had been approached by Cornell about teaching, he told Mrs. White, "I may cut my throat." Nevertheless, he was enchanted by Nabokov's warm, detailed evocations of his aristocratic childhood in Russia. For his part, the writer was delighted that Ross "hit it off so well with the ghost of my past," but he shouldn't have been surprised. Not only were Nabokov's stories beautifully rendered, but Ross always had a soft spot for personal history, which is one reason the genre flourished in *The New Yorker*—from Thurber and Clarence Day through Sally Benson (whose reminiscences became the basis for *Meet Me in St. Louis*) and Ruth McKenney *(My Sister Eileen)* to the various autobiographical pieces of H. L. Mencken.

Mrs. White worked closely not only with Nabokov but with McCarthy, Stafford, Kay Boyle, and many other of *The New Yorker's* top contributors. Since her return to the office in 1943, she and Lobrano had settled into an uneasy détente. They were two strong people, and it was awkward for both to have the onetime boss-subordinate roles reversed. Given the delicate situation, Ross wasn't always as sensitive as he might have been. "Ross would sometimes consult me for an opinion on a manuscript after Lobrano had sent it to him," Mrs. White remembered. "Sometimes I would agree with Lobrano's opinion and sometimes not, and this must have been very trying for him, but it was not my fault. For the most part, our opin-

J. D. Salinger.
(Archive Photos)

ions coincided, and we had many, many happy times together during that period." That she overstated how genial the situation was is indicative of how earnestly the fiction editors tried to play down their differences. But the tension was real, and Edward Newhouse and others close to Lobrano say that he was frustrated by the arrangement. While he would never have been so gauche as to say as much, Newhouse said, "he managed to communicate a faint distaste for her."

Nonetheless, Mrs. White was right about everyone being civil. Lobrano's fiction department, like Mrs. White's before it, was truly a collegial operation. The editors had their literary disagreements, naturally, but were not hobbled by them. One day in 1948 Shirley Jackson submitted a modern-day horror story that excited the editors, with the exception of William Maxwell, who voted against it as being too heavy-handed and gimmicky for *The New Yorker*. The others, including Ross, took Maxwell's point, yet considered the story so mesmerizing that they simply had to publish it. It was "The Lottery," which created a sensation when it appeared and went on to become one of the most anthologized short stories in history. Ross was as

Vladimir Nabokov.
(Archive Photos)

bewildered as everyone else, including the author, about the "mean-ing" of "The Lottery," but he clearly appreciated it, saying later that it was "terrifically effective" and was destined to become a classic "in some category."

Ross liked to gripe about the bumper crop of "grim" stories, of which "The Lottery" was one, that *The New Yorker* was now cultivat-ing, and this grousing gave rise to the notion that he disliked them, which wasn't true. He *was* sorry to see the corresponding falloff in humorous pieces, which no doubt provoked some of his curmud-geonly asides, but he enjoyed the darker stories too. James Geraghty recalled coming upon the editor reading a galley of Robert M. Coates's "A Winter in the Country," a melancholy but moving story about an old man who gives every indication that he is about to die, only to be revived miraculously by the onset of spring. "Well," Ross said, a little melancholy himself, "maybe that will make up for six weeks of dull publishing."

CHAPTER 14

RECLUSE

ABOUT TOWN

IN THE FALL OF 1950, GIBBS, HAVING DETERMINED TO PROVE TO HIM-self and the New York theater community that he was capable of practicing what he had preached for ten years, saw his comic play *Season in the Sun* open successfully on Broadway. With its obvious autobiographical chords, it told the story of a magazine writer who runs off to his oceanside retreat to be a novelist (a "real" writer) and slip the bonds of his brilliant, tyrannical boss, Horace William Dodd, nakedly patterned after Harold Wallace Ross. (The stage directions: "Dodd should really be played by Harold Ross of *The New Yorker* but, failing that, by an actor who could play Caliban or Mr. Hyde almost without the assistance of makeup.") Near the play's end, Gibbs has the protagonist's attractive young friend tell Dodd/Ross, "He says you're the greatest editor in America." To which Dodd/Ross replies, "Well, they're a pretty seedy bunch, generally speaking."

All through that year, Ross's peers, seedy and otherwise, had been sizing up *The New Yorker* now that it had attained the venerable age of twenty-five, and many of them frankly *did* consider him the greatest editor in America. But as undeniably gratifying as this sentiment was, Ross actually was feeling strangely at sea just then, uncharacteristically uncertain in some of his judgments. To a great extent, he sensed the modern world overtaking him. A nineteenth-century man at heart—after all, he still bore the scars of a boyhood stagecoach accident, and considered air travel so unnatural that he never once set foot on a plane—he was uneasy with the terrible realities of the atomic age, like coming up with contingency plans to publish *The New Yorker* in the event New York City was bombed. (He decided that any surviving staff would relocate to the printing plant in Greenwich if *it* was still standing.)

As intransigent and romantic as Ross could be in his worldview, largely shaped as it was by people and events prior to 1920, he was not unsophisticated. Nonetheless, the brinksmanship and Cold War emotionalism of the late Forties and early Fifties had him flummoxed. He confessed as much to Howard Brubaker, who from 1925 contributed *The New Yorker*'s Of All Things column, a collection of humorous paragraphs that was a kind of poor man's Notes and Comment. "I've never been up against a [situation] such as the present one," Ross wrote. "War doesn't buffalo me professionally, everything being black and white in wartime, and peace doesn't, although journalistically it's not as simple as war, but I'm baffled by this in-between business. I started to get out a light magazine that wouldn't concern itself with the weighty problems of the universe, and now look at me."

Ross found it "incredible" that the United States was fighting in Korea ("It's incredible for Americans, that is," he told Rebecca West. "The English . . . have been banging around the world for centuries"). He stubbornly refused to take Korea seriously as a war until or unless Soviet troops showed up at the front, which explains why he resisted his own reporters' appeals to cover it until it was almost over. He despised Communism but considered the "Red scare" in this country hysterical and overblown ("Goddammit, I have it on good authority there aren't two hundred Communists in the whole goddamn U.S.A."). As a close observer of the Alger Hiss case—Ross's friend and *New Yorker* associate Lloyd Paul Stryker defended the former State Department official—Ross had serious doubts about Hiss's guilt, though his skepticism sprang as much as anything from the fact that Hiss's accuser, Whittaker Chambers, was at bottom a "*Time* man." He appears to have had no higher opinion of Joseph McCarthy than of the many other bullies and blowhards he had come across, and he commended White and Rovere when from time to time they called the senator's demagoguery what it was. Some would later accuse *The New Yorker* of being reluctant to confront McCarthy, and it is true that the brunt of the magazine's criticism appeared in McCarthy's real heyday, 1953 and 1954, after Ross was dead. (Earlier, White in particular hadn't wanted to feed McCarthy's virulent ego with too much ink.) Still, as early as May 1950 Rovere was exposing the Wisconsin senator's bankrupt tactics and deploring the extent to which he had gummed up the works of government. He would keep up this drumbeat, in increasingly harsh terms, with Ross's approbation.

On one hand, these disorienting political currents troubled Ross the same way they troubled thoughtful people everywhere. In his view, government should feed the hungry, help widows and orphans, and pretty much leave all else alone; yet now it seemed to be mongering fear and anxiety. He brought up his personal politics so seldom in the office that most *New Yorker* staffers simply assumed from his conservatism and his disdain for Franklin Roosevelt—"the only non-phony I have ever heard you voice animosity towards," Frank Sullivan once told him—that he was a Republican. He was freer in his personal views with friends, and his letters reveal him to be less a partisan than a kind of Spencerian independent. In the 1948 election, for example, he said he couldn't support Thomas E. Dewey, by now the governor of New York, about whom Ross's feelings hadn't really changed since Gibbs's unflattering 1940 Profile. Yet neither could he vote for Harry Truman, despite the fact that the President was a devoted *New Yorker* reader. When Truman prevailed, Ross professed not to be surprised, explaining the upset to Mencken by borrowing an old Al Smith line: "Nobody ever shoots Santa Claus." (Ross held the electorate less responsible for Truman than he did Roosevelt, who the editor maintained had suppressed every capable Democratic successor. He once confronted FDR's son Elliott about this, and the young Roosevelt replied by way of explanation, "You don't think my father thought he was ever going to die, do you?")

But on another level what vexed Ross was less the political climate itself than the way it was buffeting *The New Yorker*. A conservative with an isolationist bent, he found himself running a magazine whose perspective was steadily growing more liberal and internationalist. If this paradox bothered him—and often it did—he had decided he could live with it as long as individual reporters didn't suffuse their pieces with their personal politics. The changing world hadn't changed his fundamental conviction that his job was to let intelligent people write about what interested them in a clear, entertaining way. What he found harder to swallow was the reputation his magazine was picking up in the process.

This ideological divergence between editor and magazine was not a sudden development, really, but a predictable by-product of the war. Certainly their coverage of the great conflict and its confused aftermath had helped put the "world" in the worldview of his young writers. Shawn had demonstrated more openness to political slants in journalistic pieces, and surely "Hiroshima" was nothing if not a giant billboard against nuclear war. There had also been White's high-profile campaign for "world government," an idea he propounded upon his return to New York in 1943, and *The New Yorker*'s first overtly political cause. For four years, in almost one out of three Comments, White had argued that if humanity was ever to rid itself of war, individual nations would have to subordinate themselves to some kind of global supergovernment. In some of his most eloquent writing, he tried to make people see that their deepest loyalties would have to shift from their nation to all of mankind. He argued less about the specifics of what this world government would be, or how it would work, than for its necessity and underlying principles. He was advocating not the United Nations itself, whose disappointing development he covered for *The New Yorker*, but something with more teeth in it. (Though written anonymously for Comment, White's views were later pulled together in a book under his name entitled *The Wild Flag*.)

While the world-government campaign was widely followed and admired by many politicians and opinion makers, there is no question that a great percentage of the magazine's largely conservative readership found it unsettling, even heretical. They did not expect or welcome such radical sentiments in *The New Yorker*. Especially in retrospect, the concept of world government is sweetly naïve, and Ross, calling himself a "complete cynic," thought as much at the time. Personally, he took the glum view that once the war was over the world would return to its same old belligerent ways. Yet even if he was incapable of mustering any idealism of his own, he always admired White's, and he encouraged the world-government theme. "My viewpoint is that if the people of the earth don't get a new set-up, they are being offered a very remarkable line of writing and thinking anyhow," Ross told him. "You (collective) can't lose on that basis. . . . But aside from all that and from everything else, you made the Comment page what it is, God knows, and I have for long regarded it as yours to the extent that you want to use it. That is not only the right way to look at the matter, but very sound business, I am convinced. I say carry on without hesitation or qualm." Still, both men would have to concede that they were a long way from the Penn Station information-booth campaign.

But when Ross surveyed his roster of writers from a political standpoint, he could only sigh. He saw virtually no Republicans; there were no good young conservatives out there who could write, he once lamented to Liebling. *New Yorker* writers were mostly Democrats, mostly liberal, and some, like Richard O. Boyer, outright leftist. While there is scant evidence that anyone really tried to use the magazine for aggressive proselytizing, something Ross would not have tolerated, by the same token a writer's personal interests obviously colored his choice of subject matter. In 1950 E. J. Kahn, Jr., was moved to write a Wayward Press piece defending two friends, musician Larry Adler and dancer Paul Draper, who as a result of a very public lawsuit were being roughed up by the right-wing press as pro-Communist. Shawn bought the piece, but Ross didn't see it until it was set in galleys. When Kahn ran into the editor, he was holding a proof. "Jesus Christ, Kahn, why did you have to write this goddamn piece?" he spluttered. "Now I have to run it." It was a reaction nearly identical to the one Ross had had to Rovere's controversial Washington Letter on integration, and it evoked from Kahn identical feelings of gratification and respect for his employer.

The price Ross paid for this kind of editorial scruple was watching his magazine increasingly attacked as "pink," or even deeper shades of red. In some quarters *The New Yorker* was dubbed *The New Worker*. Onetime friends of Ross's, like the influential columnist Westbrook Pegler, now blasted him in print for promoting the work of fellow travelers.

Certainly this was how the magazine was being viewed by the FBI. J. Edgar Hoover, as has been mentioned, was no fan of Ross's anyway, and any small *New Yorker* dig at the bureau could be expected to provoke a response. For instance, in 1943 a one-paragraph Talk item related a tepid joke about an FBI agent who is supposedly conducting a background check. The agent says, "I notice, in reading over back copies of your college daily, that your friend was sometimes referred to as Lefty. Was this because he was interested in communistic activities?"

For this transgression Ross heard from the great man himself. *The New Yorker*, Hoover wrote, "has again seen fit to refer to an alleged question by an FBI agent. . . . If this were labeled as a joke, I, of course, could get a good laugh out of it. Since, however, it is given such a prominent place in the Talk of the Town, I think it is right to assume that you intended that it should be considered as factually accurate. Accordingly, I feel justified in asking you for the basis upon which the item was predicated."

This was not the first or last time Hoover would harass Ross, and chances are he disdained the director less for his sanctimony and ham-handedness than for his stillborn sense of humor. According to the bureau's own files, Ross was generally "evasive" when approached for explanations about matters like the Talk joke, and he once suggested that Hoover's G-men could stand "an elemental education in politics, etc."

Of course "evasiveness" only engendered more suspicion. While the FBI didn't keep a dossier on Ross himself, it did so on many of his writers: Dorothy Parker (a thousand pages), Irwin Shaw, A. J. Liebling, Richard O. Boyer, Kay Boyle, John O'Hara, Edmund Wilson—even, amazingly, E. B. White and S. J. Perelman. They were among the hundreds of writers whose activities and attitudes the FBI was "policing" for Hoover. As Herbert Mitgang discussed in his book *Dangerous Dossiers,* files on the *New Yorker* writers were gathered for an array of reasons: Parker for her leftist causes, Liebling for making fun of Hoover in print, White for attacking McCarthyism, Perelman for advocating a fair shake for the blacklisted writers and directors known collectively as the Hollywood Ten. At bottom, however, all of them were suspected of somehow undermining what the bureau considered the American way of life.

A man who harbored so many "suspect" writers was naturally suspect himself. In a truly bizarre episode in 1949, John O'Hara decided for some reason that he wanted to become an operative for the Central Intelligence Agency and in his application listed Ross as a character witness. Charged with checking out O'Hara's background and loyalty, the FBI apparently debated for weeks whether Ross's opinion, given his own history with the bureau and the politics of his magazine, was even worth hearing. In the end they did interview Ross, who informed them that O'Hara was a "hotheaded Irishman" who hung out in bars a lot (for research), was belligerent when drunk, and was once a man of dubious morals. But he added that the writer had lately cleaned up his behavior and was in any event a patriot of the first rank. In spite of this ringing endorsement, O'Hara's application was rejected.

Ross had no problem shrugging off the likes of Hoover, but the aspersions against his magazine were more bothersome. Just *how* bothersome can be seen in separate but near-simultaneous contretemps involving two of his veteran reporters, Janet Flanner and freelancer Richard O. Boyer.

A regular contributor to *The New Yorker* since 1931, Boyer was a conspicuously adroit reporter and writer; in later years he would produce an acclaimed biography of John Brown. He was also an avowed Communist who wrote for such publications as the *New Masses* and the *Daily Worker*. He had never tried to use the pages of *The New Yorker* for political purposes, and the editors took pains to make sure that his assignments avoided any potential conflicts. Still, his mere presence in the magazine was controversial, and suddenly, in the fall of 1949, Ross terminated his association with *The New Yorker* (though not a staff reporter, Boyer apparently was receiving some sort of drawing account). It is not clear what prompted Ross's decision, though it was said he had discovered that the reporter was using *New Yorker* stationery for political purposes.

Word circulated quickly in Boyer's circles that he had been fired on account of his political beliefs. Just as Ross had been excoriated before by anti-Communists for the journalist's presence in the magazine, now he was denounced by Boyer's friends and associates for this "cowardly" act. In replying to some of these people, Ross characteristically declined to divulge details of what was in his view a personnel matter, but he did remind his correspondents of a technicality that he had also pointed out to Boyer himself: he couldn't be "fired" because he was a freelance writer.

Against this prickly backdrop, an even more painful situation surfaced with Flanner. Its seed had been planted earlier that year when she had suggested profiling Léon Blum, the venerable French socialist and, during the Third Republic, prime minister. She was an ardent opponent of Communism, but she was captivated by the burgeoning socialist movement and by Blum, its leader and a man through whom one could tell virtually the entire story of contemporary France. On this broad basis, the magazine approved her proposal. Flanner researched the piece for months, and it began shaping up as a four-part series. Then in March 1950 Blum died. Flanner had known this was a possibility, given the politician's advanced age and failing health, but it was her recollection that she had been given the magazine's assurance that the Profile would run even if he died. Ross and Shawn didn't remember it that way, and because *The New Yorker* did not run posthumous Profiles Ross wanted to kill it. Shawn offered to pay Flanner for the piece, to help her sell it elsewhere, or to get it made into a book. Flanner, though, felt double-crossed, and she attempted to find a way to have it appear in *The New Yorker.*

The two editors and the writer went back and forth for a few months about what to do with the article, until it became clear to Flanner that Ross was stalling until Blum was so cold it would be a moot point. In the process it likewise became clear that Ross's and Shawn's concern was less about the Blum piece per se than about Flanner's politics. Ross in fact was worried about her growing sympathy for socialism, how this had crept into her copy—and been expunged—and how she seemed out of touch with the mood in the United States. In the summer of 1950, they suggested to Flanner that she come back to New York for something of a "reorientation." As Ross tried to explain it, "Merely and simply . . . we want you to re-sense the temper of the country here, which is rather outlandish: witch hunts, *The New Yorker* accused of being red, etc., etc."

Flanner agreed to return, but she didn't get to New York until early November, and when she did a curious thing happened: Ross didn't want to see her. When she bumped into him in the hall on her first day in the office, he was flustered and abrupt. He didn't have time to talk just now, he said. In fact, he was "getting [out] this damned Christmas issue and I can't talk to you till next year."

But the next evening Ross made some time over coffee at "21," where Flanner had been dining with the Shawns and he with some other friends. He talked obliquely of his fear that Europe was being "lost" to "the Commies." ("Odd that he, such a patron of good writing and editing, should nickname Bolshevism so it sounds like a baseball team," Flanner wrote a friend.) Ross set no more store on socialism than on Communism, and he was concerned that she did. To Flanner's mounting irritation, it was several more weeks before they resumed their fumbling discourse, this time in Ross's office. As he talked, he began to pace nervously and become more agitated. Suddenly he blurted out that the French were not the people he had once known; they had changed, and no one could believe in them anymore. "And you don't believe in them either," he shouted at Flanner. "It shows in every goddamn word you write."

Unaccustomed to this vehemence from her patron and friend, Flanner shot back that she agreed: no one in Europe felt the same about anything anymore, she said, because nothing *was* the same. She offered to resign, but Ross calmed down and mumbled an apology, and there the matter ended.

Looking back on this frustrating home leave, Flanner would attribute Ross's erratic behavior to his genuine concern for her, and to his own marginal health. At the time, though, she felt bruised and estranged from her beloved *New Yorker* in a way she had never experienced before. Doubtless she was right in part about Ross, but just as surely his clumsy, groping performance was also about Boyer, about Hoover, about *"The New Worker,"* about writers and their politics generally, and his discomfort and despair in trying to reconcile the two. "I returned to Paris," Flanner would write, "no wiser."

———

ALL HIS LIFE ROSS HAD WORKED HARD TO KEEP HIS PUBLIC PROFILE low, but over the years there was so much fascination about the unorthodox guiding spirit of *The New Yorker* that attention was paid him anyway. The father of contemporary magazine profiles was such an irresistible character himself that by now he had been the subject of half a dozen profiles in competing publications, and he still turned up regularly in the gossip columns. Thus he could not have been altogether surprised one morning in 1948 to find that *"New Yorker* editor" was the clue to a four-letter word in the *Times* crossword puzzle.

At this point in his life it might have been said of Ross what he once said of Alan Dunn, one of his most prolific and eccentric artists. Of Dunn's many obsessions, the most pronounced was a paralyzing fear of fire. Good company though he was, the cartoonist routinely declined dinner invitations from friends if their apartments didn't have what he considered an adequate number of fire escapes. He seldom came down to the office, which he felt was a fire trap. Indeed he seldom went out at all, and as a result he began to get a reputation as a recluse. Ross found this odd, even amusing, because he always seemed to be bumping into Dunn in restaurants and theater lobbies. Said the editor, "He's some kind of recluse about town."

His friends knew that Ross was anything but a recluse, but to the reading public his resolute shunning of the spotlight only enhanced his air of mystery. He didn't mind this so much; he even cultivated it to an extent. Yet he was finding that avoiding publicity, especially when so many of his friends and acquaintances were in the media, was increasingly a challenge. Genuinely uncomfortable in public settings, he never accepted speaking engagements, attended few "functions," and rejected frequent requests to appear on the radio (he liked to tell broadcasters that whenever he got in front of an open microphone he had an uncontrollable urge to swear). Writers, on the other hand, could not be so easily dissuaded. Being written about made Ross self-conscious, but as a print journalist he felt he owed colleagues at least grudging cooperation. Yet in his view, few of the resulting pieces ever did more than perpetuate the old, mad Ross of myth—or worse, give his friends cause to rib him. After two writers double-teamed Ross unsuccessfully for *Harper's,* Mencken wrote him to say, "There was material enough to scare half the children of America to death, but all the authors managed to do is to touch the edges of it. I am almost tempted to spit on my hands and do [a profile] myself. If I ever get to I'll print it in either the Christian Herald or the Police Gazette."

In such ways Ross the private man was becoming, reluctantly, a public figure, but if he was not altogether happy about the idea, he was at least becoming more comfortable with it. More secure in himself and his accomplishments, he was finally demonstrating a willingness to drop his guard. In 1949 and 1950, this new attitude, along with some calamitous events beyond his control, combined to expose his public persona all the more.

In fact 1949 was a miserable year for Ross, and his chronic tax and marriage problems were only the beginning of it. White got the year off to an inauspicious start by giving up Comment, at least as a full-time obligation. In March, illness and exhaustion forced his friend James Forrestal to quit as Secretary of Defense, and then in May he leaped to his death from a window of the Bethesda Naval Hospital. Ross happened to be in Washington at the time, having put in a rare appearance at the annual Gridiron Dinner. The next morning a bell-boy broke the news to him about Forrestal. Ross paced the lobby of the Willard Hotel in agony and frustration for half an hour, then decided to return to New York, the suicide of another friend—one the same age as he—leaving him "low and bitter."

That summer, when O'Hara published *A Rage to Live* and Brendan Gill dissected it in *The New Yorker*, the ensuing flap drove O'Hara in a snit away from the magazine (temporarily, at least). In October, sparks from the chimney of Ross's Stamford home ignited the roof, causing a fire that resulted in extensive damage and a year's worth of insurance hassles and repairs. Only weeks later, there was more tragedy in Washington: artist Helen Hokinson died in a fiery air-plane crash at National Airport. The horrible irony—"an outrage by fate," Ross said—was that the shy Hokinson, who lived alone with her mother, virtually never traveled; her only reason for going to Washington was to appear at a Community Chest drive. Ross had an almost paternal feeling for her, having watched Hokinson grow up with his magazine, and arranging to have her body returned to New York and her mother was almost too much to bear.

Soon after, Ross went up to Boston for a one-week checkup at the Lahey Clinic. He returned to New York in time for the premiere of a new play, *Metropole*, which had been written by his onetime per-sonal secretary William Walden. Not that Ross intended to see it, since the play was about a New York magazine called *Metropole*, a thinly disguised *New Yorker*, and its manic and temperamental editor, Frederick Hill, a thinly disguised Ross. It was directed by the editor's old poker pal and sometime contributor George S. Kaufman, who realized that *Metropole* was weak but put his time (and some of his own money, it was later learned) into it so that first-time playwright Walden, who still worked at *The New Yorker*, might at least walk away from the experience with a Broadway credit. Ross was not so charitable; having disclaimed the whole project—"People write about me, but I spend my time working"—he refused to see the play, and was not sorry when it closed after only two performances. Later that week Ross and Ariane attended the opening of *Gentlemen Prefer Blondes*, sitting immediately in front of Kaufman, whom Ross needled about *Metropole* all evening.

But after this dreadful spate, in December matters took a decidedly sunnier turn. For two months *The New Yorker* had quietly but stubbornly protested the recent decision to permit broadcasting of music and commercials over the public-address system in Grand Central Terminal. To Ross, who commuted through Grand Central and thus spent a fair amount of time there, this commercial white noise was both a personal affront and a civic outrage, and almost every week *The New Yorker* commented on it somehow. One cartoon featured the terminal's statue of Commodore Vanderbilt with a sign hanging around his neck that read, "Drink Shaefer Beer." Thanks largely to the magazine's provocation, so many people complained about the broadcasts to the New York State Public Service Commission that it decided to hold a public hearing on the matter. Amazingly, Ross, as de facto leader of the opposition, agreed to testify.

Ross hadn't taken the hearing seriously, and said later that had he known how big a fuss would be made over his appearance, he would at least have prepared some remarks rather than ad lib. (In truth, he probably wouldn't have appeared at all.) As it happened, it didn't matter. True to the spirit of his magazine, the editor made his point, and provided comic relief to boot.

Before Ross testified, an attorney for the New York Central Railroad, which along with the New Haven line was sponsoring the broadcasts, described him as the editor of "an adult comic book." Hence when Ross took the stand and was asked to state his occupation, he replied sarcastically, "I am editor of an adult comic book edited by a person who commutes to and from the Grand Central Terminal—to put it heavy-handedly." He then proceeded to object to the broadcasts on almost every conceivable ground: that the screech was an invasion of privacy, and unintelligible in any case; that it made it difficult to read; even that it amounted to a "semi-swindle" of the advertisers because anyone who was reading, eating, or conducting other business in Grand Central could not be paying attention to their commercials. Mostly, however, it was simply a damned nuisance. "I just want to be let alone in the terminal," Ross said. "I can do all right with magazines and newspapers without them singing lullabies to me, or funeral dirges."

When the New York Central's attorney, Kenneth F. Stone, got his turn, he pursued Ross's contention that the broadcasts were largely unintelligible.

"You said, Mr. Ross, that these broadcasts give you a ringing in the ears. . . . Your hearing is one hundred percent?"

"It is perfect," Ross replied. "It is too good. Under the circumstances, I am thinking of having an eardrum punctured."

When Stone accused *The New Yorker* of inviting readers to complain, Ross denied it. Stone then read aloud from a Talk item that had said, "We strongly advise any person who finds himself exposed to amplified sounds in hospitals, terminals or common carriers to protest to the management or call the police."

Ross didn't hesitate. "I beg your pardon," he said. "I guess I must have read that in the Grand Central Station."

Dozens of others spoke against the broadcasts, but it was the rare public performance of the editor of *The New Yorker* that put the story on New York's front pages. A few weeks later the railroads threw in the towel, and the broadcasts stopped as abruptly as they had begun. Ross joked that the victory was premature: *The New Yorker* had intended to propose an entire elaborate sideshow for Grand Central, complete with a crystal gazer to predict when trains were arriving, and a dime-a-dance area. Nonetheless he accepted congratulations for repulsing this latest assault on civility. He even found his handsome mug plastered in *Life*—and as himself this time, not Stalin.

The star witness offers animated testimony during the public hearing on broadcasts in the Grand Central terminal, 1949. *(Archive Photos)*

Thus, 1950 dawned more promisingly for Ross, which was only fitting, for with *The New Yorker* turning twenty-five it would be a year of celebration and introspection. A wire-service reporter interviewing him for the anniversary caught him in a typically reflective moment. He asked the editor whether the years had changed his conception of *The New Yorker.* "Damned if I know," said Ross, and went on to take issue with the persisting characterizations of him as impatient and surly, and the only high-powered executive in town whose clothes looked as if he still rode to work in boxcars. "I'm a well-dressed man, dammit."

In March 1950 Ross presided over the Ritz anniversary fete, and in June the high-school dropout accepted an honorary doctorate from Dartmouth. He was a bit anxious about the occasion. The fuss and the ceremony were sure to make him uncomfortable, and he had always resisted similar gestures before. But as he confided to friends, in light of all the *"New Worker"* business, this time he thought public validation from a respected conservative institution like Dartmouth might prove useful. Still, he was gratified, and in fact found himself in respectable company: fellow honorees included Federal Judge Harold Medina, *Atlantic* editor Edward Weeks, architect Wallace Harrison, and statesman George Kennan, who gave the commencement address. As he sat on the dais awaiting his degree, Ross scanned the program, then leaned over to Weeks and said, "It says here you'll get an LL.D., but I'm to be a Doctor of Humane Letters. Means I'm a kinder man."

That fall saw the premiere of yet another *"New Yorker"* play, this time Gibbs's aforementioned *Season in the Sun,* about which Ross was in somewhat better humor. *Season* opened on September 28 at the Cort Theatre and was so well received that it ran for a year. Ross had long ago steeled himself to the idea of being stage fodder; aside from *Metropole,* Thurber had been trying to write a play about him for years. He never finished it, though others have pointed out that Ross inhabits many of Thurber's protagonists, from Walter Mitty to King Clode to his besieged cartoon husbands. Ross felt if he was going to have his character appropriated, it might as well be Gibbs doing the appropriating, for at least the result would be funny. Sure enough, *Season,* while not a great play, made audiences laugh. Staged by Gibbs's friend Burgess Meredith, it featured a thin plot that was resolved when the Ross character saves the hero's self-esteem, marriage, and career by making him see what a great life he has after all. Today it would be sitcom fodder, with the Ross character being the crazy uncle who in the end talks sense.

Ross wouldn't see the play until he was sure no one in the audience would recognize him—no mean trick, Gibbs said. Eventually he saw it twice, once with Franklin P. Adams—who was drunk, Gibbs recalled—and once with Patty. On the latter occasion he took her backstage to meet his fictional counterpart, who was played, ironically, by Broadway veteran Anthony Ross. Introducing her to the actor, Ross said, "This is what Mr. Gibbs thinks I'm like."

On the whole, the year had been a fine season in the sun for Ross, who for the first time in his life really let himself accept acclamation for his extraordinary accomplishment with *The New Yorker.* That

November, as she was about to leave New York after her "reorienta-tion" debacle, Flanner stopped by Ross's office and peered in. The editor looked up at her and smiled, all traces of the previous unpleas-antness now vanished. He asked if there was something she wanted to talk over. No, Flanner said, she just wanted to take a long look at him.

BACK TO THE ALGONQUIN

IN JUNE OF 1950, HAROLD ROSS, DAUGHTER PATTY, ONE OF HER GIRL-friends, her second cousin James Gilson (recruited to drive), Mrs. Gutzon Borglum, and her flatulent dog all piled into Ross's three-year-old Cadillac and headed west. Ariane did not come along. In South Dakota they dropped off Mrs. Borglum and the dog at the Mount Rushmore monument that her late husband had blasted out of the Black Hills, then proceeded south to Colorado. Patty had been with her father on vacations before, but this time in their three weeks together Ross was determined to really show her the West—*his* West. Its pull on him was so strong that had work not made it impractical, he would have lived there part of the year. Nothing could prevent him from retiring there, however, and he told friends that this was what he hoped to do, fully intending to grow as old and feisty as his endearing uncle John, who had died at ninety-one.

In Aspen they met up with more relatives and friends, among them Frank Capra, then headed up to a remote lake near Dillon,

Colorado, where they fished, camped, and rode the mountain trails. (Ross was not exactly an elegant horseman. Each time before climbing into the saddle, his daughter recalled, her father liked to talk with his steed and try to persuade it to be civil.)

Ross, tired and with sixty in view, was coming to terms with himself, and this trip with Patty was only a part of it. Increasingly he found himself in an uncharacteristically contemplative frame of mind. The next spring, writing Rebecca West—sympathetic and an ocean away, she would receive some of Ross's most revealing letters in his last years—he mentioned how Eleanor Roosevelt suddenly looked very old to him. He was reminded of a pleasant afternoon that the two of them had spent a few years earlier, talking for hours as they rode along in Mrs. Roosevelt's sedan. At one point the former First Lady suddenly allowed as how "old people ought to be bumped off

Ross and Dave Chasen vacationing in Aspen.
(Courtesy of Patricia Ross Honcoop)

when their usefulness is done." Since she was still a vigorous woman at the time, her remark took Ross by surprise. "I mildly raised the question of who would make the decision as to when the moment had come," he recalled, "and she didn't have a ready answer for that."

At around this same time Ross startled Patty one day by declaring, apropos of nothing in particular, "I think I believe in God—in fact, I do." Coming from a man whose only recent brush with organized religion had been to accompany his daughter to a church service at her school, where he promptly fell asleep and began to snore, this was a remarkable declaration. When Patty pressed him to elaborate, her father declined, saying only that he had come around to this point of view over the course of a long life, as people often will.

That autumn Ross left Ariane—on September 29, a Friday, the day after the Broadway premiere of *Season in the Sun* (a coincidence, apparently). She would continue to reside at 375 Park, while he took a suite at the Berkshire Hotel at Fifty-second and Madison. It is not known if any single incident prompted his departure. As usual, he said little if anything about it to colleagues, and Patty, having just begun a new school year at the Country School in Woodstock, Vermont, and therefore seldom around, was privy to no special blowup. What *is* clear is that Ross wanted an end to the marriage. He had brought up the subject of divorce many times, but Ariane had always resisted (though when Ross insisted she get an attorney a few months before he left, she did). Additionally, for the entire preceding year Ross had had Truax's associate at *The New Yorker,* Milton Greenstein, combing through his convoluted finances, tracking where every dollar in the household was going. In moving out, Ross doubtless had the prenuptial agreement in mind too, with its stipulation that if he and Ariane were living apart for any reason, her trust-fund stipend would be restricted.

Ariane would later tell Ross's friends that she was miserable during this separation, and that she continued to hope for a reconciliation. She also said that while it was plain Ross eventually intended to divorce her, he had promised to keep her whole financially. He urged her to remain in the expensive apartment and carefully log her expenses, Ariane said; he would see to it that she was reimbursed. During this period, it appeared that their contacts, if not exactly pleasant, were at least cordial.

By the beginning of 1951, then, about the only happy development in Ross's life was witnessing the fruition of an unlikely publishing project he had dreamed up years earlier. Back during the war, when he came under Sara Jordan's care for his ulcers, he was amazed to discover that he could again enjoy many foods he thought he had given up forever—lobster, for instance—as long as they were properly prepared. This had given him a brainstorm, and he prevailed on Dr. Jordan, who was also an accomplished cook, and *The New Yorker*'s food editor, Sheila Hibben, to collaborate on a cookbook devoted to people with ulcers, colitis, chronic indigestion, and other gastro-intestinal ailments. It had taken a long time to pull the project together, but now the book, *Good Food for Bad Stomachs,* was being readied for publication. *Good Food* contained five hundred appealing but dietarily correct recipes and a conspicuous introduction by H. W. Ross. It was the first piece he had written for public consumption, at least with his name attached, since World War I, which assured that *Good Food* got widespread attention when it came out in the summer of 1951.

"I write as a duodenum-scarred veteran of many years of guerrilla service in the Hydrochloric War," Ross confessed, launching into a piece that was half personal essay, half explanation. He was not pleased with the introduction—as always, he was feeling rushed when he wrote it—and in places it does seem more forced than Ross the editor would have been comfortable with in a *New Yorker* piece. Still, he put his point across with self-effacing humor and obvious empathy for his fellow sufferers. The introduction explained how he arrived at the idea for the book after having dinner one evening with Dr. Jordan. When it came time for dessert, Ross, as usual, intended to play it safe with the fruit compote.

To my astonishment Dr. Jordan suggested that I have *meringue glacée*. Now *meringue glacée* has a French name, which is bad, and it is an ornamental concoction, which is bad. It sounds and looks evil. The meringue constituents of it look, in fact, almost as evil as a couple of macaroons, which are made of almonds, which are oily, and hence evil. Dr. Jordan revealed that meringue is made from the whites of eggs and sugar—no harm in a barrel of it. I had *meringue glacée* that evening, and although I regard it as essentially a sissy proposition and nothing for a full-grown man to lose his head over, I have it now and then when I'm in the ulcer victim's nearest approach to a devil-may-care mood.

———

IN THE DISMAL WINTER OF 1951, AS FLU RACED AROUND *THE NEW Yorker*, the staff was ravaged. To keep up, everyone, including Ross, was putting in long hours altogether too reminiscent of the war. "We're getting old. The boys have taken to falling down in the hallways and hemorrhaging," the editor wrote Rebecca West in late February. "We're thinking of keeping an ambulance parked at the curb, to be in readiness." As for himself, he said he had been lucky: only a two-day cold, hardly worth complaining about. He offered an upbeat report on Rebecca's son, Anthony, who had just begun reviewing books for the magazine, but made no mention of Ariane, as he customarily had before their separation.

A month later, Ross must have thought that the flu bug had finally caught up with him, because he suddenly felt terrible—a severe pain in the chest and a bad cough. In early April, his condition having gotten worse rather than better, he took the train up to Boston for a full examination at the Lahey Clinic. There his doctors concluded he was suffering from pleurisy, a painful inflammation of the lung wall that he had first contracted as a boy. Meanwhile, Ariane decided to come up to see him when she heard he would be at the clinic longer than he had originally said. Doctors told them both that a few months of bed rest in Stamford should put him right. Ariane pleaded with her husband to allow her to oversee his care, but he refused; instead, Ross hired a male nurse and returned to Connecticut without her. She would never see him alive again.

All that May and June, under the watchful eye of his nurse, Ross spent twenty-two hours a day on his back, and the running of *The New Yorker* was left to his lieutenants. While his colleagues were anxious about his health, their larger concern was whether he would obey his doctors' orders and thereby give himself a chance to get well. His track record, after all, was abysmal. He was the kind of patient who was known to sneak out of hospital rooms and crib cigarettes from the janitors—usually getting caught—and he stubbornly refused to stop working. "Expecting Ross to take it easy and not work or worry is like expecting a poodle puppy to stay out of mischief," a concerned Thurber wrote to Katharine White that May. Yet this time he surprised them all; he actually welcomed the relaxation. He said the grounds at Stamford, in full spring bloom, were "so beautiful and restful that [the] effect is almost hypnotic." As the bed rest and antibiotics relieved his discomfort and raised his spirits, he took on a little work—reading, letter-writing, some dictation. Mostly, though, he used the forced hiatus to do something he otherwise never found time to do: actually think about *The New Yorker.* By now the circulation of his magazine was pushing 325,000, and two thirds of this was from outside greater New York. *The New Yorker* had come to represent less a city than a certain cosmopolitan state of mind, and as such there seemed no limit to its possibilities.

Ross did indulge in one bit of non–*New Yorker* business. In mid-June he quietly changed his will, bequeathing his entire estate to Patty. Nothing beyond her entitlement under the prenuptial agreement would be left to Ariane.

Toward the end of June, feeling better but not wholly recovered, Ross went back to Lahey for a follow-up examination. Dr. Jordan and her colleagues began to suspect that they were dealing with more than pleurisy. They ordered more tests, and this time their diagnosis was chilling: bronchogenic carcinoma, or cancer of the windpipe.

One can only imagine Ross's trepidation, for he betrayed little emotion himself. At the time, cancer was even more terrifying than it is today, so feared and misunderstood that it was virtually taboo as a subject of polite conversation. Given his pernicious symptoms and the fact that his father had died of cancer, he almost certainly must have considered the disease at least a possibility; yet all of a sudden here was the terrible confirmation, like a firm slap. Still, it appears he chose to entrust the news to only two other people, Truax and Julius Baer, his personal attorney of twenty years and the man who would be handling any future legal skirmishes with Ariane. Probably for strategic reasons, he didn't want his wife to know, and he elected not to tell Patty or any other *New Yorker* colleagues because he didn't want them to worry about him.

Surgery was weighed, but Ross's doctors instead opted for a still relatively novel procedure, radiation therapy. A lifelong skeptic of technology, Ross had his doubts but agreed. His general anxiety may be inferred from the fact that while he had never been one to keep a personal journal, he now bought a daybook with the apparent intention of documenting his upcoming ordeal. Throughout his sickness, he would be intrigued by its parallels with the more public affliction of George VI of England, whose own cancerous condition was never revealed to him. In coming months, when people inquired about his condition, Ross liked to grumble that he was suffering from "the same damn thing as the king of England." On July 10, 1951, the day before he was to begin the radiation series, the first note he scribbled in his journal said, "Didn't have chance of surgery, as king of England did, whether his C or not. He and I same period, same experiences, except me to bed, he to walk moors of Scotland."

On July 12, the day of the second treatment, Ross's pessimism was more apparent. According to notes in the journal, he rhetorically asked Dr. Jordan, "This is the only straw I have to clutch at, isn't it?" While she took pains to assure him of the efficacy of radiation, he noted to himself that this was "a great deal to swallow."

Ross's bleak mood was also evident in the fact that at around this time he apparently instructed Baer to tell Ariane not to contact him anymore. According to his wife's letters recounting this period, Baer also said that his client was cutting off her charge accounts and would send her no more money except what a court might order. Soon thereafter, Ariane wrote, she was mortified one day at Gristede's when the embarrassed manager pulled her aside and showed her a letter from her husband closing her account. Ross's own records tend to support Ariane's recollections, indicating that at around this time, while he continued to write checks to cover their joint taxes, Ariane's phone bill, her rent, and some other basic expenses, he stopped sending her any money directly. She was stunned by this turn of events, and would later attribute his actions to his fear, and to the sway of Baer, whom she came to despise.

Over the next eight weeks, Ross underwent thirty-nine radiation treatments, the last one on September 7. Beyond the first few cryptic entries, he noted only a sporadic countdown of his treatments in his journal. That it was a dreadful experience, however, there can be no doubt. For one thing, he was desperately alone. At the Boston Ritz-Carlton, where he stayed when he wasn't at the hospital, his only companion was his male nurse, who ate three meals a day with him, kept poking him with thermometers, and slept in the next room. Outwardly he tried to remain upbeat and nonchalant, telling friends that the pleurisy had abscessed and that a special treatment for it was keeping him in Boston. Apparently no one found this overly suspicious, which is not surprising given Ross's medical history. With his ubiquitous "suitcase full of pills," as one relative put it, he was widely regarded as a minor-league hypochondriac in any case. Besides, he had been through so many hospitalizations for his ulcers that this stay, while longer than usual, didn't seem much out of the ordinary, and certainly didn't suggest anything grave.

Finally, in mid-September, after having been away from *The New Yorker* for five months, Ross returned to work. With all the rest, he actually felt better than he had in some time. Still, a poignant update he sent to White reveals that he had the past very much on his mind:

I am back at work on a break-in, gradual basis. I am reading Newsbreaks and Talk anecdotes and doing a couple of other small things. The Newsbreaks are a pleasure. Through the years, they have remained my only weekly pleasure.

Pls. note Packard's note below this and decide how you want the item headed. Packard's first two sentences seem to contradict each other flatly, but you'll get what he means.

I marked English quote marks into this, instead of stetting the French quotes. For one thing, I doubt if Nast has French quotes on hand for the Linotype machines, and if he hasn't he would have to borrow them from a French printer here. I was in the reverse of this situation once and know how tough it can be. I undertook to get out a black market publication in Paris during the First World War and made a deal with an American Army printing company (soldiers) to do the composition. They were glad to earn some money and worked cheap. The only thing was, there weren't any English quote marks in the French print shop in which they were stationed and did their work, and my copy was full of quotes. I had to provide English quotes. I had drag with the foreman of the composing room of the *Daily Mail,* which printed the *Stars and Stripes,* upon which I was then employed, and he would lend me, for the daylight hours, the quote marks from the *Daily Mail*'s machines. I had to have them back by dusk for use at the *Daily Mail* plant, or the *Daily Mail* wouldn't get to press. The French print shop was in the outskirts of Paris, twelve miles about from the *Daily Mail* plant, and for ten days I had to make two trips a day between the two places, delivering and recovering twelve small slivers of metal. I have never been the same since.

I don't know why I pause to tell you this. I should be writing my life, which is full of such oddities.

In the meantime, for its convenience, and possibly for its pleasant memories, Ross had taken up residence in a suite of rooms that *The New Yorker* maintained across Forty-fourth Street at the Algonquin.

———

THE LAST TIME ARIANE SPOKE WITH ROSS WAS JUST AFTER LABOR DAY. All summer she had been in a state of near panic. She knew he was sick, but she couldn't seem to obtain any details. Her phone calls were always intercepted, and her letters only provoked more warnings from Baer. According to Ariane, her lawyer pleaded with her to start legal proceedings against her husband, but she refused to consider the idea until she knew he was well again. She still believed that his illness, whatever it was, had bent his judgment, and that once he recovered he would soften. Then one day she called Stamford and was surprised when Ross actually answered the phone himself. She asked after his health, and Ross assured her he was "completely cured." She then asked why he had treated her in such a hurtful fashion. When he offered no reply, she told him that she didn't want to go to court but that he seemed to be pushing her in that direction, with all the ugly publicity it implied. Ross said he would talk to Baer about her financial situation and get back to her; instead, it was Baer who called her, scolded her, and reiterated the hard line.

Ariane did not try to contact Ross again. She checked with *The New Yorker* to make sure he was in fact back at work, and then on October 4 filed suit against him in New York State Supreme Court (despite the name, a lower court). She accused Ross and the other trustee of her fund, an attorney named Jules Englander, of fiduciary irresponsibility. The suit alleged that eighty-six thousand dollars from the account that Ariane said she was entitled to had gone to Ross instead, in violation of the trust. She said that Ross and Englander had "negligently and wastefully managed" the trust and had failed to apprise her of their actions. She also sought reimbursement of seventeen thousand dollars in expenses incurred in the year since he had left.

Ross's attorneys responded by trying to get him removed as a defendant, but a judge refused. Then on November 21, Ariane filed a separation suit in the same court, charging Ross with abandonment and seeking five hundred dollars a week in alimony and five thousand dollars for legal fees. November 21 was the Wednesday before Thanksgiving, a date Ariane said was chosen in the hope that the suit would be overlooked in the preholiday hubbub. It wasn't; reporters sniffed it out and short news items appeared in the Thanksgiving newspapers. The suit could not have surprised Ross, for it certainly appeared that his strategy *had* been to provoke Ariane into making the first legal move, but in any event it got his attention. That Friday, his own records show, he released to Ariane twenty-one thousand dollars from the trust fund.

As if cancer and the public evisceration of his marriage weren't distraction enough, Ross was now visited by a third plague nearly as vexing in his view as the first two: official, book-length celebrity. In late October, Doubleday brought out a biography of Ross written by Dale Kramer, a journeyman who had been one of the coauthors of the much-maligned *Harper's* profile of Ross back in 1943. The editor had been aware of the book project for more than a year, and thoroughly deplored it. He had declined to cooperate with Kramer, as had most of his *New Yorker* colleagues. There were even rumors that he approached the publishers in an effort to derail the book. Afterward E. B. White said that Ross hadn't tried to stop it, only to protest what he considered its underhanded evolution—from a broad book about humor to one focusing on *The New Yorker* to one focusing on him. When *Ross and The New Yorker* finally appeared, all its subject had to say about it was that "I never read a book that starts with the word 'it' "—which Kramer's did. *The New Yorker's* institutional opinion was nearly as perfunctory; in a one-paragraph review, it dismissed the book as superficial, inadequate in distributing credit, and short on energy. Charitably the review added, "It is only fair to note that this is probably because Mr. Kramer got very little cooperation from members of the staff, who had no confidence in such an undertaking by an outsider. Whatever the cause, it is a conspicuously uninformed work, though a kindly intentioned one, and it makes most of the editors and contributors around the place seem as cute as performing fox terriers." The word was that Ross wrote the capsule review himself, which is just possible. There was also an in-house contest for the most succinct critique. White won, calling *Ross and The New Yorker* simply "an industrial romance."

When not at work, Ross was keeping to himself in Room 806 at the Algonquin. He had his mail and most of his meals sent up, though he ate little. He was still smoking, and he seemed preoccupied and irritable. One of his few pleasures was the company of James and

Helen Thurber, who by coincidence were also staying at the hotel at this time. This afforded Ross and Thurber the welcome opportunity to get reacquainted. Though he was synonymous with *The New Yorker* to most people, Thurber had actually left the regular staff in 1936 to become a freelancer, and he divided most of his time between rural northwestern Connecticut and Bermuda. Given this distance, not to mention his soaring celebrity and failing eyesight, he had less and less direct contact with Ross. Even then, if their communications weren't about Thurber's stories or drawings, they tended to revolve around his complaints that Talk wasn't funny anymore, or that the magazine wasn't paying him enough. Still, he had always been one of those few people who could walk into Ross's office and instantly have him laughing, and now they could rekindle this happier side of their relationship. But for the first time Thurber could appreciate how really sick his friend was. Ross did not tell him it was cancer, but Thurber said he guessed as much, partly because of the editor's wrecked appetite. One evening when the Thurbers called on him in his room, they found him eating "dinner"—sardines, right out of the can. "It's practically the only thing I can taste," he told them.

Ross's complexion was wan, but otherwise the radiation hadn't materially affected his appearance. With his sparkling eyes and crow-black hair, he still looked years younger than his age. He was telling friends that he was fine, feeling better, perhaps eighty-five percent back to normal. Yet he continued to cough up discharge, sometimes for an hour or two at a stretch, which kept him awake nights and as a result fatigued his days. By Thanksgiving weekend, even as he was being sued for abandonment, he was heading back to Boston for more tests.

First Ross stopped off in Saratoga to see Frank Sullivan and Wesley Gilson, then briefly dropped in on Patty in Vermont. It had been several months since she had seen him, and she remained unaware of his true condition. Her father tried to be blasé about the trip to Lahey, though from his demeanor she sensed that this time he was unusually nervous. He told her not to worry, he would be back in New York in a few weeks.

In the meantime, Walter Winchell had latched on to the separation suit, and in the December 3 *Mirror* he put his inimitable spin on
it: "Mrs. Harold Ross, wife of *The New Yorker* editor, according to
intimates, was forced to go to court to get money to eat; Ross cut off
all charge accounts, including groceries, to starve her into accepting
his terms. Every time the case was to be heard—Our Hero ran up to
Lahey's Clinic (Boston) and reported ill—so he didn't have to read
the N.Y. papers about it. . . . Mrs. Ross was Ariane Allen, former
actress, and one of the most beautiful women in the land. . . . It was
Mrs. Ross the literary gagmen meant—when they quipped: 'One day
she'll be the most popular widow in town.' "

Ariane later said she was scandalized by this item, and Ross's colleagues considered it a hateful all-time low, even for Winchell. But
its target was too preoccupied to care. He was at Lahey by then, getting more bad news. It appeared that while the radiation may have
mitigated the bronchial lesion, as intended, the doctors now feared
that the cancer had metastasized to the lungs. To know for certain
what they were dealing with, they would have to cut him open.
Exploratory surgery was scheduled for Thursday, December 6, at
New England Baptist Hospital.

Back at *The New Yorker* a few key people were informed that some
sort of surgical procedure was occurring that day, but its true nature
was kept from them, and they were led to believe it was just another
in Ross's continuum of treatments. Many friends were concerned
enough to call, from Dave Chasen to Jane Grant, but Ross assured
them that there was no cause for alarm. Patty didn't even know there
would be an operation. Ross phoned her at about this time, she
recalled, but said nothing about it. Their conversation was testy; he
seemed upset, even angry, as if she had done something wrong, but
she didn't know what it could be.

Truax, of course, knew why Ross was irritable, and he came up
from New York to be by his friend's side in the days leading up to the
operation. They talked, played cribbage, and generally tried to keep
their minds off the surgery. Truax would later report that the editor
faced his uncertain predicament bravely and with dignity, but at the

same time compiled a list of sundry matters he wanted Truax to take care of should things go badly.

At about one o'clock on Thursday, not long before the surgery was to begin, Ross telephoned George S. Kaufman, who he had learned was in Boston trying out a new show. "I'm up here to end this thing, and it may end me, too," Ross told him. "But that's better than going on this way. God bless you. I'm half under the anesthetic now."

As Ross had intimated to his friend, when the surgeons opened his chest they were confronted by their worst fear—a large mass of cancer in his right lung. The lung was removed, but Ross's heart failed. It was about half past six in the evening, and he never came out of the anesthetic.

———

WILLIAM SHAWN AND HIS WIFE WERE TO HAVE DINNER THAT NIGHT with the Philip Hamburgers. Mrs. Shawn was already at their apartment, and they were waiting for her husband, assuming that as usual something had come up to keep him at the office. Then the phone rang; it was Shawn, asking to speak with Cecille. She went into another room to take the call, and a few minutes later came out, ashen. "Take me home," she asked Hamburger. "Mr. Ross has just died."

Within hours, several of Ross's aides, including Louis Forster and Leo Hofeller, were at Shawn's apartment to begin disseminating the shocking bulletin—to the Whites, to Thurber, to Gibbs, to Lobrano, to dozens of others. On hearing the news, some gathered in bars for impromptu wakes; others came to the Shawns' apartment, not knowing what else to do with themselves. Among these was S. N. Behrman, who had the distinction of being the last writer to be personally edited by Ross. At the Algonquin one evening just before the editor left for Boston, he was helping Behrman rework a Profile of a man named Gabriel Pascal, a colorful Hungarian adventurer who somehow had persuaded George Bernard Shaw to give him the exclusive rights to film his plays. Behrman had been noodling with the piece for years, but the temperamental Pascal was still balking at seeing it published. Ross, however, was enchanted by the very idea of the story—a highlife-lowlife if ever there was one—and that night he and Behrman were having another go at it.

At the apartment, Behrman was so overcome that he couldn't stop wailing, and finally Shawn asked Forster to see him safely home. As it happened, the playwright was one of Forster's idols, and so the younger man remembered their taxi ride that night as almost surreal. Through his tears, Behrman told Forster many stories of Ross, none more poignant than about the first time he ever had a piece accepted by *The New Yorker,* a brief Profile of George Gershwin. The writer was just about to sail for Europe when Ross turned up at the pier. He had come to send Behrman off, and to deliver his check in person.

By nine or ten that night, the news of Ross's death was on the radio. Coming home with his wife from a party, William Maxwell was driving on the Taconic State Parkway when he heard the report and nearly veered off the road in shock. Ariane Ross had not been listening to the radio. At 11:45, she was awakened by a phone call from a *Daily News* reporter, who asked if he could have a comment from her about the death of her husband. Caught off guard and still smarting from the Winchell item, Ariane assumed the call was a spiteful practical joke and started to hang up. "Please believe me, Mrs. Ross," the reporter pleaded, "it was just on the eleven-thirty news—Mr. Ross died at six-thirty this afternoon."

Ariane immediately phoned the hospital for confirmation. The head nurse was startled: "Oh, Mrs. Ross, haven't you been told?" According to Ariane, the hospital had expected Truax to notify her, but in the confusion they hadn't spoken.

Up at the Woodstock Country School, the housemother at Patty's dormitory did hear the report. Patty was still up, busy with chores. The older woman didn't want to alarm the girl, and didn't think it was her place to tell her in any case. Still, she didn't want Patty to hear by accident, so she rounded up all the girls and told them that because they had exams the next day they were to turn off their radios. The next morning one of Patty's friends, one who had not been in the dorm the night before, telephoned to tell Patty how sorry she was. "About what?" Patty asked. Her friend was puzzled. "Why, about your father," she said. "Haven't you heard?"

At *The New Yorker* the usual quiet of the hallways was different that morning, enveloped in profound sorrow. Staffers milled about aimlessly, huddling in twos and threes to talk about Ross and, inevitably, to begin imagining life without him. Now, at a time when magazines are mass-produced like shoes or soft drinks by multi-national conglomerates, it seems hard to fathom, but Ross was so much the persona of *The New Yorker* that people inside and outside the magazine seriously wondered whether it could go on without him. The sadness, like the speculation, wasn't confined to the office. Ross's passing was front-page news around the country, and radios blared it around the world. In Paris, Janet Flanner's devastation—she told Katharine White her sense of loss was "enormous, like losing the top and walls of your house"—was ameliorated only by having so many people, even strangers, cable their regards or send her flowers of condolence. A Roman Catholic brother told Mrs. White that when he heard the news he knelt before an altar and prayed for Ross.

In his corner office on nineteen, Andy White had been at work since early that morning. More or less by common consent, the task fell to him to compose Ross's obituary for the magazine. A more difficult thing had never been asked of him. He was still in shock himself—privately, he wrote a friend that "K and I . . . have the sensation of being disembowelled"—and there was little time. Ornery to the very end, Ross died just as the next issue of *The New Yorker* was about to close. As White admitted in what would turn out to be a warm and vivid tribute, "This is known, in these offices that Ross was so fond of, as a jam. Ross always knew when we were in a jam, and usually got on the phone to offer advice and comfort and support. When our phone rang just now, and in that split second before the mind focusses, we thought, 'Good! Here it comes!' But this old connection is broken beyond fixing. The phone has lost its power to explode at the right moment and in the right way."

Gibbs and many others had drifted in and out of White's office that morning, offering help and solace, if not seeking the same.

Suddenly, from down the corridor near the bank of elevators, rose a primal wailing: "Andy! *An*-dy!" The voice, getting closer, seemed familiar and strange all at once. "Andy!" A staffer who was there remembers the sound as almost spectral, one of pain, yet tinged with fear. She ran into the hall, and there found Thurber moving slowly down the corridor, hands to the wall, groping his way from doorway to doorway. "Andy!" he called again. By now almost fully blind, Thurber seldom ventured to the magazine, and on such occasions he was never without his wife or someone else to lead him. But now, robbed of his friend and mentor, Thurber had never seemed so vulnerable, so utterly alone. Instinctively he was drawn back to *The New Yorker*, as was White, as were Gibbs and Shawn and all the rest, like children drawn to their father's grave.

THE ANGEL
OF REPOSE

AT FOUR O'CLOCK ON A DANK DECEMBER AFTERNOON, THE MONDAY after Ross died, a service in his memory was held at the Frank Campbell Funeral Home, at Eighty-first and Madison. Through the years Frank Campbell's has more or less made its reputation as a mortuary to the stars (dispatching New York celebrities from Valentino—whose opera hat fell to Ross's custody, it will be recalled—to John Lennon), but once upon a time, before it moved uptown, it advertised in the city's subways, "A dignified funeral for $95." In his last-minute instructions to Truax, Ross specified the simple service, as well as his wish to be cremated. So on that somber afternoon, four hundred mourners, including his sixteen-year-old daughter, his wives, and most of his staff, crowded into the funeral home's main chapel. Hundreds more spilled into the hall and down the steps outside.

For all their grief, the service itself was strangely impersonal. In a room wall to wall with celebrated writers, actors and politicians, almost anyone present could have, with no more notice than a tap on the shoulder, stood and delivered an eloquent tribute to Ross. The assembled looked to Thurber, to White, to Frank Sullivan, to Ralph Ingersoll, to Helen Hayes or Bennett Cerf, but in their sorrow, and in the confusion of the hastily arranged affair, none of these eminences rose. Instead everyone listened in astonishment as the chaplain of Yale University, a man who had never met Ross, offered a well-intentioned but mawkish eulogy. "He hated all tyrannies," the cleric intoned, "not least the insidious tyranny of things, and he made us feel that the world of matter or even of atoms is somehow too narrow for any one of us." After a bit more of this blather, he concluded, "On next February 26, Eustace Tilley will have a slight tear on his monocle and a tremor in his hand."

No one who heard it ever quite forgot the peculiar incongruity of the eulogist and the eulogized. It is not clear exactly who retained the Yale man, though Julius Baer later confided to Thurber that he had stepped in to help Ariane with the arrangements because he feared she would make the service private. In any case, White's view was that the real tribute that day was the almost unnerving silence that preceded the service. Only Ross, White said, could have gotten "such a bunch of normally noisy and disorderly people [to sit] so quietly, so respectfully, and so completely forlorn."

Six weeks later—a very anxious six weeks for the *New Yorker* staff—Raoul Fleischmann appointed William Shawn editor of the magazine. There is no real question that this was what Ross intended to happen. Some *New Yorker* people, especially some of the fiction contributors, thought Gus Lobrano might get the job, and he was badly disappointed when he didn't. But to almost everyone who worked at Forty-third Street and saw how the magazine functioned, Ross's second-in-command was the obvious and rightful heir. Privately Shawn thought so too, though Ross never told him as much. Indeed, despite the "succession" clause in his employment contract, it appears that Ross never formally committed himself to a replacement, however conspicuously and carefully he may have groomed Shawn. Nonetheless, those close to both Ross and Truax believed that the editor expressed his intention to his longtime confidant, meaning it to be passed along to Fleischmann.

Still, the magazine's staff, and Shawn himself, were unsettled by the delay. There is some reason to believe that Fleischmann took so long because he did not fully share the conventional wisdom about Shawn. In the collected papers of Ralph Ingersoll there is a cryptic note from this period summarizing a briefing Ingersoll or an associate received from the publisher about *The New Yorker*'s finances. According to the note, Fleischmann was moving slowly on appointing a new editor because of a "violence of personal feelings." There is no elaboration, but it should be remembered that as tragic as Ross's death was, it handed Fleischmann the one thing he had wanted for almost two decades: the chance to appoint his own editor. He knew Shawn very well—well enough to respect his vast talents, but also well enough to have seen his odd side, and to size him up as a strong-willed disciple who almost certainly would brook no more business-side input than Ross had. These factors may help explain why Fleischmann thought long and hard before capitulating to Ross, even in death, for the last time.

Meanwhile, Ariane was challenging Ross's will in a Connecticut probate court. At the time of his death his net worth appears to have been in the neighborhood of half a million dollars. This comprised cash, securities, insurance benefits, Ariane's prenuptial trust, a trust for Patty, and the Stamford home and grounds, whose value in 1952 was estimated at $131,000. The legal wrangling would take six full years, featuring a veritable conga line of attorneys—for Ariane, for Patty, for the Ross estate, for Ariane's trust, even for Chasen, who saw a parking lot that Ross still owned figure in the dispute. In the end, after all the claims and counterclaims, a compromise was struck that awarded roughly a third of the money to Ariane, a third to Patty—and a third, naturally, to the lawyers.

After the probate was finally resolved, Ariane remarried. The groom was Sir John Leigh, scion of a wealthy English family that Ariane had gotten to know in the Forties. Sir John doted on her and surrounded her with servants. Brief news accounts of the nuptials noted that his father, a longtime member of Parliament, had amassed a fortune in cotton. Raoul Fleischmann clipped one such story and sent it to Katharine White with the note, "Thus again is virtue rewarded!"

————

IN 1954, WRITING TO WHITE, THURBER SAID, "I READ A GARBLE NOT long ago for 'angle of repose' which came out angel of repose, a mighty good angel to have around these days. Angle of repose is usually applied to an angle that will let go at the slightest disturbance, causing landslides, filling up Culebra Cut, and making it necessary to start work all over again. The angel of repose, on the other hand, keeps the balance secure with nothing more than a cheerful word or an unauthorized proof sent through the mails. . . . As you and I know, H. W. Ross had dealings with the angel of repose and was good at the cheerful word of praise. . . ."

This formal portrait of Ross, taken in 1944 by Fabian Bachrach, still hangs in the *New Yorker* offices.
(© Bachrach)

Four decades after his passing, *The New Yorker*'s angel of repose remains an abiding if ethereal presence at the institution he loved so well. A flattering formal portrait taken by Fabian Bachrach during the war hangs prominently on the main editorial floor of the magazine's new offices, across Forty-third Street from its old ones. Ross's even gaze meets yours no matter from what angle you approach, and he wears a wry smile, as if he knows something about you that he shouldn't, which usually was the case. Passing him, veteran members of the staff half expect to be stopped by that flat, slightly nasal western voice that remains as vivid for them today as it was fifty years ago. Ross would say how much he enjoyed that last piece, and just perhaps suggest that it was too long. The voice is reassuring, mischievous, secure.

In 1956, in accord with his final wish, the remains of Harold Wallace Ross were dispersed not over the canyons of Manhattan or the tranquil woods of Stamford, but over the emerald mountains of Aspen, Colorado.

APPENDICES

I. THE NEW YORKER PROSPECTUS

Written and distributed by Harold Ross in the fall of 1924

ANNOUNCING A NEW WEEKLY MAGAZINE
THE NEW YORKER

The New Yorker will be a reflection in word and picture of metropolitan life. It will be human. Its general tenor will be one of gaiety, wit and satire, but it will be more than a jester. It will not be what is commonly called radical or highbrow. It will be what is commonly called sophisticated, in that it will assume a reasonable degree of enlightenment on the part of its readers. It will hate bunk.

As compared to the newspaper, *The New Yorker* will be interpretive rather than stenographic. It will print facts that it will have to go behind the scenes to get, but it will not deal in scandal for the sake of scandal nor sensation for the sake of sensation. Its integrity will be above suspicion. It hopes to be so entertaining and informative as to be a necessity for the person who knows his way about or wants to.

The New Yorker will devote several pages a week to a covering of contemporary events and people of interest. This will be done by writers capable of appreciating the elements of a situation and, in setting them down, of indicating their importance and significance. *The New Yorker* will present the truth and the whole truth without fear and without favor, but will not be iconoclastic.

Amusements and the arts will be thoroughly covered by departments which will present, in addition to criticism, the personality, the anecdote, the color and chat of the various subdivisions of this sphere. *The New Yorker's* conscientious guide will list each week all current amusement offerings worthwhile—theaters, motion pictures, musical events, art exhibitions, sport and miscellaneous entertainment—providing an ever-ready answer to the prevalent query, "What shall we do this evening?" Through *The New Yorker's* Mr. Van Bibber III, readers will be kept apprised of what is going on in the public and semi-public smart gathering places—the clubs, hotels, cafes, supper clubs, cabarets and other resorts.

Judgment will be passed upon new books of consequence, and *The New Yorker* will carry a list of the season's books which it considers worth reading.

There will be a page of editorial paragraphs, commenting on the week's events in a manner not too serious.

There will be a personal mention column—a jotting down in the small-town newspaper style of the comings, goings and doings in the village of New York. This will contain some josh and some news value.

The New Yorker will carry each week several pages of prose and verse, short and long, humorous, satirical and miscellaneous.

The New Yorker expects to be distinguished for its illustrations, which will include caricatures, sketches, cartoons and humorous and satirical drawings in keeping with its purpose.

The New Yorker will be the magazine which is not edited for the old lady in Dubuque. It will not be concerned in what she is thinking about. This is not meant in disrespect, but *The New Yorker* is a magazine avowedly published for a metropolitan audience and thereby will escape an influence which hampers most national publications. It expects a considerable national circulation, but this will come from persons who have a metropolitan interest.

The New Yorker will appear early in February

The price will be: Five dollars a year

Fifteen cents a copy

Address: 25 West 45th Street, New York City

Advisory Editors

Ralph Barton	George S. Kaufman
Heywood Broun	Alice Duer Miller
Marc Connelly	Dorothy Parker
Edna Ferber	Laurence Stallings
Rea Irvin	Alexander Woollcott

H. W. Ross, Editor

II. THEORY AND PRACTICE OF EDITING
NEW YORKER ARTICLES

This was written by Wolcott Gibbs around 1937, apparently at the request of Katharine White, who was then trying out a succession of new fiction editors. Though it has passed into New Yorker *legend, "Theory and Practice" was a working document and fairly reflected the magazine's guidelines and tastes of the time.*

———

THE AVERAGE CONTRIBUTOR TO THIS MAGAZINE IS SEMI-LITERATE; that is, he is ornate to no purpose, full of senseless and elegant variations, and can be relied on to use three sentences where a word would do. It is impossible to lay down any exact and complete formula for bringing order out of this underbrush, but there are a few general rules.

1. Writers always use too damn many adverbs. On one page, recently, I found eleven modifying the verb "said": "He said morosely, violently, eloquently," and so on. Editorial theory should probably be that a writer who can't make his context indicate the way his character is talking ought to be in another line of work. Anyway, it is impossible for a character to go through all these emotional states one after the other. Lon Chaney might be able to do it, but he is dead.

2. Word "said" is O.K. Efforts to avoid repetition by inserting "grunted," "snorted," etc., are waste motion, and offend the pure in heart.

3. Our writers are full of clichés, just as old barns are full of bats. There is obviously no rule about this, except that anything that you suspect of being a cliché undoubtedly is one, and had better be removed.

4. Funny names belong to the past, or to whatever is left of *Judge* magazine. Any character called Mrs. Middlebottom or Joe Zilch should be summarily changed to something else. This goes for animals, towns, the names of imaginary books and many other things.

5. Our employer, Mr. Ross, has a prejudice against having too many sentences begin with "and" or "but." He claims that they are conjunctions and should not be used purely for literary effect. Or at least only very judiciously.

6. See our Mr. Weekes on the use of such words as "little," "vague," "confused," "faintly," "all mixed up," etc., etc. The point is that the average *New Yorker* writer, unfortunately influenced by Mr. Thurber, has come to believe that the ideal *New Yorker* piece is about a vague, little man helplessly confused by a menacing and complicated civilization. Whenever this note is not the whole point of the piece (and it far too often is) it should be regarded with suspicion.

7. The repetition of exposition in quotes went out with the Stanley Steamer:

Marion gave me a pain in the neck.

"You give me a pain in the neck, Marion," I said.

This turns up more often than you'd expect.

8. Another of Mr. Ross's theories is that a reader picking up a magazine called *The New Yorker* automatically supposes that any story in it takes place in New York. If it doesn't, if it's about Columbus, Ohio, the lead should say so. "When George Adams was sixteen, he began to worry about the girls he saw every day on the streets of Columbus" or something of the kind. More graceful preferably.

9. Also, since our contributions are signed at the end, the author's sex should be established at once if there is any reasonable doubt. It is distressing to read a piece all the way through under the impression that the "I" in it is a man and then find a woman's signature at the end. Also, of course, the other way round.

10. To quote Mr. Ross again, "Nobody gives a damn about a writer or his problems except another writer." Pieces about authors, reporters, poets, etc., are to be discouraged in principle. Whenever possible the protagonist should be arbitrarily transplanted to another line of business. When the reference is incidental and unnecessary, it should come out.

11. This magazine is on the whole liberal about expletives. The only test I know of is whether or not they are really essential to the author's effect. "Son of a bitch," "bastard" and many others can be used whenever it is the editor's judgment that that is the only possible remark under the circumstances. When they are gratuitous, when the writer is just trying to sound tough to no especial purpose, they come out.

12. In the transcription of dialect, don't let the boys and girls misspell words just for a fake Bowery effect. There is no point, for instance, in "trubble," or "sed."

13. Mr. Weekes said the other night, in a moment of desperation, that he didn't believe he could stand any more triple adjectives. "A tall, florid and overbearing man called Jaeckel." Sometimes they're necessary, but when every noun has three adjectives connected with it, Mr. Weekes suffers and quite rightly.

14. I suffer myself very seriously from writers who divide quotes for some kind of ladies club rhythm. "I am going," he said, "downtown" is a horror, and unless a quote is pretty long I think it ought to stay on one side of the verb. Anyway, it ought to be divided logically, where there would be pause or something in the sentence.

15. Mr. Weekes has got a long list of banned words beginning with "gadget." Ask him. It's not actually a ban, there being circumstances when they're necessary, but good words to avoid.

16. I would be delighted to go over the list of writers, explaining the peculiarities of each as they have appeared to me in more than ten years of exasperation on both sides.

17. Editing on manuscript should be done with a black pencil, decisively.

18. I almost forgot indirection, which probably maddens Mr. Ross more than anything else in the world. He objects, that is, to important objects, or places or people, being dragged into things in a secretive and

underhanded manner. If, for instance, a Profile has never told where a man lives, Ross protests against a sentence saying "His Vermont house is full of valuable paintings." Should say "He had a house in Vermont and it is full, etc." Rather weird point, but it will come up from time to time.

19. Drunkenness and adultery present problems. As far as I can tell, writers must not be allowed to imply that they admire either of these things, or have enjoyed them personally, although they are legitimate enough when pointing a moral or adorning a sufficiently grim story. They are nothing to be light-hearted about. "*The New Yorker* cannot endorse adultery." Harold Ross vs. Sally Benson. Don't bother about this one. In the end it is a matter between Mr. Ross and his God. Homosexuality, on the other hand, is definitely out as humor, and dubious, in any case.

20. The more "as a matter of facts," "howevers," "for instances," etc., you can cut out, the nearer you are to the Kingdom of Heaven.

21. It has always seemed irritating to me when a story is written in the first person, but the narrator hasn't got the same name as the author. For instance, a story beginning: "George," my father said to me one morning; and signed at the end Horace McIntyre always baffles me. However, as far as I know this point has never been ruled upon officially, and should just be queried.

22. Editors are really the people who should put initial letters and white spaces in copy to indicate breaks in thought or action. Because of overwork or inertia or something, this has been done largely by the proof room, which has a tendency to put them in for purposes of makeup rather than sense. It should revert to the editors.

23. For some reason our writers (especially Mr. Leonard Q. Ross) have a tendency to distrust even moderately long quotes and break them up arbitrarily and on the whole idiotically with editorial interpolations. "Mr. Kaplan felt that he and the cosmos were coterminus" or some such will frequently appear in the middle of a conversation for no other reason than that the author is afraid the reader's mind is wandering. Sometimes this is necessary, most often it isn't.

24. Writers also have an affection for the tricky or vaguely cosmic last line. "Suddenly Mr. Holtzman felt tired" has appeared on far too many

pieces in the last ten years. It is always a good idea to consider whether the last sentence of a piece is legitimate and necessary, or whether it is just an author showing off.

25. On the whole, we are hostile to puns.

26. How many of these changes can be made in copy depends, of course, to a large extent on the writer being edited. By going over the list, I can give a general idea of how much nonsense each artist will stand for.

27. Among other things, *The New Yorker* is often accused of a patronizing attitude. Our authors are especially fond of referring to all foreigners as "little" and writing about them, as Mr. Maxwell says, as if they were mantel ornaments. It is very important to keep the amused and Godlike tone out of pieces.

28. It has been one of Mr. Ross's long struggles to raise the tone of our contributors' surroundings, at least on paper. References to the gay Bohemian life in Greenwich Village and other low surroundings should be cut whenever possible. Nor should writers be permitted to boast about having their telephones cut off, or not being able to pay their bills, or getting their meals at the delicatessen, or any of the things which strike many writers as quaint and lovable.

29. Some of our writers are inclined to be a little arrogant about their knowledge of the French language. Probably best to put them back into English if there is a common English equivalent.

30. So far as possible make the pieces grammatical, but if you don't the copy room will, which is a comfort. Fowler's *English Usage* is our reference book. But don't be precious about it.

31. Try to preserve an author's style if he is an author and has a style. Try to make dialogue sound like talk, not writing.

III. ROSS QUERY SHEETS

Harold Ross's "query" sheets were long, enumerated lists of comments, suggestions, and quibbles that occurred to him as he read over pieces planned for publication. His query sheets on a Profile or Reporter at Large piece would be much longer, but these two examples from 1948 typify the nature and tone of his editorial comments.

———

Ross's notes on Frank Sullivan's "The Cliché Expert Testifies on the Tabloids" on June 30, 1948:

1. As Hollywood stars are listed here, and as at 1b it says all people in the foregoing list are automatically included, I guess film stars shouldn't be mentioned again at 1b.

2. Haven't the tabs got a better adjective than *pretty* here. That seems ordinary. On other hand, maybe it is their word, though.

3. In view of fact that *Graphic* has been out of business many years, suggest tense change marked, to take better cognizance of this fact. It's twenty years, I think; whole generation has grown up—and gone to war.

4. Well, does the Kinsey report mention rape? Surprises me that it does, for I've heard of no rape quotes from that book (which I haven't read).

5. Here a peculiar point, and one that has long obsessed me. The tabs use *exotic* wrong, nearly always. *Exotic* means, merely, foreign. But they apply it to domestic ladies freely. A man who worked long on the *Daily News* told me that *News* rewrite men were given a list of ten or twelve words to use in stories and headlines that sounded snappy, would be thought by the readers to mean something more than they really mean, or something other than they really mean, something snappy—and wouldn't be libelous. At head of list was *exotic*. Tab readers are supposed to think that *exotic* means *erotic*. It would be libel to call a lady *erotic*. I guess. Sullivan might possibly go into this with a question or two—on this unusual use of the word, but doesn't matter. I'm just writing this to be interesting.

6. Seems to me might be cut as marked, as obvious, or something.

7. This brusqueness doesn't seem in character for Mr. A, somehow. Hasn't he always been more diplomatic, more graceful than this?

————

Ross's notes on Peter De Vries's "If the Shoe Hurts" on October 26, 1948:

I think this is a pretty darned good piece now, cleaned up a little bit, and maybe an 8. Am querying Mr. Lobrano on that.

1. One place it needs a little fix, it seems to me, is here, for this is inconsistent with the facts as revealed in the conversation narrated in the piece. Meeley didn't merely send them away with an adage. He talked almost entirely in adages, one platitude after another. Just to talk to him was to listen to these adages. He didn't merely conclude with one of them, as stated here.

2. And this garbled adage is out of character. All the adages he quotes in the conversation with Disbrow are straight, not garbled, not mixed up.

3. No real antecedent for the *it* here. Think De Vries should put in something equivalent to *these activities* in his own non-flat way. Also, if she was merely dubious, as stated at 3a, it is hardly right to say she took a view of the activities. Dubiousness is not taking a view, I think; it's lack of a view. Think what's wrong is the *dubious*, think the wife was definitely exasperated, or some such. And, the "I don't know" sentence, which seems to me to convey practically no meaning at all.

4. He didn't refuse to discuss it. He discussed it quite openly and fully after he got started, which was almost immediately. Would kill this, and also suggest that, since I (as an example) have no idea whatever what is meant by *that radio serial* the next sentence might well go, too.

5. Have no idea at all what throwing everything up for grabs means; never have heard the expression. Advocate clearer wording, unless this *is* a recognized expression.

6. He wouldn't find out she was asleep *after* he switched off the lights, presumably; couldn't see her. Suggest might just cut as marked, and duck the matter. These people seem to have bedside lights. The woman has a bedside table, it has been said.

7. This piece is slugged *Anytime,* but summer is the vacation season. Suggest that if this piece not used in summer (which unlikely) this be made to read *"He's gone away for three weeks."*

8. Think would be effective to italicize as marked. Later De Vries does this, in similar circumstances. And the *that* is definitely cluttery.

9. Don't think *fast as I could* quite right, for the robbery was during the day and he hasn't got around to the Ford agency until around 9 p.m., which has been established as the closing time. Would word as marked, or some such. The man would naturally be tied up with the police quite a while, etc.

10. Later, 10a, next galley, Meeley puts the coat back on, so it should be taken off here.

11. *Gun* includes rifles, shotguns, and everything else. Would make it a hand-weapon here, first mention. Revolvers are out of date and the word *pistol* hardly used any more. Think *automatic* the word, but maybe there's another.

12. Seems to me might be more effective if first part last clause went in Roman, as marked. Would emphasize the last part more.

13. Repeat here with *drove on* at start of paragraph.

14. I think a dash here. It's a self interruption.

15. *Slander* is better, seems to me. The man would *say* it, not print it. Libel is printed slander.

16. Why not simplify the thing and keep it rational by having the letters from Mrs. T? It isn't logical that this fellow would keep around incriminating letters that *he* had written whereas there is a little logic of his not destroying her letters.

17. I wonder if something more definite than *do this* would be better here: *do away with you,* or some such. There has been no specific statement either by Disbrow or the author that D. is going to kill Meeley, and maybe should be clinched here. It is true that they are headed for a ravine for, presumably a killing, but only D. and the reader know that. Meeley doesn't. Or, might be made more specific earlier. Might have D. tell M. that they're headed for the ravine, back at (a) Galley 2. M. would then draw the conclusion that he is going to be bumped off, and this would make the *do this* here stand up.

18. I don't get any picture from *sitting stretched out.*

19. Would duck this *said* here somehow; two others in the quotes.

ACKNOWLEDGMENTS

AND A NOTE ON THE SOURCES

Not long ago I came across a line in a book review about another of journalism's flamboyant figures that I regard as equally appropriate to my subject. The review—in *The New Yorker*, as it happens—was of a biography of British press mogul Lord Beaverbrook, and the line read, "This isn't the first life of Beaverbrook, but it's the first real one."

Dale Kramer's 1951 book, mentioned in Chapter 15, is the only other straightforward biography of Ross, and it suffered from all the shortcomings *The New Yorker* attributed to it at the time. James Thurber's memoir *The Years with Ross*, written serially for *The Atlantic Monthly* and published as a book in 1959, is a delight. As biography, however, it is dubious, and a reader could be forgiven for carrying away the impression that Ross helped Thurber make *The New Yorker* rather than the other way around. A 1968 memoir by Jane Grant, *Ross, The New Yorker and Me*, demonstrates similar myopia, without benefit of Thurber's style or wit. And Brendan Gill's otherwise charming 1975 memoir, *Here at The New Yorker*, gives Ross a real bruising.

All these books helped cement in the public mind a picture of Ross as a perpetually confused hayseed, a naïf, an uncouth provincial who succeeded almost in spite of himself. I hope this book, in some small way, counteracts that impression. Still, each of these previous works provided much insight and information about Ross and *The New Yorker*, and where appropriate I have tried to credit them in the text and notes.

Of the hundreds of people who touched this project, I must single out several for special thanks. Patricia Ross Honcoop, who appears to have inherited all her father's best qualities, was unfailingly gracious and helpful. *New Yorker* writer and editor Roger Angell responded warmly to a stranger's query and set me off in the right direction. *New Yorker* mainstays Philip Hamburger (you too, Anna), William Maxwell, and Louis Forster more or less adopted me, spending countless hours keeping me on the trail and making sure I didn't go hungry. I thank them not only for their generosity of spirit but for their valued friendship. From their unique vantage point, *New Yorker* editor Tina Brown and her predecessor, Robert Gottlieb, were kind enough to share their thoughts on Ross and the magazine, and made available its formidable resources to me.

The man they succeeded, William Shawn, spoke with me briefly on two occasions before he died. He was characteristically reticent about cooperating per se, but he told me my hypothesis was sound, and he was personally encouraging. What he said of Ross—"He was an extraordinary man, and in every way remarkable"—was just as true of Ross's heir. Cecille Shawn was giving of her time and memories, and told me much about her husband that I suspect he would never have volunteered himself.

I want to thank the late Peter Fleischmann, son of the cofounder, Raoul Fleischmann, and his successor as publisher of *The New Yorker.* Though in ill health, he made time to see me and was most gracious, as was his wife, Jeanne.

The happiest aspect of this project was the opportunity to meet and get to know so many longtime *New Yorker* staffers, who proved as charming as I imagined them to be and who, to a person, were free with their time and reminiscences. My only regret, and it is a heavy one, is that some of these lovely people did not live to see the book finished. So I thank New Yorkers present and past Joseph Mitchell, Gardner Botsford, Edith Oliver, Emily Hahn, Edward Newhouse, Leo Rosten, John Bainbridge, Mary D. Kierstead, Brendan Gill, E. J. Kahn, Jr., Dorothy Lobrano Guth, Eleanor Gould Packard (generally, and specifically for saving hundreds of Ross's invaluable query sheets), Albert Hubbell, Harriet and William Walden, Berton Roueché, Wolcott (Tony) Gibbs, Jr., Thomas Whiteside, Peter De Vries, Marcia

Davenport, Clifton Fadiman, William Mangold, Burton Bernstein, William Steig, Mischa Richter, Arthur Getz, Andy Logan, Dana Fradon, Lee Lorenz, Arne Gittleman, Peter Matthiessen, Bruce Bliven, Jr., William Buxton, Charles McGrath, Bill Fitzgerald, Sheila McGrath, Edward Chase, Helen Stark, Richard McCallister, Barbara Nicholls, Charles Baskerville, and Edith Iglauer Daly. Also such friends and family as Joel White (son of E. B. and Katharine), Peggy Day (widow of Clarence), Maude Chasen, Rebecca Bernstien, Mrs. Milton Greenstein, Daphne Hellman Shih, Jane Ellen Austin, James and Sara Gilson, Robert Gilson, Charles Porteous, Helen Hayes, Elizabeth Paepcke, Phyllis Cerf Wagner, and Al Hirschfeld. My thanks also to Augustus and Margery Hallum, Ronnie Clint, Barbara Ragland, Tony Cichielo, and fellow writers Linda H. Davis, Roy Hoopes, Steve Oney, Joan Walker Iams, Bruce Berger, and Tom Philp.

Of the many special collections consulted for this book, six proved indispensable. For their help and encouragement, and for permission to use their material, I would like to thank Mary B. Bowling and Francine Tyler at the New York Public Library's Rare Books and Manuscripts Division, which houses *The New Yorker*'s vast archival material, as well as H. L. Mencken's correspondence with Ross; Patricia Willis at Yale University's Beinecke Library, which houses the *New Yorker*–related papers of James Thurber, as well as Rebecca West's correspondence with Ross; Victoria Jones at the University of Oregon Library, which has Jane Grant's papers; Leo M. Dolenski at Bryn Mawr College's Canaday Library, which has Katharine S. White's papers; James Tyler and Lucy Burgess at Cornell University's Kroch Library, which has the papers of E. B. White and Frank Sullivan; and Charles Niles at Boston University's Mugar Library, which maintains the Ralph Ingersoll collection.

I likewise acknowledge the Library of Congress, and the libraries of the University of Wyoming; Ohio State University; Hamilton College; Syracuse University; Penn State University; Harvard University; the University of Florida; Columbia University (Oral History collection); New York University; and Princeton University, as well as the New-York Historical Society; the Aspen Historical Society; the Utah State Historical Society; the State Historical Society of Wisconsin; the

California State Library; the Museum of Television and Radio; and the New York State Public Service Commission. Thanks as well to Leigh Baker Michels at *The Advocate* in Stamford, Connecticut, and to Linda Amster and David Jones at *The New York Times,* for making old newspaper clippings available to me.

I would like to thank my agent, Peter Matson, of Sterling Lord Literistic Inc., and my editor at Random House, who eschews acknowledgment but who is widely known for his skill, for his compassion, and for smoking too much. Had I not stumbled into their sure hands, I cannot imagine this project ever happening. Virginia Avery copy-edited the manuscript with intelligence and sensitivity, and Lawrence LaRose helped me with countless details.

Most of all I would like to thank my wife, Debra, who aided me in untold ways with this book, and all my family and friends for their good humor, support and encouragement through what must have seemed a mystifying, even masochistic, process.

The aforementioned are largely responsible for whatever good things are contained herein. The errors, sadly, are mine alone.

Thomas Kunkel
August 15, 1994

NOTES

Abbreviations used in these notes:

HR	Harold Ross
JG	Jane Grant
KSW	Katharine S. White
EBW	E. B. White
JT	James Thurber
WG	Wolcott Gibbs
FS	Frank Sullivan
RI	Ralph Ingersoll
RW	Rebecca West
TNY	*The New Yorker*

PROLOGUE: A HELL OF AN HOUR

3 "In no other country": *The New York Times,* 1/7/50.

4 "Prominent persons": Edmund Wilson to Morton D. Zabel, 4/28/50.

4 "I danced with Harriet": John Cheever to Polly and Milton C. Winternitz, 3/6 [1950].

6 Mencken and Ross at the Ritz: From "Mr. Mencken, Mr. Ross," an unpublished monograph by St. Clair McKelway, 1958.

6 "like a movie film": HR to RW, 3/21/50.

8 "In retrospect I am": EBW to FS, Sunday [December 1951].

8 "The main satisfaction": Charles W. Morton to HR, 3/30/50.

8 "I guess we've made": HR to Morton, 4/3/50.

10 "All that remains": Richard H. Rovere, *Arrivals and Departures,* p. 62.

1: THE PETTED DARLING

14 George Ross–Ida Martin courtship: Jane Grant, *Ross, The New Yorker and Me,* p. 34.

18 "everybody in town": *Current Biography,* 1943, p. 634.

19 "I may well have been the boy": HR to Margaret Case Harriman, quoted in Harriman, *The Vicious Circle,* p. 175.

19 "didn't have much of a chance": HR to RW, 10/4/49.

20 The story about Ross overhearing his mother and friends talking about the madam is from an interview with Elizabeth Paepcke, 8/12/92.

21 "violent anti-Mormon": HR to Frank I. Sefrit, 1/16/50.

21 "At some time an impressive": RW in *The Sunday Times* (London), 7/19/59.

22 "a buxom old Roman emperor": This and the entire Pillar of Fire segment is from a letter from Joseph Mitchell to JT, 8/24/57.

25 Ross's fascination with Frederick Palmer: Dale Kramer, *Ross and The New Yorker,* p. 6.

25 Ross playing hooky in the library: Grant, p. 39.

26 "Jesus Christ, kid": Shelley Armitage, *John Held, Jr.: Illustrator of the Jazz Age,* p. 4.

26 "I had accumulated": *Salt Lake Tribune,* 10/6/35.

27 "But the real trouble": Ibid.

2: TRAMP

30 "The re-navigating": This and next passage, *Marysville Appeal,* 3/28/11.

30 "If I stayed anywhere": Charles W. Morton, *It Has Its Charms . . . ,* p. 208.

31 "clear, hard, classical": RW in *The Sunday Times* (London), 7/19/59.

32 "Someone had to edit": *Salt Lake Tribune,* 10/6/35.

33 "He's got them convinced": Dale Kramer, p. 11.

33 "It so happens": HR query notes on "Dry Run," 6/25/51.

33 "at the lowest pay": HR to Marjorie Roehl and Barbara Selby, 4/9/46.

34 New Orleans saloon story: Henry F. Pringle, "Ross of *The New Yorker,*" '48 *Magazine,* March 1948.

35 "the police did what they always do": This and subsequent passages, *San Francisco Call and Post,* 6/23/15.

40 "Usually these pieces": Steve Oney to author, 9/21/93.

40 "Being of that vast": *Atlanta Journal,* 7/20/13.

42 "a picture-chaser": Cyrus LeRoy Baldridge to JT, [1958].

42 Ross and Polynesian chieftain: Grant, p. 46.

43 "The generation that acclaimed": Richard Hofstadter, *Social Darwinism in American Thought,* p. 34.

44 Ross and W. Averell Harriman: Dale Kramer, p. 9.

3: *THE STARS AND STRIPES*

45 "He and a pal had put one": Cyrus LeRoy Baldridge to JT, 4/16/58.

46 "There were 2,600 troops": *San Francisco Examiner,* 9/14/17.

46 "By way of comfort": HR to parents, [1917].

47 "I was too flip": Grant, p. 49.

47 "For two hours we hunted": HR quoted in *Squads Write!* by John T. Winterich, pp. 289–90.

48 "Without saying goodbye": Dale Kramer, p. 20.

49 "military son of a bitch": HR to Samuel Hopkins Adams, Tuesday [1945].

49 "May the private have": Dale Kramer, p. 25.

49 "a human owl": Samuel Hopkins Adams, *A. Woollcott: His Life and His World,* p. 87.

50 "Where'd you work?": Grant, p. 51.

52 "trundling along in some exposed:" S. H. Adams, p. 87.

52 "Far off to the left": Winterich, p. 14.

53 "more than almost any individual": Alfred E. Cornebise: *The Stars and Stripes,* p. 124.

55 "In the cover of the bushes": HR, quoted in Winterich, pp. 147–48.

56 "The Americans were in it strong": HR to parents, 7/23/18.

56 "At home I was always": *New York Tribune,* 5/11/19.

56 "I was standing with my mouth open": *San Francisco Examiner,* 4/29/18.

57 Ross and the Ferris wheel: Marc Connelly, *Voices Offstage,* p. 95.

57 "a rough guy": Interview with Charles Baskerville, 3/24/93.

58 "As I peered at him": Grant, p. 21.

59 "I haven't laughed much": HR to JG, 2/27/19.

60 "brave and fearful": Grant, pp. 32–33.

60 "In a restaurant today": HR to parents, 11/14/18.

63 "Oh, I can't do that": The money-order story is from "The Life and Death of the Lafayette Publishing Co." by John T. Winterich, *The New Colophon,* September 1949.

64 "although my stock of shirts": HR to parents, 5/6/19.

65 "the most widely known private": *San Francisco Examiner,* 6/3/19.

65 "stood out so conspicuously": Cornebise, p. 16.

65 "Clad in these": Alexander Woollcott to Brigadier General Theodore Roosevelt, Jr., 1/14/43.

4: NEW YORKER

68 "an early manifestation": HR to Samuel Hopkins Adams, Tuesday [1945].

71 "Goddammit, it's a pretty howdy-do": Grant, p. 123.

71 "Don't you ever buy": Ibid., p. 114.

71 "his words hit the listener": Dale Kramer, p. 35.

71 "Each embraces New York": E. B. White, *Here Is New York,* p. 18.

72 "It was an intimate world": Interview with Charles Baskerville, 2/18/93.

75 "Aw, why don't you two": Harriman, p. 139.

76 This account of the formation of the Round Table is largely based on that of James R. Gaines in *Wit's End: Days and Nights of the Algonquin Round Table.* His version is generally corroborated by Grant, and by Ross in various correspondence.

76 "I was there a lot": HR to H. L. Mencken, July 27 [year unknown].

78 "Fine, this is the first time": Howard Teichmann, *George S. Kaufman: An Intimate Portrait,* p. 202.

78 "At least I'm not a *writing* soldier": Harriman, *Vicious Circle*, p. 241.

78 "a sort of adopted child": Frank Case, *Tales of a Wayward Inn*, p. 65.

79 "Frank, I feel so wonderful": Harriman, *Vicious Circle*, p. 51.

79 "teamsterlike snorts": Ben Hecht, *Charlie: The Improbable Life and Times of Charles MacArthur*, p. 97.

79 "He looked at you as if": Interview with Rebecca Bernstien, 1/14/92.

79 "daring felicity of phrase": Julie Goldsmith Gilbert, *Ferber: A Biography*, p. 110.

80 "To J. Toohey's": Franklin P. Adams, *The Diary of Our Own Samuel Pepys*, Vol. 1, p. 248.

80 "So to our inn": Ibid., pp. 455–56.

82 "a cowhand who'd lost": Harpo Marx, *Harpo Speaks!*, p. 173.

84 "I remember having dinner": Russel Crouse to JT, 9/4/57.

84 "It was Anna Case": HR to S. H. Adams, Tuesday [1945].

85 "We adored Aleck": Harriman, *Vicious Circle*, p. 115.

85 "I agree with you": S. H. Adams, p. 131.

89 "He carried a dummy": James Thurber, *The Years with Ross*, p. 304.

89 "How the hell could a man": Hecht, p. 141.

91 "That's the trouble": Corey Ford, *The Time of Laughter*, pp. 112–13.

92 "Some of them didn't really": Harriman, *Vicious Circle*, p. 180.

5: LABOR PAINS

100 "there were no proven": HR to EBW, 5/7/35.

100 "I threw it across the room": Grant, p. 136.

100 "Well, Margaret, I think": Harriman, *Vicious Circle*, p. 187.

100 "too frothy for my liking": Franklin P. Adams, *Pepys*, Vol. 1, p. 505.

101 "I, and my associates": *Time*, 2/25/25.

102 "My personal opinion": *Current Biography*, 1943; pp. 635–36.

103 "I am free to admit": *The New York Times*, 5/12/69.

103 "This feat slightly stunned": Philip Wylie to JT, 1/3/58.

105 "I told Ross to cut it": Interview with Marc Connelly in the Oral History Project, Columbia University.

107 "He never told me anything": Interview with Charles Baskerville, 2/18/93.

107 "Ross had a map in his mind": Interview with William Maxwell, 8/9/91.

109 "rubbed most of the uncouthness": Wylie to JT, 1/3/58.

109 "Irvin always knew what": RI to JT, 8/1/59.

111 "Have to dig up a thousand": Dale Kramer, p. 70.

111 "This added debt gave me": Grant, p. 188.

112 "I can't blame Raoul": *The New York Times*, 5/12/69.

113 "It is a pretty good chance": Raoul Fleischmann, "The History of the Fleischmanns," a private, unpublished family history, August 1963.

114 " 'Tilley' was the name": Ford, p. 120.

116 "doing everything—as we all": Linda H. Davis, *Onward and Upward: A Biography of Katharine S. White*, p. 60.

117 "You look a little vague": This and subsequent passages are from Ralph Ingersoll's 1925 diary.

119 "The cast of characters": E. B. White, *Letters of E. B. White*, p. 73.

120 "Ingersoll, the typewriter": HR to RI, undated.

121 "Memorandum from McGuinness": James Kevin McGuinness to HR, undated.

123 "was actually removed": RI note in his collected papers, undated.

123 "Done right, the whole": RI to JT, 8/1/59.

126 "Certainly you know your Paris": JG to Janet Flanner, [June 1925].

126 "I don't want to know": Grant, p. 7.

127 "to his eyes and ears": Ibid., p. 9.

127 "Write exactly what you see": Dale Kramer, p. 88.

128 "The only thing I had a talent": Ibid., p. 89.

128 "We do not particularly like": *TNY*, 11/28/25.

129 "Modern girls . . . marry whom": *TNY*, 12/12/25.

130 "Say it's terrible": Dale Kramer, p. 84.

131 "Peck & Peck has broken": *TNY*, 10/24/25.

6: CAVALRY

133 "I note what you say": H. L. Mencken to William Saroyan, 1/25/36.

133 "A magazine written and edited": *TNY*, 9/12/25.

136 "the chargings-about of a man": From "The Thursdays with Ross," an unpublished monograph by Robert M. Coates, 1958.

136 "I think the organization": Fillmore Hyde to RI, [1926].

136 "her own mother [had] objected": *TNY*, 5/15/26.

137 "I must get back to the office": Thurber, *Years with Ross*, p. 33.

138 "He was very earthy": Interview with Emily Hahn, 11/5/91.

139 "One day nearer the grave": Thurber, *Years with Ross*, p. 141.

140 "I'll have no mythological": *TNY*, 5/2/42.

140 "Ingersoll was a great man": Ibid.

140 "I had no right to take": Ralph Ingersoll, *Point of Departure*, p. 221.

141 "If I have been cranky": HR to RI, [1926].

141 "a nervous breakdown the likes": Ingersoll, p. 166.

142 "When he was unsure": *TNY*, 8/1/77.

144 "the highest personal comment": Scott Elledge, *E. B. White: A Biography*, p. 118.

146 "Station WJAX": *TNY*, 4/23/27.

147 "as impractical as Jesus Christ": Janet Flanner to KSW, 12/13 [1951].

147 "We noted that the *Spirit*": *TNY*, 5/28/27.

148 "the lilting name of": Thurber, *Years with Ross*, p. 34.

149 "All right then, if you're": Ibid., p. 17.

149 "The precision and clarity": Burton Bernstein, *Thurber*, p. 164.

150 "though the magazine was his": Brendan Gill, *Here at The New Yorker*, p. 288.

151 "Are you the son of a bitch": Bernstein, p. 181.

152 "I don't give a damn": Wolcott Gibbs, *Season in the Sun (and Other Pleasures)*, pp. vii, viii.

154 "The little shindig": *TNY*, 5/7/27.

155 "We thought nothing of working": Marcia Davenport, *Too Strong for Fantasy*, p. 119.

155 "When one of my writers": Carl R. Dolmetsch, *The Smart Set*, p. xxiii.

156 "Constant Reader, in the early": HR to EBW, Monday [Fall 1938?].

156 "Aw, Harold, I've been": Roy Hoopes, *Cain*, p. 205.

156 Benchley in Philadelphia: Nathaniel Benchley, *Robert Benchley*, p. 11.

157 "Fleischmann frankly said": JG to Ida Ross, [4/17/28].

157 "That was one of the factors": Ibid.

158 "I'm married to this magazine": Thurber, *Years with Ross*, p. 16.

158 "Jane just doesn't understand": Marc Connelly to JG, Monday [1928].

159 "Of course, I don't know": Ibid.

160 "We have different tastes": HR to JG, [1928].

161 "I have worried ever since": Ida Ross to JG, 4/12/28.

161 "I did not know how you would feel": JG to Ida Ross, 4/17/28.

162 "My heart ached": Ida Ross to JG, 5/16/28.

162 "The reason I left": HR to S. H. Adams, Thursday [1945].

162 "Never for a moment": Grant, p. 246.

162 "a small harem": Hecht, p. 139.

163 "there would be no *New Yorker*": HR to Lloyd Paul Stryker, 10/29/45.

164 "Go back and put your clothes on": Davis, p. 75.

165 "Occasionally she would": Marcia Davenport to author, 4/14/92.

165 "I never should have left": KSW to Geoffrey Hellman, 10/3/75.

167 "an escape from the life": Katharine Angell to EBW, [1929].

167 "On account of the fact": EBW to HR, Friday [July? 1929].

168 "I have an anguished letter": EBW to Katharine Angell, Tuesday [August 1929].

7: A CESSPOOL OF LOYALTIES

170 Ross-Schindler practical jokes: Allen Churchill, "Ross of *The New Yorker*," *American Mercury*, August 1948.

170 "Harold, of all the men": Interview with Clifton Fadiman, 11/12/93.

172 "Just as he gained": Nunnally Johnson to JT, 9/3/57.

173 "He had a wonderful kind": Interview with Edith Oliver, 1/16/92.

173 "He was bluff and funny": Interview with Daphne Hellman Shih, 9/30/91.

173 "Oh, I don't know": Grant, p. 260.

174 "Ross sent me a thing": Sally Benson to JT, 5/5/58.

174 "They ought to have covers": St. Clair McKelway to JT, 4/11/58.

177 "Her instincts, as usual": Ginger Rogers, *Ginger: My Story*, p. 84.

178 "You know, Ginger is also": Ibid., p. 95.

179 "People in California": HR to RW, 7/24/47.

179 "We had quite a long session": Harpo Marx to Groucho Marx, 5/7/58.

180 "Nobody is going to leave": Thurber, *Years with Ross*, p. 225.

180 "Instantly he was on the alert": Stanley Walker to JT, 8/14/57.

181 "There was a slight benefit": *TNY,* 11/9/29.

182 "was simple and, theoretically": Russell Maloney, "Tilley the Toiler," *The Saturday Review of Literature,* 8/30/47.

182 "In our inattention": *Women's Wear Daily,* 7/1/68.

183 "We walked over to Union": *TNY,* 3/5/32.

184 "In the class war": Dwight Macdonald, "Laugh and Lie Down," *Partisan Review,* December 1937.

184 *"The New Yorker* was, of course": EBW to Charles Morton, 5/6/63.

186 "I was chattering away": This and entire Charles Morton segment is from Morton's *It Has Its Charms . . . ,* pp. 206–20.

188 "They droop off his wrists": James M. Cain to Allen Churchill, 8/16/47.

192 *"The New Yorker* is a cesspool": JT to HR, August 1947.

192 "It built him up": Grant, p. 219.

193 "We got to Park Avenue": WG to JT, Monday [1957].

193 "The day at the office": Ogden Nash to Frances Leonard, 1/5/31.

194 "was about as miserable": Hoopes, *Cain,* p. 213.

196 "O'Hara's in us for three hundred": Bernard A. Bergman, "O'Hara and Me," *John O'Hara Journal,* Winter 1978–79.

196 "You, I believe, had warned me": Bergman to JT, 9/4 [1957].

197 "In the beginning, he kept on": WG to JT, 8/12/57.

197 "We laughed about which one": St. Clair McKelway to JT, 5/31/58.

199 "the most succinct and accurate": RI memo in his collected papers, 6/6/66.

199 "Well, I am as bitter": HR to Eugene Spaulding, 3/12/30.

201 "The front office boys": Cain to Allen Churchill, 8/16/47.

203 "Hell, Ingersoll, *Fortune* was invented": RI to JT, 8/1/59.

8: FLEISCHMANN

209 "We never went to Sunday school": This and subsequent passages are from the Raoul Fleischmann family history.

210 "because then the Jewish clientele": *Variety,* 12/12/51.

211 "a hatred which is almost": Fleischmann to EBW, 7/2/45.

212 "Fleischmann et al.": HR to Lloyd Paul Stryker, 10/29/45.

212 "My father used to say": Interview with Peter Fleischmann, 1/15/92.

212 "The publisher was to have": William Shawn to *TNY* staff, 11/11/76.

213 "I did a thing no decent": Dale Kramer, p. 170.

213 "I was sorry not to come": Edmund Wilson to JT, 3/22/58.

215 "Harold just had a great distaste": Fleischmann to JT, 3/28/58.

216 "ring of stupid fumblers": HR to Stryker, 7/4/45.

219 "I got onto the *Stage* thing": HR to KSW, [1942].

219 "his resentment was almost": Fleischmann to JT, 3/28/58.

220 "I could understand your spending": HR to Fleischmann, 4/5/38.

221 "I'm not going to work myself": Ik Shuman to JT, 8/22/58.

221 "Unless, before 5 p.m.": HR to Fleischmann, 4/5/38.

221 "If this demand is not met": St. Clair McKelway to JT, 4/2/58.

222 The account of Shuman's meeting with Fleischmann is from Shuman's letter to JT, 8/22/58.

223 "I . . . find myself in what": HR to Fleischmann, 5/24/38.

223 "to Florida, California": F-R Publishing Corporation to HR, 11/17/38.

224 "we have another little mouth": HR to EBW, [Fall 1937].

224 "weren't exactly parallel": HR to KSW, [1942].

226 "As I get it, this new board": Stryker to Peter Vischer, 7/3/42.

226 "Ross was a constant irritation": Interview with Peter Fleischmann, 1/15/92.

228 "It makes [your] place look like": Howard Teichmann, *Smart Aleck*, p. 156.

228 "She was a simple, beautiful": KSW note in her collected papers, [1973?].

228 "the primary purpose of baseball": WG to JT, Monday [1957].

228 "Conceived in an absent-minded": Allen Churchill, "Ross of *The New Yorker*," *American Mercury*, August 1948.

229 "As I reached to do so": FS to JT, 10/5 [1957].

231 "Ross didn't want me to come": Interview with Peggy Day, 9/15/92.

232 "He is a man of substance": HR to RW, 8/24/48.

232 "The second they got into": FS to the Whites, [10/19/38].

233 "I was hit on the head": Dale Kramer, p. 265.

234 "As I have said," HR to Stryker, 7/25/44.

235 "The little bastard": FS to JT, 10/5 [1957].

235 "The poor son of a bitch": McKelway to JT, 5/25/58.

235 "which recently allowed me to be forged": HR to Alexander
Woollcott, Tuesday [April 1942].

236 "Any American can be taken": Thurber, *Years with Ross,* p. 250.

237 "the king of England": Hoopes, *Cain,* p. 211.

9: LIFE ON A LIMB

240 *Sunset Boulevard* story is from an interview with Philip Hamburger,
8/8/91.

241 "Magazines are about eighty-five": HR to George Jean Nathan,
12/27/49.

242 "diligence in looking at": EBW in personal notes on *TNY,* in his
collected papers, undated.

242 "By being hospitable": Gill, p. 391.

243 "I wish I were a writer": HR to Geoffrey Hellman, July 1949.

243 "I . . . think he thought": "The Art of Fiction: William Maxwell,"
Paris Review, Fall 1982.

243 "When publishers wrote": Edmund Wilson to JT, 3/22/58.

244 "who looks at them with a bleary": HR to Mencken, 3/19/45.

245 "I think the attraction": Interview with John Bainbridge, 9/29/91.

245 "I didn't read [it]": HR to S. H. Adams, 4/5 [1943].

245 "Several of you writers": HR to Arthur Kober, 12/9/46.

246 "For instance, what in God's": Margaret Case Harriman, *Blessed Are
the Debonair,* p. 150.

246 "I could have asked Joe Mitchell": HR to Nunnally Johnson,
6/17/47.

246 "I am enormously relieved": HR to William Maxwell, 9/3/47.

246 "I am not God": HR to EBW, Monday [September 1938].

247 "stop writing letters to me": FS to Charles Morton, 10/19/57.

247 "Long life to the legal": HR to Messrs. Chadbourne, Wallace, Parke
& Whiteside, 9/17/43.

248 "He didn't like his facts": Thurber, *Years with Ross,* p. 98.

248 "What about this Hemingway": Interview with Roger Angell,
1/16/92.

249 "What kind of writer": WG to JT, 8/12/57.

250 "America's great contribution": Peter De Vries to JT, 10/31/57.

251 "What do the voices say": EBW, personal notes on *TNY*, undated.

252 "Oh, are you still there": Interview with Patricia Ross Honcoop, 2/21/92.

252 "I'm surrounded by a bunch": James Geraghty's notes on *TNY*, undated.

254 "With what, for God's sakes?": John Hersey, *Life Sketches*, p. x.

254 "I think Ross is wonderful": Mary McCarthy to KSW, 1/10/51.

254 The Liebling "WHO HE" story is from Joseph Mitchell's letter to JT, 8/24/57.

255 "Which *side* of the fireplace?": Interview with Emily Hahn, 11/5/91.

256 "Write me a cold piece": S. N. Behrman, *The Suspended Drawing Room*, pp. 14–15.

257 "You know, this is kind of like": Interview with Berton Roueché, 4/21/93.

257 "I herewith pass the idea": HR to Joseph Mitchell, 2/13/45.

258 "I'm getting sick and tired": Interview with Roueché, 4/21/93.

259 "I could explain that one": Thurber, *Years with Ross*, p. 267.

260 "the lightest of light": *The New York Times*, 1/11/80.

260 "Be more debonair": Interview with John Bainbridge, 9/29/91.

263 "Gibbs, you're *fucking* my story": Interview with Louis Forster, 9/13/92.

264 "Commas in *The New Yorker*": "The Art of the Essay: E. B. White," *Paris Review*, Fall 1969.

264 "what [we] do is query": HR to Mrs. Norton Baskin (Marjorie Kinnan Rawlings), 11/30/45.

265 "I am gradually starving": James M. Cain to WG, 8/18/34.

265 "the editors are so afraid": Edmund Wilson to KSW, 11/12/47.

265 "something that deserves high": Mencken to KSW, 4/27 [1934].

267 The Eisenhower-Columbia story is from an interview with William Mangold, 3/11/92.

268 "Ross didn't mean he didn't": McKelway to JT, 5/29/58.

269 "is just inviting Harlem": HR to Governor Robert A. Hurley, 11/5/41.

270 "There are thousands of those": *The New York Times*, 6/21/42.

271 "*The New Yorker* . . . if you'll": HR to James J. Lyons, 6/23/42.

271 "I was certainly indiscreet": HR to FS, Friday [1942].

272 "I meet many modern Abraham Lincolns": HR to Emily Hahn, 1/5/48.

272 The Letter from Washington story is from Rovere, *Arrivals and Departures,* pp. 68–70.

274 "I think probably your piece": HR to RW, 1/7/48.

274 "He was a man following": EBW to JG, 4/6/67.

10: SKIRMISHES

275 "built like the first joint": JT to McKelway, 4/14/58.

276 "You know, I was Aleck's": Teichmann, *Smart Aleck,* p. 316.

276 "He was a friend who demanded": HR to S. H. Adams, 2/4/43.

277 "All the time [Woollcott] wrote": Ibid.

278 "With certain reservations": S. H. Adams, p. 221.

279 "Nothing would happen": HR to Alexander Woollcott, Tuesday [April 1942].

279 "To me you are no longer": S. H. Adams, p. 222.

279 "He was rebuffed as man": FS to EBW, 5/16 [1939].

280 "I've tried by tender": Woollcott to HR, 4/18/42.

281 "You're a flatfoot": Interview with Phyllis Cerf Wagner, 4/12/94.

282 "In the interests of avoiding": HR to *TNY* staff, 9/6/40.

284 "Dear Bennett": Gill, p. 273.

284 "I herewith swear": HR to Marshall Best, 11/20/42.

284 "They have a selection": JT to Edward Aswell, 3/16/45.

285 "This is the first time": This and subsequent citations are from a letter from Shuman to JT, 9/22/57.

286 "You are a man who should not": HR to EBW, 5/7 [1943].

290 "It's not true": McKelway to JT, 5/25/58. There have been various accounts of the Luce-Ross meeting, published and unpublished. This draws mainly from McKelway's letter to Thurber, from an Ingersoll letter to Thurber (8/1/59), and from W. A. Swanberg's book *Luce and His Empire.*

291 "I assume it is up": HR to Henry Luce, 11/23/36.

292 "Nobody over there": McKelway to JT, 5/25/58.

293 "Life does story on the placid": HR to EBW, [1951].

294 "Ross was so furious": Interview with Al Hirschfeld, 12/7/92.

294 "Is this thing going to be": Robert T. Elson, *Time Inc.: The Intimate History of a Publishing Enterprise, 1923–1941*, p. 268.

11: WORDS AND PICTURES

297 "As to your sharpshooting": HR to KSW, [1939].

298 "I think it's a crime": WG to EBW, [September 1937].

299 "We've got to have more": McKelway to JT, 4/2/58.

299 "Where are you?" Interview with Philip Hamburger, 8/8/91.

301 "as indeed it should have": McKelway to JT, 4/2/58.

302 "million-word book": Raymond Sokolov, *Wayward Reporter: The Life of A. J. Liebling*, p. 106.

303 "George Baker, who by a process": *TNY*, 6/20/36.

304 "On her walk, Mazie": *TNY*, 12/21/40.

304 "You know, you write": Interview with Joseph Mitchell, 1/13/92.

304 "Back in the twenties": *TNY*, 10/5/35.

306 "You wouldn't get rich": HR to F. Scott Fitzgerald, 4/26/29.

306 "in the early days I never": HR to Martha Gellhorn, 2/15/43.

308 "Ah yes, those wonderful": Jerome Weidman, *Praying for Rain*, pp. 21–22.

311 "All I can say is that any man": FS to HR, 10/14/33.

312 "slight, tiny, mood story": KSW to Mrs. Miller, August [ca. 1947–48].

313 "Do you want to say a little prayer": Davis, p. 103.

313 "the most beautiful letter": Interview with Helen Stark, 12/3/92.

314 "You are one of the people": KSW to Clarence Day, 10/22/35.

317 The "Chutzbah" story is from Weidman, pp. 112–13.

318 "People [were] working for what": Interview with John Bainbridge, 9/29/91.

319 "Ross . . . would no more have thought": A. J. Liebling, "Harold Ross—The Impresario," *Nieman Reports*, April 1959.

319 "I have been a party to robbing": HR to JT, 3/23/45.

319 "The magazine is having a slight": HR to EBW, 4/22 [1943].

320 "A dollar bonus on each": John O'Hara to HR, 1/5/34.

320 The story of O'Hara's pawnshop watch is from *The O'Hara Concern,* by Matthew J. Bruccoli, p. 190.

322 Ross on "highlife-lowlife" stories is from "Joseph Mitchell and *The New Yorker* Nonfiction Writers," by Norman Sims, in *Literary Journalism in the Twentieth Century,* Norman Sims, editor, p. 103.

322 "I must write you in connection": HR to FS, Thursday [year unknown].

323 "It's Ross's old wall-tearing-down": JT to KSW, 4/19/38.

326 "This magazine is run on ideas": HR to Gluyas Williams, 8/7/34.

326 "Thurber's people have no blood": Thurber, *Years with Ross,* p. 63.

326 "Well, if it's a fad": JT interview on *Omnibus* television program, 3/4/56.

327 "Wait a minute, Hubb": Interview with Albert Hubbell, 4/28/93.

329 "You looked like a gentleman": James Geraghty's notes on *TNY.*

329 "Miss Terry, I want you to meet": Ibid.

330 "He would come back and say": Interview with Dana Fradon, 3/19/93.

331 "Ross approached drawings": Geraghty *TNY* notes.

331 "Delete what": Interview with Peggy Day, 9/15/92.

333 "The checking of the names": HR to JT, 12/13/44.

333 "and how much constant stimulation": Gluyas Williams note in his collected papers, undated.

334 "You don't think the father": HR to Gluyas Williams, 12/19/47.

334 "I am writing this at home": Ibid., Friday [1948].

335 "I don't know what the hell": Ibid., 5/20 [1948].

12: WAR

340 "when Hawley and Shawn": EBW to KSW, Thursday [Summer 1948].

342 "I haven't been an astonishingly": Fleischmann to KSW, 1/12/61.

343 "It was practically starvation": *The New York Times,* 12/9/92.

344 "he's bright, by all indications": HR to EBW, [Summer 1936].

346 "The ten million men": *TNY,* 9/9/39.

347 "Great pressure is being": HR to EBW, 5/31/40.

347 "Democracy is now asked": *TNY,* 6/22/40.

348 "My very great fear": HR to Paul Hyde Bonner, 9/11/40.

348 "My decision is that we have": HR to EBW, 6/24 [1941].

349 "has suddenly shrunk": *TNY,* 6/1/40.

350 "coming away from a story": Brenda Wineapple, *Genêt: A Biography of Janet Flanner,* p. 165.

351 "In effect, Liebling treated": Sokolov, p. 152.

351 "anybody who loved Paris": *TNY,* 12/7/40.

351 "War, after all, is simple": HR to EBW, Sunday [May 1941].

353 "They rejected me for everything": Interview with Albert Hubbell, 4/28/93.

354 "God bless you, Hamburger": Interview with Philip Hamburger, 9/15/92.

354 "Youth! Youth!": Hamburger to author, 5/1/94.

354 "I am up to my nipples": HR to Alexander Woollcott, 5/19/42.

354 "The magazine is running us": HR to KSW, [1942?].

356 "I guess I will have to start writing": Ring Lardner, Jr., *The Lardners: My Family Remembered,* p. 311.

356 "He left England": HR to RW, 12/6/45.

357 "I have taken it every few": HR to Mencken, 8/3/42.

357 "I have done everything right": Ibid., 4/8/43.

358 "The giants have come down": Geraghty *TNY* notes.

358 "*The New Yorker* is a worse madhouse": EBW to Stanley Hart White, 3/2/44.

358 "Nobody knows what war is": HR to FS, 12/17/46.

358 "hot love hole": HR to FS, 1/20/47.

359 "Is she active?": Interview with William and Harriet Walden, 8/12/91.

359 "You're a loss to American industry": From Geoffrey Hellman speech, 5/14/75.

360 "There was a certain amount of wine": *TNY,* 2/26/44.

361 "I asked the boy what": *TNY,* 7/1/44.

362 "As the hours went by": *TNY,* 7/8/44.

364 "We were no more in the house": Nunnally Johnson to JT, 9/3/57.

365 "Don't thank me, Hellman": Hellman speech.

366 Ross–Kip Orr elevator story is from an interview with Philip Hamburger, 9/14/92.

366 "No pretty woman like that": Janet Flanner to Natalia Danesi Murray, 12/11/51.

366 "Advertisers are running around": HR to EBW, 5/7 [1943].

368 "a historical moment": Flanner to Murray, 1/21/45.

368 "Where is that goddam pope?": Philip Hamburger speech, 11/21/91.

370 "The more time that passes": William Shawn to John Hersey, 3/22/46.

371 "one of the most remarkable": HR to RW, 8/27/46.

372 "Hersey has written thirty thousand": HR to EBW, [1946].

372 "Can something that is two-dimensional": Hersey, p. x.

374 "There was never any magazine story": HR to FS, 9/5/46.

374 "I don't think I've ever got as much": HR to Irwin Shaw, 9/16/46.

374 "the most famous magazine article": *TNY*, 4/5/93.

13: SQUIRE

375 "Twenty years ago this week:" *TNY*, 2/17/45.

376 "One is that the major owner": HR to Lloyd Paul Stryker, 7/4/45.

377 "It's downright ridiculous": Draft of 1945 letter from JG to Stryker; not sent.

377 "She got a sucker": This and next passage from HR letter to Stryker, 10/29/45.

378 "the hardest-working": HR to RW, 11/25/47.

379 "the whole editor emeritus": HR to Julius Baer, 11/12/45.

380 "He thought I ought to know": Interview with Patricia Ross Honcoop, 1/31/92.

383 "Patty, try not to annoy": Ibid., 2/21/92.

384 "How about a nice vegetable": Ford, p. 130.

384 "When I came in he said": Interview with Patricia Ross Honcoop, 3/9/92.

385 "mired like a wounded bird": S. J. Perelman to JT, 9/6/57.

385 "no-limit stud poker": HR to RW, 10/4/49.

386 "damned well had to catch a train": Ibid.

387 "Nothing to it": Richard H. Rovere, *Final Reports*, p. 87.

387 "a wise and remarkable man": HR to RW, 8/16/49.

387 "Ross got more and more nervous": Interview with Daphne Hellman Shih, 9/30/91.

388 "Goddammit, I forgot": Interview with Patricia Ross Honcoop, 2/7/92.

389 "There was a standing rule": United Press report, 12/7/51.

389 "had something of the same idea": FS to KSW, 4/25/48.

389 "Their gay plans curled": HR to Elmer Davis, 9/13/49.

389 "Thank God we can relax": Interview with Elizabeth Paepcke, 8/12/92.

390 "Dear Sir (or Madam)": Interview with Tony Gibbs, 11/19/92.

390 "He was a person who was almost incapable": Ibid., 1/14/93.

390 "Maybe he doesn't like anything": Thurber, *Years with Ross*, p. 128.

391 "glided past like a ghost": Edmund Wilson to JT, 3/22/58.

391 "I've always felt that play": *The New York Times*, 8/17/58.

391 "Well, think about it for a second": Interview with Tony Gibbs, 1/14/93.

392 *"Pretty Little Parlor": TNY*, 4/29/44.

394 "We may sound provincial to you": HR to W. Averell Harriman, 11/15/49.

395 "Your sports parable": WG to EBW, [October 1947].

396 "Edmund Wilson once explained": KSW note in her collected papers, 1972.

396 "I may cut my throat": HR to KSW, [1948].

396 "hit it off so well with the ghost": Vladimir Nabokov, *Speak, Memory*, introduction to 1966 edition, p. 10.

396 "Ross would sometimes consult me": Davis, p. 142.

397 "he managed to communicate": Interview with Edward Newhouse, 3/10/94.

398 Ross on "The Lottery": HR to Stanley Edgar Hyman, 8/9/48.

398 "maybe that will make up": Geraghty *TNY* notes.

14: RECLUSE ABOUT TOWN

399 "Dodd should really be played": Wolcott Gibbs, *Season in the Sun* (play), p. 92.

399 "He says you're the greatest": Ibid., p. 167.

400 "I've never been up against": HR to Howard Brubaker, 1/22/51.

400 "It's incredible for Americans": HR to RW, 8/8/50.

400 "Goddammit, I have it on good authority": Janet Flanner to Solita Solano, 10/9/52.

401 "the only non-phony": FS to HR, 6/30/42.

402 "Nobody ever shoots Santa Claus": HR to Mencken, 11/10/48.

402 "You don't think my father": HR to FS, 10/18/48.

403 "My viewpoint is that if the people": HR to EBW, Sunday [October 1943].

404 "Jesus Christ, Kahn, why did you": Interview with E. J. Kahn, Jr., 8/9/91.

404 "I notice, in reading over": *TNY,* 9/4/43.

404 "has again seen fit to refer": J. Edgar Hoover to HR, 9/13/43.

405 "an elemental education": FBI memorandum, 7/18/49.

407 "Merely and simply": HR to Flanner, 6/9/50.

407 "getting [out] this damned Christmas issue": Flanner to JG, 12/9/51.

407 "Odd that he, such a patron": Flanner to Natalia Danesi Murray, 11/15/50.

408 "And you don't believe in them": Flanner to KSW, 11/1 [1953].

408 "I returned to Paris": Ibid.

409 "He's some kind of recluse": Interview with Albert Hubbell, 4/28/93.

409 "There was material enough": Mencken to HR, 3/30/43.

411 "People write about me": Interview with Philip Hamburger, 8/8/91.

411 "I am editor of an adult": This and following passages are from Ross's testimony before the New York State Public Service Commission, 12/21/49.

413 "I'm a well-dressed man": Associated Press report, February 1950.

414 "It says here you'll get": Edward Weeks, *Writers and Friends,* p. 211.

414 "This is what Mr. Gibbs": WG to JT, 8/12/57.

15: BACK TO THE ALGONQUIN

417 "old people ought to be bumped off": HR to RW, 6/20/51.

418 "I think I believe in God": Interview with Patricia Ross Honcoop, 2/7/92.

419 "I write as a duodenum-scarred": This and next excerpt are from Ross's introduction to *Good Food for Bad Stomachs,* by Sara M. Jordan, M.D., and Sheila Hibben, pp. 6–7.

420 "We're getting old": HR to RW, 2/27/51.

421 "Expecting Ross to take it easy": JT to KSW, 5/14/51.

421 "so beautiful and restful": HR to RW, 6/20/51.

423 "I am back at work": HR to EBW, [September 1951].

426 "It is only fair to note": *TNY,* 11/17/51.

427 "It's practically the only thing": Thurber, *Years with Ross,* p. 191.

429 "I'm up here to end this thing": Ibid., p. 304.

429 "Take me home": Interviews with Philip Hamburger, 9/15/92; and Cecille Shawn, 2/4/93.

430 "Please believe me, Mrs. Ross": Ariane Ross to JT, 11/16/57.

430 "Oh, Mrs. Ross, haven't you": Ibid.

431 "Why, about your father": Interview with Patricia Ross Honcoop, 2/7/92.

431 "enormous, like losing the top": Janet Flanner to KSW, 12/13 [1951].

431 "K and I ... have the sensation": EBW to H. K. Rigg, 12/11/51.

431 "This is known, in these offices": *TNY,* 12/15/51.

432 The Thurber story is from an interview with Mary D. Kierstead, 3/10/92.

EPILOGUE: THE ANGEL OF REPOSE

434 "He hated all tyrannies": *The New York Times,* 12/11/51.

434 "On next February 26": *Variety,* 12/12/51.

434 "such a bunch of normally noisy": EBW to Elmer Davis, 12/16/51.

435 "violence of personal feelings": File note from 1952 in Ralph Ingersoll's collected papers.

436 "Thus again is virtue": Fleischmann to KSW, 10/1 [1958].

436 "I read a garble": JT to EBW, 2/20/54.

SELECTED
BIBLIOGRAPHY

Adams, Franklin P. *The Diary of Our Own Samuel Pepys* (Vols. 1 and 2). New York: Simon and Schuster, 1935.

Adams, Samuel Hopkins. *A. Woollcott: His Life and His World.* New York: Reynal and Hitchcock, 1945.

Armitage, Shelley. *John Held, Jr.: Illustrator of the Jazz Age.* Syracuse: Syracuse University, 1987.

Ashley, Sally. *F.P.A.: The Life and Times of Franklin Pierce Adams.* New York: Beaufort, 1986.

Baldridge, C. LeRoy. *Time and Chance.* New York: J. Day, 1947.

Behrman, S. N. *The Suspended Drawing Room.* New York: Stein and Day, 1965.

————. *People in a Diary.* Boston: Little, Brown, 1972.

Benchley, Nathaniel. *Robert Benchley.* New York: McGraw-Hill, 1955.

Bernstein, Burton. *Thurber: A Biography.* New York: Dodd, Mead, 1975.

Bode, Carl. *Mencken.* Carbondale: Southern Illinois University, 1969.

Brown, John Mason. *The Worlds of Robert E. Sherwood.* New York: Harper and Row, 1965.

Bruccoli, Matthew J. *The O'Hara Concern: A Biography of John O'Hara.* New York: Random House, 1975.

Capra, Frank. *The Name Above the Title.* New York: Macmillan, 1971.

Case, Frank. *Tales of a Wayward Inn.* New York: Stokes, 1938.

Cerf, Bennett. *At Random.* New York: Random House, 1977.

Cheever, John. *The Stories of John Cheever.* New York: Knopf, 1978.

————. *The Letters of John Cheever.* Edited by Benjamin Cheever. New York: Simon and Schuster, 1988.

Churchill, Allen. "Ross of *The New Yorker.*" *American Mercury,* August 1948.

Clarke, Gerald. *Capote: A Biography.* New York: Simon and Schuster, 1988.

Connelly, Marc. *Voices Offstage.* Chicago: Holt, Rinehart and Winston, 1968.

Cornebise, Alfred E. *The Stars and Stripes.* Westport: Greenwood, 1984.

Cowley, Malcolm. "The Grammar of Facts." *The New Republic,* 7/26/43.

————. *The Flower and the Leaf.* New York: Viking, 1985.

Davenport, Marcia. *Too Strong for Fantasy.* New York: Scribner's, 1967.

Davis, Linda H. *Onward and Upward: A Biography of Katharine S. White.* New York: Harper and Row, 1987.

Dolmetsch, Carl R. *The Smart Set.* New York: Dial, 1966.

Donaldson, Scott. *John Cheever: A Biography.* New York: Random House, 1988.

Elledge, Scott: *E. B. White: A Biography.* New York: Norton, 1984.

Elson, Robert T. *Time Inc.: The Intimate History of a Publishing Enterprise, 1923–1941.* New York: Atheneum, 1968.

————. *The World of Time Inc.: The Intimate History of a Publishing Enterprise, 1941–1960.* New York: Atheneum, 1973.

Ferber, Edna. *A Peculiar Treasure.* Garden City: Doubleday, 1960.

Flanner, Janet. *Darlinghissima: Letters to a Friend.* Edited by Natalia Danesi Murray. New York: Random House, 1985.

Ford, Corey: *The Time of Laughter.* Boston: Little, Brown, 1967.

Frank, Elizabeth: *Louise Bogan.* New York: Knopf, 1985.

Gaines, James R.: *Wit's End: Days and Nights of the Algonquin Round Table.* New York: Harcourt Brace Jovanovich, 1977.

Gibbs, Wolcott. "A Very Active Type Man (Part I)." *The New Yorker,* 5/2/42.

————. *Season in the Sun (and Other Pleasures).* New York: Random House, 1946.

————. *Season in the Sun* (play). New York: Random House, 1951.

————. *More in Sorrow.* New York: Henry Holt, 1958.

Gilbert, Julie Goldsmith. *Ferber: A Biography.* Garden City: Doubleday, 1978.

Gill, Brendan. *Here at The New Yorker.* New York: Random House, 1975.

Glendinning, Victoria. *Rebecca West: A Life.* New York: Knopf, 1987.

Golden, Harry. *A Little Girl Is Dead.* Cleveland: World, 1965.

Goldstein, Malcolm. *George S. Kaufman: His Life, His Theater.* New York: Oxford, 1979.

Grant, Jane. *Ross, The New Yorker and Me.* New York: Reynal, 1968.

Hamburger, Philip. *Curious World: A New Yorker at Large.* San Francisco: North Point, 1987.

Hamilton, Ian. *In Search of J. D. Salinger.* New York: Random House, 1988.

Harriman, Margaret Case. *The Vicious Circle.* New York: Rinehart, 1951.

————. *Blessed Are the Debonair.* New York: Rinehart, 1956.

Hecht, Ben. *Charlie: The Improbable Life and Times of Charles MacArthur.* New York: Harper and Brothers, 1957.

Heidenry, John. *Theirs Was the Kingdom.* New York: Norton, 1993.

Herrmann, Dorothy. *S. J. Perelman: A Life.* New York: Putnam, 1986.

Hersey, John. *Life Sketches.* New York: Knopf, 1989.

Hofstadter, Richard. *Social Darwinism in American Thought* (revised edition). Boston: Beacon, 1955.

Holmes, Charles S. *The Clocks of Columbus.* New York: Atheneum, 1972.

Hoopes, Roy. *Cain.* New York: Holt, Rinehart and Winston, 1982.

————. *Ralph Ingersoll: A Biography.* New York: Atheneum, 1985.

Hoyt, Edwin P. *Alexander Woollcott: The Man Who Came to Dinner.* London: Abelard-Schuman, 1968.

Hyman, Stanley Edgar. "The Urban New Yorker." *The New Republic,* 7/20/42.

[Ingersoll, Ralph]. "The New Yorker." *Fortune,* August 1934.

————. *Point of Departure.* New York: Harcourt Brace and World, 1961.

Jordan, Sara M., and Sheila Hibben. *Good Food for Bad Stomachs.* With an introduction by Harold W. Ross. Garden City: Doubleday, 1951.

Kahn, E. J., Jr. *About The New Yorker and Me.* New York: Putnam, 1979.

Kluger, Richard. *The Paper: The Life and Death of The New York Herald Tribune.* New York: Knopf, 1986.

Kramer, Dale. *Ross and The New Yorker.* Garden City: Doubleday, 1951.

Kramer, Dale, and George R. Clark "Harold Ross and *The New Yorker:* A Landscape with Figures." *Harper's,* April 1943.

Kramer, Hilton. "Harold Ross's *New Yorker:* Life as a Drawing-Room Comedy." *Commentary,* August 1959.

Lardner, Ring, Jr. *The Lardners: My Family Remembered.* New York: Harper Colophon, 1977.

Liebling, A. J. "Harold Ross—The Impresario." *Nieman Reports,* April 1959.

————: *Back Where I Came From.* With a foreword by Philip Hamburger. San Francisco: North Point, 1990.

Literary Journalism in the Twentieth Century. Edited by Norman Sims. New York: Oxford, 1990.

Macdonald, Dwight. "Laugh and Lie Down." *Partisan Review,* December 1937.

Mahon, Gigi. *The Last Days of The New Yorker.* New York: McGraw-Hill, 1988.

Maloney, Russell. "Tilley the Toiler." *The Saturday Review of Literature,* 8/30/47.

Marx, Harpo (with Rowland Barber). *Harpo Speaks!* New York: Bernard Geis Associates, 1961.

Maxwell, William. *The Outermost Dream.* New York: Knopf, 1989.

Meade, Marion. *Dorothy Parker: What Fresh Hell Is This?* New York: Villard, 1988.

Mencken, H. L. *The New Mencken Letters.* Edited by Carl Bode. New York: Dial, 1977.

Meryman, Richard. *Mank: The Wit, World and Life of Herman Mankiewicz.* New York: William Morrow, 1978.

Miller, Donald L. *Lewis Mumford: A Life.* New York: Weidenfeld and Nicolson, 1989.

Mitgang, Herbert. *Dangerous Dossiers.* New York: Donald I. Fine, 1988.

Moorhouse, Geoffrey. *Imperial City: New York.* New York: Henry Holt, 1988.

Morton, Charles W. "A Try for *The New Yorker.*" *The Atlantic Monthly,* April 1963.

———. "Brief Interlude at *The New Yorker.*" *The Atlantic Monthly,* May 1963.

———. *It Has Its Charms. . . .* Philadelphia: Lippincott, 1966.

The Most of John Held, Jr. Introduction by Carl J. Weinhardt. Brattleboro, Vt.: Stephen Greene Press, 1972.

Mumford, Lewis. *Sketches from Life.* New York: Dial, 1982.

Nabokov, Vladimir. *Speak, Memory* (revised edition). New York: Putnam, 1966.

Nash, Ogden. *Loving Letters from Ogden Nash.* Edited by Linell Nash Smith. Boston: Little, Brown, 1990.

"A New York Diary." *The New Republic,* 9/14/27.

"The New Yorker." Time, 2/25/25.

The New Yorker Book of War Pieces. New York: Schocken, 1988.

O'Hara, John. *Selected Letters of John O'Hara.* Edited by Matthew J. Bruccoli. New York: Random House, 1978.

Peterson, Theodore. *Magazines in the Twentieth Century.* Urbana: University of Illinois, 1964.

Pinck, Dan. "Paging Mr. Ross." *Encounter,* June 1987.

Pringle, Henry F. "Ross of *The New Yorker.*" *'48 Magazine,* March and April, 1948.

Rogers, Ginger. *Ginger: My Story.* New York: HarperCollins, 1991.

Rohrbough, Malcolm J. *Aspen: The History of a Silver-Mining Town.* New York: Oxford, 1986.

Ross, Lillian. *Takes.* New York: Congdon and Weed, 1983.

Rovere, Richard H. *Arrivals and Departures.* New York: Macmillan, 1976.

———. *Final Reports.* Garden City: Doubleday, 1984.

The Saturday Review Gallery. New York: Simon and Schuster, 1959.

Sokolov, Raymond. *Wayward Reporter: The Life of A. J. Liebling.* San Francisco: Donald S. Ellis, 1984.

Starr, Roger. *The Rise and Fall of New York City.* New York: Basic Books, 1985.

A Subtreasury of American Humor. Edited by E. B. White and Katharine S. White. New York: Coward-McCann, 1941.

Swanberg, W. A. *Luce and His Empire.* New York: Scribner's, 1972.

Tebbel, John. *The American Magazine: A Compact History.* New York: Hawthorne, 1969.

Tebbel, John, and Mary Ellen Zuckerman. *The Magazine in America, 1741–1990.* New York: Oxford, 1991.

Teichmann, Howard. *George S. Kaufman: An Intimate Portrait.* New York: Atheneum, 1972.

———. *Smart Aleck: The Wit and World of Alexander Woollcott.* New York: William Morrow, 1976.

Thomas, Bob. *Winchell.* Garden City: Doubleday, 1971.

Thurber, James. *The Years with Ross.* Boston: Atlantic Monthly/Little, Brown, 1959.

———. *Selected Letters of James Thurber.* Edited by Helen Thurber and Edward Weeks. New York: Penguin, 1982.

Trilling, Lionel. "New Yorker Fiction." *The Nation,* 4/11/42.

Tunis, John R. "My Friends, the Editors." *The Saturday Review of Literature,* 1/9/43.

Updike, John. *Hugging the Shore.* New York: Knopf, 1983.

———. *Odd Jobs.* New York: Knopf, 1991.

Wainwright, Loudon. *The Great American Magazine: An Inside History of Life.* New York: Knopf, 1986.

Weeks, Edward. *Writers and Friends.* Boston: Atlantic Monthly/Little, Brown, 1981.

Weidman, Jerome. *Praying for Rain.* New York: Harper and Row, 1986.

Weiner, Ed. *Let's Go to Press.* New York: Putnam, 1955.

White, E. B. *Here Is New York.* New York: Harper and Brothers, 1949.

———. *Letters of E. B. White.* Edited by Dorothy Lobrano Guth. New York: Harper Colophon, 1978.

———. *Writings from The New Yorker: 1927–1976.* Edited by Rebecca M. Dale. New York: HarperCollins, 1990.

Wilson, Edmund. *Letters on Literature and Politics, 1912–1972.* Edited by Elena Wilson. New York: Farrar, Straus and Giroux, 1977.

Wineapple, Brenda. *Genêt: A Biography of Janet Flanner.* New York: Ticknor and Fields, 1989.

Winterich, John T. *Squads Write!* New York: Harper and Brothers, 1931.

————. "The Life and Death of the Lafayette Publishing Co." *The New Colophon*, September 1949.

Woollcott, Alexander. *The Letters of Alexander Woollcott.* Edited by Beatrice Kaufman and Joseph Hennessey. New York: Viking, 1944.

Yardley, Jonathan. *Ring: A Biography of Ring Lardner.* New York: Atheneum, 1984.

INDEX

ABOUT THE AUTHOR

THOMAS KUNKEL has worked for the *San Jose Mercury News,* the *Miami Herald, The New York Times,* and other newspapers, and was editor and publisher of *Arizona Trend* magazine. This is his first book. He lives in Indiana with his wife and four daughters.

ABOUT THE TYPE

The text of this book was set in Janson, a misnamed typeface designed in about 1690 by Nicholas Kis, a Hungarian in Amsterdam. In 1919 the matrices became the property of the Stempel Foundry in Frankfurt. It is an old-style book face of excellent clarity and sharpness. Janson serifs are concave and splayed; the contrast between thick and thin strokes is marked.